A People of Two Kingdoms II: Stories of Kansas Mennonites in Politics

by James C. Juhnke

Bethel College
North Newton, Kansas
2016

Library of Congress Cataloging-in-Publication Data

Cover design by John Hiebert
Wedel Series logo by Angela Goering Miller
ISBN-13: 978-1-889239-11-8
Copyright 2016 by Bethel College.
This edition distributed by Pandora Press.

This publication may not be reproduced, stored in a retrieval system, or transmitted in whole or in part, in any form or by any means, electronic, mechanical, photocopying, recording, or otherwise, without the prior written permission of Bethel College.

Cornelius H. Wedel Historical Series

1 Rodney J. Sawatsky, *Authority and Identity: The Dynamics of the General Conference Mennonite Church*, 1987
2 James C. Juhnke, *Dialogue with a Heritage: Cornelius H. Wedel and the Beginnings of Bethel College*, 1987
3 W. R. Estep, *Religious Liberty: Heritage and Responsibility*, 1988
4 John B. Toews, ed., *Letters from Susan: A Woman's View of the Russian Mennonite Experience (1928-1941)*, 1988
5 Louise Hawkley and James C. Juhnke, eds., *Nonviolent America: History through the Eyes of Peace*, 1993, 2004
6 Al Reimer, *Mennonite Literary Voices: Past and Present*, 1993
7 Abraham Friesen, *History and Renewal in the Anabaptist/Mennonite Tradition*, 1994
8 James C. Juhnke, *Creative Crusader: Edmund G. Kaufman and Mennonite Community*, 1994
9 Alain Epp Weaver, ed., *Mennonite Theology in Face of Modernity: Essays in Honor of Gordon D. Kaufman*, 1996
10 Sjouke Voolstra, *Menno Simons: His Image and Message*, 1996
11 Robert S. Kreider, *Looking Back into the Future*, 1998
12 Royden Loewen, *Hidden Worlds: Revisiting the Mennonite Migrants of the 1870s*, 2001
13 Jean Janzen, *Elements of Faithful Writing*, 2004
14 H. G. Mannhardt, *The Danzig Mennonite Church*, 2007
15 Jaime Prieto, *Mennonites in Latin America: Historical Sketches*, 2008
16 Jaime Prieto, *Menonitas en América Latina: Bosquejos Históricos*, 2008
17 Wilhelm Mannhardt, *The Military Service Exemption of the Mennonites of Provincial Prussia*, 2013
18 Mark Jantzen, Mary S. Sprunger, and John D. Thiesen, eds., *European Mennonites and the Challenge of Modernity over Five Centuries: Contributors, Detractors, and Adapters*, 2016
19 James C. Juhnke, *A People of Two Kingdoms II: Stories of Kansas Mennonties in Politics*, 2016

Series editor: vols. 1-4, David A. Haury
vols. 5-19, John D. Thiesen

Contents

	Series Preface	vii
	Author's Preface	ix
1	A People of Two Kingdoms 1874-1940	1
2	Coming of the War	10
3	World War II: Crisis and Revitalization	29
4	Postwar Mobilization	56
5	Civil Rights and Cold War Antimilitarism	77
6	Vietnam War	103
7	Campaign for Congress, 1970	126
8	1970s: Party Politics, Wheat Centennial	139
9	Bicentennial 1976	154
10	Mennonite Politicians I	177
11	Mennonite Politicians II	195
12	Activity Church	216
13	1980s: Farm Crisis, Legislative Awareness	232
14	1990s: Desert Storm, Summer of Mercy	252
15	Turn of Century: Flags, Same-Sex Marriage	269
16	A People of Dual Citizenship	286
	Appendix A: State and National Candidates	297

Appendix B: Voting Statistics 1940-1976	300
Bibliography	301
Index	318

Series Preface

The Cornelius H. Wedel Historical Series was initiated by the Mennonite Library and Archives at Bethel College as part of the college centennial celebration in 1987. Cornelius H. Wedel, the first president of Bethel College from the beginning of classes in 1893 until his death in 1910, was an early scholar of Mennonite studies. His four-volume survey of Mennonite history, published from 1900 to 1904, helped to rescue Anabaptism and Mennonitism from their marginal and denigrated portrayal in standard works of church history. Wedel saw Anabaptism and Mennonitism as part of a tradition of biblical faithfulness going back to the early church.

Wedel also believed in the cultivation of the intellect in all fields of knowledge. The current college mission statement continues the commitment to intellectual, cultural, and spiritual leadership for the church and society. The Wedel Series furthers these goals by publishing research in Mennonite studies with a special emphasis on works with a connection to Bethel College, such as campus lecture series and projects based on the holdings of the Mennonite Library and Archives.

Of the eighteen volumes published in the series prior to this time, twelve have originated in campus lecture series or symposia, four arose out of library or archival holdings at Bethel College, and two had both ties. One volume has been reprinted since its original publication. Topics in the series have included Mennonite identity, biography and autobiography, Bethel College history, nonviolent interpretations of United States history, Menno Simons, Mennonite literature, and theology.

The volume you have before you comes from a Kansas Mennonite historian whose name is on three previous Wedel Series volumes. He extends into the recent past a central focus of the series, on Kansas Mennonites.

John D. Thiesen
Series Editor

Author's Preface

This book is the second volume in a project that began a half century ago. My Ph.D. dissertation at Indiana University, completed in 1967, was about Kansas Mennonites in politics from the 1870s to the 1940s–immigration until World War II. In 1975 a version of the dissertation was published with the title *A People of Two Kingdoms: The Political Acculturation of the Kansas Mennonites*.[1] This book picks up where that first volume left off. The first chapter includes a brief summary of volume one.

The field of Mennonite studies has been transformed in the half-century since I began work on my Ph. D. dissertation. In the 1950s and 1960s scholars of Mennonite history had written mostly about sixteenth century European Anabaptism. American Mennonite studies was in its infancy, confined mostly to officially-sponsored books about denominational institutions. *A People of Two Kingdoms* was an early attempt at inter-Mennonite social history. Today we have a number of excellent general inter-Mennonite studies that insightfully explore the social and intellectual course of Mennonite political attitudes and behavior. Four of these most valuable for this volume are Leo Driedger and Donald A. Kraybill, *Mennonite Peacemaking: From Quietism to Activism*; Perry Bush, *Two Kingdoms, Two Loyalties: Mennonite Pacifism in Modern America*; Paul Toews, *Mennonites in American Society, 1930-1970: Modernity and the Persistence of Religious Community*; and Royden Loewen and Steven M. Nolt, *Seeking Places of Peace*.[2] It has been my privilege to work with Mennonite historians Theron Schlabach, Richard MacMaster, and Paul Toews on the four-volume Mennonite Experience in America Project.[3] To

---

[1] James C. Juhnke, *A People of Two Kingdoms: The Political Acculturation of the Kansas Mennonites* (Newton, KS: Faith and Life Press, 1975).

[2] Leo Driedger and Donald B. Kraybill, *Mennonite Peacemaking: From Quietism to Activism* (Scottdale, PA: Herald Press, 1994), Perry Bush, *Two Kingdoms, Two Loyalties: Mennonite Pacifism in Modern America* (Baltimore: Johns Hopkins University Press, 1998), Paul Toews, *Mennonites in American Society 1930-1970: Modernity and the Persistence of Religious Community* (Scottdale, PA: Herald Press, 1996), Royden Loewen and Steven M. Nolt, *Seeking Places of Peace*, Global Mennonite History Series: North America (Intercourse, PA: Good Books, 2012).

[3] Richard K. MacMaster, *Land, Piety, Peoplehood: The Establishment of Mennonite Communities in America* (Scottdale, PA: Herald Press, 1985); Theron Schlabach, *Peace, Faith, Nation: Mennonites and Amish in Nineteenth-Century America* (Scottdale, PA: Herald Press, 1988); James C. Juhnke, *Vision, Doctrine, War: Mennonite Identity and*

these and to other secondary studies acknowledged in footnotes I am deeply indebted.

In many ways this book tells my own story. I was born (1938) and reared in the Kansas Mennonite heartland. My academic career was as a teacher of American history and Mennonite history at Bethel College in North Newton, Kansas. As an adult I was actively involved in the Mennonite church and in local party politics. In 1970 I ran for political office as the Democratic candidate for Kansas' fourth congressional district. One of my students teased me that my motive in campaigning for office was to live out something interesting to include in a prospective second volume of *A People of Two Kingdoms*. At some level the student's charge may have been accurate. A careful reader will discover that my experience and point of view lie not far below the surface of the text in each chapter. I chose to write about the 1970 campaign in the third person--an attempt to gain some objective distance.

The field of historiography in the decades since my Ph.D. dissertation has seen a postmodern assault on the reliability of all historical narratives. Some critics have even challenged the assumption that events of the past bear any relationship to each other apart from the mind of the historian. At Bethel College our senior history students wrestled with this challenge as we read such books as *Telling the Truth About History* by Joyce Appleby, Lynn Hunt, and Margaret Jacob (1994).[4] One lesson was that historians should remain humble about the final completeness of their constructed narratives. Nevertheless, a historian's task is to take account of as many facts as possible in a framework as appropriate as one can muster. In the face of deconstructionist historiography, I claim that this book is more than emotional autobiography. I have not intentionally disregarded any information or hidden any skeletons from this story in order to preserve or promote my own identity as a Mennonite and a

---

Organization in America 1890- 1930 (Scottdale, PA: Herald Press, 1989); Paul Toews, *Mennonites in American Society*.

[4]Joyce Appleby, Lynn Hunt, and Margaret Jacob, *Telling the Truth About History* (New York: Norton, 1994).

Christian. The ultimate value or meaning of Mennonite involvement in politics is beyond my purview.[5]

One challenge in counting Mennonite voters or describing Mennonite politicians is the definition of "Mennonite." For this book the primary marker of Mennonite identity is formal membership in a Mennonite church congregation. In two exceptional cases, I counted persons to be "Mennonite politicians" if they regularly attended a Mennonite congregation, were married to a Mennonite, and shared Mennonite values—even though they were not officially baptized members. However, I have noted every Mennonite who ran for state or national office, whether or not they were elected. From 1940 to 2016 that list includes thirty persons.

At the grass roots, "Mennonite" has both ethnic and religious meaning. Many Kansans identify themselves as Mennonites on the basis of their ancestry or family upbringing, even though they do not belong to a Mennonite congregation. On the other hand, there have been politically active members of Mennonite congregations who have kept themselves on the margins of the Mennonite heritage. Some have consciously reflected Mennonite values in their political positions. Others have not.

Another challenge is to define "politics." In this book, as in volume one, I define political identification and behavior broadly to include more than partisan activity of Democrats, Republicans, or third parties. Mennonites were behaving politically when they refused military service or war tax payment, when they protested against the Vietnam War, when they lobbied government officials against building reservoirs that threatened their farms, when they wrote to state legislators about property taxes or abortion policies, and when they attempted to display the Anabaptist martyr tradition in the Smithsonian Museum in Washington, D.C.

Mennonites in Kansas also contributed significantly to civic life through membership on local public school boards, township offices, and small town and county government. For this book I have not attempted to identify by name the hundreds of Mennonites who participated in local politics. A few examples of

---

[5] I addressed the question of historical objectivity in a section, "History as Autobiography," in a memoir, *Small Steps Toward the Missing Peace* (N.p.: Flying Camel Publications, 2011), 120-8.

locally prominent officials have had to suffice. However, I have told something about the story of every Mennonite who ran for state or national office, whether or not they were elected. From 1940 to 2014 that list includes twenty-nine persons.

From 1952 until the present, Mennonites had at least one representative in the Kansas House of Representatives. From 1982 onward typically two or three Mennonites served in the Kansas House. In one election, November 1990, four Mennonites were elected to the legislature. Given the population of Kansas, each member of the 125 total in the House of Representatives represented some 20,000 residents.[6] That is roughly the number of Mennonites in south-central Kansas. Thus it can be said that the two or three Mennonites in the Kansas legislature represented somewhat more than their religious-ethnic group's fair share. This over-representation was a great shift from the early years after immigration when Kansas Mennonites were reluctant to become involved in politics.[7]

In America, Mennonites became a denomination, or a group of splintered denominations. It is possible to view Mennonite political attitudes and behavior in terms of the statements of denominational institutions–resolutions of official church conferences, findings of gatherings of church leaders, statements of faith, or editorials in church publications. In this book I often quote such official sources. I have been aware, however, that Mennonite political attitudes and behavior are not individualistic, but are rooted in the life of families and of church congregations.

The Mennonite Library and Archives at Bethel College, where John Thiesen serves as archivist and James Lynch as assistant archivist (retired 2014), has served as my primary source of information. John's careful editing improved the writing and accuracy of the text. I also received generous help from the Center for Mennonite Brethren Studies at Tabor College, Peggy Goertzen, director, and Anita Boese, assistant. The county clerks in Harvey, McPherson and Marion Counties guided me to voting data. Staff members at the Kansas Historical Society Archives in Topeka

---

[6]http://www.ballotpedia.org/Kansas_State_Legislature (accessed 23 April 2015). That number has changed with population increase.

[7]Juhnke, *A People of Two Kingdoms*, 153-57.

helped my research. Robin Ottoson, fellow scholar of Kansas Mennonite history, pointed me to key information. John Hiebert, graphic designer of volume one, also designed the cover and some illustrations for this volume. A version of chapter two was first published in *Mennonite Quarterly Review*, October 2010, with the title "Kansas Mennonites and the Political Order on the Eve of World War II."

I am indebted to hundreds of informants in the Mennonite community, especially my colleagues and students at Bethel College, only some of whom are adequately identified in the endnotes. The opportunity to tell the stories on these pages has been a great privilege in my retirement years.

Chapter 1

A People of Two Kingdoms 1874-1940

Volume I of *A People of Two Kingdoms* in 1975 documented the political attitudes and behavior of the Mennonites who in the 1870s and 1880s immigrated to south central Kansas. These immigrants were not highly politicized people. Most of them came from scattered communities in Eastern Europe, with smaller numbers moving west from the eastern United States. They were all inheritors of the Anabaptist dissenting tradition in the sixteenth century Reformation. They were a people of two kingdoms who sought a place where they could live together in obedience to their understanding of the kingdom of Christ. They were attracted by the opportunity to own and to work on land on the American frontier.

Mennonites were conscientious objectors to warfare. Many left Russia in the 1870s because the Russian government threatened to withdraw their traditional exemption from military service. President Ulysses S. Grant told Mennonite delegates that military service would not be an issue because the United States did not intend to get into any future wars. Officials in Kansas told the Mennonites their young men could be exempted from any military service if they registered yearly as conscientious objectors at the county seat. Mennonites in 1898 became alarmed when the United States went to war against Spain in Cuba and the Philippines, but that war did not involve military conscription. The promise of military exemption held good until 1917 when the United States entered the world war in Europe.

Immigrant Mennonites were notably hesitant to apply for formal U.S. citizenship and to vote in local or national elections. Compared to Swedish immigrants who lived in northern McPherson County, Mennonites voted in smaller numbers from immigration in the 1870s until World War II. But voting records also show that some Mennonites voted in elections from the beginning. They served in local township offices as early as 1877. American politicians recruited Mennonites in 1878 and 1879 to vote in railroad bond elections. But conservative groups such as the Mennonite Brethren and Krimmer Mennonite Brethren adopted church resolutions that forbade voting and office holding.

2 People of Two Kingdoms II

Kansas was a predominantly Republican state where reform movements such as Populism in the 1890s and Progressivism in the early twentieth century had a strong impact. Mennonites fit into the Kansas pattern—a Republican majority, Democratic minority, and a few radical reformers. During the presidential election of 1888, for example, Mennonite political engagement was on display in Hillsboro when John J. Funk, a free-trade Democrat from Peabody, squared off in public debate about free trade and patriotism against H. D. Penner, schoolteacher Republican, before a packed schoolhouse audience. In the decades before World War I, Mennonite voting patterns corresponded remarkably closely with the Kansas pattern. In McPherson and Marion counties a small group of Mennonites ran for local office as Populists and voted for that party. The Mennonites were not a solid block of voters. Those of Swiss-Volhynian background in McPherson and Reno Counties tended to vote Democratic. Those of Dutch-Russian background in Marion County tended to vote Republican.

Kansas Mennonite German-language community newspapers in the Progressive era before World War I provided vigorous coverage of national and international news. Jacob Gerhard Ewert, editor and writer for the Hillsboro *Journal* and *Vorwärts* from 1909 onward, challenged the community with his socialist, pacifist, and prohibitionist viewpoints. In Newton Henry Peter Krehbiel, Mennonite pastor and businessman, spoke and wrote from a more conservative capitalist perspective. In 1908 Krehbiel was elected to the Kansas House of Representatives. He served one term.

The outbreak of war in Europe in 1914 and the United States' entry into the war in 1917 shocked the comfortable course of Kansas Mennonite political acculturation. When Germany became the national enemy, patriotic Americans were not tolerant of German-speaking Mennonites who refused military service. The Defense Department conscripted young men into military camps, where they had to make their claims for military exemption in the face of hostile army officers. Some Mennonites were convicted at courts martial for their refusal to obey orders, and were imprisoned at Fort Leavenworth until after the war. Meanwhile Mennonites at home who refused to buy war bonds were subjected to intense social pressure and mob violence. The war experience was a turning point for the Mennonite experience in America. Their claim to productive American citizenship had come under question. Their German accents had become a badge of shame. More than a few of them gave up their pacifism and their Mennonite identity.

Under pressure for their failure to meet the demands of citizenship in wartime, and having benefitted from wartime economic prosperity, Kansas Mennonites reached for a positive civic identity during and after the war. They contributed generously to benevolent programs for victims of war. A Mennonite Central Committee, founded in 1920, became the primary agency for Mennonite voluntary service and financial contributions. Major efforts went into providing aid for Mennonite victims of famine and civil war in Russia. Meanwhile, in the postwar years, Mennonites became more proactive in opposing American militarism and in preparing for the possibility of another war in the future.

Kansas Mennonites never recovered their Progressive-era self-confidence as German-Americans in American public life. After the war their newspaper editors refrained from political commentary and reduced their coverage of secular news. The English-language *Mennonite Weekly Review* in 1923 marked a shift not only to another language but to a more non-political community consciousness. The numbers of Mennonite elected officials in county offices nearly died out during the war, and made a slow recovery. The most notable trend in Mennonite voting was disaffection from the Democratic Party—the party whose president had led the country into war contrary to President Woodrow Wilson's pre-election promises. In 1924 Kansas Mennonites voted distinctively higher than other Kansans for Robert LaFollette, the Progressive Party presidential candidate who in 1917 had opposed American entry into the war.

Judged by voting statistics, the Mennonite response to the Great Depression and the New Deal of the 1930s was not markedly different from that of other Kansans. Kansas Mennonite newspaper editors did not comment passionately or extensively on Roosevelt and the New Deal. However, in 1930 they voted in unusually high numbers for an independent gubernatorial candidate, Dr. John R. Brinkley. Brinkley was a quack doctor who attacked both Republicans and Democrats. He promised the people free school textbooks, a lake in every county, lower taxes, and medical care at cost. In Mennonite precincts Brinkley won the three-way election with 42.3 percent of the vote. The result reflected Mennonite mistrust of politics and politicians.

The numbers of Mennonites running for local and country offices picked up in the 1930s. In 1934 J. A. Schowalter, a Mennonite farmer and businessman from Harvey County, was elected on the Democratic ticket for the state legislature. Also elected to the Kansas House in the 1930s was Leon H. Harms, a Republican businessman from Hillsboro. Kansans in 1934 voted decisively (55.7%) to repeal the Prohibition of the sale of alcohol. Among Mennonites the vote was 75.3% against repeal.

Mennonites at times were attracted to right-wing Christian evangelists who had their own political agendas. In the 1930s an anti-Semitic and anti-Communist fundamentalist preacher, Gerald B. Winrod, leader of "The Defenders of the Christian Faith," got the support of many Kansas Mennonites. In 1938 Winrod ran a third-party campaign for the U.S. Senate and won 60% of the Mennonite vote, while getting only 21.4% of the vote statewide. In 1942 the U.S. government indicted Winrod for sedition. Mennonite support for Winrod had been more religious than political, but it was another example—along with support for Robert LaFollette in 1924 and for John R. Brinkley in 1932—of Kansas Mennonite willingness to support political candidates outside of the two-party establishment.

Mennonites originally migrated to Kansas in quest of community autonomy rather than in quest of individual freedom as understood in American democracy. By the coming of World War II a basic irony had appeared. Mennonites who had come to Kansas to maintain autonomous German-speaking separate-from-the-world communities were being acculturated into their adopted environment more rapidly and completely than were their German-speaking cousins who had remained in Russia. The boundaries of Kansas Mennonite communities became far more porous than the immigrant generation had intended. American democracy was a powerful solvent.

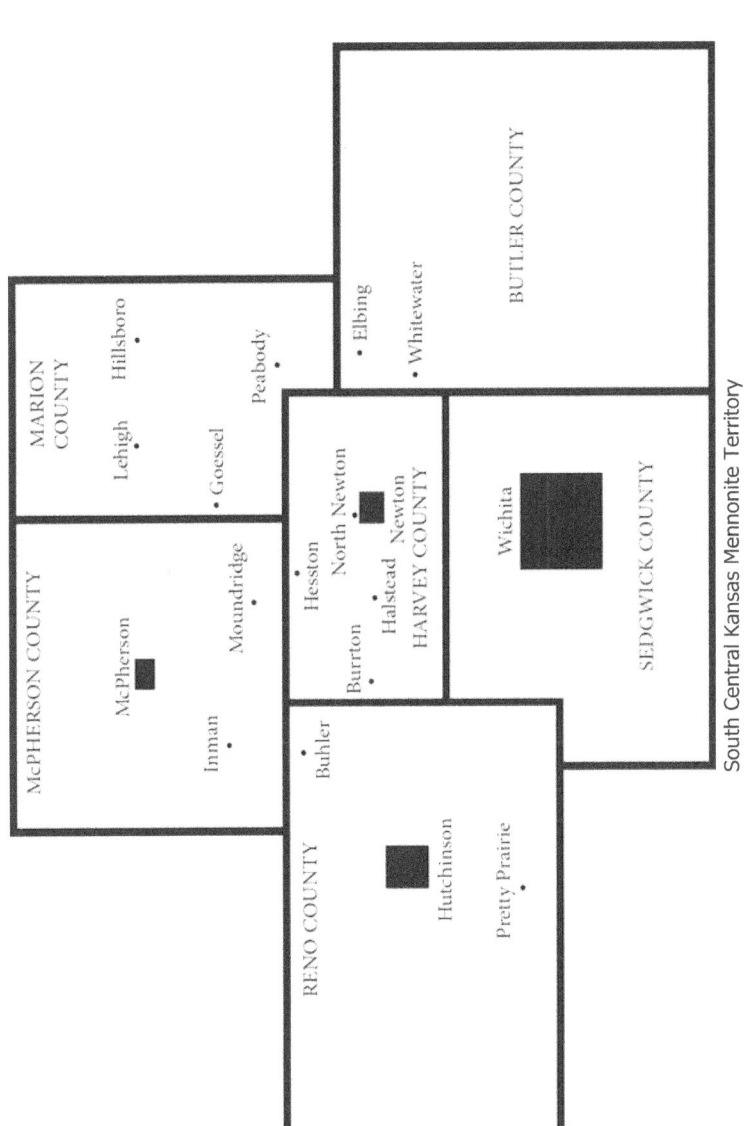

South Central Kansas Mennonite Territory

6 People of Two Kingdoms II

Kansas Mennonites in 1940

In 1940, before the United States entered World War II, there were 12,676 Mennonites in south central Kansas, spread over six counties.[8] Mennonites were overwhelmingly rural. They lived on family farms and in small towns of southern McPherson county, western Marion county, and northern Harvey county. Other more isolated congregations were located on the periphery of the settlement in Reno, Butler, and Sedgwick counties. Despite their small numbers, their presence helped make the region as a whole distinctively pluralistic. Elsewhere in the United States people tended to settle and live with their own kind, whether Congregationalist, Methodist, Baptist, Lutheran, Anglican, Mormon, or other religious groups. Single denominations were dominant in the vast majority of counties in the United States.[9] Mennonites also clustered together where they settled in Pennsylvania, Virginia, Ohio, Indiana, Iowa, and Kansas. But they were always too few in numbers to become the dominant social/religious group. As of 1950, the Mennonites were a minority of less than 25% in any county of south central Kansas. Despite their relatively small population, Mennonites kept any one other group from dominating.

Mennonite institutional development—colleges, newspapers, hospitals, retirement homes, business enterprises—strengthened the Mennonite impact on the region. Mennonite colleges within a thirty mile radius at North Newton (Bethel College), Hillsboro (Tabor College), and Hesston (Hesston College) contributed significantly to the educational and cultural level of the region. Mennonites had public visibility and influence beyond their numbers. Many people considered south central Kansas to be

---

[8]The number was compiled from the church directories of Mennonite conferences in or around 1940. It includes the following counties: McPherson, Marion, Harvey, Reno, Butler (Peabody and Fairmont townships), and Sedgwick (Wichita city). It does not include smaller, more isolated congregations such as the Amish in Reno County and other congregations in western Kansas.

[9]See the map "Religion in America: 1950" accompanying Edwin Scott Gaustad, *Historical Atlas of Religion in America* (New York: Harper & Row, 1962). Figure C10. Thanks to John A. Lapp for pointing out this pattern of American religious group settlement.

"Mennonite country." Steven Foulke, in a geographical study of "Mennonitism in South Central Kansas," concluded that the region was "strongly influenced by a Mennonite presence for well over a century." In Foulke's view, "Despite the strong presence of Catholic, Methodist, and other churches in the area, the public and often contrary nature of Mennonite ideology makes Mennonitism visible locally in ways not observed in other faiths."[10]

Between World War II and the early years of the twenty-first century, Kansas Mennonites received both compliments and criticisms in the local press. Stuart Awbrey, editor of the *Hutchinson News*, wrote in 1976, "No Central Kansan can escape the Mennonite influence. Few Central Kansans will question the Mennonite conviction and devotion, not only to doctrinal faith but also to their fellow men."[11] Whenever America went to war, however, central Kansas Americans were not so complimentary. They resented the Mennonite refusal of military conscription and their public peace witness. Indeed, the Mennonite public peace identity seemed to generate a distinctively strong response by patriotic veterans' organizations. Robert Kreider, Mennonite scholar and church leader, observed that American veterans' organizations throughout the country in small towns with substantial Mennonite population—in Ohio, Indiana, and Virginia as well as Kansas—were more energized and vigorous than veterans in average American towns.[12] The ambivalent attitudes of the non-Mennonites toward Mennonites were a major influence on the history of Mennonite involvement in American politics chronicled in this volume.

Outsiders often viewed the Mennonites as a singular and more or less homogeneous group. In fact, they were divided into subgroups that were quite different from each other. Their differences had to do with decisions they made about the extent of acculturation to their host American society. The south central

---

[10]Steven Vail Foulke, "Shaping of Place: Mennonitism in South-Central Kansas," Ph.D. dissertation in geography, University of Kansas, 1998, 30-1.

[11]*The Hutchinson News*, 31 January 1976, 4.

[12]Robert Kreider, interview by James C. Juhnke, July 22, 2008. Kreider noted the Veterans Day parade organized in 1967 in Newton in opposition to an antiwar "Repentance Walk" at Bethel College.

8 People of Two Kingdoms II

Kansas Mennonites were divided into five separate organized larger bodies.

Group	1940 membership	percentage
Western District of the General Conference Mennonite Church	8,355	66%
Mennonite Brethren	1,666	13%
Church of God in Christ Mennonite (Holdeman)	1,216	9.6%
(Old) Mennonite, South Central Conference of the Mennonite Church	890	7%
Krimmer Mennonite Brethren	549	4.3%
Total	12,676	100%

More than ninety percent of the Mennonites of south central Kansas were descendants of German speaking immigrants of the 1870s and 1880s, mostly from Poland and Russia. The (Old) Mennonite group, whose larger communities were east of the Mississippi River, were a small minority in Kansas, although they had their own private academy and two-year college in Hesston. Nearly all Kansas Mennonites had begun to speak the English language, but most of them had grown up in families that spoke a north German dialect known as Low German or *"Plautdietsch."* The levels of political awareness and involvement of these groups varied widely. The largest group, the Western District General Conference, was more politically engaged than the other four groups. The Holdeman Mennonites, on the conservative edge of the Mennonite complex, kept themselves separate from the world through the wearing of beards by men and distinctive dress by women—and by not voting in political elections.

This book is a study of Mennonite engagement in the American political world. It is not a general and balanced study of the social, economic, and cultural life of all Kansas Mennonite groups. Not included here, for example, is the Mennonite community in Meade

County in western Kansas.[13] Most attention in this book is given to the Western District of the General Conference Mennonite Church. The General Conference (bi-national–U.S. and Canada) denominational headquarters and four-year liberal arts college (Bethel College) were located in Newton and North Newton in Harvey County. These institutions helped ensure that the General Conference Mennonites, the majority group in Kansas, would remain the most progressive and politically active of Mennonites leading up to—and after—World War II.

---

[13]Royden Loewen has written two excellent studies which include Mennonites in Meade County in western Kansas: *Family, Church and Market: A Mennonite Community in the Old and New Worlds* (Urbana: University of Illinois Press, 1993), and *Diaspora in the Countryside: Two Mennonite Communities and Mid-Twentieth Century Rural Disjuncture* (Urbana: University of Illinois Press, 2006).

Chapter 2

Coming of the War

On the hot Kansas afternoon of August 4, 1940, at a time normally dedicated to Sunday afternoon naps or to visiting with friends and relatives, the men of the Eden Mennonite Church in southern McPherson County gathered to talk about the impending military draft.[1] Three visiting members of the Western District Mennonite peace committee presented to the Eden men information about the Burke-Wadsworth Bill then before Congress. The peace committee visitors were Jesse N. Smucker, pastor of the Bethel College Mennonite Church in North Newton; Peter H. Richert, pastor of the Tabor Mennonite Church near Walton; and Emmet Harshbarger, history professor from Bethel College. Earlier that year, along with other leaders of historic peace churches, Harshbarger had met with President Franklin D. Roosevelt in Washington, D.C., to represent the interests of religious pacifists. After discussing the matter in August, the men of Eden Mennonite Church voted to send telegrams opposing the draft "to officials at Washington," and to encourage members of the congregation to send letters and cards, "stating our views on military service." Robert Wuthnow, noted scholar of faith and politics in Kansas, has observed, "Houses of worship in the nation's heartland have always been places to discuss political issues."[2]

On August 3, the day before the gathering at Eden, President Roosevelt had for the first time endorsed the Burke-Wadsworth Bill. A wily politician, Roosevelt had let others advocate for the controversial measure until after the Democratic Party Convention had nominated him for an unprecedented third term as president. Never before in American history had the country enacted military conscription in peacetime. Roosevelt now argued that a military draft would help keep the United States out of the war that was raging in Europe. Harshbarger, along with many other Mennonites,

---

[1] Eden Mennonite Church Record Book, Congregational Meeting Minutes 1926-1980, 70.
[2] Robert Wuthnow, *Red State Religion, Faith and Politics in America's Heartland* (Princeton: Princeton University Press, 2012), 361.

was convinced military conscription would be another step *toward* war.

Kansas Mennonite congregations and individual church members who sent telegrams and wrote letters to Congress in 1940 acted not only in response to their regional Western District Conference peace committee recommendations. They were carrying out a mandate from the bi-national (U.S.-Canada) General Conference Mennonite Church denomination. At the 1938 triennial meeting in Saskatoon, Saskatchewan, the denomination's Peace Committee had recommended that members "write to their Representatives and Senators urging them to support legislation favorable to peace and to oppose measures that are unfavorable to peace."[3] The Peace Committee had offered an optimistic and pragmatic reason for their recommendation: "It is a fact that our national legislators do give heed to the convictions of their constituency."

In 1940 Kansas Mennonites could indeed assume that "national legislators" who represented them in Washington, D.C., were spokesmen for peace, rather than for war and war preparations. Kansas Senator Arthur Capper, a Republican of Quaker background, vigorously promoted peace from the mid-1930s until December 1941 when the Japanese attacked Pearl Harbor. Capper supported nationalizing the munitions industries, restricting the profits that business corporations could make on war, and amending the constitution to require a popular referendum before the declaration of war.[4] In 1937 when the Kansas Institute of International Relations at Bethel College came up $200 short of meeting its budget, Institute director Harshbarger sent a letter to Capper in Washington asking him to make up the difference.[5] Apparently Capper did not send money to the Kansas Institute, but it was clear that peace advocates believed the Senator was on their side.

---

[3]*Minutes and Reports of the Twenty-Eighth Session of the General Conference of the Mennonite Church of North America, 1938*, 141.

[4]John W. Partin, "The Dilemma of 'A Good, Very Good Man': Capper and Noninterventionism, 1936-1941," *Kansas History* 2 (Summer 1979): 87.

[5]Letter from Harshbarger to Capper, June 23, 1937. International Relations Institute Collection, V.14, Mennonite Library and Archives.

John M. Houston, a Democrat Congressman from Newton (1934-42), spoke out against "sending American soldiers to foreign battlefields." The National Council for the Prevention of War reported that Houston had an excellent, though not perfect, record on peace issues. Edmund G. Kaufman, president of Bethel College, was a good friend of Houston and invited him to speak at Bethel on a number of occasions. In 1939 Houston responded to one of Kaufman's appeals, saying, "under no circumstances will I vote to send American soldiers to foreign battle fields."[6] Kaufman wrote to both Houston and Capper about peace issues, and also sent the senator Christmas greetings and congratulations after election victories. Houston and Capper both voted against the Burke-Wadsworth conscription bill.[7]

Some non-Mennonite newspaper editors in Kansas towns with substantial Mennonite population also spoke out for peace. Vernard Vogt, the editor of the *Moundridge Journal*, was a member of the Methodist Church and of German Evangelical background. Vogt warned against insidious pro-war propaganda. On January 13, 1938, he recalled the official lies about the sinking of the *Maine* (1898) and the *Lusitania* (1915) that had misled the United States in the Spanish American War and World War I. "Every sane man abhors war," wrote Vogt, "Every good American abhors it." Even after Germany had invaded Poland in September 1939, Vogt wrote that, despite sympathies for the allies, "we are not going to do any killing if we can help it." By the spring of 1941 the *Moundridge Journal* shifted its editorial position to support the war. But it is clear that Kansas Mennonites who made a public witness for peace before the 1940 election were expressing widely held popular views, rather than speaking as a small and separate minority.

Three young men, Bill Juhnke, Elmer Ediger, and Robert Kreider, illustrate the Mennonite political witness against war. Bill Juhnke in 1940 was a high school social science teacher in Moundridge, where Vernard Vogt was a school board member.[8] In September

---

[6]John M. Houston to Edmund G. Kaufman, October 26, 1939, folder 187, box 50, E. G. Kaufman presidential records, III.1.A.1.g, Mennonite Library and Archives.

[7]James C. Juhnke, "Edmund G. Kaufman, Minister of Peace in a World of War," *Kansas History* 18 (Spring 1995): 52-3.

[8]James C. Juhnke, *So Much to be Thankful For: The Bill and Meta Juhnke Story* (Wichita, KS: Juhnke, 2009), 77, 89-94.

Coming of the War   13

1940, after the wheat harvest and the annual Western District Mennonite Youth Retreat, Juhnke had begun a systematic file that he labeled "clippings on compulsory military service." He pasted and stapled newspaper stories, mostly from the *Wichita Eagle*, onto scrap pages of 8 ½ by 11 inch paper. On the first page of Juhnke's clippings file was an Associated Press release of July 23 that said the Burke-Wadsworth bill would provide for "registration of 42,000,000 men, of whom 1,500,000 would be drafted in the first year."[9]

Juhnke was alarmed. He was subject to the draft—twenty-eight years old, married, and father of a two year old son. He was convinced that a peace-time military draft would be a step toward war. He and his wife, Meta Goering Juhnke, lived near Elyria four and a half miles north of the Eden Church on a farm he inherited as the oldest son in a family of ten children. Bill spent part of each summer at Kansas University (Lawrence) working toward a master's degree in public school administration. He was a popular teacher at Moundridge High School, noted for his quick wit, love of debate, and willingness to defend controversial causes. His master's thesis was about the teaching of controversial issues in Kansas high schools.

Bill and Meta Juhnke with Jimmy, 1938. Both Bill and Meta wrote to public officials against war.

Juhnke was the president of the Western District Young People's organization, and the editor of its quarterly youth publication that he had founded, *Western District Tidings* (circulation 1,500). In the summer of 1940, living at Kansas University in Lawrence, Bill and Meta wrote letters to Washington, D.C., against military conscription. Meta regularly listened to the "Farm and Home Hour" radio program, where commentator H. R. Baukhage held forth on leading issues of the day. Meta wrote to Mr. Baukhage that "peace-time compulsory military training" was "not democratic

---

[9] William E. Juhnke Collection, Folder "Clippings on Conscription," author's collection.

but is based on the Hitler type of regimentation." Bill wrote letters to President Franklin D. Roosevelt; to Kansas senators Clyde M. Reed and Arthur Capper; to Kansas 5th district congressman John M. Houston, and to Kansas governor Payne Ratner. He told them he agreed with aviator Charles Lindbergh's "idea of staying at home. We do not want to spill more American blood on European soil."

Bill and Meta Juhnke were Christian pacifists whose peace convictions were grounded in the life and teachings of Jesus. But in their letters to public officials they did not quote the Bible or use religious arguments. They spoke a secular language and used practical arguments about the futility of war. In some of his letters, Bill bolstered his authority by writing on Moundridge Public School letterhead and signing as "Head of Social Science Dep't Moundridge High School." Mr. Curt Siemens, the Moundridge superintendent of schools, whose name appeared on the letterhead, was also a Mennonite pacifist.

Elmer Ediger, social studies teacher at Buhler High School, drafted 1942.

Elmer Ediger, of Buhler, Kansas, had been inspired by Bill Juhnke's youth leadership. Elmer was born in Greensburg, Kansas, raised on a farm near Buhler, the seventh of eleven children in his family. His eight fun-loving brothers saw him as the most serious and scholarly of the large family. When Elmer attended Buhler High School, his school principal had been Edward E. Kaufman. Like Curt Siemens at Moundridge, Kaufman was a peace-minded Mennonite school administrator. He advocated the teaching of Bible in public schools.[10] As school principal, Kaufman allowed some students to put up an outdoor stand with military posters. Ediger and others in the Buhler school Hi-Y club, a Christian young men's organization, asked to put up a counter-poster in support of the Kellogg-Briand

---

[10]Edward E. Kaufman, "The Bible in Public Schools," *Mennonite Weekly Review* (30 October 1940), 3.

Peace Treaty for the outlawry of war as an instrument of national policy.[11] Kaufman was the advisor of the Hi-Y club and agreed to the request. As the Hi-Y student leader, Ediger wrote to Charles M. Sheldon, famous author and social gospel advocate of Topeka, Kansas. Ediger asked Sheldon for the text of a peace "pledge" that the Hi-Y club could use in their meetings. With his response, Sheldon enclosed an anti-war tract that called for a national popular referendum "on this war business."[12]

Elmer was a peace idealist eager to become involved in the world crisis. During his senior year at Bethel College, in February 1939, he applied (but did not go) to join an American Friends Service Committee program that was helping Jews leave Germany. He joined the Fellowship of Reconciliation. After graduating from Bethel in 1940 he taught sixth grade at Ellis in western Kansas. He wrote to the Ellis County draft board an extended rationale for his conscientious objection to military service. The heart of the matter was that "the spirit and teaching of Jesus are irreconcilable with war." The alternative to war was "Non-Violent Direct Action," a method that Mahatma Gandhi had proved to be effective in South Africa and in India. War was, Elmer wrote to the draft board, "an enemy of all of us, greater than Nazism, and an enemy against everything that is precious to the best interests of mankind." Even if nonviolence were not a practical alternative in the present case, "I would still be true to the fundamental truths that Jesus voiced."[13] He wrote in the same vein

Pro-war (left) and anti-war (right) posters at Buhler High School.

---

[11]Transcript of interview by Roger Juhnke, October 9, 1978. Elmer Ediger Collection, Mennonite Library and Archives.

[12]Charles M. Sheldon letter to Elmer Ediger, 16 Oct 1935. Sheldon, "A Vote on War." Carol Ediger Peters Collection..

[13]Elmer Ediger, "To the Local Board of Ellis County," 20 Sept 1941. Carol Ediger Peters Collection.

to his Congressman, Clifford R. Hope, claiming to be both "a Christian and a sincere patriot of the United States."[14]

Elmer spent part of the summer of 1941 in New York, visiting two experimental communitarian "frontier" groups he had learned about at Bethel College. One was a Christian Ashram in Harlem. There he experienced group discipline, silence, practical sharing, street "riots" and recreation, and study of the history and religious basis of pacifism and non-violent direct action. Another community was the rural "School of Living" in Suffern led by Ralph Templin. The school was "combination of church and agricultural station." Templin advocated "decentralism—from city factory to home factory, from large farms to small farms." Elmer talked with Ed Kaufman, Bethel College President, and with his friends Esko Loewen and Robert Kreider about implementing School of Living ideas at Bethel College or in his home town of Buhler.[15] He encouraged the director's son, Lawrence Templin, to attend Bethel College in the 1941-2 school year. While in New York Elmer attended the triennial meeting of his denomination, the General Conference Mennonite Church. There he got "a much better picture of Mennonitism." He was encouraged by visits with both the "more enlightened leaders" as well as those who were "conservative but tolerant." As a result, and especially in aftermath of his contacts with the communitarian experiments, they all "seemed much closer to me."[16] In January 1942 Elmer began teaching social science at Buhler High School, his alma mater. He was drafted in August 1942 and assigned to a Civilian Public Service camp at Colorado Springs, Colorado.

In the summer of 1940 Robert S. Kreider was between two years of graduate study in Chicago and earning money at the Ford Motor Company in Detroit, Michigan. Kreider, like Bill Juhnke and Elmer Ediger, was a graduate of Bethel College. But Kreider did not come from a large rural Mennonite family. His father, Amos E. Kreider, taught Bible classes at Bethel College. He also co-taught a class

---

[14]Elmer Ediger to Clifford R. Hope, July 22, 1940. Elmer Ediger Collection, Mennonite Library and Archives

[15]Letters to Elmer Ediger from Robert Kreider, 2 Jan 1942, and from Esko Loewen, 14 Jan 1942. Carol Ediger Peters Collection.

[16]Elmer Ediger letter to Mildred Gerbrandt, 18 Oct 1941. Carol Ediger Peters Collection.

titled "Peace Principles." There were two children in the Kreider family, a sign of the lower birth rate that the Mennonite transition from farm to town to city would bring. Robert Kreider was an intelligent and brash student leader. As editor of the Bethel College student newspaper, he had challenged the president of the college (Edmund G. Kaufman) on athletic policy. He also critiqued John Thierstein, the editor of the denomination's official periodical, *The Mennonite*, for his inadequate understanding of Hitler and National Socialism. Kreider had traveled in Europe the summer after graduating from Bethel. He eagerly read the Detroit daily newspapers for news of the European war and the progress of the Burke-Wadsworth conscription bill.

In the fall of 1940, Kreider became more directly involved in national electoral politics than did any other Kansas Mennonite. He was elected president of the Socialist Club on the University of Chicago campus. In that capacity he had opportunity to meet Dr. Robert Hutchins, the anti-war president of the university. He also met the Socialist Party candidates for president and vice-president in 1940—Norman Thomas and Maynard Krueger. As club president, Kreider chaired a well-attended public meeting with Thomas and Krueger as main speakers. In the November elections, Kreider voted for the Socialist ticket. He said it was a "protest vote" against Democrat and Republican national political leaders who lacked the wit or will to resist the drift toward war.[17]

Robert Kreider, with pick-ax in International Voluntary Service for Peace in England, July 1939.

Despite the heady cultural and political environment of the University of Chicago, Robert Kreider was not seduced away from his Mennonite community of origin by the promises of upward academic mobility and urban worldly glory. In letters to his parents and to his fellow students at Bethel College, he wrote of a deepening appreciation for his Anabaptist-Mennonite heritage. His

---

[17]Robert S. Kreider, *My Early Years, An Autobiography* (Kitchener: Pandora Press, 2002), 265-68.

teachers at the university were indeed inspiring, but he also realized that he had gotten an excellent undergraduate education at Bethel College.[18] He fantasized about the prospect of returning to teach there. To his idealistic student friends back at Bethel, Kreider wrote that the Socialist Party did not have all the answers. Nor was the liberal theology of the social gospel necessarily adequate to the dire world crisis.[19]

Bill Juhnke, Elmer Ediger, and Robert Kreider were part of a remarkable generation of idealistic peace activists at Bethel College. These future denominational leaders were unusually aware of world political and social events, and convinced of the relevance of Mennonite ideals for addressing world problems. In the late 1930s the Bethel campus became, in the judgment of historian Perry Bush, "a hubbub of peace and service activism that would not appear on Mennonite campuses again until the 1960s."[20]

At the center of activist peace idealism on the Bethel campus was Dr. Emmett L. Harshbarger, professor of history and social sciences from 1933 to 1942. He was something of an outsider to the insular Kansas Mennonite community. Born in Ohio to an acculturated Mennonite family, he could not speak either Low German or High German, the mother tongues of most of his students. His Ph.D. dissertation at Ohio State University (1933) was on a non-Mennonite topic, "African Slave Trade in Anglo-American Diplomacy." Bethel students were dazzled by his political sophistication, his knowledge of international affairs, and his dynamism in the classroom. Esko Loewen, one of Harshbarger's student admirers, reported that by 1941 a quarter of the entire student body had become history majors.[21]

In his teaching and public speaking, Harshbarger's passion was for a Christian peace witness to public order. He was an internationalist, not an isolationist or an "America Firster." In a summary of his personal "Stand on Peace," Harshbarger wrote,

---

[18] Kreider, *My Early Years*, 271.
[19] Esko Loewen, interview by Keith Sprunger, Oct. 9, 1973, 940.5316 #1-2, MLA.
[20] Perry Bush, *Two Kingdoms, Two Loyalties*, 51.
[21] Esko Loewen interview.

Realizing that the Christian conscience is the strongest personal and social motivation for righteousness, I believe that the spread of the Christian ideal for peace is an all-important factor in achieving world peace. . . . We must use our privileges as citizens to influence Congressmen and other leaders to formulate national policy in harmony with peaceful relations; we must educate youth away from the glories of war to the glories of peace; we must build a strong permanent international organization which can settle peaceably the inevitable international disputes; we must consolidate the mighty influence of the Christian Church on the side of peace; and, we must, in every way possible, increase the agencies and occasions for cooperation instead of friction in our social and economic relationships.[22]

Harshbarger had a double mission. One task was world-transformation—to carry the gospel of Christian peace to a war-making world. Another task was to awaken the Mennonites to their political responsibilities. Some traditionalist Mennonite church leaders, including some who had been influenced by American fundamentalism, were inclined to be suspicious of political activity and to focus on change through personal religious conversion. Some Mennonites worried that modern pacifism "seems to be aligned, if not identified, with political movements, such as Communism and the like."[23] In answering such fears, Harshbarger typically did not build primarily upon Bible texts, theological analysis, or Mennonite history in a traditional Mennonite fashion. He was rather a modern

Emmett L. Harshbarger, academic peace activist and history teacher at Bethel College, 1933-1942.

---

[22]Statement in the summary for a Bethel College class, "The Peace Principle," 1937-8, box 33, folder 418, MS.108, Edmund G. Kaufman papers, MLA.<check this>

[23]Western District Conference Report of 45th annual meeting, Beatrice, Nebraska, 21-23 October 1936, "Peace Committee Report," 2167<?>.

Christian social scientist who used the language of sociology and politics.[24] He was a mediator of new ways of thinking to traditionalist Mennonites in rural churches. In connection with the annual Bible Week lectures at Bethel College in 1934 Harshbarger offered a five-session daily "course for ministers on modern social movements and their religious implications." His topics were Communism, Fascism and Hitlerism, Socialism, Recent American Trends, and The Peace Movement.[25]

The anti-war spirit did not find as strong political expression in the town of Hillsboro and Tabor College as it did in North Newton and Bethel College. But some folks in Hillsboro did speak out for peace. In the fall of 1938, George S. Klassen, a local dentist and outspoken pacifist, spoke to the Hillsboro High School Hi-Y Club. Klassen had been a conscientious objector in World War I, and had collected war artifacts. The high school newspaper noted his "word or two denouncing the terrible scourges of war." Klassen convinced the club "that patriotism changes during a war crisis. When our country is at peace it is patriotic to protect the life and interests of man, but during a war patriotism changes to a policy of killing and destroying for the good of the nation."[26] In May 1940 the "Tabor College Bulletin," also published in the *Hillsboro Vorwaerts*, included an anti-war article, probably by student editor Ernest Schellenberg, arguing for neutrality. "(No) matter which side wins, both sides will have suffered and lost more than victory is worth. . . . Then again we ask, why favor either side for in doing so, one is favoring destruction."[27] Shortly before the 1940 election Vernon Vogt, editor of Tabor's student newspaper, wrote a fervent editorial insisting that American young people had rejected war. They were not showing up at military recruiting offices. Why not? Wrote Vogt, "It is the result of education. Young people . . . have their own ideas of democracy and they want to live it out. They don't want to stoop

---

[24]For an example of Harshbarger's language for a scholarly academic audience, see his essay, "Can America Be Neutral?" *The Southwestern Social Science Quarterly* (March 1938), 1-10.

[25]"Program for the Bible Week at Bethel College," *Bethel College Bulletin* (Feb. 1934), n. p.

[26]*Vorwaerts*, Nov 18, 1938, 4. "Hillsboro High School Oracle," ed. Marjorie Klassen.

[27]*Vorwaerts*, May 3, 1940, 7, "Tabor College Bulletin," ed. Ernest Schellenberg.

to war as a means to stop war; neither do they believe that dying for our democratic principles will save them."[28]

The official statements of the General Conference and Western District peace committees, on which Emmett Harshbarger served, reflected a compromise of competing voices. On one hand was the traditional Mennonite pietistic language of conservative leaders such as Peter H. Richert and Henry P. Krehbiel. On the other hand was Harshbarger's more political language. In September 1939 the Western District Peace Committee adopted a letter to send to members of Congress, and published the letter in the denominational periodical, *The Mennonite*. The letter contained specific policy recommendations, surely drafted by Harshbarger, regarding the war in Europe. It called for "positive neutrality" between the warring nations, a prohibition on sending military supplies, and the exertion of national influence "in a non-partisan spirit toward the peaceable adjustment of all differences." But the statement also had traditional Mennonite language supplied by other committee members: "As followers of Jesus Christ we are convinced that war is sin, both against God and Man." It also called the nation to live by a Christian ethic: "as a Christian nation our country should not engage in war with any other nation."[29]

Kansas Mennonite letters and statements to government on the eve of World War II, mostly written by second generation immigrants, did not have clear positions about Mennonite identity and about church-state relations in a democratic society. Was the United States a Christian nation or was it not? Cornelius H. Wedel, first president of Bethel College, had provided a theology for Mennonites before World War I.[30] But Wedel had died untimely in 1910, and his writings had not been translated from German into English. The most extensive peace statement by a Kansas Mennonite before World War II was Henry P. Krehbiel's book, *War,*

---

[28]"Youth Accepts Challenge," Tabor College Bulletin, *Hillsboro Journal*, (17 October 1940), 7.

[29]"Letter to Members of Congress," *The Mennonite* (3 Oct 1939), 3.

[30]On Wedel's theology see J. Denny Weaver, *Keeping Salvation Ethical, Mennonite and Amish Atonement Theology in the Late Nineteenth Century* (Scottdale, PA: Herald Press, 1997), 78-91, 221-224, and James C. Juhnke, *Dialogue With a Heritage, Cornelius H. Wedel and the Beginnings of Bethel College* (North Newton, KS: Bethel College, 1987), 63-75.

Peace, Amity (1937). Krehbiel before World War I had served a term in the Kansas House of Representatives. He was a progressive optimist who believed that international warfare was passing away. But he rejected political and economic efforts to end war as inevitably coercive. Peace would come by spiritual transformation, through a worldwide revival of Christian peace-minded teaching and behavior. In the judgment of a later critic, the thinking of men such as Krehbiel and Harshbarger, as different as they were from each other, undermined Mennonite minority consciousness and proved inadequate to the crisis of a world war.[31] To be sure, Kansas Mennonites were not theologically sophisticated. Nor can it be said that Christian theology in general, in America or in Europe, was prepared for the crisis of global warfare.

In their peace witness to the national government, first to keep the United States out of the war and then to protect the interests of conscientious objectors in case of the military draft, Mennonites worked together with the two other largest pacifist denominations—the Friends/Quakers and the Church of the Brethren. Groundwork for cooperation of the historic peace churches had been laid in a meeting held in Newton, Kansas, in the fall of 1935, at the invitation of Henry Peter Krehbiel. Harshbarger served as vice-chairman of a new "Mennonite Central Peace Committee" created in 1939. On January 10, 1940, a historic peace church delegation met with President Franklin Roosevelt and delivered two statements about the prospects for military conscription and military service. The Friends, more than the Mennonites, were concerned about policies to protect absolutist and non-religious conscientious objectors. President Roosevelt charmed the delegation and led them to believe, mistakenly as it turned out, that he appreciated their position and would help to protect their interests.[32]

Mennonite weekly newspapers in Hillsboro and Newton in 1940 reflected a readership in rapid transition from the German language to the English language. The *Hillsboro Journal*, an eight-

---

[31] Rodney James Sawatsky, *History and Ideology: American Mennonite Identity Definition through History* (Kitchener, ON: Pandora Press, 2005). 107-114,

[32] Albert N. Keim and Grant M. Stoltzfus, *The Politics of Conscience: The Historic Peace Churches And America at War, 1917-1995* (Scottdale, Pa: Herald Press, 1988), 77.

page paper edited by Peter H. Berg and A. J. Voth, was a dual language paper. Until July 1940 it had been named *Vorwaerts*, with the sub-heading "A family paper for the German house." Even after changing its name to *Hillsboro Journal,* nearly half of the text was in the German language. Most of its readers were from the Mennonite Brethren church. The Herald Publishing Company in Newton, reaching a primarily General Conference Mennonite constituency, published separate newspapers in German and English. Henry Peter Krehbiel had founded *Mennonite Weekly Review* in 1923. Gerhard H. Willms, who in 1922 had immigrated to Kansas from the Mennonite Molotschna colony in South Russia, edited the German language newspaper, *Der Herold*. Most of *Der Herold's* readers were in Canada. It ceased publication at the end of 1941. Menno Schrag, who had attended Hesston Academy, Bethel College, and Wheaton College, after 1935 edited the *Mennonite Weekly Review*. None of these Mennonite editors commented extensively on the presidential candidates, or upon issues in the campaigns. But these editors all chose news articles that favored the Republican Party and its candidates.

In issues before the election, Berg (and perhaps also associate editor A. J. Voth) revealed their partisan preferences with a gratuitous insult of Eleanor Roosevelt (who allegedly told reporters, "I've nothing to say about anything."), and with news items favorable to Willkie ("He Stands for Peace" and "More Jobs, Less taxes is Willkie's Pledge"). The front page of the issue before the election featured photographs of Willkie and of Payne Ratner, Republican candidate for governor of Kansas. "Vote for Wendell Willkie and Payne Ratner, and rest assured that our national and state problems will be solved properly."[33] The paper did not identify this as a paid political advertisement. The *Hillsboro Herald* also announced a "Republican Rally" to be held in Hillsboro City Hall on Saturday evening.

Meanwhile editor Willms in Newton ran front page news reports of Wendell Willkie's claim that President Roosevelt was associating with "little Hitlers" (October 17), and that a third term for Roosevelt would be "the last step toward dictatorship" (October 24). On October 30 editor Schrag of *Mennonite Weekly Review*

---

[33]*Hillsboro Journal,* 17 October 1940, 4; 24 October 1940, 7; 31 October 1940, 1.

obliquely endorsed Willkie on the basis of the third term issue. "It is an especially fateful decision," wrote Schrag, "because of the totalitarian trends which have been set in motion all over the world. It is not the personalities involved that counts. Neither Republican or Democratic candidates will be able to guarantee prosperity or peace.... But it is the trend which is all important."[34]

In the 1940 election Jacob V. Friesen of Hillsboro was elected to the Kansas legislature on the Republican ticket without Democratic opposition. He was just the second Mennonite since immigration in the 1870s in that office. The first had been Henry Peter Krehbiel of Newton in 1909. Friesen was a graduate of Bethel College, former public school superintendent, and owner of the Home Furnishing Store on Main Street in Hillsboro. He was a member of the First Mennonite Church of Hillsboro (GC) and married to Renetta Schultz, teacher of English at Tabor College. Like Krehbiel, Friesen served just one term in the Kansas legislature, a sign of general Mennonite disinterest in wider state politics. His decision not to run in 1942 apparently had less to do with anti-Germanism in wartime than with Friesen's primary interest in local public welfare. Long active in civic affairs, he served as mayor of Hillsboro from 1943 to 1951.[35]

The actual votes in precincts with substantial Mennonite population reveal that the 1940 election was a watershed in Kansas Mennonite political identity. From the time of their immigration to Kansas in the 1870s and 1880s, Mennonites had generally distributed their votes to Republicans and Democrats in numbers that did not diverge widely or consistently from the voting patterns of other Kansans.[36] But in 1940 Mennonites voted overwhelmingly and distinctively for the Republican ticket. After 1940 Mennonites quite consistently returned a Republican majority that was about fifteen percent higher than the Kansas state average.[37]

---

[34] *Mennonite Weekly Review*, 30 October 1940, 5.

[35] "Election Results," *Hillsboro Journal*, 7 November 1940, 1; Jacob V. Friesen file at Center for Mennonite Brethren Studies at Tabor College. Ray Wiebe, interview by James C. Juhnke, Hillsboro, April 4, 2014.

[36] Juhnke, *People of Two Kingdoms*, 3-7, 125-6.

[37] See Appendix B.

	1940 Presidential Vote in selected precincts of substantial Mennonite population		1940 presidential vote in Kansas overall	
Republican – Willkie	3,607	81%	489,169	56.8%
Democrat – Roosevelt	783	17.6%	364,725	42.4%
Socialist – Thomas	37	.8%	6,403	.8% (Thomas & Babson combined)
Prohibition – Babson	26	.6%		

Four years earlier, in the 1936 presidential election, these same Mennonite precincts had voted for the Republican candidate, Alfred M. Landon, by a majority of only 55.4%. Landon had been governor of Kansas. What can account for this radical shift from 1936 to 1940 of more than twenty-five percentage points to the Republican candidate? And why was this shift so much more dramatic than the Kansas statewide shift of only eleven points? The answer must be that the pacifist Mennonites thought that the Democrat president, Franklin D. Roosevelt, was leading the country toward war. The convincing evidence was the national draft registration of young men between ages 21 and 35 on October 16, 1940. The subsequent draft lottery was conducted October 29, just one week before the election. Editor P. H. Berg of the *Hillsboro Journal* wrote, "Not even the presidential campaign overshadowed the dramatic draft lottery in Washington."[38] Presidential candidates Willkie and Roosevelt both said they would not send Americans to fight in European wars, but Berg said he was more inclined to

---

[38] *Hillsboro Journal*, 7 November 1940, 1.

believe Willkie's sincerity. Even so the Mennonite vote was more a protest against the Democrats than an embrace of the Republicans. It set an enduring pattern.

Mennonite communities did not all vote exactly alike. As in previous elections, in 1940 the strongest Republican majorities were in the Dutch-Russian townships in Marion County. Menno and West Branch townships voted 97% Republican. These were primarily Mennonites of Low-German background (originally from Prussia and Russia) in the Alexanderwohl settlement. The Republican majority was smaller among the Swiss-Volhynian Mennonites in southern McPherson County. Albion township in Reno County, which included the town of Pretty Prairie and a minority of Swiss-Volhynian Mennonites, actually gave a 56% majority to the Democrat Roosevelt.

More evidence of Mennonite diversity surfaced on the Bethel College campus in North Newton. A student straw poll, taken after a meeting at which two Newton attorneys made their cases for the Democrat and Republican parties, resulted in 146 votes for Willkie (R), 42 votes for Roosevelt (D), and 65 votes for Thomas (Socialist). The Bethel vote of 30.5% for the Socialist candidate may have reflected the activity of the student Socialist club on campus, and a greater awareness that Norman Thomas was the only strong anti-war candidate. A few Bethel faculty members, including Amos E. Kreider, Bible professor, probably also voted Socialist as a protest.[39] In any case, despite the larger undeniable Republican trend, there was some variety among Mennonites in their political preferences. Conservative Mennonites who feared the allegedly corrupting and radicalizing tendencies on Bethel's liberal arts campus apparently had good reason for their fears. There was a gap between Mennonite farm and Mennonite college campus.

On the county and local level, Mennonites were not strongly represented in comparison to their numbers. Their people were settled on the edges of four counties (McPherson, Marion, Harvey, and Reno), rather than primarily in one county.[40] They were far from a majority in any county, less than 25% of the population. The evolution of Mennonite involvement in local and county politics

---

[39]Robert Kreider interview by author, 11 November 2008.
[40]See map, chapter 1.

would have been significantly different if any one or two county boundaries had enclosed a strong Mennonite majority. McPherson County had three commissioners elected according to district, and the Mennonites were a majority in the southern district. In that district Gerhard Zerger, a member of the Eden Mennonite Church and a member of the Democrat party, served as commissioner for sixteen years—from 1934 to 1952. In 1940 three additional Mennonite Democrats of Swiss-Volhynian background, ran for office in McPherson County and were defeated: J. D. C. Goering (state representative), Jacob A. Wedel (county treasurer) and David T. Stucky (county clerk).

The passage of the Burke-Wadsworth conscription bill and the approach of the general election in 1940 prompted a higher level of political commentary and activity among Kansas Mennonites than at any time since their immigration. Some Mennonites had been arguing about American politics and voting in elections already in the 1870s and 1880s. A new generation of leaders in the 1930s and 1940s–men such as Emmett Harshbarger, Bill Juhnke, Elmer Ediger, and Robert Kreider–were generally better informed about national politics, and more likely to write letters to their national legislators than were Kansas Mennonites a quarter century earlier in the run up to World War I. The disillusioning experience of that Great War, both for Kansas Mennonites and for political leaders such as Arthur Capper and John Houston, had made opposition to war and military conscription an attractive political option in the late 1930s. Kansas Mennonite activism surely belies the typical image of Mennonites as a withdrawn and apolitical people. The dominant General Conference majority of immigrants from Eastern Europe and Russia were more inclined toward political involvement than were (Old) Mennonites and Amish folk east of the Mississippi River. An image of Mennonites as energetic political activists must be qualified by the presence of smaller groups in Kansas, such as the (Old) Mennonites and Church of God in Christ (Holdeman) Mennonites, who held to a stronger dualism of church and world and who were reluctant to speak out politically.

In the wake of Roosevelt's victory in the November election of 1940, editor Menno Schrag of *Mennonite Weekly Review* warned that the country was abandoning the individualism of its forefathers: "A more socialistic society is in the making."[41] Meanwhile Peter H. Berg of the *Hillsboro Journal* expressed a typical Mennonite distaste for politics. "As a nation," wrote editor Berg, "we can be thankful that Presidential elections only occur once every four years."[42] Berg was heartily tired of noisy political meetings, garish posters, and unsightly political buttons on the coat lapels of men walking the streets of Hillsboro. Kansas Mennonites did not generally have high expectations from the decisions of government. In the fall of 1940 their voices registered a protest rather than an affirmation of the course of public policy—both in their witness to government about impending military conscription, and in their rejection of President Roosevelt and the Democrat party at the polls on November 5.

---

[41] *Mennonite Weekly Review*, 6 November 1940, 5.
[42] *Hillsboro Journal*, 7 November 1940, 4.

Chapter 3

World War II: Crisis and Revitalization

Mennonites in World War II struck a new balance of separation from, and involvement with, the American political and social order. Their pacifism and their ethnic German background made them aliens in a country at war against Germany. After Pearl Harbor, it was not an option to work within the political system to influence public policy. The war empowered conservative Mennonites who in principle opposed involvement in politics and supported separation from the world. At the same time it disempowered progressive Mennonites who prior to Pearl Harbor had advocated a more aggressive and proactive political witness. The war forced the core of peace activists at Bethel College to abandon their political witness. America in wartime had no room for pacifists who wanted to shape public policy.

At the same time, Mennonites came into an unprecedented cooperative relationship with the United States government. They agreed to undertake alternative service work "of national importance" under government supervision in Civilian Public Service (CPS) camps. The CPS camps taught Mennonites that America, though the country scorned pacifists in wartime, was able to accommodate constructive religious nonconformists. Mennonite leaders could argue that their separated rural communities exhibited a form of authentic American patriotism. The war fostered both a new separation from American politics, and a new engagement with the political order in a wider context.

The Kansas Mennonite experience with the political order in World War II resulted in a revitalization of communal identity. As in World War I, Mennonite religious pacifists were set apart from their war-crusading American neighbors. They experienced enough exclusion and persecution to be reminded that they were a peculiar people. The war strengthened their separate religious identity, even as war-induced economic recovery increased their financial resources. The church lost many of its young men who chose, against official denominational policy, to accept military service. For those who rejected participation in war, CPS turned into a leadership laboratory for the denomination's future, and helped generate the basis for new programs of Mennonite benevolence.

The Mennonite Settler: Symbol of Civic Acceptability in a Time of Rejection

Mennonite Settler monument in Newton Athletic Park, dedicated September 10, 1942

In the summer of 1940, at the dawn of a wartime era of public shame and embarrassment for Mennonite pacifists, the Newton Junior Chamber of Commerce (Jaycees) announced a project to celebrate the Mennonite contribution to the Kansas economy.[1] Behind the project were three Jaycee members who were of Mennonite background and had attended Bethel College: John C. Suderman, Irvin E. (Dutch) Toevs, and Paul Kliewer.[2] The Jaycees promoted the project in the style of small town boosterism–"the biggest thing ever undertaken in Newton." Mennonite farmers in the area donated wheat to put the project fund drive over the top. Funds to employ the sculptor, Max Nixon, a native of Butler County and recent graduate of the University of Kansas, came from the government's Works Progress Administration (WPA).

The result was an eleven-foot limestone sculpture of a Mennonite settler, set atop a six-foot pedestal and located at Athletic Park in Newton. At the base was a circular tile mosaic with stylized images of a church in Russia; of migration over sea by ship and land by

---

[1] Reinhild Janzen, "The Mennonite Settler Receives National Register Nomination," *Kansas Preservation* (March-April 1998), 1, 4-5. Keith Sprunger, "The Most Monumental Mennonite," *Mennonite Life* (September 1979), 10-15.

[2] Sprunger, "Most Monumental," 11.

World War II 31

railroad; and of a farm that helped turn the Kansas grasslands into wheat fields. An inscription around the images read, "Commemorating entry into Kansas from Russia of Turkey Red hard wheat by Mennonites, 1874."

The Mennonite-affirming statue was dedicated on September 10, 1942, after a series of anti-Mennonite incidents. In the wake of the U.S. declaration of war in December 1941, ruffians vandalized two downtown Mennonite businesses. Popular outrage in town against pacifism at Bethel College prompted the Newton Chamber of Commerce to withdraw sponsorship of the annual Bethel Booster Banquet. In this context the dedication of a statue in the honor of Mennonites was anomalous. According to the newspaper account, "several thousand farmers and businessmen" and representatives from *The Topeka Capital* and from *Life* magazine attended the dedication. Seldom had the paradoxes of Mennonites in public life been more starkly symbolized.

The Jaycee Newton boosters had not anticipated the change of attitudes that would come in the two years between the birth of the Mennonite Settler idea and the actual dedication of the statue. One way to hide the newly embarrassing Mennonite theme was to call the statue a "Wheat Memorial."[3] But the statue itself had been designed to represent a Mennonite farmer. The mosaic caption specifically mentioned the Mennonites. Paul Kliewer, president of the Jaycees in 1942, presided over the dedication. The Mennonite Settler, of mixed private and public origin, was uneasy in its "Mennonite" identity. That same kind of nervous cooperation between Mennonites and the American public characterized the larger Civilian Public Service program for Mennonite draftees in World War II.

Government Alternative Service for Pacifist Draftees–Civilian Public Service

From both the Mennonite and the government viewpoint, the Civilian Public Service program in World War II was a great

---

[3]"Local News," *Mennonite Weekly Review*, (17 September 1942), 5.

improvement over the conflicted arrangements of 1917-1918. This time the government did not send conscientious objectors to military camps or subject them to military court trials. Instead of being inducted into the army, conscientious objectors did non-military work of "national importance" under civilian direction. When local draft boards denied a draftee his requested conscientious objector classification, the draftee had the right of appeal.[4] When a Mennonite refused to appear for induction he was arrested and tried in a civilian court.

The Mennonites accepted overall administration of Civilian Public Service by Selective Service, a military branch of the government. President Roosevelt turned out to be quite hostile to conscientious objectors. He opposed using government funds for civilian service and said he thought all conscientious objectors should be drilled by army officers. The military drills did not materialize, but close associations between Mennonites and military officials were unavoidable. Uniformed military officers (and some civilian officials) from Selective Service offices in Washington, D.C., decided where the CPS camps should be located, assigned CPS workers to the various camps, accepted and rejected peace church proposals for camp administration, and investigated camp operations on official visits. Although the CPS program amounted to a vast operation of unpaid conscript labor of their young men, Mennonites were generally happy to take responsibility for funding the daily normal expenses of CPS camps. They hoped that if they paid the bill for camp operations, they

---

[4]On Mennonites, conscription, and Civilian Public Service, see Melvin Gingerich, *Service for Peace: A History of Mennonite Civilian Public Service* (Akron, PA: Mennonite Central Committee, 1949); Albert Keim, *The CPS Story: An Illustrated History of Civilian Public Service* (Intercourse, PA: Good Books, 1990); Mulford Q. Sibley and Philip Jacob, *Conscription of Conscience: The American Sate and the Conscientious Objector, 1940-1947* (Ithaca, NY: Cornell University Press, 1952); Steven J. Taylor, *Acts of Conscience: World War II, Mental Institutions, and Religious Objectors* (Syracuse, NY: Syracuse University Press, 2009); Rachel Waltner Goossen, *Women Against the Good War: Conscientious Objection and Gender on the American Homefront, 1941-1947* (Chapel Hill: University of North Carolina Press, 1997); and Perry Bush, *Two Kingdoms, Two Loyalties*. See also online http://www.civilianpublicservice.org/.

might have greater church denominational independence and control over CPS.

Coherent cooperation between the peace churches and the government required unprecedented unified action among the historic peace churches (Mennonites, Friends, and Brethren) as well as among multiple Mennonites and Amish bodies. Mennonite groups had divided along a liberal-conservative spectrum with markedly divergent attitudes about ways to keep separate from the world. The conservative groups were wary of losing identity through inter-Mennonite relationships. The historic peace church groups came together, partly as a result of government initiative, in an agency that came to be known as the National Service Board for Religious Objectors (NSBRO). The NSBRO offices were in Washington, D.C., while the denominational groups had separate offices that took responsibility for different assigned camps. The Mennonite Central Committee offices for the Mennonite part of CPS administration were in Akron, Pennsylvania.

While policies for conscientious objectors in World War II were an improvement over World War I, the loosely defined relationship between cooperating military and civilian pacifist agencies was inevitably beset with confusion and misunderstanding. When did the labor of conscientious objectors cross the line from the civilian national interest to contributing to the war? How intrusive was the control by Selective Service officials over camp operations allowed to be? A generation of young Mennonite leaders received an accelerated education in the ways of government bureaucracy and in civilian/military relations. Mennonites, more than Quaker or general Protestant pacifists, were inclined to accept the government's authority and to see their unpaid labor as service to humanity. Albert Gaeddert, first director of the camp near Colorado Springs, wrote, "Through the generosity of a democratic government, it is possible to offer our services for constructive purposes. . . . Although we refuse to become a part of the war machine, we are willing and eager to give our service where we

34   People of Two Kingdoms II

Civilian Public Service Camp No. 5 near Colorado Springs

feel it is employed toward the harm of no one and to the upbuilding of the abiding interests and welfare of humanity."[5]

A total of 740 Mennonites in Kansas served in Civilian Public Service. Of these 617 came from congregations in South Central Kansas included in this study.[6] This was a small group compared to the 215,000 men and women from Kansas who served in uniform during the war, more than 3,500 of whom were killed in action.[7] There were no CPS camps in Kansas. The first Kansas Mennonite draftees went in June 1941 to a former Civilian Conservation Corps (CCC) camp near Colorado Springs, Colorado, to work on soil conservation projects. Later draftees worked under the United States Forest Service, the National Park Service, the Bureau of Reclamation, the Public Health Service, state mental hospitals, and other agencies.

---

[5] Albert Gaeddert, "Why Civilian Public Service Work?" *Pike View News* 1.3 (4 Oct. 1941), 5. Cited in Theodore Glenn Grimsrud, "An Ethical Analysis of Conscientious Objection to World War II" (Ph. D. dissertation, Graduate Theological Union, 1988), 165.

[6] http://www.civilianpublicservice.org/workers/ (accessed 25 March 25 2013).

[7] Robert Richmond, *Kansas: A Land of Contrasts*, 4th ed (Wheeling, IL: Harlan Davidson, 1999), 277.

Although the official position of all Mennonite denominational groups opposed military service, only about half of drafted Mennonites nationally chose to serve in CPS. Young men from urban and small town congregations tended to be more Americanized and acculturated, and more inclined toward military service. In the Eden Mennonite church, a rural congregation near Moundridge, sixty-eight members were drafted. Of these, forty-four (65%) served in CPS; thirteen (19%) were in regular military service; and eleven (16%), accepted noncombatant military service.[8] In the Bethel College Mennonite Church in North Newton, a small town, most of whose young men had attended the more patriotic Newton High School, fifty-seven members were drafted. Of these, twenty (35%) served in CPS; thirty-four (60%) went into regular military service; and three (5%) accepted noncombatant military service.[9] In the Lorraine Avenue Mennonite Church, a more cosmopolitan urban congregation in Wichita, of twenty-one draftees sixteen (76%) were in regular military service and five (24%) were in Civilian Public Service.[10] All three of these congregations were in the Western District of the General Conference Mennonite Church. Congregations with stricter discipline and more separation from the world, such as the Old Order Amish and the Church of God in Christ Mennonite, had a higher percentage in CPS. The Mennonite Brethren congregations, more influenced by evangelical Protestantism, had a lower percentage in CPS.

---

[8]Eden Mennonite Church record book, entry for 13 Nov 1945, 131. Mennonite Library and Archives.

[9]Keith Sprunger, *Campus, Congregation, and Community: The Bethel College Mennonite Church 1897-1997* (North Newton: Bethel College Mennonite Church, 1997), 48.

[10]Unlike the Eden and Bethel College congregations, the Lorraine Avenue Mennonite Church did not publish a summary listing of the choices of their conscripted men. These figures were compiled from notes in Lorraine's church newsletters, bulletins, and other church records. They may not be complete or fully accurate.

Percentage of selected rural, small town and urban drafted men in selected congregations who chose Civilian Public Service

Eden Mennonite Church (rural)	65%
Bethel College Mennonite Church (small town)	35%
Lorraine Avenue Mennonite Church (urban)	24%

Civic Identity in CPS Camps

In Civilian Public Service Camps an entire generation of young Mennonite conscientious objectors learned what it meant to be an American. They learned who they were in relation to the political order from their peers (Amish, Mennonite, and non-peace church pacifists) in camp, from their American work supervisors, from the public in nearby towns and cities, and from the CPS camp leaders. Mennonite denominational leaders quickly realized that CPS camps offered an unprecedented opportunity to teach large groups of potential church leaders (4,536 drafted men in CPS overall) the first principles of Christian discipleship and Anabaptist-Mennonite history and identity.

Robert Kreider arrived at the Colorado Springs CPS Camp No. 5 in August 1941 and served there until September 1942. A month after arriving he was appointed Educational and Assistant Director for the camp. Kreider had a grand vision for the CPS camps to become "blessed communities" that would teach Christian cooperation along the lines taught by Jesus and lived out in Anabaptist-Mennonite history at its best. Kreider's high view of cooperative community came in part from his major professor at the University of Chicago, Arthur E. Holt, and from Winfield Fretz, a promoter of Mennonite mutual aid who had graduated from the University of Chicago and was teaching at Bethel College. Together with Albert Gaeddert, pastor and former school teacher, who was Camp No. 5 director, Kreider organized social, recreational, and educational programs for the draftees. Their education committee created a "Core Course" with four units of study, each six weeks long. The units covered the teaching of peace, church history, the rural community, and church-state issues ("Christian Citizenship").

World War II 37

Guest lecturers from Mennonite colleges and from local churches supplemented instruction by the camp staff.

But Mennonites did not agree on what constituted good "Christian Citizenship." Did it involve voting in elections, holding public office, and attempting to influence public policy in other ways? General Conference Mennonites, the largest group in Kansas and at the Colorado Springs camp, were inclined toward political participation. Those influenced by Emmett Harshbarger and Ed G. Kaufman at Bethel College favored prophetic engagement. "Old" Mennonites, and especially Amish and Holdeman Mennonites, were more inclined to separation from politics. Harold S. Bender of Goshen College, "Old" Mennonite leader and dean of educational programming for the MCC-related CPS camps, strongly criticized the Colorado Springs Camp No. 5 Core Course. He thought it neglected the Mennonite heritage and reflected a liberal activist Fellowship of Reconciliation viewpoint. Bender proposed that Kreider be transferred away from Colorado Springs to an overseas assignment in England. Kreider, deeply offended, wrote home to his parents, "I do not want Old Mennonite leaders to gain the impression that the young men of our (GC) group are wishy-washy liberals with no keen appreciation of our Mennonite heritage."[11]

The conflict between Kreider and Bender did not last long. Part of Bender's agenda, early in the development of CPS educational programming, may have been to establish his own authority over the process. Eventually, Kreider won Bender's approval. In September 1942, MCC-CPS invited Kreider to transfer to MCC headquarters in Pennsylvania to serve as administrative coordinator of CPS educational programs nationwide. Bender chose the authors and supervised the editing of a six volume, 70-page booklet series, "Mennonites and Their Heritage," for use in CPS camp education. Bender wrote the first booklet, "Mennonite Origins in Europe." Guy F. Hershberger, Bender's colleague at Goshen College, wrote booklet No. 5, "Christian Relationships to

---

[11]Robert Kreider, "CPS: 'A Year of Service with Like-Minded Christian Young Men': CPS Camp No. 5, Colorado Springs, Colorado, 1941-42," *Mennonite Quarterly Review* (October 1992), 567-68.

State and Community." Hershberger in 1941-42 was writing *War, Peace, and Nonresistance*, a book that after its publication in 1944 became the most comprehensive and influential exposition of the Mennonite peace position.[12]

In his CPS booklet, Hershberger wrote that "coercive authority" was the "fundamental and characteristic function" of the state. He believed that Mennonites should not participate in government, apart from a few civil functions that did not involve violence or coercion, such as the post office. He did not mention the issue of voting in elections. In fact, he quietly voted for Norman Thomas, the Socialist candidate in 1940. Hershberger believed that people who entered high political office tended to abandon their peace convictions. Despite his negative definition of "the state," Hershberger summarized the history of American democracy in thoroughly positive Jeffersonian terms. "Democracy in America," he wrote, "owes much to Christianity and the Bible."[13] Christians could contribute most to the body politic by establishing strong rural family-oriented communities that were the essential base of American democracy, especially in an era when democracy was threatened by rapid urbanization, industrialization, and secularism. Hershberger strongly endorsed the CPS program of alternative service and rejected both military service and noncombatant service in the military. He also respectfully rejected the option of refusing to register for the draft.

How much influence did Hershberger's writings have? Robert Kreider has noted that when CPS workers in later years reminisced about their wartime camp experiences, they did not talk about what they had learned in the educational courses. But there is evidence that Mennonites were reading Hershberger and applying his views to specific situations. William Juhnke quoted Hershberger in correspondence with his younger brother, Walter, in CPS camp. Walter wrestled with the contradiction that if his CPS work was really "in the national interest," it had the effect of freeing up

---

[12] Theron F. Schlabach, *War Peace and Social Conscience: Guy F. Hershberger and Mennonite Ethics* (Scottdale, PA: Herald Press, 2009).

[13] Guy F. Hershberger, *Christian Relationships to State and Community* (Akron: PA: Mennonite Central Committee, 1942), 29.

another young man to go to fight in the war. Walter dramatically set a date when he would walk out of CPS, return home and wait for the authorities to arrest him and bring him to trial. Walter's cousin and fellow church member, Carl J. Stucky, had refused cooperation with Selective Service and was awaiting such a trial. Prison was the proper place for a pacifist in wartime. William urged Walter to consider Hershberger's viewpoint that the CPS program was a good way to express both pacifist separation from a violent world and also a positive patriotic American identity.[14]

Robert Kreider faced the dilemmas of separation and cooperation in his role as Assistant Director of the Colorado Springs CPS camp. Despite his youth, only age twenty-three, Kreider found himself in administrative charge when the director, Albert Gaeddert, a thirty-four year old pastor, was called away for special assignments. Kreider soon learned about the problems and complexities of relating to four different agencies: Selective Service and NSBRO in Washington, D.C.; Mennonite Central Committee in Akron, PA; and Soil Conservation Service (SCS) agents who supervised the work projects. The four agencies did not always agree on proper rules for work hours and furloughs, or on what work constituted civilian rather than military service. Nor did Conservation Service supervisors show respect to CPS workers: "And yes sir, Mr. Idiot, I'm talking to you."[15]

The CPS program embraced a dilemma that required careful and patient negotiation. On one hand the work had to be of national importance, or as the Selective Service law said, "important to the government in the emergency." On the other hand, the work could only indirectly contribute to the war effort or the conscientious objectors would refuse to do it. For their own identity and self-respect, the Mennonites had to participate in the choice of what work qualified. As they negotiated these issues, neither the Selective Service officials nor the conscientious objectors wanted publicity.

---

[14]William Juhnke letter to Walt Juhnke, September 12, 1944. Author's collection.
[15]Robert Kreider, "The 'Good Boys of CPS,'" *Mennonite Life* (September 1991), 4-11.

Tensions at Camp No. 5 reached a peak in the summer of 1942. The Soil Conservation Service staff wanted to prove its patriotism by putting CPS crews on a series of war emergency projects. They brought in film makers and photographers to publicize work on large beet farms. Billboard advertisements lauded beet-raising as war work, with beet sugar used for making explosives. At the same time the SCS Project Superintendent asked for CPS workers to help collect scrap rubber and to drive trucks at the army airport. Kreider, Assistant Director in charge while Gaeddert was absent from the camp, refused to cooperate. He reported to the MCC CPS office in Pennsylvania that the SCS was attempting to draw CPS men into war work. Meanwhile the SCS reported to Selective Service in Washington, prompting an investigative visit by Victor A. Olsen from the Washington office. Olsen gave the youthful Kreider a "sustained, vicious tongue-lashing" and later spoke to the assembled CPS men: "He barked at us; growled at us; snarled at us."[16]

Despite such hostile confrontations, relationships between the Mennonite leaders and the Selective Service System proved to be manageable overall. Indeed, the Mennonite CPS workers, compared to those in the camps operated by Quakers, gained the reputation of the "good boys of the system."[17] It was important that Lewis B. Hershey, the Director of the Selective Service System, was committed to the validity of alternative service and had a generally sympathetic understanding of conscientious objectors to war.[18] Hershey had been reared in rural Indiana and learned that in friendly conversations with Mennonites he could trade on the fact that Hershey was a common Mennonite name. Henry A. Fast, Bethel College Bible teacher who became director of the MCC CPS Program, emphasized Hershey's basic respect for religious objectors. "I don't think he was unfair to anybody who had a sincere conviction of conscience. We took a good many cases to

---

[16]Kreider, "The 'Good Boys,'" 9.

[17]Perry Bush, "We have Learned to Question Government," *Mennonite Life*, (June 1990), 13-17.

[18]Nicholas A. Krehbiel, *General Lewis B. Hershey and Conscientious Objection during World War II* (Columbia, MO: University of Missouri Press, 2011).

him, and . . . you could be sure that he would bend over backwards to be fair with them."[19]

Kansas Mennonites in CPS camps learned that government officials had their own idiosyncracies and normal fears and problems. David C. Wedel had interrupted his post as pastor of the First Mennonite Church in Halstead, Kansas, to open and direct a new CPS camp in Marietta, Ohio. Wedel found that Colonel Lewis F. Kosch was an "intimidating figure" when visited in his office in Washington D.C. But later, when Kosch visited the camp at Marietta, the officer was not so secure and self-assertive. Recalled Wedel, "When he was not in his home office, he was as timid as a lamb."[20]

Mennonite draftees loved to tell stories of holding the moral high ground in relation to the government officials. Roland Bartel, from the Alexanderwohl Mennonite Church, told one of these triumph tales about a Quaker camp where the "government people" took their meals in the common dining room where the conscientious objectors were in charge. After each dinner a CO camp leader read excerpts from pacifist literature. Reported Bartel, "Those government people would just squirm." But one after-dinner reading was thoroughly nationalistic and militaristic. The government people cheered. "So when they were through cheering he said, 'What I read to you was from Hitler's *Mein Kampf.*'"[21] Such stories exposed the contradictions of nationalistic militarism and justified the pacifist rejection of war.

Despite some tense relationships with Selective Service officials, Mennonites reported that they faced more hostility from the American public than from the government. In Mennonite minds they often were the winners in arguments with Selective Service officials. Erwin Goering, from the Eden Mennonite Church, directed camps in Nebraska, California, and the Rocky Mountain

---

[19]Henry A. Fast, interview by Keith Sprunger, March 21, 1973, 940.5316 #3, MLA.
[20]David C. Wedel, interview by Fred Fransen, March 24, 1988, 940.5316 #160, MLA (transcription p. 5).
[21]On the Mennonite "Triumph Tale Tradition," see James C. Juhnke, "The Victories of Nonresistance: Mennonite Oral Tradition and World War I," *Fides et Historia* (Fall 1974): 19-25.

region. He discussed pacifism and war with Colonel Franklin A. McLean, a friendly "government inspector." McLean was willing to grant that COs had "the right values" but insisted that those values were not practical. Goering used the example of Gandhi, who challenged British imperialism in India with "moral spiritual courage." McLean said, "Well, maybe you'll convince me someday." "No," replied Goering, as he told about it years later, "You'll convince yourself."[22]

CPS and Mental Health Reform

CPS men who worked in state mental hospitals often were shocked by the inhumane and brutal treatment of inmates at state mental hospitals.[23] Edwin Schrag, member of the Eden Mennonite Church near Moundridge, Kansas, joined with others in documenting and exposing the appalling mistreatment that was common in mental health institutions. Schrag and his roommate, Ralph Lehman, were assigned to the acute treatment ward at Hudson River State Hospital at Poughkeepsie, New York. There they saw orderlies brutally intimidate patients by binding them to chairs and beds for long periods, by assaulting them and pinning them to the floor, and, in one case, by shoving a catatonic patient down a flight of concrete steps, breaking his leg. One sadistic attendant sat in a large arm chair and disciplined an inmate by demanding that he put his fingers on the wooden arm of the chair and by striking the fingernails with an eight-inch heavy ward pass key. The other attendants laughed. Then the abuser demanded that the inmate put his penis on the chair arm for the same treatment. This happened on a daily basis.[24]

---

[22]Erwin Goering, interview by Trent Shipley, November 13, 1987, 940.5316 #146-147, MLA (transcription, 15).

[23]The story of CPS and mental health reform is most fully documented by Steven J. Taylor, *Acts of Conscience*.

[24]Edwin Schrag, interview by Tim Schrag, Sept 13, 1974, 940.5316 #17, Mennonite Library and Archives, cited by Taylor, *Acts of Conscience*, 257. Ralph Lehman, interview by author 23 September 2013. Edwin Schrag, in *The Eden Peace Witness, A Collection of Personal Accounts*, ed. by Jeffery W. Koller (Jebeko Publishing, 2004), 134-38.

Schrag and Lehman reported the abuse to supervisors but were told to "mind your own business." The system was designed to protect the abusers. They were so distressed that they considered leaving the CPS program, "going AWOL," rather than continue to observe and to be complicit in the abuse. Bert Smucker, assistant director of the CPS unit, managed to get an interview with Dr. John Ross, superintendent of the hospital. Ross was interested in getting reliable information about abusive orderlies. At Ross's direction the CPS men for several weeks, without talking to each other about their observations, daily documented the abuse in detail: "patient's names, attendant's names, time and duration of each incident, and a detailed description of just what had happened."[25] Based on this evidence Superintendent Ross fired four attendants, three of whom were union members and two of whom were military veterans.

The local American Legion and labor union jumped to the defense of the dismissed attendants, accused the hospital of giving special privileges to the CPS workers, and demanded that the CPS unit be shut down. The incident got wide press coverage. The local *Poughkeepsie New Yorker* editorialized that the CPS workers should be investigated, and the dismissed attendants be given fair trials. But Eleanor Roosevelt, widow of President Franklin D. Roosevelt, intervened and influenced public opinion in favor of the CPS men. Mrs. Roosevelt lived at Hyde Park, just four miles from the Hudson River State hospital. She and her secretary accepted an invitation from a women's summer service unit at the hospital to visit the institution. In her nationally syndicated column, "My Day," on July 11, 1945, Mrs. Roosevelt wrote of her visit and reported that Superintendent Ross had gotten evidence from the CPS men that he could not get otherwise. Public opinion shifted. The CPS men testified in civil hearings against the attendants, and the firings were confirmed.[26] The incident revealed one of the most creative outcomes of the CPS program upon national public policy–the reform of mental hospital practices.

---

[25]Ralph Lehman, "Civilian Public Service and the Poughkeepsie Story," in *The Eden Peace Witness*, 296.

[26]Taylor, *Acts of Conscience*, 257-59.

The U.S. Congress denied peace church pacifists the opportunity to work overseas. That issue was not settled until the spring of 1943 when a conservative Democratic Congressman from Alabama, Joe Starnes, attached a rider to an appropriations bill forbidding CPS work overseas. The bill passed, and plans under way to for a CPS unit to work in China were aborted. Robert Kreider was in that China-bound group. They got as far as Durban, South Africa, before being recalled. Kreider had been in Akron, Pennsylvania, as administrator for CPS camp education programs. (Elmer Ediger replaced him in that position.) Upon returning, Kreider returned to Akron as assistant director of the MCC CPS hospital program. The "Ill-Fated Mission" to China, as Kreider called it, was a grievous disappointment, though he had had an "eventful trip over the globe's surface, packed with educational value."[27] It was also a lesson in ways that popular resentment against conscientious objectors in wartime could be expressed in government restrictions.

General Conference Mennonites from Kansas had a strong role in the administration of CPS, disproportionate to their numbers in the country generally. All four directors of Mennonite Central Committee CPS, administered from Akron, Pennsylvania, were graduates of Bethel College–Henry Fast, Albert Gaeddert, Erwin Goering, and Elmer Ediger. (Fast was originally from Mountain Lake, Minnesota, but after the war joined the staff at Bethel College.) Moreover, a significant number of camp directors spread across the country were from Kansas. In the view of Robert Kreider, General Conference men typically were more open minded and able to cope with the new situations and social diversity of the CPS camps than were leaders from more conservative Mennonite groups.[28]

Tensions on the Home Front

Public hostility against pacifist Mennonites in Kansas was not as severe during World War II (1941-45) as it had been in World War

---

[27]Kreider, *My Early Years*, 352.
[28]Robert S. Kreider, interview by Keith Sprunger, 19 October 1988, 940.5316 #178, MLA (transcript, 9).

I (1917-18), when violent mobs had attacked Mennonites in McPherson, Harvey, and Butler counties. As in World War I, the most serious confrontations came later in the war, after supporters of military service received news of casualties and deaths of their young men overseas. The conscientious objectors seemed to get off free.

The Japanese attack on Pearl Harbor and the American declaration of war (December 7-8, 1941) transformed the national attitudes on war and peace. In Moundridge, Kansas, Mennonite peace advocates at the public high school came under severe public pressure.[29] Selma Rich Platt, English and psychology teacher, refused to attend a war rally where the newly energized patriots burned an effigy of Hirohito, the emperor of Japan. She became the focus of popular hostility. A sign in a downtown drugstore window identified her with Hirohito; her car was vandalized; the school board called her in and demanded that she stop showing opposition to war. Platt was a widow with three young children and had no prospects for alternative employment. But she resigned her job at Moundridge at the end of the 1941 fall semester.[30]

William Juhnke, Moundridge High School social studies teacher, had been an active peace promoter in his classes and as sponsor of the Hi-Y, a student Christian organization whose national leaders had been outspoken against U.S. intervention in the war. When Dave Roth, a downtown car dealer, complained to the high school principal about Juhnke's peace activism, Juhnke went directly to Roth and defended himself. The car dealer had to be careful, because he knew Juhnke (unlike Platt) had wide family and church connections in the Moundridge area. Roth did not want to do anything to discourage Mennonites from buying Ford cars. Juhnke did not lose his job for expressing peace convictions, as had Platt, but he did move to a new position at Buhler High School for the following school year (1942-43).[31]

---

[29]James C. Juhnke, *So Much to be Thankful For*, 94-97.
[30]Selma Platt, interview by James Juhnke, 25 January 1975, 940.5316 #31a, MLA. Perry Bush, *Two Kingdoms, Two Loyalties*, 96-7.
[31]Juhnke, *So Much to be Thankful For*, 95-6.

Lawrence Templin

In the spring of 1942 another town-gown crisis exploded between Newton and Bethel College. Lawrence Templin, a Methodist pacifist student from New York, had learned about Bethel College from Elmer Ediger in the summer of 1941 when Elmer attended the "School of Living" in Suffern, New York, where Templin's father was director. Lawrence wrote in the March 27 Bethel school paper that some men were refusing to register with Selective Service: "The state has no right in forcing the will of individuals. It might be a good thing if a few of our more daring souls would go to jail over a hot issue and awaken some of the drowsy pacifists."[32] News of this apparent endorsement of nonregistration spread like wildfire. Patriotic resentments flared in downtown Newton. Chamber of Commerce officials summoned Bethel administrators to a meeting that was "almost like a court of law." Edmund Kaufman, Bethel College president, refused to dismiss Templin from school, but did place him on probation, remove him from the *Collegian* staff, and had him sign a statement of apology asserting his intention to register for the draft when he came of age. The Chamber withdrew its sponsorship of the annual Bethel Booster Banquet. On the night of April 2 vandals ransacked and smeared yellow paint on Mennonite businesses in downtown Newton and hung an effigy of Templin on the Bethel College flagpole. Kaufman invited Templin to spend the nights at the Kaufman house for his personal safety. The situation in 1942 had been totally transformed from the 1930s when Kaufman was on good terms not only with local Newton dignitaries, but also with U.S. Congressman John M. Houston (a Newton businessman) and with U.S. Senator Arthur Capper, whose anti-war and internationalist views aligned with those of Kaufman.

---

[32]"On the serious side, on registration," *The Bethel Collegian*, 27 March 1942, 4.

On August 16, 1944, six young Mennonites traveled on a bus with thirty-three draftees from McPherson to Leavenworth for pre-induction physical examinations. Three of the Mennonites were members of the "Holdeman" branch (Church of God in Christ Mennonite) that required the wearing of beards.[33] Enroute to Leavenworth the regulars and the Mennonites began to argue about war and peace: "What will you do when the Nazis overrun America and rape your grandmothers?" "Do you CO Germans deserve American citizenship at all?" One of the Mennonites talked back belligerently. The argument snowballed into violence. The patriots got out a razor (supplemented with a scissors purchased during a stop at Emporia) and cut the beards and hair of the Mennonites. John M. Dyck, one of the Holdeman Mennonites, later recalled, "They made us take off our belts and also our trousers. They tried to make us commit immoral acts and called us all kinds of dirty names. They beat us with our belts."[34] By the time they arrived in Leavenworth, all six Mennonites had suffered cuts and bruises, two had split lips, two had broken or loose teeth, and all had had their hair and beards roughly cut.

The pre-induction physical examinations in Leavenworth revealed the abuse. Officials at the Induction Station identified eight of the regulars as ringleaders. The Kansas State Attorney General's office initiated a process to bring the offenders to trial. The news travelled fast. "When we got home everyone seemed to know about it," said one of victims. Newspapers around the state covered the investigation and subsequent trial in detail. The men were tried in a civil court in Emporia. They pleaded guilty and were fined ten dollars each, plus $1.25 court costs. The minimal fines seemed to reflect a public opinion that was ready to accept a token slap on the wrist for perpetrators of violence against Mennonite conscientious objectors. The outcome was different from World War I when violent mobs were able to attack Mennonites with complete impunity. But it was clear that in

---

[33]Roger Juhnke, "The Perils of Conscientious Objection: An Oral History Study of a 1944 Event," *Mennonite Life* (September 1979), 4-9.

[34]John M. Dyck, *Faith Under Test: Alternative Service During World War II In the U.S. and Canada* (Moundridge, Ks: Gospel Publishers, 1997), 24.

wartime Mennonites were second class citizens, if not despised outsiders.

The most dramatic legal confrontation in Kansas between Mennonite pacifism and American wartime justice came when Carl J. Stucky on June 7, 1944, refused to show up for his pre-induction physical in McPherson County.[35] Stucky had registered as a conscientious objector on his eighteenth birthday in August 1942. As a student at Bethel College 1942-44, he enrolled in Bible and "Practice Preaching" classes and qualified for a IV-E deferment for divinity students. While at Bethel, Stucky decided that any cooperation with the war system compromised his Christian pacifist values. When his ministerial deferment was withdrawn, he refused to cooperate with Selective Service. On June 12, 1944, he was put in jail and then released on a $2,500 bond put up by his parents. On September 7, one week before his impending trial, he was severely burned in a gasoline tractor fire. The burns made him unfit for military service, but he refused to register for exemption. The U.S. District Court judge refused to excuse him as long as he disobeyed the Selective Service Law. His trial in Wichita was held on September 11, 1945, a year after the fire. His wounds had not fully healed and, indeed, remained an affliction for many years.

Although Stucky's noncooperation deviated from the official position of the church, six prominent Mennonite leaders came to the trial as character witnesses in his behalf. These included Christian E. Krehbiel, president of the General Conference Mennonite Church of North America; Edmund G. Kaufman, president of Bethel College; and Gerhard Zerger, County Commissioner in McPherson County. Stucky's older brother, Harley, a divinity student in Chicago, wrote to the judge of Carl's sincerity and honesty: "Even as a small boy, he would not molest

---

[35]This account is drawn from two unpublished papers in the author's possession: Debra L. Dirks, "The United States vs. Carl J. Stucky" (n.d.), 26pp; Harley J. Stucky, "Carl J. Stucky's Witness for the Christian Gospel of Love and Non-resistance," (n. d.).

farm animals, because of a personal attachment and devotion for living creatures."[36]

After pleading guilty to charges, Stucky made a statement to the court regarding his religious pacifist convictions. He said that his training at home and in church convinced him that military force was "not in harmony with the Christlike way of life." He referred to Bible texts from the Old and New Testaments–"most of all (Jesus') prayer on the cross when He pleads for his enemies saying, 'Father, forgive them for they know not what they do,' prescribing a way of life so pacifistic that it has no place under Selective Service and military organizations." Stucky's statement referred to early church history, and ended with a quotation from General Douglass MacArthur in the current issue of *Time* magazine (September 10, 1946) stating that military solutions had failed and that civilization could be saved only by spiritual renewal. What Stucky said was not unlike the personal credos written by Bethel College students in peace studies classes. The difference was his conclusion of separation from a military system: "Men ought to follow Christ and love, live and let live. It is for this reason that I sever relations with the Selective Service."

The judge sentenced Stucky to two years in prison, plus a one thousand dollar fine and court costs. Stucky served just over nine months of his sentence in the Federal Reformatory in El Reno, Oklahoma, before he was paroled. At the time of his release, a local draft board in Oklahoma changed his classification to IV-F, "Rejected for military service, physical, mental or moral reasons." Two years and three months later he was called to register under a new Selective Service Act of 1948. On September 7, 1948, at the beginning of a new school year at Bethel College, Stucky went to the courthouse in Newton and registered with Selective Service. He did not explain why he had changed his mind, nor did he talk about his wartime experience in subsequent years.

---

[36]Harley J. Stucky letter to United States District Court Office of the Clerk, 14 September 1944. A copy of the letter is attached to Harley Stucky's account of the case.

Carl Stucky was a lonely representative at the radical separationist end of a continuum of Mennonite responses to the military draft. His example impressed itself most strongly upon members of his own Hopefield congregation and satellite Swiss-Volhynian congregations. The Mennonite denomination in general ignored him. Despite his isolation, he had taken a place in a tradition of non-registration for the draft that came to flower during the Vietnam War. In the 1970s a new generation of Mennonite non-registrants convinced the leading church bodies to accept non-registration along with alternative service as valid Christian responses to the military draft.

After the war Mennonites still felt the pressures in their local communities. David C. Wedel, pastor of the First Mennonite Church at Halstead, returned home from his job as CPS camp director and noted that sometimes "there were people who would cross the street rather than pass me on the sidewalk."[37] Gene Yoder, from McPherson, reported that he lost job opportunities at two businesses because he was a CO. And then "a bunch of businessmen got together... and went around to all the businesses trying to get... everybody that had hired a CO to lay him off."[38] Dale Stucky, from Elyria and a member of Hopefield congregation, had been in CPS for nine months. He graduated from the University of Chicago Law School in the spring of 1945 and made arrangements to take the bar exam. A judge and three attorneys endorsed his nomination, but someone intervened to get the endorsements withdrawn because Stucky had allegedly "deceived" them about his military service. He was not allowed to take the bar exam. Stucky managed to get a job as a clerk with a law firm in Wichita and, after a year, was sponsored by a leading partner in the firm to take the bar exam. He passed the exam and spent his career as an attorney in Wichita and as an active member of the Lorraine Avenue Mennonite Church.[39]

---

[37]David C. Wedel oral interview, 24 March 1988.
[38]Gene Yoder, interview by Tim Schrag, 19 January 1975, 940.5316 #23b, MLA.
[39]Dale Stucky, interview by James Juhnke and Keith Sprunger, 3 August 1993, 940.5316 #258-259, MLA.

Although Kansas had no CPS camps, the state did have eight camps for German prisoners of war. One of the branch camps was in Peabody. German-speaking Mennonite farmers in the area were among those who hired the POWs as farm laborers. The military administration rules forbade American farmers from talking about politics or war issues with their POW laborers. But Louis Janzen, a Mennonite farmer near Elbing, engaged his POW workers in discussions about the nature of American democracy. Apparently Janzen spoke to the German POWs in the German language, out of the hearing of the American guards. At the time of President Roosevelt's death, Janzen gave the POWs a lesson in American freedom of speech by using a prescribed national three minutes of prayer to make some critical remarks about Roosevelt. The POWS, said Janzen later, "were shocked and amazed that anyone could be so critical of his government."[40]

Marian Claassen, twelve years old when her father employed German POWs, was afraid not of the 'enemy' soldiers, but of their American guards. "In total terror," she later recalled, "I watched as one, upon being urged, demonstrated how to attach his bayonet for action. No gun intended to kill people or to spear stomachs had ever before been near our home." In time, both the guards and the POWs relaxed in the Claassen home. Guards stopped bringing guns to the table. "After meals we all gathered around the piano to sing hymns and folksongs in both German and English. In one case of friendship, the German prisoners, seeing an approaching army jeep with inspection officers, awakened a sleeping guard to keep him from being disciplined." From this event, and, no doubt, from her family and church traditions, Claassen drew the lesson that German and U.S. soldiers were not natural enemies. The real enemy was "the system of war."[41]

---

[40]Joseph S. Miller, "German POWS at Peabody and Concordia, Kansas During World War II," Bethel College Social Science Seminar paper, 1978, 34.

[41]Marian Claassen Franz, "Enemies," from *Persistent Voice: Marian Franz and Conscientious Objection to Military Taxation*, ed. by David R. Bassett, Steve Ratzlaff and Tim Godshall (Telford, PA: Cascadia Publishing House, 2009), 80-1.

1944 Election

In the 1944 presidential election, Franklin Roosevelt ran for a fourth term. The Republican candidate was Wendell Willkie. The Mennonite newspaper editors, no doubt intimidated by anti-Mennonite wartime pressures, gave less attention to the election than four years earlier. Menno Schrag, editor of *Mennonite Weekly Review* in Newton, did not again decry the drift under Roosevelt toward authoritarianism and socialism. His pre-election editorial in 1944 said, "There is not much a small group like ours can do by getting very much exercised over politics." In a post-election editorial Schrag quoted Roger W. Babson, a "nationally known statistician and economist," who warned against the rising national debt and possible bankruptcy. Babson called for "wholesome, industrious, Godly living" as a solution. Schrag's point, though made obliquely, may have been that the ungodly war was the greatest generator of national debt. But he did not dare to be openly critical of the government, given popular hostility against Mennonites in Newton during the war.[42]

The *Hillsboro Journal* in 1944 was still a dual language German and English paper, with Orlando Harms as editor. Harms wrote that "It has been our policy to refrain from exerting influence which would direct people how to vote." But he then proceeded to tell his readers to vote against Roosevelt: "It is an established fact by this time, however, that our present administration is under foreign influence of the most subversive kind, trying to undermine our democratic form of government.... A change in the administration is essential at this time if we keep the welfare of our nation in mind."[43] On page three was a full-page Republican advertisement.

The 1944 presidential vote in precincts of substantial Mennonite population was a Republican majority of nearly 90%. That was over 20% higher than the Republican vote generally in the state of Kansas. It was also the highest Republican majority in the history of Kansas Mennonite voting in presidential elections since their

---

[42]*Mennonite Weekly Review*, November 2 and 7, 1944.
[43]*Hillsboro Journal*, November 2, 1944, 4.

arrival in Kansas. As usual, Mennonites of Swiss Volhynian background voted Democrat in greater numbers. A handful of Mennonites, including the brothers Walter and William Juhnke, registered their protest against President Roosevelt and the war by voting for the Socialist candidate, Norman Thomas. But even among Swiss Volhynian Mennonites, the Democrat numbers were down from elections held before 1940–the turning point in Kansas Mennonite voting preferences.[44]

World War II and Mennonite Revitalization

The Mennonite experience in World War II revitalized the denomination and refocused its place in the American democratic system. The Civilian Public Service system was an essential element in the changing Mennonite civic identity. Mennonites came to accept CPS as an opportunity affirm both the role of worldly government and the responsibility of Christians to be of service in the world. Elmer Ediger's rationale for CPS service expressed the Mennonite viewpoint. Ediger's CPS career had included work at the Colorado Springs Camp #5, a role as assistant director and education director at Weeping Water, NE (outside Lincoln), and then the position of national education director for Mennonite camps, with office in Akron, PA. The challenges were exhilarating. "Here we were just out of college, two, three, four years, and we had opportunity to manage national programs. Fantastic!"[45] Ediger came to see CPS work as Christian service, despite its roots in national military conscription. Unlike Carl Stucky and other radical critics of conscription, Ediger was able to "reconstruct this compulsion into a voluntary service of good will." Thus he applied the Bible's "second mile" and "good for evil" principles. "I believe government (not anarchy) is desired by God to make for orderly group living, and therefore I obey government except when I am asked to sin."[46]

---

[44]Juhnke, *People of Two Kingdoms*, 6, 147-51, 163.
[45]Elmer Ediger, interview by Roger Juhnke, 9 October 1978.
[46]Elmer Ediger, "Is It Right to Accept CPS?" *The Snowline* 3.4 (Apr 1945), p. 2. Cited in Grimsrud, "An Ethical Analysis," 173.

54 People of Two Kingdoms II

Most of the Mennonites who went into regular military service drifted away from the church in subsequent years. Some, like Marvin Juhnke of the Eden Mennonite Church, returned home and retained membership, but suffered social marginalization. Some of them returned home from the military and became strong peace advocates. Leland Harder was in the U.S. navy (noncombatant service) for twenty months and enjoyed the public status in his home town: "to walk around Hillsboro with that uniform, I was somebody."[47] After the war Harder attended Bethel College with GI Bill funding and became a convinced conscientious objector to war. He later taught at the Mennonite seminary in Elkhart, Indiana.[48]

If the more liberal or open-minded General Conference and Bethel College folk were well adapted to the challenges of CPS camp administration, it is also true that the more conservative Old Mennonites at Goshen College supplied a theological and intellectual rationale for Mennonite identity that became ascendant in the wartime and postwar years. Two publications in 1944, Harold Bender's "Anabaptist Vision" essay and Guy F. Hershberger's book, *War, Peace and Nonresistance* became central "Goshen School" manifestos for Anabaptist/Mennonite renewal in the postwar era.[49] In the sobering context of World War II, a separatist and conservative theology was more persuasive than the progressive idealism represented by Emmett Harshbarger and Edmund G. Kaufman of Bethel College. Symbolic of the progressive decline was the untimely death of Harshbarger in 1942–the removal of a key Kansas spokesman for proactive Mennonite witness to government.

At one level the war led to disillusionment with the political order. Bill Juhnke, earlier a champion of the peace witness, wrote to a friend in 1943 that the war and military conscription "sort of

---

[47] Leland Harder, interview by Fred Fransen, 10 March 1988, 940.5316 #155, MLA.
[48] Leland Harder, *The Houses I Lived in: Memoirs of my Life* (North Newton, KS: Harder Graphics, 2008).
[49] Harold S. Bender, "The Anabaptist Vision," *The Mennonite Quarterly Review* (April 1994), 67-88; Guy F. Hershberger, *War, Peace and Nonresistance* (Scottdale, Pa: Herald Press, 1944, rev. ed. 1953).

broke my enthusiasm for democratic government."[50] Robert Kreider's CPS contacts with Selective Service and state mental health institutions made him "increasingly displeased with governmental bureaucracies, despite my youthful leanings toward socialism." Kreider decided that if he wanted to affect social change, "then I should invest my energies in non-governmental agencies."[51]

At another level, the broadening experiences of alternative service away from home led to ever expanding visions for service and witness in the post-war years. The CPS experience produced peace movement activists, many of whom returned to their home congregations where they became long-term peace-minded church members. John Gaeddert, from the Hoffnungsau congregation near Inman, came out of Civilian Public Service committed to activist pacifism. The war, he believed, had caused incredible destruction and human suffering while it fostered militarism and the notion "that all things are settled by military means."[52] Former CPSers became not only local church and community builders and founders of new social welfare institutions such as Prairie View mental hospital and Mennonite Disaster Service. They became leaders of a Mennonite peace witness to the government in the era of Cold War militarization. The Mennonite version of what journalist Tom Brokaw called "The Greatest Generation" carried its service and anti-war ethic to new heights after returning home from CPS.[53]

---

[50]Juhnke, *So Much to be Thankful For*, 96.
[51]Robert Kreider, *My Early Years*, 389.
[52]John Gaeddert, interview by Trent Shipley, 14 May 1988, 940.5316 #167, MLA, transcript page 17.
[53]Tom Brokaw, *The Greatest Generation* (New York: Random House, 1998).

Chapter 4

Postwar Mobilization 1945-1960

"War is good for Mennnonites," said Cornelius J. Dyck, Mennonite seminary teacher of church history.[1] Dyck's provocative statement was only partly serious. It certainly was not true for Mennonites in Europe whose families and communities were devastated in World Wars I and II. But Dyck could make the case that in North America the great wars enhanced Mennonite identity, strengthened institutions, and fostered mission efforts. War-generated economic prosperity enabled Mennonites to build new churches and to give generously to war victims. The world wars of the twentieth century enhanced Mennonite identity as a people of peace and service. To be sure, there were conflicts between pacifist Mennonites and war-crusading Americans during the wars. But those conflicts were generally manageable.[2]

World War II, and especially the Civilian Public Service program, taught Mennonites new lessons on how to relate to government. In the early twentieth century they had been more involved in politics than their commonly accepted reputation as separated from the world. From 1941 to 1945, their pacifism pushed them to the margins as the United States engaged in a popular war. But on one public policy issue they used their newfound familiarity with national government to undertake a role of political lobbying. The issue was "Peacetime Conscription." Progressive Kansas Mennonites–men such as Elmer Ediger, Robert Kreider, and William Juhnke–took leadership that moved Mennonites toward political witness. The war may have closed off opportunities for Mennonites to seek election to public office in America's democratic system. But their war experience, especially in Civilian Public Service, taught them how to relate to government.

---

[1]Cornelius J. Dyck, unpublished presentation at the Mennonite Central Committee 75th anniversary symposium, "Unity Amidst Diversity," Fresno, CA, March 10, 1995.

[2]On the peoplehood "revitalization" wrought by World War I, see James C. Juhnke, "Mennonite Benevolence and Revitalization in the Wake of World War I," *Mennonite Quarterly Review* 60 (January 1986) 15-30.

Peacetime Conscription

In the summer of 1944, more than a year before the end of the war, American veterans' organizations and pro-military politicians began to plan for military conscription after the war. The Selective Service Act was due to expire May 15, 1945. Leading the charge for conscription was the Citizens Committee for Universal Military Training, a body that had promoted peacetime conscription in 1940 before the war started. Peace organizations pushed back. In August of 1944 *Fellowship* magazine, published by the Fellowship of Reconciliation, included statements against "peacetime conscription" that had been adopted by four Protestant denominations (Methodist, Baptist, Presbyterian, Church of the Brethren) and by a number of secular agencies.[3] Editors of *The Christian Century* attacked the pro-conscription arguments and asked, "Where is the justification for this American adoption of militarism?"[4]

Mennonite leaders took courage from the mainline peace advocacy. Reynold Weinbrenner, editor of *The Mennonite*, the official General Conference periodical edited in Newton, Kansas, in December 5, 1944, listed twenty groups that were opposing peacetime conscription. "The idea of war and more preparation for war has been loosed," warned Weinbrenner. "We are again seeing a repetition of those slow-moving steps that led us into this war."[5]

The Executive Committee of the General Conference Mennonite Church wrote a letter to President Roosevelt, to Vice-President Wallace, and to all members of both houses of Congress opposing peacetime conscription. They published their letter in *The Mennonite* and urged readers to write to their own members of Congress. The letter applied Christian values to national life as well as personal life: "The Mennonite Church . . . holds that . . . righteousness, goodwill, justice, mercy, and love must be the basis

---

[3] "Here is What Others Say About Peacetime Conscription," *Fellowship*, August 1944, 142.

[4] "Peacetime Conscription," *The Christian Century*, 18 October 1944, 1190-1.

[5] Reynold Weinbrenner, "Peacetime Conscription," *The Mennonite*, 5 December 1944, 3.

of national as well as of individual conduct and durable peace and well being."⁶ This view of public and individual morality differed from Guy F. Hershberger's church/state theology in his book, *War, Peace and Nonresistance*. Hershberger had drawn a sharp distinction between Jesus' teaching of love in his Sermon on the Mount and the ethic of justice required by the state. "Mercy and love" were not political virtues.

In opposition to peacetime conscription, Kansas Mennonites claimed religious and political warrants in the same breath. J. W. Vogt, editor of *The Christian Leader*, Mennonite Brethren publication in Hillsboro, wrote, "Every Christian ought to be deeply concerned about the matter which if carried through will make our nation a militaristic nation equal to and exceeding European militarism. . . . This cannot be God's will nor is it the spirit of democracy."⁷ At Bethel College, President Edmund G. Kaufman condemned peacetime conscription as not only unchristian but as "anti-American to the core."⁸ Conscription, Kaufman wrote, undermines democratic liberty. It calls for "blind obedience which is preparation for totalitarianism." Leona Krehbiel, youthful librarian at Bethel College, offered a woman's voice that also combined nationalistic and religious arguments. Conscription, she wrote, was "a radical departure from the ideals of our founding fathers, and directly contrary to Christ's teaching regarding the sacredness of human personality."⁹

Perhaps the most remarkable Mennonite invocation of a nationalistic argument against peacetime conscription came from Harold S. Bender, chairman

Leona Krehbiel, Bethel College librarian 1932-1970

---

⁶C. E. Krehbiel, "Peacetime Conscription," *The Mennonite*, 2 January 1945, 4.

⁷J. W. Vogt, "Peacetime Military Conscription," *The Christian Leader*, November 1944, 2.

⁸Ed. G. Kaufman, "Editorial," *Bethel College Bulletin*, 15 March 1945, 1.

⁹Leona Krehbiel, "Peacetime Military Conscription," *The Mennonite*, 17 April 1945, 1-2.

of the Mennonite Central Committee Peace Section, in testimony, June 12, 1945, before a congressional committee. Bender lauded America as "the greatest (and one of the last) nations of the world with a record of genuine moral and spiritual idealism and devotion to peace and the arts of peace." Bender said that peacetime conscription would betray the peace-loving heritage of a nation "which has never had a military caste, and in which the ideal of constructive achievement in peace has always been cherished above that of military prowess."[10] In retrospect, there is no little irony in a pacifist Mennonite leader lauding America's peace heritage in the context of the most devastating war the nation had ever fought. Bender delivered his testimony just two months before the United States president decided to drop atomic bombs on Hiroshima and Nagasaki.[11]

Some Kansas Mennonite congregations had peace committees that mobilized church members to write letters to Congress. During the war the Lorraine Avenue Mennonite Church (LAMC) in Wichita had had three times as many young men in regular military service as in Civilian Public Service. But the congregation also created a "peace committee" that diligently promoted Mennonite peace identity and witness. At the war's end, September 1945, the LAMC peace committee urged congregation members to write their U.S. Senators Arthur Capper and Clyde Reed, and their U.S. Representative, Edward H. Rees, regarding three public policy issues: peacetime conscription, postwar relief, and fair employment practices. Relief aid, said the committee, should go to "all the hungry," including the defeated Germans. "If thine enemy hunger, feed him." In a bulletin/newsletter of September 30, 1945, the peace

---

[10]"Mennonites Testify at Hearings on Post-War Military Policy," *The Mennonite*, 10 July 1945, 5-6.

[11]Bender's nationalist/pacifist testimony of June, 1945 is not mentioned in the major scholarly treatments of Mennonite peace witness: Perry Bush, *Two Kingdoms, Two Loyalties*; Leo Driedger and Donald B. Kraybill, *Mennonite Peacemaking*; or in the biography by Albert Keim, *Harold S. Bender, 1897-1962* (Scottdale, PA: Herald Press, 1998). Robert Kreider has suggested that Bender's statement may reflect "the kind of politically conditioned argumentation one is inclined to strengthen one's case when one is seeking to be influential in the public square." Email message from Robert Kreider to James Juhnke, 3 June 2003.

committee reported that "quite a number of members" had already written to the politicians.¹²

The Mennonite anti-conscription witness even found a place at King City Grade School in the small town of Elyria in McPherson County. King City was a two-room public school where both teachers and nearly all the pupils were Mennonites. William Juhnke, teacher of the upper grades 1944-46, five years earlier had been an outspoken opponent of going to war. In the face of American wartime enthusiasm he had moderated his anti-militarist statements. But Juhnke remained convinced that a primary goal of public school teaching was preparing students to be active citizens. So even before the war was over, he had his students write letters to Congressman Rees about peacetime conscription.

In April 1948, with a new conscription law hurrying toward passage, Bethel College dismissed classes for one day and held an "all-day peace conference"–what would be called a "teach-in" twenty five years later. The speakers included Bethel faculty and students, as well as two local Newton pastors who spoke on opposite sides of the question. Advocating the "absolutist" position was Lawrence Templin, former student who had spoken out for non-registration during World War II.¹³

Two months later, in June 1948, Congress passed a new Selective Service Law. For three years, due to "a fit of Congressional carelessness," religious objectors, though required to register, were indefinitely deferred from service of any kind.¹⁴ Despite the deferment, some Mennonites recommended non-cooperation with the registration requirement. In a fifteen month period, 1948-1949, seven articles appeared in *The Mennonite* about the option of noncooperation.¹⁵ Gordon Kaufman, son of Ed. G. and Hazel Kaufman and a former CPS man then doing graduate work in sociology at Northwestern University (Evanston, Illinois), wrote an anti-registration article published in *The Mennonite*. He made three

---

¹²Lorraine Avenue Mennonite Church bulletin/newsletter, 30 September 1945. LAMC archives.
¹³*Bethel College Bulletin*, 1 May 1948, 3.
¹⁴Keim and Stoltzfus, *Politics of Conscience*, 147.
¹⁵Toews, *Mennonites in American Society*, 239.

points. (1) "The sole purpose of registration is to raise an army." (2) Military conscription undermines the Christian tenet of "the sacredness of personality." (3) "Conscription is the last and biggest step necessary to announce to the world that we are ready and willing to fight another war."[16] Kaufman said he had not decided whether or not to register. But he suggested that a massive popular refusal of registration could be an effective witness against the nation's current military mobilization. Eventually Kaufman did register with Selective Service.

Four Kansas Mennonites refused to register and spent time in prison for their disobedience. Austin Regier, like Gordon Kaufman, was a former CPS man who had second thoughts about registration. He had grown up on a farm in northwest Harvey County and was a member of the Hebron Mennonite Church. He had voted for the Socialist candidate, Norman Thomas, in the election of 1944. Inspired by A. J. Muste, executive director of the Fellowship of Reconciliation, Regier was critical of CPS. "Not only did the men not have a good, strong basis for pacifism, but the Church, too, was weak and inconsistent."[17] CPS men did not have the courage of their convictions, in Regier's view, as demonstrated in the Fort Collins Camp #33 where forty-four men signed a statement against work in the beet fields but then, except for six holdouts, went and did the work after all.[18] Now, with peacetime conscription in 1948, Regier, a single man more independent than Gordon Kaufman, who was married, refused to register. He was arrested and on January 10,

Austin Regier, imprisoned six months in 1949 for refusal to register with Selective Service

---

[16] Gordon Kaufman, "Should Mennonites Register for the Draft?" *The Mennonite*, 8 June 1948, 4-5.

[17] Austin Regier, "The General Conference and World War II," student paper for Mennonite history class taught by Cornelius Krahn, Bethel College, May 1948, 17.

[18] Austin Regier, *The Courage of Conviction: The Correspondence of a Conscientious Objector* (North Newton, KS; Raymond Regier, 2000), 23-24.

1949, sentenced to a year and one day in prison. His eloquent statement to the judge set forth his Mennonite heritage, his Christian theology, and an insightful analysis of the ethical issues involved. The statement was published in *The Christian Century* with an ironical editorial comment that Regier's was "the type of mind which the United States thus classifies as criminal." It was also published in *The Mennonite* and in *The Youth's Christian Companion*.[19]

The official Mennonite denominational position, a legacy of Civilian Public Service, called for registration and alternative service. But Jacob J. Enz, acting editor of *The Mennonite*, endorsed Regier's witness as a valid Christian challenge to American militarism. "DOES CAESAR MEAN MARS?" asked Enz in an editorial just before Regier's courtroom date. "The line is becoming an exceedingly fine one that marks the end of our Christian and Biblical responsibility to 'the powers that be' and the beginning of the worship of the Twentieth Century idol–Mars."[20] Enz did not specifically call for the church to change its official policy regarding registration. But he leaned in that direction: "The mark of the true Church, the mark of the true Christian, is their willingness to be the 'voice' for truth, love, and righteousness at times when it is popular to evade the issue and compromise a clearcut stand, succumbing to the forces of immorality, hatred, selfishness and greed." Erland Waltner, pastor in Mountain Lake, Minnesota, attended Regier's court hearing and wrote an article for *The Mennonite* that obliquely compared Regier with Christ as "Numbered With the Transgressors" (Luke 22: 37).[21] He was paroled after six months in prison.

Three additional non-registrants sentenced to prison for a year and a day were Ralph Bargen (1949), Dwight Platt (1951), and Eldon Bargen (1953), all of whom had attended Bethel College and had been inspired by Austin Regier. The judge at Ralph Bargen's

---

[19] Austin Regier, "Christianity and Conscription as Viewed by a Nonregistrant," *The Mennonite*, 30 November 1948, 13-15.

[20] Jacob J. Enz, "Editorials," *The Mennonite*, 7 December 1948, 3.

[21] Erland Waltner, "Numbered with the Transgressors," *The Mennonite*, 1 February 1949, 4.

hearing in Wichita said he had read three "editorials and articles" about the Austin Regier case sent to him by editor Jacob Enz. The judge said he had "utmost respect" for the Mennonites as "God-fearing law-abiding people." But the Mennonite church, he said, did not officially advise young men not to register. Bargen had pleaded guilty so the judge had no alternative to send him to prison.[22] Ralph, Dwight, and Eldon were all paroled after serving about half their sentences. The government could have brought them to trial again for their continuing disobedience, but was not inclined to do so. Platt refused to sign a registration form, but did sign a statement, "I agree to obey all laws insofar as God gives me the light."[23] That statement, plus three years of voluntary service in India, apparently satisfied Selective Service. In late 1953, however, Eldon, younger brother of Ralph Bargen, was arrested for failing to report for a physical examination. This time the judge sentenced him to three years of alternative voluntary service, most of which he fulfilled at Brook Lane Farm psychiatric center near Hagerstown, Maryland. But he consistently refused to sign a registration document.[24]

In 1951 Congress put the Selective Service System on a permanent basis. All American men between age 18 and 26 were required to register for the draft and, if called, to serve for two years. Conscientious objection was limited to men who "by religious training and belief" were "opposed to participation in war and in any form." Secular pacifists and objectors to only "unjust wars" were excluded. Mennonites would have preferred a broader inclusion, or no conscription at all. The new conscription program took shape, as Ed. G. Kaufman had predicted, in the context of massive militarization. The president's "Truman Doctrine," designed to contain Soviet imperialist expansion, involved the

---

[22] Transcript of Proceedings, U.S. District Court, Wichita, Kansas, 11 March 1949, 16-17. Helen Bargen collection.

[23] Sue Schroeder and Michelle Friesen, "A Case of Non-Registration," Bethel College research paper, 21 March 1972.

[24] Helen Bargen and David Habegger, "The Life of Eldon Bargen," unpublished paper, 28 August 2010 (MLA). Conversation with Helen Bargen, North Newton, KS, 17 February 2014.

projection of American military power in Europe and Asia. He used the Korean War (1950-1953) to justify a vast increase of military forces, new military technology, and military budgets. The growth of the American "military/industrial complex," and above all the nuclear arms race with the Soviet Union fostered a fearful militarization of American society and politics.[25]

The Mennonite witness against American militarism, stated so strongly in the face of approaching peacetime conscription, receded into the background in the face of popular Cold War alarm about Communist expansion. It became clear that the government's system would treat religious objectors with unprecedented tolerance. The term of service was set at two years, unlike the indefinite "for the duration" requirement in CPS. Approved religious conscientious objectors were required to work for two years in an approved civilian public or other nonprofit agency. The Selective Service System, directed by General Lewis Hershey, was remarkably generous in approving more than 2,000 agencies as recognized I-W employers. The draftees could make their own arrangements with approved employers quite apart from church or denominational direction. They did not need to live in camp units. They could serve as volunteers or be paid for their work. Overseas work was allowed, unlike World War I, and known as "Pax Service." Government Selective Service officials had minimal contacts with the workers. The program became known as I-W, often pronounced and written "1-W."[26]

From 1952 to 1955 nearly 10,000 conscientious objectors worked in the I-W program, some 70% from Mennonite and Brethren in Christ churches. More than 80% of them worked in hospitals or other health work. Unlike World War II when there had been no CPS camps in Kansas, one of larger places of I-W employment was in Topeka, Kansas (125 men). However more Kansas draftees

---

[25]James Carroll, *House of War: The Pentagon and the Disastrous Rise of American Power* (Boston: Houghton Mifflin, 2006).

[26] "I-W" was the classification in 1951 conscription bill. For a review of the I-W system see Toews, *Mennonites in American Society*, 240-55; and Dirk W. Eitzen and Timothy D. Falb, "An Overview of the Mennonite I-W Program," *Mennonite Quarterly Review* 56 (October 1982), 365-81.

Postwar Mobilization 1945-1960   65

probably served in Denver, where the largest number of I-W men were employed (180 men). In addition some I-W workers took jobs at Prairie View Mental Hospital in Newton, and at the approved Mennonite colleges. The percentage of young Mennonite men who went into civilian alternative service increased significantly from World War II to the post-war system. In 1944 43% of GC Western District draftees went into civilian alternative service (as opposed to combatant or noncombatant service in the military). Ten years later, in 1954, 60% percent were in civilian alternative service. Opinions differed as to why more young men made decisions that conformed to the official teaching of the church. Elmer Ediger, then serving as the general secretary of the GC Board of Christian Service, suggested that some of the improvement may have been due to diligent denominational efforts at peace education.[27] Perhaps more convincing was the fact that "I-W was so easy."[28]

I-W service represented a diffusion of Mennonite forces. In CPS the draftees had served in camps or other places where they lived in community where the church-appointed leaders were in charge. In I-W the churches were relieved of organizational and management responsibility for drafted pacifists. The Selective Service System approved jobs that would qualify as alternative service and assigned draftees to places of service. The drafted men could make arrangements for assignments without consulting local or denominational leaders. The program had freedom and flexibility, but compared to CPS the church lost control. Even so, I-W was a creative endeavor that resulted in a new service theology, movement into new careers, planting of new churches, assistance to Mennonite institutions, and personal religious assessment and action by each draftee. The end of the military draft in 1973 during the Vietnam War meant the loss of this moment of commitment and decision.

---

[27] Elmer Ediger, "Board of Christian Service General Secretary's Annual Report to the Board, 1954," 2. Mennonite Library and Archives.
[28] Eitzen and Falb, "An Overview," 381.

Peace Conferences

In the post World War II era Mennonites gathered repeatedly for special conferences and earnestly wrote and adopted statements on issues of war and peace, church and state. In November 1950 twelve Kansas Mennonite leaders, all men, joined others from across the country in a "Study Conference on Nonresistance" at Winona Lake, Indiana, sponsored by the Mennonite Central Committee Peace Section. The "Peace Section" had been created during the war to address military draft issues. In the post-war era it became something of a Mennonite think tank on war and peace. The Peace Section's theological range reflected the great diversity of participating groups. The Kansas delegates at the 1950 Winona Lake conference included General Conference Mennonites, who were interested in political engagement, as well as Church of God in Christ Mennonite (Holdeman) leaders who were more strictly separated from politics. Also present from Kansas were delegates from the Mennonite Brethren, Evangelical Mennonite Brethren, and "Old" Mennonite groups, as well as other delegates from across the United States and Canada.[29]

Robert Kreider, who had just completed his preliminary examinations for a Ph.D. degree at the University of Chicago, wrote a paper for the Winona Lake conference, "The Disciple of Christ and the State." Kreider sketched out what he called a "more aggressive out-going approach to community responsibility than has characterized our Mennonite tradition." He framed his call for Mennonite political witness cautiously. Among other recommendations, he proposed that Mennonite service workers overseas should stop in Washington, D.C,. at the end of their service terms and go from office to office with information and recommendations to policy makers.[30] But the kind of radical

---

[29]"Declaration of Christian Faith and Commitment," a flyer with the delegates and resolutions of the Study Conference on Nonresistance, Winona Lake, Indiana, November 9-12, 1950. Akron, PA: MCC Peace Section, 1950.

[30]Kreider, *My Early Years*, 581-2. Anna Juhnke, notes from a panel of participants at the Winona Lake Conference, Bethel College Mennonite Church, November 14, 1993, author's collection.

challenge to militarism that Gordon Kaufman and Austin Regier were calling for was not on the inter-Mennonite table.

It was clear to everyone at the Winona Lake conference, including the conservative separationists, that Mennonites would do what they could to influence public policy on the military draft. Beyond that, however, the final Winona Lake statement disclaimed any "blueprint for peace" or any assumption "that human endeavor alone can bring about a warless world within history." The statement did acknowledge a vague general "obligation to witness to the powers that be of the righteousness which God requires of all men, even in government." The statement focused on the issue of warfare. It did not include the concept of "justice," or any reference to the civil rights issue that would emerge in the coming decades.

In their post-war peace conference dialogues, some Mennonites insisted that "peace" was a matter of the Christian's individual spirituality while others claimed political relevance for the "peace position." The Mennonite Brethren, with their center at Hillsboro, were inclined to a more spiritual pacifism. In March 1953, at an annual peace conference at Tabor College, Frank C. Peters, Tabor president, concluded two lectures with the statement, "If I have accepted Jesus Christ as the center of my life, and if I must conclude that Jesus Christ did teach the way of peace, then it is up to me to take up my cross and follow in the Master's steps."[31] Also on the program was Erland Waltner, Bible teacher at Bethel College, who spoke on "God's Love and Our Peace." Like Peters, Waltner made no specific references to conscientious objection or to politics. Listeners and readers could draw their own conclusions to the theological and biblical exposition.

Milo Kauffman, president of Hesston College, at the same conference made more practical claims for what he called "Second Mile Religion." Noting that many believed "we are approaching a third war far more catastrophic than the two preceding ones,"

---

[31]Frank C. Peters, "Principles of Peace" and "The Maladjusted Christian," in a booklet, "Peace Conference Lectures," printed by Tabor College. Copy in the Wesley Prieb collection at the Center for Mennonite Brethren Studies, Tabor College.

Kauffman suggested that pacifism had "worked" for William Penn in his American colony. He concluded, "As a peace-loving people, we must not grow weary in preaching love and nonresistance. Other groups are joining us in holding that hate and war are impractical and wrong, and that the way of Christ is the way of peace and power."[32]

Winfield Fretz, teacher of sociology and church history at Bethel College, in the spring of 1953 attended a conference in Missouri on "Preparing College Men and Women for Politics." The conference sponsors, from the University of Kansas and the Citizenship Clearing House, addressed the question, "How can colleges and universities help the student obtain better preparation for active participation in the political affairs of their community?"[33] The focus was on local community political engagement rather than on national politics. That emphasis fit with Fretz's interests. He was a leader in a wider Mennonite "community movement" that affirmed a future for Mennonites in rural communities rather than in cities.[34]

J. Winfield Fretz, professor of sociology at Bethel College 1933-1960

But Fretz was cautious. In his report to David C. Wedel, Bethel College president, he respectfully acknowledged the traditional Mennonite view that Mennonites should not be involved in politics. Among the 100+ conference participants he was a fish out of water, "the only one who did not smoke and one of the very few who did not imbibe a cocktail." But he nevertheless returned to Bethel College with a vision for Mennonite church engagement with the civil order. "I feel more strongly than before that we in the General Conference should launch forth,

---

[32] Milo Kauffman, "The Challenge of the Second Mile," in booklet "Peace Conference Lectures," Tabor College, 1953.

[33] "Conference on Preparing College Men and Women for Politics," brochure for conference at Excelsior Springs, MO, April 17-18, 1953, J. Winfield Fretz papers, MS.69, MLA.

[34] Toews, *Mennonites in American Society*, 100-1, 195-7.

perhaps in a small but quiet and effective way, to try to do what we can to make better citizens; this by way of cooperation with local county committees of both parties to study issues that confront voters and to assist in gathering information about candidates for election to public office."[35]

Three years later, in the spring of 1956, Fretz and Harley Stucky, history professor at Bethel College, organized the first of two conferences on "education and responsibility." Attending were Mennonite church pastors, Bethel College students and faculty, and a few local politicians. Although Fretz and Stucky designed the conferences to make the theological and practical case for increased Mennonite involvement in politics, their arguments for participation were hedged with caution and warning. In his opening keynote address Fretz argued that the case for nonparticipation, which arose out of church persecutions in the first and sixteenth centuries, was not valid in the context of American democracy.[36] Non-Mennonite local politicians who had been invited to the conference wondered why refusal to participate in politics was even an issue. Walter Neufeld, a Mennonite pastor, suggested that Mennonites should take political office and remain there until faced with a situation of moral compromise. Then their Christian witness would be made by resigning from office.

Harley Stucky summarized the arguments both for and against participation in politics. Christianity, he said, was foundational for democracy. "Christianity has given us the basis of our moral and legal codes in the Ten Commandments and the Sermon on the Mount, our respect for human life and

Harley Stucky, professor of history and government at Bethel College 1948-1960

---

[35]Winfield Fretz to D. C. Wedel, 29 April 1953, Fretz papers, MS.69, MLA.

[36]See the following articles in *Mennonite Life* (July 1956): J. Winfield Fretz, "Should Mennonites Participate in Politics?" 139-40; Esko Loewen, "Church and State," 141-2; Elmer Ediger, "A Christian's Political Responsibility," 143-4.

the sacredness of individual personality. (I)t has influenced our concepts of brotherhood, justice, equality, and liberty." Nevertheless, a Christian's primary allegiance is to the Kingdom of God. A Christian politician who "sees the state reflecting values other than God's, will exercise his judgment as to where and how far he must withdraw."[37] Stucky did not give any historical examples of such withdrawal. The Bethel College conferences on education and political responsibility were designed to foster intelligent engagement with the political order. Decades later the presentations as published in *Mennonite Life* seem to be more on the side of caution than on the side of engagement.

Ernest Arthur "Ernie" Unruh, Republican

Strangely absent from the 1956 and 1958 Bethel College conferences was Ernie Unruh, a Mennonite from Newton who was then serving in the Kansas House of Representatives. Though he was the most prominent case of the conference topic, Unruh was not present in person and not mentioned by any of the speakers. He was a member of the Bethel College Mennonite Church, where conference speakers Fretz, Stucky, and Ediger were members. In 1952 he had successfully campaigned on the Republican ticket for a seat in the Kansas legislature. He went on to serve ten two-year terms. Unruh had served as an Air Force pilot during World War II, and was proud to be one of four military pilots from his North Newton church congregation. He claimed that he was "not ostracized in any way by the pacifists at the church." Nevertheless his absence from Mennonite pacifist conversations at Bethel College in 1956 and 1958 about political involvement demonstrated the wide distance between the pacifist and non-pacifist members of Mennonite churches.

Unruh's military credentials helped his political standing in his district. The district included all of Harvey County, with its substantial Mennonite minority but strong non-Mennonite

---

[37] Harley Stucky, "Should Mennonites Participate in Government?" *Mennonite Life* (January 1959), 34-8, 12.

majority. He was a businessman who owned and operated a gasoline station on Main Street between Newton and North Newton. Unruh was a Republican–the party that supported free enterprise and private property. Republicans, in his view, were farmers and family men who held strong moral values. The Democrats were for liquor by the drink and for gambling. Although Unruh was a long-term member of the Harvey County Chamber of Commerce, he said his support came more from the rural areas than from Main Street. He always favored "the little guy, the working man." In 1958 he did vote for an anti-union Right to Work law that Kansas adopted as a Kansas constitutional amendment. The law prohibited unions from requiring workers to pay dues as a condition of their employment. But Unruh also introduced minimum wage bills "that upset the businessmen in town."[38]

Unruh served on different committees in the legislature, including the powerful Education and Ways and Means committees. He took pride in his positions for a reformed drivers license renewal system, against a Republican bill for funding road improvements, and for a proposed Arkansas River Watershed Act that would have given taxing authority to build dams along the river. He supported two education measures that seemed less substantive and more reactionary: to require that everything that appeared on a school examination must also appear in the textbook, and to outlaw Communists from appearing on the campuses of Kansas state colleges and universities.[39] In general, he did not take major roles of strong leadership or advocacy in the state legislature.

Ernie Unruh was a common man, an affable gasoline station owner, more than an articulate and prominent local citizen. In Newton he did not hold any positions or serve on any committees in the Chamber of Commerce. He attended his local church, but did not attend or teach Sunday School classes or serve on church committees. He occasionally played a role in local Republican Party

---

[38]Ernest Unruh, interview by James Juhnke, Newton, KS, 24 February 2005.
[39]James Juhnke to Anna Kreider, 28 January 1962, author's collection.

infighting. One such battle was for removal of John McCuish from his long-term role as Harvey County Republican Party chairman. Unruh's father, Henry F. Unruh, ran an under-the-radar campaign for precinct committeeman and defeated McCuish by a few votes. McCuish, a Newton journalist, had been elected lieutenant governor of Kansas, and in 1957 had participated in a controversial "triple play" which elevated him temporarily to the governor's office where he immediately appointed the ex-governor, Fred Hall, to the recently vacated office of Chief Justice of the Kansas Supreme Court.

Walter W. "Sprig" Graber, Democrat

Walter W. "Sprig" Graber, an active member of the Pretty Prairie First Mennonite Church in western Reno County, had a greater influence on local and state politics than did Ernie Unruh. Graber belonged to the Swiss-Volhynian ethnic group, with its centers in Pretty Prairie and Moundridge, Kansas, and in Freeman, South Dakota. From their early years in the United States, the Swiss-Volhynians had been more drawn to the Democrat Party than were the Mennonites of Dutch-Russian ethnicity. This difference was enhanced during the New Deal of President Franklin D. Roosevelt. "Sprig" Graber became a Democrat. After graduating from Bethel College and a time as public school teacher and sports coach, he in 1936 started what became an 800-acre farm "devoted to wheat, soil-building legumes and feed and pasture for the 80 head of Guernsey cows."[40]

In 1939 Graber was elected to the Roscoe Township Board, and subsequently to the Pretty Prairie School Board. He helped to organize the first Pretty Prairie Rodeo, which grew into a major widely-attended event of local entertainment. In 1949 he took initiative to organize a group of western Kansas wheat farmers into the "Kansas Wheat Growers Association." He joined the Reno County Farm Bureau and became the chairman of its legislative

---

[40]"Farmers Start Tour European Countries," undated and unidentified newspaper clipping (Feb 1950), in scrapbook of Helen Graber Unruh (Graber's daughter), Hutchinson, KS.

committee. In 1949 he testified at the state capitol in Topeka for the Farm Bureau in favor of a severance tax on the oil industry. He was a vigorous advocate:

> Without a doubt the most powerful force in Kansas politics is an oil Industry which determines Kansas legislation as well as its executive with the same dictatorial power that Huey Long ruled the state of Louisiana. . . . Their work is carried on by lobbyists with virtually unlimited financial backing, and they will use money, far-fetched reasoning, and a system of promoting taxes on everything under the sun except oil and gas to carry on the work of tax supported institutions.[41]

In 1950 Graber went on a month long tour of Europe with a group of farmers. In Germany he was able to make use of the German language he had learned in his childhood home. The newspaper account did not report on his agricultural business contacts, but did report his comments on the Cold War: "Marshall aid has been the salvation of western Europe. . . . Isolation is a thing of the past and something we cannot hope to maintain. We must accept our responsibility as a world power if our civilization is to survive, or we will be absorbed by communism."[42] This was the first of Graber's numerous overseas trips to support agricultural development. For sale at home and abroad he promoted new wheat-based products such as "Redi-wheat," a whole kernel processed wheat food sold in cans, and bulgur (de-branned) wheat made into wafers.

Kansas governors Fred Hall (Republican) and George Docking (Democrat) appointed Graber to the Kansas State Board of Education for consecutive three-year terms (1956-62). In 1957, Docking appointed Graber one of the seven commissioners of the

---

[41]"Oil Interests Said Holding Up Severance Tax," undated, unidentified newspaper clipping, March 1949, in scrapbook of Helen Graber Unruh, Hutchinson, KS.

[42]"Better Understanding Gained by Farm Tour," undated, unidentified newspaper clipping, Feb 1950, in scrapbook of Helen Graber Unruh, Hutchinson, KS.

Kansas Wheat Commission. In 1968 he won an upset victory in Kansas' 104th legislative district over a Republican incumbent, Dick Vanlandingham. He served in the legislature until 1976, and was defeated that year in a race for the Kansas Senate.

Walter Graber, in contrast to Ernie Unruh, was an active and outspoken legislator. He was most passionate about the Kansas tax system that, in his view, depended too much on local property taxes and sale taxes while allowing unfair loopholes for wealthy persons and businesses. He undertook to reform the probate court code by eliminating excessive costs and delays connected with settling estates–an effort that was opposed by attorneys, bankers, and bonding company executives. He served on the House Agriculture and Livestock Committee and the Assessment and Taxation Committee. He wanted to limit state funding for higher education.[43]

In his final term, Graber became known for the "Graber Amendment" to a majority Republican Party bill to finance highway construction. Many Republican legislators, not realizing how popular that amendment would be with the public, voted against it. John Carlin, Graber's fellow Democrat in the legislature and later governor of the state, recalled that the Democrats had "caught 'em napping." The Democrats used the "Graber Amendment" as a major issue against the Republicans in the 1976 election. The result was a Democratic majority in the legislature. That did not happen often in Kansas, and it lasted for just one term. Unfortunately for Graber, he was not in the legislature for that term and missed his chance to be a committee chairman for the Democratic majority.[44]

---

[43]Clippings from scrapbook in possession of Helen Graber Unruh, Hutchinson, KS. "Taxes," unidentified paper, 16 January 1971; "Move to Bar Local Sales Tax Defeated," *Topeka State Journal*, 15March 1973; Dave Macgruder, "Farming was best of all," *Kingman Journal*, 9 January 1973.

[44]Bob Beatty, ed., "Be Willing to Take Some Risks to Make Things Happen: A Conversation with Former Governor John Carlin," *Kansas History* 31 (summer 2008): 114-140.

Postwar Mobilization 1945-1960 75

Lydia Ewert, Mennonite Woman Activist

From the 1940s to the 1980s, Lydia Siemens Ewert was one of the most persistent Mennonite commentators on militarism, race relations, and other current events.[45] Ewert attended Bethel College, taught high school at Goessel and Hillsboro, and served as president of the Ladies Aid Society of the First Mennonite Church in Hillsboro. In 1956 she was elected president of the bi-national General Conference Mennonite Church Women's Missionary Association. She kept up a stream of letters to national political figures, to Kansas newspapers, and to denominational publications–often invoking her "Ladies' Aid" credentials and signing "Mrs. D. P. Ewert." In 1940 she wrote to Senator Arthur Capper favoring neutrality and peace. Immediately after the war she urged that "everything be done to see that food and other necessities of life be supplied to all the distressed peoples of the world, including those of the Axis countries."

In 1954 Ewert wrote to the editor of the *Hutchinson News Herald* defending Mennonites against the charge that they falsely imagine they avoid compromise by not taking part in military service. In a later retrospective reflection she regretted that critics said her stands were "anti-government." "If I didn't care about my government, I'd have an easy life. . . . To me good citizenship parallels being a wise parent. You're not going to be okay with everything a child does. We must have constructive criticism for good government, because having good government rests with us."[46] She did not speak and write as a political partisan, but her progressive-liberal convictions guaranteed that Democrat-leaning ideas were well covered in local newspapers and denominational publications.

---

[45]Lydia Siemens Ewert, *Lydia's Letters & Messages* (Hillsboro, KS: author, 1984).
[46]Don Ratzlaff, "Speaking Her Mind," *Hillsboro Star-Journal*, 26 September 1979, pp. 99-100 in *Lydia's Letters & Messages*.

The American Flag as Religious Symbol

Mennonite churches traditionally did not use the American and the Christian flag at the front of their sanctuaries. But pressures from the outside and from within some congregations, especially in wartime, resulted in the use of flags. Gerhard Friesen, a graduate of Witmarsum Seminary, a Mennonite school in Ohio, and pastor of several Mennonite congregations, noted that the flags had gone up in World War I as "an effort on the part of our people to prove that they were patriotic."[47] The First Mennonite Church in Newton put up American and Christian flags in church in 1942 and 1959. The Eden Mennonite Church put up flags during the war, but took them down quietly in the 1950s under the leadership of Peter J. Dyck, pastor from Canada. Both General Conference and Mennonite Brethren publications advertised American flags. From Oct 1940 through December 1942, *Mennonite Weekly Review* ran ads "in behalf of the Herald Book Store" for American and Christian flags.

In 1948 the Mennonite World Conference was held in North Newton, attended by many overseas visitors. Reportedly some European visitors took offence at seeing American flags in Mennonite churches.[48] Gerhard Friesen suggested that if American Mennonites were to visit churches in other countries and see their national flags in church, they would ask, "Do they worship something else here than I do? . . . Is this state worship? . . . Would it not indicate that national allegiance is valued above the allegiance to the Divine Lord, above the ecumenical nature of the church?"

Apart from the issue of flags in churches, Mennonites faced the question of how to respond on occasions of flag veneration such as the playing and singing of the national anthem at public school athletic events. In the winter of 1973-74, Walt Neufeld, pastor of the Eden Mennonite Church stayed seated with a hat on his head while everyone else rose for the playing of the national anthem. He

---

[47] Gerhard Friesen, "The Flag in the Church," *The Mennonite*, 26 June 1945, 8.

[48] Michael Bogard, "The Flag: A Symbol of Patriotism Among American Mennonites," seminary paper for Great Plains Seminary, December 1990, 18-19.

bowed forward and clasped his hands in prayer. Someone who was offended wrote a letter to the editor of the local newspaper. Neufeld wrote a response explaining why he did what he did. One Moundridge student, at least, Doug Krehbiel was deeply moved and instructed by Neufeld's witness.[49]

Resisting a Military Base in Marion County

In the summer of 1959 concrete evidence of the Cold War arms race arrived in the rural Kansas Mennonite heartland. The US Air Force proposed to build a Nike Hercules missile base in southwestern Marion County. The proposed site was four miles northeast of the small town of Goessel. The Air Force did not give out details about the proposed missile base, but the Nike Hercules missile was an anti-aircraft weapon with a range of about one hundred miles and carrying a twenty-kiloton nuclear warhead.[50] (The Hiroshima blast had been equivalent to sixteen kilotons of TNT.)

The Mennonites were alarmed. Leo L. Miller, pastor of the Goessel Mennonite Church and a member of the Western District Peace Committee, led the organization of "Operation 600," a plan to write six hundred protest letters to Air Force and Defense Department officials. Letter writing appeals appeared in the Sunday morning bulletins of at least five local congregations, and in the June 23, 1959, issue of *The Mennonite*.[51] James Waltner and Peter W. Goering, local pastors who were also on the Western District Peace Committee, made a special trip to Omaha, Nebraska, to learn what they could from an anti-missile protest action there.

Menno Schrag, editor of *Mennonite Weekly Review*, wrote that "Paradoxically, the peace-loving Mennonites who have for four centuries said they are placing their trust in God rather than

---

[49]Doug Krehbiel, interview by James Juhnke, North Newton, Ks, 11 Nov 2012.

[50]"Project Nike," Wikipedia, http://en.wikipedia.org/wiki/Project_Nike (accessed 15 Oct 2015).

[51]The congregations were First Mennonite, Goessel; First Mennonite, Hillsboro; Brudertal Mennonite; Tabor Mennonite; and Alexanderwohl Mennonite. "Operation 600," *The Mennonite*, 23 June 1959, 400.

armaments, are now to be defended–together with the rest of the population–with the most destructive weapons in existence." In Schrag's view, "life-giving wheat fields will still prove a safer way to peace and security in the world than missile launching sites."[52]

"Operation 600" was a success. Colonel Vernon L. Hastings of the Air Force wrote a letter to Leo Miller acknowledging the blizzard of letters he had received from the folks around Goessel. He justified the missile program as a force for peace. "Our efforts to strengthen defensive might of the United States have only one purpose," Hastings wrote, "that of avoiding armed conflict. . . . The selection by the Air Force of your area for missile sites is based on the essential needs of the country."[53] The Air Force was accustomed to local protests and often had used federal power to get control of the land they needed. But in this case, they decided to build not in Mennonite country but rather on two alternative sites near the Kansas towns of Bennington and Smolan.

By the end of the 1950s the military threat from Russia was shifting from manned bombers to inter-continental ballistic missiles. The Nike Hercules missile was not effective against ICBMs. The Air Force, apparently working with a surplus of Cold War military funds, began construction of missile sites at Smolan and Bennington, closer to Schilling Air Force Base near Salina where the program was administered. Work was suspended when the sites were 80% finished. Neither site became operational.[54] "Operation 600," had been launched by Mennonites who did not have inside information to refute the propagandistic claims of military officials. But it did keep the Air Force from scarring the land near Goessel with non-operational missile sites.

Further to the southern fringe of the Kansas Mennonite settlement were Titan II missile sites built by the Strategic Air

---

[52]Menno Schrag, "Wheat Fields and Missiles," *Mennonite Weekly Review*, 9 July 1959, 6. See also "Missile Sites Under Study," *Mennonite Weekly Review*, 3 September 1959, 7.

[53]Hastings' letter to Miller appeared on the back page of the Goessel Mennonite Church bulletin, 30 August 1959.

[54]"List of Nike missile sites," Wikipedia, http://en.wikipedia.org/wiki/List_of_Nike_missile_sites#Kansas (accessed 15 Oct 2015).

Postwar Mobilization 1945-1960 79

Command beginning in the spring of 1962.[55] The Titan II missiles were offensive weapons (unlike the defensive Nike missiles) with giant nuclear-armed intercontinental ballistic missiles aimed at targets in Russia. The nuclear warheads had explosive power 250 to 300 times that of the bombs dropped on Hiroshima and Nagasaki. Eighteen Titan II missiles, administered by McConnell Air Force base in Wichita, were located in an irregular ring around the city. One site was across the road from a Mennonite-owned field of pasture land near the town of Potwin in Butler County. Another site was two miles from Camp Mennoscah in Kingman County, a camp owned and operated by the Western District of the General Conference Mennonite Church. The Mennonites were apparently unaware of these military installations, and did not protest until 1979 when the aging Titan II missiles in their turn had outlived their usefulness and were more dangerous to people in Kansas than to people in Russia.

State and National Elections

The presidential election of 1940, held less than two months after the passage of the Burke-Wadsworth Bill for universal compulsory military training, had marked a turning point in Kansas Mennonite political party preferences.[56] In previous decades, through the 1920s and 1930s, a modest majority of Mennonites had voted for the Republican Party, but in numbers quite similar to the overall vote in Kansas. From the 1940s through the 1950s and beyond, Kansas Mennonites consistently voted ten to fifteen percent higher than Kansans in general for Republican gubernatorial and presidential candidates. The Mennonites did not all vote alike. The Swiss Volhynians in the Moundridge and Pretty Prairie areas were more inclined to vote a Democrat ticket, but even there the Democrat numbers declined. One marker of the Democrat decline came in 1952 when Gerhard Zerger, member of the Swiss Volhynian Eden Church and a long term Democrat member of the McPherson

---

[55] David K. Stumpf, *Titan II: A History of a Cold War Missile Program* (Fayetteville, AR: University of Arkansas Press, 2000).

[56] Juhnke, *People of Two Kingdoms*, 124-26.

County Commission, was defeated by John P. Franz, a Dutch-Russian Mennonite Republican from the Inman area.

President Truman's military "police action" in the summer of 1950 to repel the North Korean invasion of South Korea alarmed the Mennonites. Menno Schrag, editor of *Mennonite Weekly Review*, expressed skepticism that this was a "police action," not a "war" as the government claimed. Schrag hoped that it wasn't "the beginning of World War III."[57] It turned out not to be a world war, but it did involve a massive escalation of military armaments and budgets designed to protect the U.S. and the world against Communist expansion.

In the presidential campaign of 1952 Dwight D. Eisenhower used his high reputation as a military leader to imply that he had an answer to end the war in Korea. He said, "I will go to Korea," an attractive but vague commitment for which the Democrat candidate, Adlai Stevenson, had no answer. After the election Eisenhower did go to Korea and helped to broker an end to the fighting on the 38th parallel armistice line where the war began. For decades after, peace-minded Mennonite Republicans held a trump card in inter-Mennonite political arguments: "Democrats get the country into war; Republicans get the country out of war."[58] The litany was impressive. Woodrow Wilson got us into World War I; Franklin Roosevelt got us into World War II; Harry Truman got us into the Korean War; and then (later) Lyndon Johnson got us into the War in Vietnam.

Eisenhower was attractive to Mennonites because of his origins as a Kansas farm boy from nearby Abilene and because of his low-key, non-belligerent personal style. Yes, he was a military hero, but seemed inclined to keep the United States out of war. William Juhnke, who had earlier been a crusading pacifist progressive, was one Mennonite leader who voted for Eisenhower in both 1952 and 1956. Juhnke in the 1950s was a high school principal at Lehigh Rural High School and president of the Western District Mennonite

---

[57] Menno Schrag, "Which Is It?" *Mennonite Weekly Review*, 6 July 1950, 4.
[58] I have not seen this argument in print, but I heard it often in the 1950s and 1960s as a young Kansas Mennonite who discussed politics with friends.

Men. He was annoyed that he had to sign a loyalty oath that he had never been a Communist. He remained a progressive internationalist, and warned against narrow nationalism in public speeches. But he thought, without great enthusiasm, that Eisenhower was better than the political alternatives.[59]

Electoral politics was not high on the Kansas Mennonite political agenda in the 1950s. Churches put more energy and money into overseas mission programs, into benevolent programs for war sufferers and refugees, and into local church building and renovation projects. Relationships with the national government focused almost exclusively on the issue of military conscription. The only Mennonite in the Kansas legislature in the 1950s, Ernie Unruh of Newton, was not someone for whom traditional Mennonite peace values were politically relevant. Kansas Mennonites in the 1950s were overwhelmingly and distinctively Republican. In 1956 students at Bethel College organized political clubs prior to the election, the first such political activity on the campus since 1940. Perhaps that was a sign of the upcoming cultural and political changes among Kansas Mennonites in the 1960s and 1970s.

---

[59]Juhnke, *So Much to be Thankful For*, 144-145.

Chapter 5

Civil Rights and Cold War Antimilitarism

Between 1954 and 1965–the Supreme Court decision in Brown vs. Topeka Board of Education and the passage of the national voting rights law–race relations in America underwent tectonic change. Kansas Mennonites were on the margins of this social movement, but it did affect them in ways no one could have predicted. In the background were deep-seated racial biases that Mennonites shared with white Europeans and Americans. Blackness in the German and English languages carried negative connotations. Black Africa was a mysterious and backward continent. The legacy of slavery and segregation lay heavy upon all of American society. In Newton, Kansas, as in the rest of the of the country, white barbers refused haircuts to African Americans, and the city swimming pool was reserved for whites. Most Mennonites lived in rural areas and had no personal contact with African Americans. In 1953 when Harold Regier of rural Burrton went to work at the Mennonite mission at Gulfport, Mississippi, he met African Americans for the first time. "It was like going to a foreign country," he said.[1]

Racist language and images from American culture made their way into Mennonite families. In 1926 Emma Juhnke, in a letter to her brother, William, proudly reported that their three-year-old brother, John, was learning the English language quickly and had even learned to recite an amusing poem: "Teacher, teacher, don't whip me. Whip that nigger behind the tree. He stole money and I stole honey. Teacher, teacher, isn't that funny?" William later orally reported with some chagrin another racist poem that was circulating among his peers: "God made man and man made money. God made bees and bees made honey. God made the nigger in the dead of night. Made him in a hurry and forgot to make him white."[2] Mennonite engagement with the civil rights movement in the 1950s and 1960s took place against a background of prejudiced attitudes and separatist assumptions at the grass roots. These attitudes changed slowly.

---

[1] Harold Regier, interview by James Juhnke, 10 April 2014.
[2] Juhnke, *So Much to be Thankful For*, 45.

Civil Rights and Cold War Antimilitarism 83

Over the years Mennonite leaders in the colleges, denominational offices, church publications, and congregational pastorates gradually developed a "quietly progressive" attitude on race relations that influenced average church members.[3] Missionary work among Africans, African Americans, and other people of color played an important role in this process. As early as 1886 Krimmer Mennonite Brethren from Kansas began the first Mennonite mission to African Americans when Henry V. Wiebe and Elizabeth Pauls Wiebe established a mission at Elk Park in the Blue Ridge Mountains of North Carolina.[4] In the KMB periodical, the *Christian Witness*, the Wiebes described local racist opposition to their orphanage and schools.[5] In the MC (Old) Mennonite periodical, the *Gospel Herald,* Kansas Mennonites of that branch could read occasional articles about their group's mission to African Americans, the Welsh Mountain Mission in Pennsylvania.

Especially important for General Conference Mennonites, the largest group in Kansas, was the Camp Landon mission at Gulfport, Mississippi, that grew out of a World War II Civilian Public Service Camp.[6] Orlo Kaufman, director of the Camp Landon mission from 1947 to 1974, had grown up in the Eden Mennonite Church near Moundridge, Kansas. Camp Landon

Orlo Kaufman, director of Camp Landon, with a class of learners

provided many social services, especially released time Bible School classes and summer Bible school. More than 150 Mennonites from Kansas participated in voluntary service programs that gave

---

[3]The phrase "quietly progressive" is from Perry Bush, *Two Kingdoms, Two Loyalties*, 210.
[4]Lois Barrett, "Wiebe, Elizabeth Pauls (1876-1957) and Wiebe, Henry V. (1871-1943)." *Global Anabaptist Mennonite Encyclopedia Online*, http://gameo.org/index.php?title=Wiebe,_Elizabeth_Pauls_(1876-1957)_and_Wiebe,_Henry_V._(1871-1943)&oldid=78817 (accessed 17 Jan 2014).
[5]Le Roy Bechler, *The Black Mennonite Church in North America, 1886-1986* (Scottdale, Pa: Herald Press, 1986), 38-9.
[6]David A. Haury, *The Quiet Demonstration: The Mennonite Mission in Gulfport, Mississippi* (Newton Ks: Faith and Life Press, 1979).

them their first direct contacts with black people. At its peak, volunteers taught a thousand children in Bible school in different communities in the Gulfport area. In 1960 Kaufman initiated a "Fresh Air" program to send black children from Gulfport to spend several vacation weeks with Mennonite hosts in Kansas.

The program started with twenty-one children in the Goessel and Moundridge, Kansas, areas, and later extended to South Dakota. According to one historian, "Fresh Air programs brought more white Mennonites into intimate contact with African Americans than any other church initiative."[7] The program broke down common stereotypes. Mennonite hosts were invariably impressed by the black children's cleanliness and intelligence. A few promising young scholars from Gulfport attended Mennonite colleges. Charles and Dorothy Flowers actively contributed to student life as black students at Bethel College. Charles was a writer for the student newspaper, *The Collegian*. In 1959 and 1960 he wrote enthusiastic reports of his contacts with national black leaders Martin Luther King Jr. and Vincent Harding when they spoke at Bethel. Of King Flowers wrote, "To discuss with Dr. King his doctrine of Love is to glimpse the eternal; for it transcends race, creed, nationalism, prejudice, sect and the numerous obstacles of life. "[8] Dorothy Flowers returned from Bethel to Gulfport, had a successful teaching career, and served on the Bethel College board of directors.

As the civil rights movement heated up in the 1960s, Camp Landon leaders did not engage in activist anti-segregation marches or street protests. The local black religious leaders with whom Camp Landon cooperated were not inclined to activism and did not welcome the founding of a new Mennonite congregation that would compete for church members. Camp Landon's very existence as a white owned and white directed space to which blacks came for instruction and fellowship was in itself an offense to the prevailing segregationist ethos. Blacks were not supposed to

---

[7]Tobin Miller Shearer, *Daily Demonstrators: The Civil Rights Movement in Mennonite Homes and Sanctuaries*. (Baltimore: Johns Hopkins University Press, 2010), 94.

[8]Charles Flowers, "Services Well Attended," *Bethel Collegian*, 16 October 1959, 3; and "King Well Received," *Bethel Collegian* , 19 January 1960, 3.

Civil Rights and Cold War Antimilitarism 85

gather on white turf. On occasion local bigots threatened violence: "Is this the place where they teach those damn gorillas to be civilized?" In the face of one telephoned bomb threat, the Camp Landon staff stayed overnight in homes in the black community.

Harold and Rosella Regier at Camp Landon

From 1961 to 1970 staff member Harold Regier, originally from the Burrton Mennonite Church, was the speaker on a local weekly radio broadcast, "Sunday School of the Air." Regier used the broadcast as a low-key soapbox to "translate the relevancy of Scripture to life in Mississippi this decade." His attempts to undermine the popular use of the Bible in defense of segregation sometimes elicited hostile telephone calls to the radio station. The most dramatic response came in April 1968 after Regier's message in the wake of the murder of Martin Luther King, Jr. Regier appealed to his audience to "pledge to work, with unprecedented courage and haste, to realize the goals of the dream for which Dr. King gave his life." The radio station received twenty calls and the announcer asked a nearby air base to send a patrol to watch Camp Landon for a week.[9]

Vincent Harding, a black Mennonite pastor originally from the Bronx, New York, was the pre-eminent bridge between the Mennonites and the wider civil rights movement. He was a charismatic youthful church leader, studying for an advanced history degree at the University of Chicago, when he became interested in Anabaptism and started attending the Woodlawn Mennonite Church in Chicago. Convinced of the truth and power of the Anabaptist witness and message, Harding accepted an invitation to be associate pastor together with Delton Franz, who had grown up in Inman, Kansas. Harding was the first black pastor in the General Conference Mennonite Church. He quickly became the primary interpreter of Anabaptist values and the civil rights movement for all Mennonites, not just for the General Conference.

---

[9] Haury, *The Quiet Demonstration*, 66. Harold Regier interview, 10 April 2014.

He helped organize conferences on race issues, travelled to speak in Mennonite communities, and took a seat on the General Conference Board of Christian Service. In 1961 Harding and his wife, Rosemarie Freeney, took a position with the Mennonite Central Committee Voluntary Service Unit in Atlanta. The unit house was in a black section of Atlanta, just a block away from the home of Martin Luther King, Jr. Harding collaborated with King. His Mennonite influence was most notable in his drafting of the landmark speech opposing the Vietnam War that King presented April 4, 1967, in New York City.[10]

Vincent Harding (speaking at Bethel College in 1976)

Harding was deeply committed to both Anabaptist-Mennonitism and to the civil rights cause. Over time, however, he became impatient with Mennonite conservatism and reluctance to become actively engaged in movements for political and social change. In his first speaking tour in Kansas, a series of outdoor evening presentations to large crowds at the rural Tabor church in February, 1957, he had to deal with persistent arguments and fears about interracial marriage.[11] Was speaking in rural Mennonite venues the best use of time for someone who could be directly engaged in nonviolent resistance in the South? Harding arranged for many "study tours" of Mennonite leaders to the South, but eventually wanted his adopted church to get beyond "study" and into more direct action.

In the spring of 1963 Harding visited the mission at Camp Landon and recommended fundamental changes. There should be, he said, an integrated church worship group to resolve the "schizophrenia of week day work with Negroes and Sunday

---

[10]Tim Huber, "Pastor Nudged Church to Act on Civil Rights," *Mennonite World Review*, 9 June 2014, 1, 13.

[11]Folder 899, "Harding, Vincent, 1957-61," General Conference Mennonite Church Board of Christian Service correspondence, I.C.1., MLA.

worship where Negroes cannot go." The white leaders should become "spokesmen for (or bewith community leaders, officials and merchants" and "walk with the Negroes into the bus terminals, and to sit by them at the lunch counters."[12] Harding was imagining a more aggressive activism than either the local black leaders or the Camp Landon white leaders had contemplated. Orlo Kaufman and Harold Regier, administrators at Camp Landon, were convinced that local opposition in such a case would force them to close their mission and to leave the area.

The presence of a few African and African American students at Bethel, Tabor, and Hesston Colleges brought race issues to the surface. At Bethel some students quietly confronted barbers in the city of Newton who refused service to African Americans. There was mild protest over the exclusion of black students from a local private picnic facility (named "Yentrouc") where the Student Christian Fellowship had planned an event. In the spring of 1961 a more tense campus controversy emerged when some white Bethel Peace Club students attended an Inter-Collegiate Peace Conference in Nashville, Tennessee. The students stayed at a segregated hotel even after the hotel had denied admission to Enos Sibanda, a Bethel student from Rhodesia (Zimbabwe). John Opiyo, a Bethel student from Uganda, criticized the white students in the student newspaper, the *Collegian*. He said that Africans studying in the United States would remember such incidents when they became leaders in their own countries.[13] Lawrence Hart, a senior Cheyenne Indian student who later became a Mennonite pastor and denominational leader, wrote that the so-called "Peace Club" members did not represent *him* in Nashville.[14]

Bethel student awareness of the civil rights movement gradually increased over the years, and culminated in March 1965 when a group of twenty-five, including some adult church leaders, drove from Kansas to participate in a march from Selma to Montgomery, Alabama. One Bethel student, William Juhnke, Jr., carried a sign,

---

[12]Folder 900, "Harding, Vincent 1962-68," I.C.1.
[13]John Serapi Opiyo, "Wheat and Chaff," *Bethel Collegian*, 14 April 1961.
[14]Lawrence Hart, "Student Protests," *Bethel College Collegian*, 30 March1961, 2. Juhnke, *Small Steps Toward the Missing Peace*, 40-43.

"Kansas Mennonites for Freedom."[15] The event in Montgomery focused on voting rights. In Kansas that same spring Bethel students demonstrated for fair housing. In an event organized by the Kansas Collegiate Civil Rights Council, ten students, one faculty member, and one person from the GCMC offices in Newton, went to Topeka, the state capital, to demonstrate (including a "sit-in" in Governor William Avery's office) in behalf of fair housing for minority groups.[16]

In 1960 a Tabor College soccer team, including a Kenyan student, Hannington Pamba, on a trip to the NAIA national soccer tournament insisted on service that integrated two formerly segregated public facilities. Pamba graduated from Tabor and eventually became dean of the faculty of medicine at the University of Nairobi Medical School.[17] Local racism remained a problem into the late 1960s and the 1970s. In 1977 an African American staff member at Tabor, hired to relate to black students, had to live on campus because the town of Hillsboro still had a sunset law that said no black person could stay in town overnight. That same year a white Tabor professor, in charge of administering grant funds for black students, accused a black student of breaking and entering his house. The professor took the student to court in the county seat of Marion. The student was able to prove that he was out of town at the time of the alleged offense. The jury acquitted the student.[18]

The Hesston College student newspaper addressed the problem of racism on campus in 1969. "Yes, we have racial prejudice on the Hesston College campus," wrote black student Tony Brown, who later was hired to the faculty. "As idealistic as it may seem, with the help of God and the application of Christian principles, we can live happily together, putting emphasis not on color but on character."

---

[15]William Juhnke, Jr., "Christians for Freedom: From Kansas to Montgomery and Back," sermon text, 18 January 2009, author's collection. Clayton Koppes, "Students March in South," *Bethel Collegian*, 2 April 2 1965, 2.

[16]"Students March in Topeka," *Bethel Collegian*, 14 April 14 1965, 1.

[17]Lynn Jost, "A Time of Stability and Growth (1956-1980)," in *Tabor College A Century of Transformation 1908-2008*, ed. by Douglas B. Miller (Hillsboro, Ks: Center for Mennonite Brethren Studies, 2008), 131.

[18]Scott Chesebro, telephone interview by James Juhnke, 14 December 2011.

A critical white student noted the cultural difference between colorful black students and inhibited white Mennonites. "(W)e have nearly succeeded in psychologically suffocating our 'soul' brothers and sisters."[19]

Mennonite involvement in the efforts led by President Lyndon Johnson to pass the Civil Rights Acts of 1963 and 1964 was limited. Mennonites had learned how to exercise political influence on the issue of conscientious objection. They were not as highly motivated or equipped on the issue of civil rights. They had been major stakeholders on questions of military service. But on civil rights they were marginal and relatively passive bystanders–not invited to present testimony before congressional committees. In 1963 Vern Preheim and Esko Loewen, in behalf of the GCMC Board of Christian Service, went from Kansas and spent one day in Washington, D.C., to contact senators and congressmen from Mennonite-populated districts. They sent a copy of "A Christian Declaration on Race Relations" to every senator and congressman, and got sixty-three responses, mostly sympathetic.[20] Some local Mennonites wrote letters to their senators and representatives. An article in the *Wall Street Journal,* September 17, 1963, titled "Church Pressure Aids Chances for a Strong Civil Rights Measure," quoted Kansas Senator James Pearson that his mail was running "heavily for civil rights" and that it came from remote small towns such as Pretty Prairie, Fredonia, and Parsons. It is likely that Ben Rahn, pastor of the Pretty Prairie Mennonite Church and member of the Western District Mennonite Peace and Service Committee, was the writer and organizer of some of those letters from Pretty Prairie to Senator Pearson.[21] Kansas Mennonites clearly welcomed the landmark civil rights legislation of the Johnson administration.

---

[19]Cited by John Sharp, *A School on the Prairie, A Centennial History of Hesston College* (Telford, Pa: Cascadia Publishing House, 2009), 293.
[20]Board of Christian Service reports, December 4-6, 1963, "The Church Facing the Race Crisis," B-22, MLA.
[21]Jerry Landauer, "Church Pressure Aids Chances for a Strong Civil Rights Measure," *The Wall Street Journal,* 17 September 1963, 1.

Cold War Peace Activism

Mennonites were deeply affected by prevailing American attitudes toward Communism and the Cold War arms race in the 1950s and beyond. Convincing evidence of the evils of Soviet-style Communism came from stories of Mennonite suffering under Josef Stalin's collectivization of Russian agriculture and from refugees who escaped from the chaos after World War II. The polarization of international relations between the Soviet Union and the "Free World" led by the United States made it difficult for anyone to oppose the expanding American military establishment without seeming to be on the side of the Communists. Ernie Unruh, member of the Kansas legislature, like his fellow Mennonites, was a believer in free-market economics and in the Christian faith and hence a fervent opponent of "atheistic Communism." In January 1962 Unruh joined others in introducing a bill to the Kansas House of Representatives to make it unlawful for any Communist to appear on the campuses of Kansas state colleges and universities. The bill protested the appearance at the University of Kansas of Alexander Fomin of the Soviet embassy in Washington D.C. along with Arthur Schlesinger of President John F. Kennedy's staff.

But fear of Communism did not keep Kansas Mennonites from protesting against Cold War militarism. During the Cold War central Kansas Mennonites were on the map for the wider peace movement in the country. Mennonite congregations and colleges invited prominent speakers, such as the pacifist Methodist pastor Henry Hitt Crane and civil rights leader Martin Luther King, Jr., for special lectures. Itinerant volunteer pacifists like "Peace Pilgrim," whose blue jacket proclaimed she was "WALKING 10,000 MILES FOR WORLD DISARMAMENT," found hospitality in the homes of local peace activists. In the spring of 1961 Kansas Mennonites hosted a group of pacifists, sponsored by the Committee for Nonviolent Action, who were walking all the way from San Francisco to Moscow. The walk covered 5,767 miles in 307 days. The walkers left San Francisco December 1, 1960, and arrived in Moscow October 3, 1961. Both in the "free world" and behind the "Iron Curtain" the marchers preached their message of universal brotherhood. In both the United States and Russia they called their audiences to unilateral disarmament. On both sides they were told to preach their message to the enemy who was to blame.[22]

Students at Bethel College were greatly inspired by the marchers' message. A handful marched along for several days, and two of them, Mardy Rich and Judy Hilty, decided to drop out of school and join the group. Hilty, who was from Ohio, made a "tough decision" to leave the group in Philadelphia in late May after three months of walking. She said the walk had made her more "political," after her Mennonite upbringing had taught her to see pacifism in almost exclusively religious terms. For the first time she began to understand the implications of "unilateral disarmament."[23] Rich, who had grown up on the Bethel College campus, stayed with the group all the way to Moscow. Along the way on August 7, 1961, she was married to another marcher, Barton Stone, who was at that time a Buddhist. Relationships among the strong-willed and politically diverse pacifists occasionally were strained, but the main message of the project was effectively communicated to the world by A. J. Muste, the chairman of the Committee for Nonviolent Action and the most prominent pacifist in America. In communist East Germany, Poland, and the Soviet Union, the marchers faced the manipulation of government-approved official peace committees, but they were finally allowed to criticize Soviet military policy as vigorously as they had criticized America's policy in the United States. In Washington, D.C., officials in President Kennedy's administration had predicted the marchers would not be allowed into the Soviet Union. Instead, in the judgment of two peace scholars, the marchers "provided the crucial ingredient for a substantial act of political liberalization. Defying the odds and most expectations, they did succeed in lifting the Iron Curtain."[24] Meanwhile members of the peace club at Bethel

---

[22]Bradford Lyttle, *You Come With Naked Hands: The Story of the San Francisco to Moscow March for Peace* (Raymond, NH: Greenleaf Books, 1966); Günther Wernicke and Lawrence S. Wittner, "Lifting the Iron Curtain: The Peace March to Moscow of 1960-1961," *The International History Review* (December 1999): 900-917.

[23]Judy Hilty Kingsley, telephone interview by James Juhnke, September 8, 1996.

[24]Wernicke and Wittner, "Lifting," 917.

92 People of Two Kingdoms II

College in Kansas were meeting weekly, getting the latest news on progress of the march, and praying for the success of the project.

A major concern during the early Cold War was the proliferation of nuclear weapons and the environmental hazards of the testing of nuclear bombs. In August 1959 the triennial meeting of the General Conference Mennonite Church, meeting in Bluffton, Ohio, adopted a resolution on "The Christian and Nuclear Power." The statement condemned the United States for spending "billions of dollars for missiles and missile bases." It called for a permanent ban on the testing of atomic weapons.[25] Two years later, in December 1961, after the Kennedy administration signaled plans to resume atmospheric nuclear testing, a group of seventeen Bethel College students and one adult (Robert Carlson, associate pastor of the Bethel College Mennonite Church), travelled to Washington D.C. to join students from other colleges who were serially over several weeks picketing at the White House. The students published an attractive four-page flyer, with art work by Robert Regier and an "Open Letter to President Kennedy" by visiting history professor Robert Friedman, explaining their concern in some detail. They warned about "the possible devastating effect of radioactive fallout on the health of all humanity," and about the increasing "probability of nuclear war."[26] During the protest in Washington, D.C., some sixty students back at the Bethel campus engaged in a three-day fast. On the first day of the fast, ninety-six students and faculty signed up for a "14-Hour Peace Action Prayer Vigil," with each person praying for fifteen minutes.

The editor of a local newspaper, the *Peabody Gazette Herald*, mocked the Bethel students for thinking that the U.S. might "'conquer' the heathen Reds with Christian love." In the editor's opinion, "that path would mean turning the U.S. and the world over to Communism as the first step. The strength of the U.S. is the only thing that has contained the Reds this far."[27] The editorial was reprinted in the *Hutchinson News*. Defenders of the Bethel students

---

[25]"The Christian and Nuclear Power," General Conference Mennonite Church Minutes, 1959, 24-5.
[26]"Bethel's Concern," four-page flyer, *We Protest*, n.d.
[27]"To What Lengths?" *Peabody Gazette-Herald*, n.p., n.d.

Civil Rights and Cold War Antimilitarism 93

noted that they were asking the Kennedy administration to *continue* its present policy. The critics hadn't bothered to pay attention to the student's arguments. One Bethel student noted that the Peabody editor's argument identified the movement with total unilateral disarmament, a strategy "to ignore the point at issue and kill a straw man." As for the meaning of Christian love, the student doubted that it would "find fulfillment in pollution of the atmosphere and further preparation for war when we already know that we can wipe out civilization with our present weapons."[28] The exchange revealed the powerful fear of Communism in the American public, and the difficulty of having meaningful dialogue about modest policy changes regarding nuclear arms.

While some students were mounting protests against militarization in ways that foreshadowed student protests against the Vietnam War in the late 1960s and early 1970s, some local Mennonite congregations struggled with new issues related to "Civil Defense." In December 1961, the same month that Bethel students protested against atmospheric nuclear testing, the U.S. Department of Defense and Office of Civil Defense published a new booklet, "Fallout Protection: What to Know and Do About Nuclear Attack." The booklet was distributed in post offices across the country. It spoke about community fallout centers, and gave advice on what food and supplies were needed in shelters. In central Kansas, as in other parts of the country, Civil Defense officials investigated churches and other buildings that might serve the purposes of fallout shelters. Leo Driedger, administrator in the General Conference Mennonite Church office in Newton, summarized fallout information and Mennonite concerns in a mimeographed report, "Fallout Shelters," published in August 1962.[29]

The local Civil Defense office in McPherson County was exceptionally diligent in carrying out the new civil defense

---

[28] James C. Juhnke, letter to the *Hutchinson News*, with copy to the *Peabody Gazette-Herald*, 19 December 1961.
[29] Leo Driedger, "Fallout Shelters," 1962.

programs. On April 9, 1962, the Western District Peace and Service Committee (Walter Neufeld, chair) sent "An Open Letter to the Office of Civil Defense." It protested that engineering firms had investigated some churches without approval from the church governing councils. Neufeld was pastor of the Eden Mennonite Church north and west of Moundridge. "We see the construction of and participation in providing fallout shelters as further preparation for war. We choose not to be identified with such a program." In case of disasters, wrote Neufeld, we help through Mennonite Disaster Service.[30]

The McPherson County Civil Defense office investigated the church building of First Mennonite Church of Christian in Moundridge and determined that the facility qualified to serve as a community civil defense facility. They sent the church an official fallout shelter license and asked for a signature of approval that the building would be available "for use in a possible emergency." Ralph Weber, pastor of the congregation, returned the letter unsigned, and received a "nasty" response. The congregation's strongly stated position was signed by the pastor, a deacon and a trustee. It said, "1. We believe that the shelter program is part of preparation for war, increasing rather than decreasing the probability of attack. 2. We believe that the shelter program is an effort to condition the minds of American citizens to accept the inevitability of war, thus lessening positive efforts toward peace. . . . (and) 4. We believe that use of the church as a fallout shelter is a misuse of the church which was founded by the Prince of Peace to reconcile men to God."[31]

The attempt to pressure Mennonites to "volunteer" their church facilities for civil defense purposes was reminiscent of American public solicitations in World Wars I and II for "volunteer" war bond contributions. But in 1962 America was not at war. The government's civil defense program did not have the same public support. Even so, Mennonite congregations who pointedly refused

---

[30] See Driedger, "Fallout Shelters."
[31] See Driedger, "Fallout Shelters."

Civil Rights and Cold War Antimilitarism 95

to cooperate with civil defense programs risked good relationships with their patriotic neighbors.

Reservoir Destroys Bruderthal

In 1968 the Army Corps of Engineers completed the Marion Dam and Reservoir along the North Cottonwood River west and north of the town of Marion. It was a flood control project that inundated about 6,000 acres of farm land, including the Bruderthal Mennonite Church and its Ebenezer cemetery and a dozen church members' family farms. The Bruderthal congregation had been founded at the time of the Mennonite migration to Kansas in 1874. The long term economic and social changes that threatened small family farms in Kansas and across the country would have been a challenge to Bruderthal in any case.[32] The reservoir forced the congregation to disband in 1968, well before a normal decline.

For decades the congregation had fought against the project. Arnold Funk, native son and elder of the congregation from 1931 to 1956, served as secretary of the Cottonwood Valley Farmers Association. That group devised an alternative plan for 150 small reservoirs on individual farmers' land in the larger watershed area. The small dams would, as they said, "keep the rain where it falls," provide better flood control, and cost less money than the "big dam foolishness," and keep more farm land in agricultural production. Funk went to Washington, D.C., to testify at a congressional hearing on the Marion Reservoir Project. He sought the legal services of Dale Stucky, a Mennonite attorney in Wichita. He mobilized farmers to meet with visiting politicians, and to write to government representatives. Senator Andrew Schoeppel was ambivalent. He reportedly said, "I will vote for the reservoir, but I will *never* vote to appropriate money for it." The anti-big dam effort was frustrated by lack of an ongoing lobbying presence before government, and by the challenges of getting unified support from the potential small-dam farmers upstream. It was a

---

[32]Leland Harder, "A Joint Study of Four Hillsboro-Lehigh Area Churches in Kansas," 1964.

relatively rare case of Mennonite political engagement on environmental issues, sparked by the threat to their own community. In the extended struggle against the big dam, the Bruderthal Mennonites and their allies received an education in the futility of opposing big government powers such as the Army Corps of Engineers.[33]

Candidates from Hillsboro

In 1966 and 1968 three Mennonites from Marion County ran for state office in campaigns that had nothing to do with race or war issues. Marjorie Klassen Peters and Paul W. Hiebert, both of whom attended the First Mennonite Church in Hillsboro in their youth, ran respectively in 1966 for the state legislature and for the office of secretary of state. Both were Democrats. Marjorie Peters was a long-term Democratic Party activist, along with her husband, Jim, a farmer and cattle feeder. She had been chairperson of the Marion County Democratic Party, president of the Marion County Federation of Women's Democratic Club, and secretary to the Fourth District Democratic Organization. In 1966 her opponent in the 90th Kansas House district, which included all of Marion County, was a long-term Republican incumbent, Lawrence Slocombe. Although the Democratic candidate for governor, Robert Docking, defeated the incumbent Republican, Peters came in a distant second in her race.[34] Two years later, in 1968, Marjorie's husband, Jim, took his turn as the losing Democratic candidate in the 90th district. He got a slightly higher percentage of the vote than had Marjorie, perhaps because he ran more newspaper ads that had him wearing an attractive cattleman-cowboy hat.[35] Jim and Marjorie Peters attended the Lehigh Mennonite Church.

---

[33]Verda Epp, "The End of a Community," in *Bruderthal 1873-1964 90th Anniversary*, Ray N. Funk, compiler (Hillsboro: Bruderthal Mennonite Church, 1964), 52-7.

[34]"Harvey Political Campaign in Last Lap," *The Newton Kansan*, 2 November 1966, 3. "Docking Sweeps Aside Tradition to Defeat Avery," *The Newton Kansan*, 8 November 1966, 1.

[35]*Hillsboro Star-Journal*, 17 Oct, 1968, 8; 24 Oct, 1968, 8; 31 Oct, 1968, 3.

Paul Hiebert, after graduating from Hillsboro High School, attended Washburn University and became involved in both the local and national Young Democrats organization. For two years he served as national secretary. Although he was just twenty-three years old in 1966, he won the Democratic primary for secretary of state. After losing in the general election he worked on patronage issues with the Democratic Party transition team. Later he and his wife moved to St. Louis, Missouri.[36]

Presidential Elections

In 1960 when John F. Kennedy, a member of the Catholic Church, won the Democrat Party nomination for president, Mennonites faced a new religious issue. The Republicans nominated Richard Nixon, a Protestant of Quaker background. Menno Schrag, editor of *Mennonite Weekly Review*, was besieged with letters and telephone calls from readers who wondered when he would speak out on the dangers of electing a Catholic president. Schrag knew that most of his subscribers were Republicans. He himself had been critical of President Roosevelt's New Deal of the 1930s, and appreciated the Republican Party ideal of limited government. But in 1960 he decided to maintain a discrete and cautious silence on the "inflammable" religious issue. In recent months, Schrag said, Mennonites had shown that they were hardly capable of having a reasonable discussion regarding the new Revised Standard Version of the Bible. If Mennonites attacked other religious groups such as the Catholics they might expose themselves to attack. He wrote, "This writer could cite speeches he has heard in which it was argued that because of their nonresistant belief, Mennonites are dangerous to the very life and security of the nation, and an opening wedge for Communism."[37] Why stir the volatile waters of inter-religious relationships?

---

[36]Paul Hiebert, telephone interview by James Juhnke, 1 April 2015.
[37]Menno Schrag, "The Religious Issue," *Mennonite Weekly Review*, 13 October 1960, 6.

Menno Schrag, editor of *Mennonite Weekly Review*

However, Schrag was willing to identify in nonpartisan language what he considered to be the most important issues in the 1960 election. In foreign policy it was Cold War militarism–"the inadequacy of a policy based so largely on massive retaliatory power, rather than winning the under-privileged and under-developed peoples through our understanding and help." That issue applied to both parties, although Schrag may have had in mind candidate Kennedy's demand for more military spending to close what he called a "missile gap" with the Soviet Union. Schrag identified two primary domestic policy issues: civil rights and the "rush to bigness" in both government and business. Schrag's readers knew that Kennedy was in the Democratic New Deal tradition.[38]

Orlando Harms, editor in Hillsboro of the *Christian Leader*, the official publication of the Mennonite Brethren denomination, was more explicitly anti-Catholic than was Schrag. Harms said he did not intend to endorse any party or candidate. But he found the prospect of a Catholic president alarming. The Catholic Church was inherently authoritarian. The presidential election of 1960 "may determine whether we maintain a 'government by the people' under God or whether we will allow ecclesiastical totalitarianism to become even more forceful in our government than it is today." Perhaps this was not a specific political endorsement, but Harms indicated to his readers which presidential candidate *not* to vote for.[39]

Kansas Mennonites in 1960 voted overwhelmingly for Richard Nixon over John F. Kennedy. At Bethel College a straw poll of students and faculty showed 73.4% for Nixon, 14.6% for Kennedy, and 12% undecided. As in other Bethel straw polls, freshman

---

[38]*Mennonite Weekly Review* (27 October 1960), 6.
[39]Orlando Harms, *The Christian Leader*, 20 September 1960, 2.

Civil Rights and Cold War Antimilitarism 99

students voted most strongly for the Republican, with Democrat votes increasing among sophomores, juniors, and seniors. Eighteen faculty members voted. They were split nine to nine.[40] In fourteen rural precincts of substantial Mennonite population in Marion, McPherson, Harvey, and Reno counties, 87% of the votes were for Nixon, 12.2% for Kennedy, and .4% for the Prohibition candidate. This was the highest percentage for the Republican candidate in all the presidential elections since 1880. The percentage of votes for Nixon in Mennonite-populated townships was nearly eighteen points higher than for voters in the state of Kansas generally. This is not a precise measure of Mennonite votes, because an increasing number of non-Mennonites were living in these townships. Nevertheless, it seems safe to conclude that Mennonites were distinctively inclined to vote against a Catholic candidate. More than a few agreed with Allen J. Burkhart of Newton who referred back to sixteenth century Anabaptist history: "(W)e remember that we are the heritage of men who could no longer stand the intolerances of the Catholic Church."[41]

The American political landscape was transformed in the four years between the presidential elections of 1960 and 1964. President Kennedy was assassinated in November 1963. His successor, Lyndon Johnson, pushed through the landmark civil rights bill of 1964, legislation popular among Mennonites. The Republicans in 1964 nominated Barry Goldwater, a right-wing conservative who had voted against the civil rights bill because in his view it violated state sovereignty. Goldwater championed anti-communism and total victory in war. In his acceptance speech at the Republican convention he said, "Extremism in the defense of liberty is no vice." He criticized Johnson for being too cautious in the war in Vietnam. Goldwater would be willing, he said, to use nuclear weapons in Vietnam if necessary. Alarmed by Goldwater's positions, Mennonite editors Menno Schrag and Orlando Harms shifted more toward the Democratic candidate than they ever had in the past.

---

[40]"Presidential Poll Conducted on Campus," *The Bethel Collegian*, 11 November 1960, 1.

[41]Allen Burkhart, letter to the editor, *Mennonite Weekly Review*, 3 November 1960, 6.

For the first time in his life, Schrag voted for a Democratic candidate for president.[42]

From Schrag's viewpoint, Goldwater was on the wrong side of the two most important issues–civil rights and militarism. For the first time in his long editorship of *Mennonite Weekly Review*, Schrag guided his readers to vote for a Democrat Party national candidate. As always, Schrag did not explicitly endorse either candidate. He observed that in 1960 and again in 1964 Mennonites were becoming increasingly involved with politics. He warned readers "against the delusion that we can save the world through social action or the ballot box." Prayer was more important than campaigning. But Schrag was disturbed by signs of extremism. On the highway between Newton and Wichita, he noted, was "a large official sign by the John Birch Society which read: 'The United Nations is of the Commies . . . By the Commies . . . For the Commies.' etc. People (no matter how sincere) affiliating themselves with such organizations of the Right or Left share responsibility in any extremist statements which the leaders of such organizations make."[43]

Schrag decided to publish an essay by Paul Peachey distributed by the Mennonite Central Committee Peace Section. Peachey, a professor at Eastern Mennonite College in Virginia, warned against the "new radical wing of the (Republican) Party" behind which were the John Birch Society and the Minutemen. Peachey agreed with Schrag that Mennonites should not expect too much from the political order. But the right wing currents in the Republican Party "pose a real peril. They entail an idolatrous nationalism which seeks to play God among the nations of the world."[44] The Republican Party platform of 1964, in Peachey's view, crossed the line into idolatry. Orlando Harms printed the same article in *The Christian Leader*. When that article elicited a storm of protest, editor Harms defended himself by saying he had also published an essay

---

[42]Robert Schrag, interview by James Juhnke, 15 October 2014.

[43]Menno Schrag, "Reader Response About the Problem of the Right and Left," *Mennonite Weekly Review*, 24 September 1964, 5.

[44]Paul Peachey, "Church Cannot Align with Any Political Program," *Mennonite Weekly Review*, 1 October 1964, 9. Peachey, "The Church Cannot Align Herself, The 1964 Elections," *The Christian Leader*, 27 October 1964, 3, 21.

on the other side, "This *is* a Christian Nation," by J. L. Goetz.[45] Editors Harms and Schrag attempted by their own lights to be scrupulously non-partisan. But their choice to print Peachey's article tilted their publications to the Democratic side in the 1964 presidential election as surely as they both had tilted to the Republican side in 1960.

The 1964 voting results in rural precincts of substantial Mennonite population revealed a substantial shift to the Democrats, while the Republicans still claimed a majority. Where John F. Kennedy in 1960 had gotten only 12.3% of these votes, Lyndon Johnson in 1964 got 40%. Meanwhile the Republican votes declined from 87.3% (Richard Nixon) to 57.7% (Barry Goldwater). It is clear that in 1964 hundreds of Kansas Mennonites voted for a Democrat presidential candidate for the first time in their lives. At the same time there were some Mennonites who moved in the opposite direction. Joseph D. C. Goering of Elyria had been an early New Deal Democrat because that was the party of the oppressed and the underdog. But by 1964 he had decided that the great political issues were the threats of socialism at home and Communism from abroad. He voted for Goldwater.[46] Goering was an exception. In presidential elections through the 1940s and 1950s Mennonite populated precincts had usually voted 80% or more for the Republican candidates. In the three elections after 1964 that majority gradually declined: 77.4% for Nixon in 1968, 68% for Nixon in 1972, and 53% for Gerald Ford in 1976.[47]

Mennonites who in 1964 voted for Lyndon Johnson because he was less militaristic and extremist than Goldwater were disappointed when President Johnson in 1965 decided to escalate America's military presence in Vietnam. Johnson drew the country into an unwinnable destructive land war in Asia. Insofar as

---

[45]Orlando Harms, "The Editor's 'Uneasy Chair,'" *The Christian Leader*, 24 November 1964, 1.

[46]Joseph D. C. Goering, interview by James Juhnke, 31 July 1966.

[47]Barbara Thieszen, "Voting Trends in Selected Mennonite Townships," student research paper, Bethel College, 6 December 1979, 6. The percentage of actual Mennonite population in these townships declined over these years, making the data less accurate for tabulating Mennonite votes.

Mennonite votes represented an interest in peace, the lesson of history seemed obvious. Democratic presidents who promised peace proceeded after their election to get the country into war: Woodrow Wilson into World War I; Franklin Roosevelt into World War II; Harry Truman into Korea; and Lyndon Johnson into Vietnam. Mennonites would remain predominantly Republican.

Chapter 6

Vietnam War

The American war in Vietnam (1965-1973) prompted a new wave of Kansas Mennonite peace activism. The peace movement in Kansas reflected the thinking and behavior of the anti-war movement across the country. Kansas Mennonites also participated in trends typical of their denomination throughout North America.

In January 1969 the Peace Section of the Mennonite Central Committee established a new office in Washington D.C., located a few blocks from Capitol Hill. Delton Franz, a Kansas Mennonite native and graduate of Bethel College, was the new director of the Washington office. This was not a registered lobby but a "legislative observer... a facility through which the Church can express its convictions in witnessing to the way of peace and to the cause of brotherhood, love and justice to which Christ has called it." The new office had optimistic goals for influencing national legislation. They would mobilize political forces in ten congressional districts "densely populated by Mennonites." The "densely populated" description was misleading. Mennonites were not a majority in any district. Nevertheless the Peace Section newsletter claimed that a strong concerned minority could have "constructive influence on the thinking and the decision-making of these Congressmen." To that end the Washington office kept Mennonites informed of their Congressmen's votes on bills of special interest. They organized political seminars for Mennonites to visit Washington, to become acquainted with the political process, and to meet personally with their representatives in the national capitol. With one of their favorite sons in charge, Kansans took special interest in the work of the Washington office.[1]

Kansas Mennonite political activism during the Vietnam War was most intense at Bethel College and among General Conference Mennonites. But other Mennonite branches also had become more politically involved. The Mennonite Brethren Church indicated growing openness to political witness in an official statement

---

[1] *Memo from the Peace Section Washington Office*, January and June 1969.

adopted in November 1966. Political involvement must be "selective" and "redemptive," the statement said, but it can be exerted at the local level of school boards and city councils as well as on wider "social institutions and political structures." The statement did not mention the Vietnam War, but it did say, "The prophetic voice of the church will be a voice of protest against racial discrimination, social injustice, economic exploitation and political corruption. . . . Above all it will be a voice that will call men to repentance, faith, and Christian commitment."[2] Young peace-minded radicals criticized the Mennonite Brethren church for its primary emphasis on spiritual piety and for failing to take risks or to speak out forthrightly against the Vietnam War.[3]

The intensified awareness about Vietnam was akin to that a quarter century earlier about American entry into World War II (1938-1941). Much had changed in the twenty-five years from 1940 to 1965. Above all the anti-Vietnam War peace activism among Mennonites was affected by a wider counter-cultural movement that alienated young people from the older generation. Nationally the opposition to war was associated with youth experimentation with drugs and sex. Mennonite student war-protesters often found their political message rejected because the people in their audience identified war protest with youth movement "hippie" ways of talking, dressing, and living. Kansas Mennonites, long divided into separate ethnic/religious sub-groups, now were afflicted by a new fracture between a stable/comfortable middle class older generation and a restless/angry younger generation.

Another difference in twenty-five years was the relation of the peace movement to modern media. The anti-Vietnam war protesters, more than the generation that opposed entry into World War II, were intent upon influencing public opinion. Anti-war demonstrations on the Bethel College campus received national publicity in both televised and print media. In 1970, a Bethel College teacher, running a "peace campaign," won the Democrat

---

[2] Mennonite Brethren Statement Regarding Political Involvement Accepted at the 26-29 November 1966 General Conference, Corn, Oklahoma.

[3] See an undated (1960s) letter from Dale Suderman to "Rev. Dick." Dale Suderman papers, MS.560, MLA.

Party nomination for a seat in the U.S. Congress. In 1976 a Mennonite Central Committee worker from Kansas who had stayed in Vietnam after the April 1975 communist takeover got national media attention when he returned home.

Opposition to the Vietnam War was made up of different groups who disagreed on other issues. The unusual alliances showed up in newspaper advertisements. In a full-page anti-war ad ("The War Is Your Burden") in the *Wichita Eagle*, April 14, 1970, twenty Mennonite individuals and couples constituted a third of the signers/sponsors. Most of the others were from the Wichita peace community, including a number of prominent Libertarians. Also signing was Charles G. Koch, who had been a member of the John Birch Society but had left because that organization supported the Vietnam War.[4] Kansas Mennonites also participated with "(Western) Kansans Concerned About Vietnam," an anti-war group organized by Ellen Mae Stanley and others in western Kansas.[5]

Repentance Walk 1966

The first anti-Vietnam war protest at Bethel College that garnered regional press attention was a "Repentance Walk" on November 11, 1966.[6] That was more than two years after the U.S. Congress had passed the Tonkin Gulf Resolution giving President Lyndon Johnson power to wage war. The U.S. Air Force had begun bombing North Vietnam. The U.S. involvement had proceeded by small steps over a decade. By the end of 1966 nearly 400,000 U.S. troops were in Vietnam. The Johnson administration defended the war as a Cold War struggle against the spread of communism. They argued that if Vietnam were united under the leadership of the north, as foreshadowed in the Geneva Convention of 1954, the

---

[4] *The Wichita Eagle*, 14 April 1970, 8A; Matea Gold, "'Sons of Wichita' explores Koch brother's lives," *The Wichita Eagle*, May 23, 2014, 3B.

[5] The records of "Kansans Concerned About Vietnam" are located at the MLA, VI.2.

[6] Terence Goering, "A History of the Bethel College Peace Club" (Social Science Research Paper, Bethel College, 1975), 24-33.

communists would be poised to overtake all of Southeast Asia. But the American military was unable to achieve its objectives in Vietnam, nor was President Johnson successful in convincing the American public to support and pay for the war.

In Kansas the earliest strong opposition to the war took shape at Kansas State University in Manhattan.[7] In the fall of 1966 Arthur Peine, a retired businessman from Manhattan, ran an independent write-in campaign for the U.S. Senate. He received seventy-three write-in votes in Newton township, the precinct that included Bethel College. The "Repentance Walk" a few days later showed that the peace movement at Bethel College rivaled that at Kansas State University, and was more aggressive than that at other Kansas liberal arts colleges.

November 11 was a national holiday, marking the end of World War I in 1918. Until 1954 it had been known as "Armistice Day." After the official change to "Veterans Day," Bethel College, in quiet resistance to American militarism, continued to use the earlier designation. Each year the chapel committee invited the school's peace club to be in charge of the chapel service on the day closest to "Armistice Day." In 1966 the peace club took advantage of the invitation to plan additional anti-war activities on November 11. They invited John Swomley, professor of social ethics and religious philosophy from a Methodist seminary in Kansas City, to speak at the student convocation and at a peace rally. And they planned a mile-long march from the Bethel campus to the downtown Newton post office for people to mail letters to national leaders calling for a changed national policy of repentance. "Repentance" was religious code for national policy changes. In this case the peace club urged policies recommended by U Thant, secretary general of the United Nations: "a halt to the bombing of North Vietnam, mutual reduction of military activity, and admission of the National Liberation Front to any peace negotiations."[8] The peace club, at this point, was not so radical as to call for United States

---

[7]Calvin Trillin, "A Reporter at Large, The War in Kansas," *The New Yorker*, 2 April 1967, 82.

[8]Maynard Shelly, "Peace Walk Baffles Peace Church," *The Mennonite*, 13 December 1966, 758.

military withdrawal from Vietnam. Dwight Platt, biology teacher who had served time in prison for refusing to register for the military draft, was faculty advisor to the peace club.

Both on the Bethel campus and in the town of Newton, intense opposition to the planned march emerged. President Vernon Neufeld, faced with reports that the repentance walk might result in violence and in reduced financial contributions, asked the peace club to call off the event. Jay Franz, editor of the student newspaper, *The Collegian,* agreed with the president: "We do not believe a march enhances the prospects for peace." The peace club students insisted on moving forward, but agreed to cancel the plan to march into Newton. They would go only a few blocks to the nearby North Newton post office. In his convocation address, John Swomley made a strong case for the right of dissent. "It makes no sense to demand freedom for Russians and Chinese and Vietnamese if we do not defend it here."[9] About eighty people participated in the walk. Joining the Bethel students and faculty were a number of local pastors (Melvin Schmidt, Arnold Funk, Howard Kunkel, D. D. Unruh, James Waltner) and Bethel's academic dean (Orville Voth) and his secretary (Delia Graber).[10]

Patti Burnette, commander of the Newton American Legion, was outraged that Bethel was violating the veterans' sacred day. She said the question for her wasn't what to do in Vietnam or the right to protest. The issue rather was respect for national symbols. "We weren't denying them their right to march. . . . But on that day! Downtown!" Burnette and others organized a veterans' parade in downtown Newton for the afternoon of November 11. The veterans' parade dwarfed the Bethel repentance walk: "color guards from the National Guard, the American Legion, the Gold Star Mothers, the Daughters of Union Veterans, and the V.F.W. Auxiliary; four Vietnam veterans; a Spanish-American War veteran; the Newton Blue Angels; the Scarlet Lancers of Wichita;

---

[9] John M. Swomley, Jr., "Vietnam – Veterans and Freedom," folder 1, "Repentance Walk and Mail 1966," box 1, Bethel College Peace Club records, III.1.A.29.e, MLA.

[10] Ruth Goertz, student research project for History of Civilization II class, February 26, 1969. The *Bethel Collegian*, November 15, 1966, reported that "about 90 persons" walked in the march.

and a .50-calibre machine gun firing blanks from the bed of a truck."[11] The veterans arranged for a flight of noisy military jets to fly over the Bethel campus at about the time of the morning peace march. The press statewide covered the dramatic events in Newton and North Newton.

Bethel's repentance walk exposed fractures in the Mennonite constituency. Maynard Shelly, editor of the bi-national denominational newspaper, *The Mennonite*, had long opposed the war and published many articles, including some from Mennonite mission and relief workers in Vietnam, showing the costs and the horrors of the war. He devoted eight pages of the December 13, 1966, issue to the repentance walk and its consequences. For *The Mennonite*, it was an unprecedented focus upon a single event. In an anguished editorial Shelly judged the college's and church's mixed response to the repentance walk to have been a failure to live by the Anabaptist spiritual ideals of discipleship: "(W)hen the chips are down the Mennonite church will not put its money and its middle-class reputation where its preaching is."[12]

Accompanying the article was an editorial cartoon by Robert Regier portraying a frightened Mennonite hiding in box marked "fragile" and holding onto a copy of *The Martyrs Mirror*.[13] The issue elicited twenty-one letters to the editor, seventeen of which took the side of the students and of editor Shelly. Paul L. Goering, pastor of the Lorraine Avenue Mennonite Church in Wichita, said the event showed that obedience to Christ could cause conflict. "The plans for the Repentance Walk and Mail, born out of prayer and concern, impressed me as imaginatively conceived."[14] One letter from

Robert Regier cartoon critique of Mennonite timidity in the face of American militarism. *The Mennonite*, 31 December 1966.

---

[11]Trillin, "A Reporter at Large," 131.
[12]Maynard Shelly, "Editorial," *The Mennonite*, 13 December 1966, 765.
[13]Shelly, "Peace Walk Baffles," 757-65. Robert Regier cartoon, 762.
[14]Paul Goering, "Not Peace But a Sword," *The Mennonite*, 20 December 1966, 780.

President Vernon Neufeld scolded Shelly for giving excessive attention to the event. In Neufeld's words, "One is tempted to conclude that the editor either has run out of news and articles, has an obsession about peace marches, or is trying to convince himself of his own views."[15] Both before and after the repentance walk, members of the peace club put substantial time and energy into efforts to meet with members in Mennonite churches. Between March 19 and April 30, 1967, peace club delegations visited eight churches, including congregations in Denver and Kansas City.[16] The peace club also worked hard to open lines of communication with veterans' organizations and civic clubs in Newton.

Moratorium 1969

In the succeeding months and years, Bethel's peace club continued protesting in various ways–fasts, dramas, marches, political campaigning for Eugene McCarthy, and reading the names of war dead.[17] On January 31, 1968, the North Vietnamese and the Vietcong launched a "Tet Offensive" that attacked South Vietnamese cities and towns. The American public turned against the war. Two months later, March 31, President Johnson announced he would not run for re-election. In November the Republican candidate Richard Nixon was narrowly elected over Hubert Humphrey, partly on the strength of the promise that he had a secret plan to end the war. Nixon's secret bombing of Cambodia had no effect on North Vietnam's resolve to reunify their country. By the fall of 1969, with more than a half-million troops in Vietnam and, in the slogan of the time, "no light at the end of the tunnel," nationwide anti-war demonstrations reached a new peak. A Vietnam Moratorium Committee in Washington, D.C., planned protests for October 15 and November 16, 1969. The national television and print media chose to cover the protests at Bethel–more national media attention than the college had ever

---

[15]Vernon Neufeld, letter to the editor, *The Mennonite*, 27 December 1966, 799.
[16]"Supplementary and Revised Visitation Schedule," folder 1, Peace Club records."
[17]Goering, "A History," 32-38.

received. "Armistice Day," the 11th, was on Tuesday of that week, but the issue of Veterans Day vs. Armistice Day was swallowed up in the larger national moratorium events.

Robert Mayer, an intrepid Bethel student from Wadsworth, Ohio, was key to Bethel's day in the national media sun. In the summer of 1969 Mayer worked in Washington, D.C., with the moratorium committee leaders. Back in Kansas in September, Mayer served as state coordinator for the committee.[18] He informed moratorium leaders that the Bethel peace club planned to take a large bell from the college museum and to ring it once every four seconds in honor of every American who had died in Vietnam. It would take four twelve-hour days of ringing to reach the total of 40,000. The moratorium leaders, eager to show that the protest movement extended nationwide far beyond the urban centers of New York, Chicago, and Berkeley, began to include Bethel College in their litany to the press: "Even in conservative rural Kansas a small college will ring a hundred-year-old bell for the dead in Vietnam."

The Bethel College press office, overwhelmed by the unprecedented attention, was besieged with telephone calls and requests for interviews. *The New York Times* mentioned the Bethel event on the front page. *Life* magazine published a dramatic photo of a Bethel student ringing the bell while other students sadly looked on.[19] That photo later appeared in an English-language publication of the National Liberation Front in South Vietnam, showing how widespread was the opposition to war in the United States.[20] The national press rushed to cover the event in Kansas. The three major television networks (ABC, NBC, and CBS) all sent reporters and cameramen to Bethel and featured the anti-war event on the moratorium day October 15 evening news. Gregory Jackson,

---

[18]"Kansas Campuses Will Participate In Vietnam Plans on October 15," *Bethel Collegian*, 10 Oct 1969.

[19]"America Gathers under a Sign of Peace," *Life*, 24 October 1969, 34-35.

[20]*South Vietnam in Struggle* (10 April 1970), 1. Copy in Peace Club records, folder 29.

ABC reporter, spent three days in Kansas. His report emphasized the conservative pushback from the Newton community.[21]

Kirsten Zerger ringing the bell on Vietnam Moratorium Day

Bethel's moratorium was a religious event. The Western District Conference, meeting in Wichita a month before Moratorium Day, adopted a resolution commending "the constructive peace efforts of our young people" and urging congregations to arrange for special religious services in connection with the moratorium.[22] The resolution was moved by Ed G. Kaufman, former president of Bethel, after another resolution by Kirsten Zerger, Kaufman's granddaughter and peace club leader, had been hotly debated and narrowly defeated. Before the bell ringing began on the 15th, Alvin Beachy, professor from the Bible department, presented a

---

[21]See the transcribed text of Gregory Jackson's report in the Peace Club records, folder 28.
[22]*Minutes and Reports of the Seventy-Eighth Annual Session of the Western District Conference, October 10-12, 1969.* 17.

devotional meditation and a "quiet prayer of confession." The peace club's instructions to bell ringers recommended that they spend the time in "repetitive meditation," suggesting twenty-four phrases that fit the four-second time frame: "Continue as long as that phrase helps you to concentrate on the lives of those for whom we ring the bell, and on the Life which permeates all of life."[23] Critics of the students also spoke in religious terms. Orville Voth, Bethel College president, said, "Motivation must be in the name of Jesus Christ. Political arguments are insufficient for committing our lives."[24] Voth observed that students seemed more interested in getting publicity than in making a witness for Christ. For some of the protesters, indeed, whether the protest used religious or political language, the more urgent practical goal was to change American policy in Vietnam. It was a heady thing for Bethel people to play a highly visible role in the national anti-war movement.

Tabor College began moratorium activities on Monday, November 10. Speakers there included Alvin Beachy from Bethel; John Lapp, history professor from Eastern Mennonite College in Harrisonburg, Virginia; and (on Saturday) Doug Hostetter, who had worked for three years in Vietnam as a community development worker sponsored by Mennonite Central Committee.[25] Bethel College cancelled classes on Moratorium Day and held a Vietnam War "teach-in". Then on that Saturday, the 18th, about two hundred students and community people (including students from Hesston College, McPherson College, and McPherson public high school) walked twenty miles from the Harvey County Courthouse in Newton to the 81 Drive-In Theater on the north side of Wichita. The Newton police provided protection, but there were no incidents apart from a group of young fellows who displayed a sign, "If You Can March You Can Fight," and threw eggs at the walkers.[26] Bennie Bargen, retired

---

[23]Untitled mimeographed instruction sheet, in the author's files.

[24]Quoted in an article by Maynard Shelly, "For us the bell tolled," *The Mennonite* 4 November 1969, 663.

[25]"Campuses Set for Moratorium," *The Wichita Eagle*, 13 November 1969.

[26]Jeanette Jackson, "Jeers Greet Protest Marchers," *The Hutchinson News*, 19 October 1969). Clipping from Peace Club records, folder 28.

business professor at Bethel, was disabled and walked with crutches. He kept up with the main group by car rides between the mile lines. At the conclusion Alvin Beachy led another memorial service. Vern Bender, a vocal independent anti-communist pastor from Newton, also showed up and attempted to engage the tired and blistered walkers with his own patriotic message.

The National Moratorium Committee invited the Bethel peace club to bring the Bethel bell, now a national anti-war symbol, to Washington, D.C., for the culminating moratorium protests November 13-15. Thirty-four Bethel students were among the estimated 250,000 anti-war protesters. The bell, placed at the Arlington Memorial Bridge, rang out as thousands of marchers passed by on a "March Against Death." Bethel students who attended the moratorium events were impressed by the joyous "celebration for peace," even as some of them smelled the tear gas used to break up an unauthorized rally by the Weathermen, a militant faction of the anti-war Students for a Democratic Society.[27]

Hesston 1968-70

If a national holiday (Armistice Day vs. Veterans Day) was the contentious symbol in Newton and North Newton, the American and North Vietnamese flags became the focus at Hesston. Seven miles northwest of North Newton on US Highway 81, Hesston was a small but growing town of about fifteen hundred people. It was home to three Mennonite church congregations, to Hesston College (a two-year school sponsored by the MC (Old) Mennonite denomination), and to Hesston Corporation, a Mennonite owned manufacturer of farm equipment. In 1969 four of five of Hesston's city councilmen were Mennonites. In the 1968 presidential election the Republican ticket (Nixon-Agnew) received eighty-one percent of Hesston's votes. The conservative and stable town was shocked as the Vietnam War politicized the Hesston College student body. The students began demonstrating for peace. In early September

---

[27]Javan Shelly, "Peace Marchers Converge in Washington for Protest," *The Bethel Collegian*, 21 November 1969, 1, 5.

1969, Earl Martin and Pat Hostetter Martin, who had served in Vietnam, spoke on the campus. During their visit news arrived that Ho Chih Minh, the leader of North Vietnam, had died. The Martins put on black armbands to express Jesus' teaching of love for the enemy.[28] A few students decided to commemorate Ho's death and to make a statement against the war by improvising a homely North Vietnamese flag. They sewed a yellow star onto a red field of fabric from a Hesston dry goods store and ran the flag up the college flagpole. There it waved from midnight until morning when college officials discovered it and took it down.

Vern Bender, a crusading anti-Communist pastor from Newton, seized upon the flag incident for a protest of his own. He demanded that Hesston College officials give him the flag to be destroyed. When they refused he outfitted his station wagon with loudspeakers, American and Christian flags, and an eight-foot sign, "PEACE (?) MARCHERS REFUSED TO SURRENDER VIET CONG FLAG." Bender drove through the towns of Harvey, McPherson, and Marion Counties playing patriotic music and informing the public that a communist flag had flown over Harvey County for eight hours. He publicized the scandal through advertisements in the *Newton Kansan*, and in a series of meetings at his church. Eventually, Hesston College officials agreed to burn the offensive North Vietnamese flag and to let Bender have the ashes and a few burned fragments. Bender put the ashes on display in his church.

In February 1970 Hesston city officials responded to the anti-war protests from Hesston College students with a ritual of their own. They held a public ceremony outside a new municipal building to dedicate a new American flag that had flown over the national capitol in Washington D.C. Congressman Garner Shriver supplied the flag. The Newton VFW color guard attended the ceremony. The Hesston high school band played the national anthem. After some patriotic opening remarks by Sergeant Stanley Corcum from McConnell Air Force Base in Wichita, Peter Wiebe, pastor of the Hesston Mennonite Church, presented the main dedicatory address. Contrary to the wishes of the event organizers, Wiebe

---

[28]Earl Martin, *Reaching the Other Side* (New York: Crown Publishers, 1978).

used the occasion to speak out against the Vietnam War and to warn against misuse of the American flag. "Not a narrow patriotism or nationalism—but a new and international spirit needs to emerge," said Wiebe. "The flag is not a whip for lining people up." Wiebe quietly refused to join the crowd in the pledge of allegiance to the flag. He gave a copy of his speech to Harold Sommerfeld, a member of his congregation who was editor of the *Hesston Record* and who published it without comment.

Wiebe's controversial speech had consequences for the major public policy issue then facing the community–low cost housing. The Hesston city administration had applied for funds under the Federal Housing Administration. Opponents of the proposal argued that a low cost housing project would bring unwanted black and poor people into the community. Wiebe tied the issue of low cost housing to patriotism and the flag. If we fail in this, he said, the flag will be "a sham, a farce, it ought to be torn down." To Wiebe's dismay, the flag went up and low cost housing went down. The government approved twenty units of low-rent housing for Hesston, but on March 6, 1970, the Hesston City Council voted to refuse the money and to abandon the project. Not far below the surface of the decision were the anti-Vietnam war protests, the flag dedication controversy, and racial fears in the community. Two months later, May 7, 1970, a delegation from *Time* magazine visited the town of Hesston as part of a wider effort to find out what people in the Midwest grass roots thought about the government's policy in Vietnam. This was just six days after President Nixon's "incursion" into Cambodia and three days after the National Guard killed students at Kent State University. The *Time* officials could barely skim the surface of a very complex Hesston situation. Nor did they mention Hesston in their published report. But they did say, "Even in the Midwest . . . the Silent Majority may prove thin. *Time* correspondents around the nation found little enthusiasm for the president's new policy."[29]

---

[29]*Time.* 11 May 1970, 10; *Wichita Eagle,* 8 May 1970.

116   People of Two Kingdoms II

Options: Enlistment, Nonregistration and MCC Service in Vietnam

The experiences of draft-age Mennonites during the Vietnam War varied widely. Most conscripted conscientious objectors served in I-W assignments that were much like such placements before the Vietnam War. Many Kansas Mennonites worked in I-W units in Denver, Colorado. Three young men not in I-W had very different experiences. Dale Suderman enlisted in the army and was sent to Vietnam in military uniform. Dennis Koehn refused to register for the draft and served time in prison. And James Klassen worked in Vietnam as missionary and service worker for three and a half years under the sponsorship of Mennonite Central Committee.

Dale Suderman

Dale Suderman graduated from Tabor College in 1965, served with the U.S. Army in Vietnam in 1968, and became an anti-war activist after returning home.

Dale Suderman, farm boy and member of the Ebenfeld Mennonite Brethren Church near Hillsboro, was a Tabor College graduate of 1965. He enlisted in the army in 1966. Years later he said "I joined the army because I had been reading too much of Reinhold Niebuhr, and because I was frustrated with the '*Stillen im Lande*' ['Quiet in the Land'] position of Mennonite pacifism." He was not impressed with local fellows who said they were going into I-W service to satisfy their parents, to earn money, or to avoid the rigors of army life. From his high school days, Suderman was something of a rebel. He described himself as the "smart alec in the back row who piped up, 'Yea, I'm a conscientious objector, I object to

Dennis Koehn

The MC (Old) and General Conference branches of the Mennonite denomination made a momentous shift during the war in their official policy regarding conscription to military service.[36] The legacy of World War II and the Civilian Public Service system had been a cooperative arrangement between Selective Service and the Mennonites. Mennonites agreed to register for the military draft and the government agreed to let them perform alternative civilian service. It was a generally satisfactory and productive compromise for both church and state. The Vietnam War led some Mennonites to question the terms of the compromise.

Dennis Koehn, while a student at Bethel College, was tried in district court for refusal to register for the draft. He was imprisoned for eighteen months, 1972-73.

Had the Mennonites, grateful for their exemption from military service, abandoned their prophetic witness against militarism at a time that America had vastly increased its nuclear-armed military establishment and its neo-imperialist interventions around the world?[37]

A number of young Mennonites challenged the church to officially support them in the public civil disobedience of refusing to register with Selective Service. The youthful radicals were small in number but held the high moral ground with their claim to the church's prophetic tradition going back to its sixteenth century Anabaptist origins. But not everyone agreed on the relevance of

---

[36]Perry Bush, *Two Kingdoms, Two Loyalties*, 248-56. Paul Toews, *Mennonites in American Society*, 324-32. For a general survey of the draft during the war see Lawrence M. Baskir and William A. Strauss, *Chance and Circumstance: The Draft, the War and the Vietnam Generation* (New York: Knopf, 1978).

[37]See the papers by J. R. Burkholder and James Juhnke in *Conscience and Conscription: Papers from an MCC Peace Section Assembly, November 20-22, 1969* (Akron, PA: MCC, 1970).

Anabaptism. One anti-radical, grateful for religious freedom in American democracy, insisted, "The Bill of Rights in the U.S. Constitution has made the Anabaptist tradition obsolete."[38]

In August 1969 the MC (Old) Mennonite Church, in a dramatic meeting in Turner, Oregon, officially and overwhelmingly agreed to accept non-cooperation with Selective Service as a valid position. Two months later the Western District Conference meeting in Wichita, three days before the October national moratorium, adopted a controversial "Resolution on Christian Action" that recognized "'**total noncooperation'** with the Selective Service System as a meaningful witness of one's beliefs and as a witness compatible within the historical traditions of the Mennonite church." The resolution passed 180 to 146.[39] The Mennonite Brethren and the Church of God in Christ Mennonite (Holdeman) churches did not officially endorse non-registration.

The church's official position constituted an endorsement of civil disobedience. It soon became an issue in the U.S. District Court in Wichita. Dennis Koehn of North Newton decided not to register with Selective Service on his eighteenth birthday, January 15, 1970.[40] He made his decision public. Koehn, unlike Dale Suderman, was not a restless rebel. In Newton High School he was a class president, excellent student, and member of the tennis and basketball teams. He was president of the youth group at the Bethel College Mennonite Church. He won the respect of his teachers and church leaders. In his statement to his local Selective Service board in Newton, Koehn quoted Gandhi, Jesus, and Thoreau. He did not in that statement identify himself as a Mennonite or refer to the recent decision of his church denomination that supported his position. He included statistics about the costs of American

---

[38]Curt Siemens, "Outside power structure," letter to the editor, *The Mennonite,* February 17, 1970, 118.

[39]*Minutes and Reports . . . Western District Conference . . . 1969.* 18. The resolution also reaffirmed an earlier 1968 GCMC resolution of support for young men who had left the country because of their opposition to the Vietnam War.

[40]On the story of Dennis Koehn's resistance, see "The Cup of Noncooperation—An Opportunity for Witness," chapter 3 in Melissa Miller and Phil M. Shenk, *The Path of Most Resistance* (Scottdale, Pa: Herald Press, 1982), 66-94.

militarism, as well as personal experiences: "Just recently I read a letter from a soldier in Vietnam, whom I had gone to school with. He said that he enjoys hunting down VC just as he liked to shoot rabbits in the pasture back home. The Armed Forces teach–contrary to Christian values–that the best soldier is the most efficient killer. The feeble voice of the Sunday School teacher–'Thou shalt not kill'–is drowned out by the sergeant's roaring 'Thou shalt kill and kill well.'"[41] Koehn made an appointment to visit Colonel Junior Elder, the Kansas state director of Selective Service. Elder was cordial and interested in Koehn's motivation. Koehn kept in touch with Elder and with his local draft board as he joined a harvest crew during the summer of 1970.[42] That fall, during his first week of classes at Bethel College, an FBI agent and the local sheriff came to the campus to arrest Koehn.

Koehn's trial was in April 1971. He had planned to plead guilty, but his attorney, Gerrit Wormhoudt, wanted to make the trial into a constitutional test case. If Selective Service registration was a means to gather information about potential draftees, Koehn had met that requirement by informing his draft board. Perhaps a judicial challenge could be helpful to other draft resisters. In court questioning, Judge Wesley Brown dismissed Wormhoudt's argument that informing Selective Service constituted virtual registration. Instead Brown pursued the issue of whether Koehn was culpable, given his church's teaching that non-registration was legitimate. Wormhoudt protested that he was "somewhat dismayed by the feeling I get that the Mennonite Church itself might be on trial here this morning."[43] Brown pushed Mennonite leaders testifying in Koehn's behalf (William Keeney, academic dean at Bethel; and Esko Loewen, pastor at Bethel College Mennonite Church) to say that the church was responsible for Koehn's decision. Brown found Keeney and Loewen's responses evasive and unsatisfactory. The question, Brown said, was "Can a

---

[41]Dennis Koehn to Selective Service Local Board No. 29, February 21, 1970. Copy in author's files.

[42]"The Cup of Noncooperation," 70.

[43]Transcript of Trial Proceedings held April 15, 1971 in United States District Court for the District of Kansas, p. 34, folder 3, Dennis Koehn papers, MS.137, MLA.

person do something in the name of religion and still have criminal intent?" He found Koehn guilty as charged and sentenced him to an indefinite time not to exceed six years under the Federal Youth Corrections Act.

An editorial in the *Bethel Collegian* picked up on Judge Brown's advice to "go to the cemeteries" and reflect on the sacrifice of those who died for freedom. The writer, Sue Dick, recommended that the judge go to the cemeteries of war dead himself, including that of My Lai, Vietnam, where Americans had massacred hundreds of Vietnamese civilians. Judge Brown in his sentence, wrote Dick, "had approved and perpetrated a system which makes champions of murderers . . . and which buries problems under the ground in neat rows of crosses."[44] Koehn was in prison at the Federal Youth Center in Englewood, Colorado, for eighteen months, May 1972 until November 1973.

The controversial issue of non-registration had a major role in Mennonite thinking and dialogue during the Vietnam War. The church made a difficult decision, but the effect on the actual behavior of most draft age Mennonites was minimal. Dennis Koehn was the only Mennonite from Kansas to refuse registration. A few other young men may have returned their draft cards or refused induction into the military, but none were brought to trial. According to historian Paul Toews, writing about Mennonites across the country, "what is most striking is the gap between Mennonite rhetoric and the small number who resisted registration."[45] That judgment could also apply to the handful of non-registrants in World War II and immediately following. Progressive Mennonites were more inclined to radical prophetic verbal witness than to the risks of actual civil disobedience.

---

[44]Sue Dick, "Court Decision Questioned," *Bethel Collegian*, 30 April 1971, 2.
[45]Toews, *Mennonites in American Society*, 329.

James Klassen

In October 1972, while Dennis Koehn was in prison in Colorado and ex-army man Dale Suderman was a seminary student in Indiana, James Klassen went to Vietnam as a relief worker and Bible teacher sponsored by the Mennonite Central Committee. Klassen was a member of the Alexanderwohl Mennonite Church, a graduate of Bethel College, and a fervent Christian pacifist. He had a bushy black beard and a "foreigner" mentality that may have been in part due to growing up in 1960s America. But Klassen's nonconformity was more profoundly an embrace of the Anabaptist-Mennonite beliefs that God is love, that Jesus is Lord, and that Christians should follow after Jesus.[46] He went to Vietnam intending to be an apolitical presence, but he soon learned that he could not avoid the political complexities of being an American in Vietnam, first under the South Vietnamese government of Nguyen Van Thieu and then, after April 1975, the victorious communist Provisional Revolutionary Government.[47]

James Klassen, graduate of Bethel College 1969, served in Vietnam under Mennonite Central Committee 1972-76.

Klassen spent three and a half years in Vietnam, most of that time in Saigon as administrator of medical drugs sent from the U.S. for hospitals in Vietnam, and as Bible teacher for the Gia Dinh Mennonite Church. He quickly mastered the Vietnamese language. He taught a catechism class titled "The Foundations of Mennonite Life and Thought," with units on the Bible, Jesus, Grace, Discipleship, the Individual, the Christian Community, Suffering,

---

[46]James R. Klassen, *Jimshoes in Viet Nam: The Eyewitness Account of an American Christian Who Stayed Behind after the "Fall" of Saigon* (Scottdale, Pa: Herald Press, 1986), 352.

[47]Klassen, *Jimshoes*, 367-8.

Nonviolence, and Evangelism.[48] Some people, amazed at his excellent speaking of Vietnamese, assumed he was a CIA agent. Working daily with Vietnamese people, many of whom had relatives fighting on opposite sides of the civil war, Klassen learned a great deal about the struggles and compromises for survival in country at war.

In 1973 President Richard Nixon completed the withdrawal of U.S. troops, while continuing to send massive amounts of money and military supplies to prop up the South Vietnamese government led by Nguyen Van Thieu. Most Americans, victims of anti-communist propaganda, expected that a communist victory would result in a "bloodbath" of Americans who stayed in Vietnam and of Vietnamese who worked for them. In April 1975 the war ended when the National Liberation Front took over all of Vietnam. James Klassen, along with three other MCC workers (Max Ediger, Earl Martin, and Yoshihiro Ichikawa) decided not to flee the country in the general panic of those on the losing side.[49] Inspired by John Howard Yoder, his seminary teacher, Klassen saw an opportunity for Christian truth-telling. He wrote, "Maybe the firsthand experience and the courage to share it could provide some alternative to the impressive propaganda systems which both sides and the United States are still using today."[50] Klassen and the other MCC workers who stayed were besieged by desperate Vietnamese who begged to be taken along out of the country.

Klassen had the support of his family back in Kansas. One neighbor asked his mother if she was worried–a reasonable question given the prevailing American images of Vietnam. She answered, "No . . . When he walked down the aisle wearing cap and gown at his high school graduation, I put him into the Lord's hands and said, 'Thank you, Lord, for letting us have him for 18 years,' Why should I take him back? I have given him to the Lord. . . . If something happens to him, it's no farther to heaven from Vietnam than it is from Goessel, Kansas.'"[51]

---

[48]Klassen, *Jimshoes*, 229.
[49]Martin, *Reaching the Other Side*, 255-61.
[50]Klassen, *Jimshoes*, 156.
[51]Klassen, *Jimshoes*, 180-1.

Klassen extended his term in Vietnam by six months to help support the Mennonite church there and to gain more experience under the new government before leaving. Before they departed the MCC workers were honored with a farewell luncheon by the new government's Ministry of Foreign Affairs–an expression of appreciation for MCC's ministries in Vietnam. When Klassen's flight out arrived at Bankok, an ABC television crew met him and demanded an interview before he could get through customs. The next weeks and months were filled with press interviews and public presentations.[52]

Klassen challenged the American narrative of the war: "First of all, I don't regard the changeover of governments in Vietnam as a takeover by communists from the North. The bulk of the resistance to the Saigon government always was in the South, and certainly not all of the resistance was communist." He told of his experiences during the change of governments: "I was never threatened, with a gun pointed at me. We never lost our electricity or our water service."[53] The war itself had been the bloodbath. The transition to peace had gone smoothly. An Associated Press article published in newspapers across the country quoted Klassen, "I come from the wild west but, as a pacifist, I knew I wasn't going to have a gun in my hand. I felt an amazing degree of peace at heart and serenity in those days."[54]

Klassen's return home in the spring of 1976 coincided with the national celebration of the bicentennial of the declaration of independence. That event was clearly designed to counteract the trauma of the Vietnam War disaster. Klassen's message was an uncomfortable counterpoint. His effort to "tell it like it is" surely had an impact, but he was not always successful. Some Vietnamese

---

[52]"No Bloodbath, Executions in Saigon, Four Mennonite Missionaries Report," *The Ephrata Review* (19 June 1975), B-5. "Kansan 'Never Captive' Missionary Leaving Vietnam," *The Kansas City Star*, 23 Jan 1976, 4. "Mennonite Worker says No Blood Bath," *The Hutchinson News*, 19 May 1976, 1. Mennonite Central Committee archives, Akron, PA. Thanks to Robin Ottoson.

[53]Klassen, *Jimshoes*, 331.

[54]"Missionary Saw No Reprisals in Saigon (AP)," *Kansas City Times*, 11 May 1976, 47.

refugees in the U.S. said his picture of the changeover was too rosy. Even in his own Alexanderwohl Mennonite community, some folks wondered if he had become a communist.[55]

Six years after returning home, Klassen married Tran thi Ly, a Vietnamese women he had first met in Nhatrang in 1973 when she came to him to ask for help in translating a nursing text. She had come to the US in an MCC cultural exchange program, but was unable to return to Vietnam. She studied at Hesston College and was employed as a registered nurse. The couple spent the next decades close to the Vietnamese refugee community. Beginning January 2013 Klassen served as main pastor of a Vietnamese immigrant church in the Dallas, Texas, metroplex. He preached in both the English and Vietnamese languages.[56]

---

[55]Klassen, *Jimshoes*, 224.
[56]James Klassen, interview by James Juhnke, 21 May 2014.

Chapter 7

Campaign for Congress, 1970

Not until nearly a full century after the Mennonite immigration to Kansas in the 1870s did a Kansas Mennonite run for national political office.[1] In 1970 James "Jim" Juhnke, son of Bill and Meta Juhnke, ran for the Kansas Fourth District Congressional seat. Juhnke was an academic more than a serious politician looking for a career in public office. He undertook the campaign to make a prophetic peace witness against the Vietnam War.

Juhnke's father, Bill, a school teacher and part-time farmer, had socialized his son toward peace-minded political witness. In 1948, when Jim was in the fourth grade, his father prompted him to write a letter to Andrew Schoeppel, Kansas Senator in Washington, D.C. The letter expressed concern about the pending North Atlantic Treaty Organization (NATO), a possibly dangerous military alliance. In the presidential campaign of that year, Bill told his son that he would vote for Henry Wallace, the third party (Progressive) candidate rather than for President Harry Truman or for the Republican challenger, Tom Dewey.[2]

Ten years later, 1958-60, Jim was in Frankfurt, Germany, as a conscientious objector against military service. Between his sophomore and junior years at Bethel College, he worked in the Pax refugee relief program of the Mennonite Central Committee. There he observed German peace movement protests against the growing U.S. military presence and against the deployment of tactical nuclear weapons. NATO's threat to peace, at least in the eyes of the peace movement, remained relevant.

Back at Bethel College in the fall of 1960, Jim attended a debate between two candidates for the U.S. Congress, Garner Shriver (R)

---

[1] James C. Juhnke, "A Mennonite Runs for Congress," *Mennonite Life* (January 1971): 8-11. See also Juhnke, *Small Steps*, esp. 4-6 and 75-93. Mark E. Stucky (1971) and Keith R. Henley (1975) wrote substantial Social Science Seminar papers on the 1970 Juhnke campaign; Mark E. Stucky, "James C. Juhnke and Political Involvement" (seminar paper, Bethel College, 1971); Keith R. Henley, "The Jim Juhnke Congressional Campaign of 1970" (seminar paper, Bethel College, 1975).

[2] Juhnke, *Small Steps*, 5-6.

and Thomas Robinson (D). After their speeches, Juhnke asked the candidates about the Peace Corps, a new idea promoted by John F. Kennedy, the youthful Democratic candidate for president. The Peace Corps seemed to be modeled after the MCC Pax program. Robinson, the Democratic candidate, endorsed the Peace Corps. Shriver, the Republican, had not heard about it. Shriver was elected that November. In his first term he voted against Kennedy's Peace Corps.

By the mid-1960s the Vietnam War had become the central issue for the peace movement in the United States. Jim by then was married to Anna Kreider and working toward a Ph.D. in American history at Indiana University in Bloomington. He attended meetings of the Students for a Democratic Society (SDS). He spoke for the "Christian Pacifist" viewpoint at an anti-war rally at Dunn Meadow on campus. In the fall of 1966 the Juhnkes moved to Bethel College where Anna took a position in the English department and Jim did the research and writing for his PhD dissertation on Kansas Mennonites in politics. He also participated in Peace Club protests.

Richard Nixon was elected president in 1968. Juhnke had joined with other reform-minded Kansas Democrats to support the anti-war candidacy of Senator Eugene McCarthy. Disappointed by that election, a "New Democratic Coalition" undertook to recruit and support anti-war candidates nationwide in the off-year election of 1970. The head of the Wichita chapter of "Newdeck," Paul Andreas, a medical doctor of Mennonitebackground, approached Juhnke to run for the congressional seat held by Garner Shriver. Juhnke countered that he was too young (32), politically inexperienced, and identified with unpopular peace demonstrations. But in May 1970, when President Nixon decided to invade Cambodia and escalate the war, Juhnke changed his mind and agreed to file for office. "Newdeck" paid the filing fee and rent for a campaign office on Murdock Street in Wichita. A Vietnam War widow, angry about the war, donated a large American flag that had covered her husband's coffin to be placed on the wall behind the receptionist/secretary's desk.

Juhnke was a political neophyte. He had not met any of the six Democratic county chairmen in the Fourth District. Nor did he know any labor leaders, Chamber of Commerce officials, or elders in the African-American or Mexican-American communities. No one believed he had a chance of winning or that financial support would be forthcoming for such a lost cause. Garner Shriver, after ten years in office, had become a respected conservative Congressmen who was skilled in cultivating his constituency. Two years earlier, in 1968, the Fourth District Democratic candidate had been Patrick Kelly, an articulate Wichita attorney. Kelly had spent $70,000 in his campaign and had gotten only 35% of the vote. Warner Moore, dispirited leader of the Sedgwick County Democrats, told Juhnke, "We've tried everything we know against Shriver. You young people might as well give it a try." A Hutchinson *News* reporter asked Juhnke if he was ready to play the role of the Democratic Party's next "sacrificial lamb."

What Juhnke had was energetic peace movement activists, the Mennonites, and his own extended family and friends. Two graduate students from Wichita State University, Lynn Coker and Mike Nossaman, dropped out of school to work on subsistence salaries with the Juhnke campaign. Coker was campaign director and Nossaman communications coordinator. Melvin Schmidt, pastor of the Lorraine Avenue Mennonite Church in Wichita, volunteered to solicit contributions from peace-minded Mennonites around the country. "For years we've called Mennonites to make a prophetic political witness," said Schmidt. "Here's a chance to make it happen." Several Mennonite dairymen pressured their "Milk Producer's Association" political committee to give $750 to the Juhnke campaign–the largest gift from any lobbying group. Bill and Meta Juhnke hosted a pork barbecue in the "Juhnke grove" along the Dry Turkey Creek at their farm near Elyria. That event attracted 350 people and raised $2,600. The campaign was able to buy a few television advertisements before the August primary.

Juhnke addressed his first major campaign speeches to the people he knew best–the churches and the young people. He had been identified with radical student protesters. Now he needed to re-invent himself as a concerned mainstream patriotic citizen. He bought a new blue suit and a red, white, and blue tie. He spoke in more measured and serious tones than he had in his earlier angry peace-demonstration speeches. Where he had once denounced President Nixon as a "liar" who expanded the war he promised to shrink, Juhnke adopted a more conservative rhetoric of restoring the "authority" of the U. S. government.

Juhnke's first speech, delivered in the Sedgwick County Courthouse, was titled "The Churches and the Meaning of the Vietnam War." He quoted the Gettysburg Address, and reposed Lincoln's question: "How can Americans honor the memory of those who died in this war?" The answer was to "fulfill the great tasks which remain unfinished." How? "We must commit ourselves to building up, not destroying. We must resolve to feed, to clothe, to educate, to house those who are in need." Those tasks required a reordering of national priorities, including military withdrawal from Vietnam. Would that involve a humiliating capitulation to the Communists? Juhnke insisted that the U.S.-backed government leaders in South Vietnam, Nguyen Van Thieu and Nguyen Cao Ky, were totally corrupt and must be replaced. But there was still hope, he thought, for an alternative non-Communist "Third Force," that would commit to "land reform, economic development, and honest democracy." In any case, U.S. military withdrawal must be complete. Such was required by a new "politics of repentance."[3]

Another speech, at the Wichita State University Ballroom, was titled "Youth and the 1970 Elections: A Call to Action." Juhnke began with the generation gap. "America is uptight about students. . . . Everybody today is worrying about the young people. . . . Your parents are afraid of you." Having gotten the nation's attention, Juhnke said, it was time for students to offer constructive alternatives, to be less polarizing "even if it means

---

[3] Jim Juhnke, "The Churches and the Meaning of the Vietnam War," folder 91, "Campaign Speeches," James C. Juhnke papers, MS.136, MLA. The speech appeared in four religious periodicals as "Vietnam and the Politics of Repentance." *The Mennonite*, 13 October 13 1970, 616-18; *Lutheran Forum*, February 1971, 16, 25-27; *The Presbyterian Outlook*, 5 October 1970, 5-6; and *The Guardian: A Christian Weekly Journal of Public Affairs*, 28 January 28 1971, 7-8.

trimming our hair style." We should honor the American flag and political system, and to "translate our concerns into meaningful political action."

The speech included a litany of Shriver's lamentable votes in Congress–from his opposition to the Peace Corps ten years earlier to his recent vote against lowering the voting age from 21 to 18. "Between the Peace Corps and the Voting Age votes," said Juhnke, "Garner Shriver has compiled a legislative record which should make all progressive Kansans blush." He voted against the Civil Rights Act of 1968, against clean air and pure water, against extension of the Voting Rights Act, and against President Nixon's new Family Assistance program. While posing as a fiscal conservative, said Juhnke, Shriver voted consistently for lavish military budgets, for the antiballistic missile system, and for the "expensive and inflationary Vietnam War." Juhnke concluded:

> We now have an opportunity to demonstrate our concern for our country, our belief that reform and improvement are possible, our dedication that America shall find her truer destiny by turning away from war and toward the solution of human needs for dignity and a better life. Let us respond to the challenge with a commitment that future generations of young people may face a brighter, more hopeful world than our own.[4]

Juhnke's early campaign speeches were the product of a college history professor–freighted with big words, long sentences, and historical allusions. The candidate soon realized that if he wanted to get the attention of ordinary people, he would need to change his style. He needed to incorporate more humor and more memorable sound bites. The campaign staff thought his early focus was too religious. Was "national repentance" a marketable strategy? As the campaign unfolded, the candidate's rhetoric became less academic and more secular. He gave increasing

---

[4] Jim Juhnke, "Youth and the 1970 Elections: A Call to Action," folder 91, "Campaign Speeches," Juhnke papers, MS.136, MLA.

attention to economic issues rather than focusing solely on the peace issue.

In early June a Wichita attorney, Robert G. Martin, came to the Juhnke campaign office with his young son and said he would shortly announce that he was entering the Democratic primary. Moreover, he would, without question, win the nomination in August. The people of Wichita, including Democrat voters, were American patriots and would not vote for someone who proposed to accept military defeat. Yes, the United States should get out of Vietnam. But first we should win the war. Martin was being gracious to inform the youthful campaigners about their upcoming defeat before it happened.

The appearance of a pro-war candidate energized the Juhnke campaign. The primary election in August would be a referendum on the Vietnam War. It would be an opportunity to show that Kansans, contrary to popular opinion, were turning against the war. Robert Martin was not necessarily a strong candidate, even though he earlier had been involved in Democratic Party politics. He was middle aged (46) and bald, a contrast to the youthful Juhnke team. He was overconfident. He did not take much time off from his law practice for campaigning, nor did he match the blizzard of campaign activities, press releases, radio spots, brochures, and yard signs of the Juhnke campaign. Martin accepted Juhnke's challenge for two public debates, and used the occasions for excessive red-baiting. Juhnke, he said, in league with "adult revolutionaries" who "preach Communism."[5] Martin's charges alienated the audiences.

Juhnke won the August 3 primary with 60% of the vote. His claim that the result demonstrated that Kansans, contrary to popular opinion, were turning against the Vietnam War, was only partly convincing. The result may have had more to do with the style and energy of the opposing candidates and their campaigns.

The Juhnke campaign consciously chose to project an aggressive and youthful image to contrast with the older (58) Shriver. The

---

[5]Darrell Morrow, "Two Demos Completely at Odds," *Wichita Eagle*, 10 July 10 1970, 5c.

Juhnke campaign brochure designed by Robert Regier

campaign logo, designed by Robert Regier of the Bethel College art department, featured bold and upward-pointing arrows. Juhnke's press releases and speech rhetoric were energetic and forward-looking, often on the attack. Popular reaction to the campaign's style was mixed. Curt Siemens, retired school principal and member of the First Mennonite Church in Buhler, wrote to Juhnke, "I am glad to see you come out slugging. . . . I feel the Mennonite Church should support you wholeheartedly." On the other side was Clarence Hiebert, Bible and Religion teacher at Tabor College, who wrote that people in Hillsboro took literally St. Paul's "exhortation to be subject to the higher powers. Therefore they take unkindly to severe, open criticism of governmental policy." From an entirely different perspective, Carson Baird, an official in the Machinist's Union, listened to Juhnke's attacks on Shriver's voting record and told him, "You're gettin' good radio coverage. But you don't have to stack the shit so high. You know what I mean?"[6]

At times economic issues rivaled war/peace issues. In the fall of 1970 the unemployment rate in Wichita rose to ten percent, and Wichita became eligible for special funding as a "Redevelopment Area" under the Public Works and Economic Development Act (EDA) of 1965. Shriver arranged for federal EDA officials to come to Wichita for a highly-publicized meeting. Three days before the meeting, Juhnke held a press conference to point out that Shriver in 1965 had voted against the EDA and had no right to take credit for EDA benefits in Wichita. Shriver was "tardy in getting federal aid to Wichita because he has opposed the very legislation under which that aid is authorized and funded."[7] Juhnke's role as an educator, and his insistence that the Vietnam War was limiting federal funds for education, helped win the endorsement of the Wichita Chapter the National Education Association for his candidacy. He publicized Shriver's low rating by environmental organizations on key votes related to the environment.

Mennonite Republicans in the Fourth District in Shriver's first ten years in office, 1960-1970, had come to know him as a congenial and approachable Congressman. He showed up to congratulate local communities at local occasions such as the dedication in January 1966 of a new post office in North Newton. "Bethel College constitutes an important asset to your community and to our state," he told the locals. "The presence of the Mennonite Press in North Newton also contributed to the merit of your case for a new Post Office building."[8] For North Newton, as well as for a new Post Office flagpole in Hesston in 1970, Shriver provided American flags which had flown "over the Capitol and over the Post Office Building in Washington." Some leading Mennonites who were

---

[6]Juhnke, *Small Steps*, 81, 87.

[7]Press Release, 31 July 1970, p. 1, folder 5, "Economy," Juhnke papers, MS.136, MLA.

[8]Garner Shriver, "Suggested Remarks, Dedication of North Newton, Kan., Post Office, Saturday, January 29, 1966, Box 191, Speeches—1966, Garner E. Shriver Papers, MS 77-01, Wichita State University Libraries Special Collections.

Juhnke got 27.4% and Shriver got 72.6%. Thus a "Mennonite" town rejected Juhnke more than the 4th District as a whole. The Hillsboro results may have been due to inter-Mennonite differences. Juhnke was a General Conference Mennonite who taught at Bethel College; Hillsboro Mennonites belonged mostly to the Mennonite Brethren. Tabor College, an MB school in Hillsboro, was a competitor to Bethel College. The vote in Hillsboro may have been in part due to reverberations from a controversial speech Juhnke had given at an anti-war rally at Tabor College after the invasion of Cambodia.[15]

In "Mennonite" precincts generally, apart from Hillsboro, Juhnke did cut into Shriver's normal strong majority. In the town of Hesston, for example, since 1960 Shriver had never gotten less than 81% of the vote. In 1970 Juhnke cut that majority to 59%.[16] In 1968 in Mound township, McPherson County, Shriver had defeated Kelly 422 to 139. In 1970 Shriver defeated Juhnke 278 to 269. Although it is impossible to identify and tabulate actual Mennonite votes, it is likely that Juhnke got somewhat less than one half.

Despite his loss at the polls, Juhnke claimed to have achieved his objectives. He had won in the primary over a war hawk, showing there was "a constituency for peace in Central Kansas." He had run an issue-oriented campaign, addressing "the Vietnam War, the economy, environmental control, disarmament, education, and congressional reform." The campaign, with a very limited budget, had attracted a host of energetic peace-minded volunteers.[17]

Some of Juhnke's supporters encouraged him to run against Shriver again in two years. Charles Pearson, editor of the editorial pages of the *Wichita Eagle* and his wife, Betty Pearson, who had been raised a Mennonite, had contributed to the campaign. Pearson suspected that Shriver was politically more vulnerable than most people realized. He said Juhnke's first campaign was a successful introduction to the electorate. He could well be elected on a second, or even a third, attempt. But Juhnke was not convinced. In a confidential letter to his campaign director, Lynn Coker, he wrote,

---

[15] Juhnke, *Small Steps*, 75-6.

[16] James Juhnke, "Clashing Symbols in a Quiet Town: Hesston in the Vietnam War Era," *Kansas History* (Autumn 2000): 152.

[17] Folder 73, Juhnke papers, MS.136, MLA.

"Although we did fairly well at the polls, considering available resources, I presently doubt whether we did well enough to really convince people that we could unseat Shriver in a future election."[18] Although he had enjoyed the accelerated education that his campaign provided, he was more inclined to be a teacher than a politician. If prophetic witness for peace was his Christian calling, he would try to do it as a college teacher.[19]

Six years later, in 1976, Dan Glickman, a young Jewish Democratic candidate with more campaign funding and with more mainstream political viewpoints than Juhnke's, upset Shriver in a very close race. The next Mennonite to run for national office would be Eric Yost, a Republican and a member at the Lorraine Avenue Mennonite Church in Wichita, who challenged Dan Glickman in 1990 and 1992.

---

[18] Juhnke to Coker, 23 November 1970, folder 17, Juhnke papers, MS.136, MLA.
[19] Juhnke, *Small Steps*, 92.

Chapter 8

1970s: Party Politics, Wheat Centennial

Harvey County Democrats

Individual Mennonites had long been active as minority voices in the Republican and Democratic political parties of Harvey County, Kansas. The political controversies in the Democrat Party created by the Vietnam War brought new energy to peace-minded political activists, especially during Senator Eugene McCarthy's campaign against President Lyndon Johnson in the presidential primary of 1968, and during Senator George McGovern's presidential campaign of 1972. From 1972 to 1974 the peace reformers, with strong Mennonite leadership, took control of the local Democratic Party.

Merrill Raber, who was employed at Prairie View Community Mental Health Center, was the leader of the local McGovern supporters.[1] Raber's job required him to cultivate relationships with Newton community leaders. One good friend was Tom Reid, probate judge who was active in the Democrat Party. Reid nudged Raber into political involvement. In 1970 Raber ran for the state legislature against Ernie Unruh, who had been in office for nine two-year terms. Raber and Unruh were both members of the Bethel College Mennonite Church. Unruh had been in the Air Force and Raber lacked a military background. They maintained a cordial relationship and appeared on candidate forums together. Raber was personally committed to diversity, and proud that members of his church congregation supported both him and his opponent. He assumed he got most of the votes from the liberal-minded congregation, but it was not enough to get him

Merrill Raber

---

[1] Merrill Raber, interview by James Juhnke, 15 May 2013.

elected. Unruh won by a narrow margin of 211 votes, a result that showed Unruh's political vulnerability. Two years later, Richard Walker, a Bethel College graduate and member of the Methodist church, defeated Unruh in the Republican primary and was elected to the Kansas legislature.

In the Democratic primary of August 1972 in Harvey County, Raber ran for precinct committeemen. In that primary the energized reformers who supported George McGovern won a majority on the Democratic central committee. They elected Raber to the post of Democratic Party county chairman, effectively wresting control from the conservatives who had long controlled the local party. Especially aggrieved was Jenilee Miller, a conservative traditional Democrat who had been an officer in the state Democrat Women's Federation. She had attended the volatile 1968 Democratic convention in Chicago that nominated Hubert Humphrey, and was angry at the youthful radicals who disrupted the convention and contributed to Richard Nixon's victory over Humphrey in the general election. She was offended by the Bethel College students who had been among the protesters at that convention.

Raber attended the 1972 national Democratic convention in Miami as an alternate delegate. He was a McGovern supporter in a divided Kansas delegation. Governor Robert Docking, head of the delegation and supporter of Senator Henry "Scoop" Jackson, won Raber's respect by his generosity and openness to dialogue with the McGovernites. As Raber remembered, "Perhaps the most significant impression of the entire convention was the profound sense of being involved, along with others from a cross section of the nation, with a tremendous amount of political power and a feeling of having some influence on that power." After the Democratic convention, the McGovern supporters in Harvey County were greatly energized. Ruthann Dirks, a Mennonite and relative newcomer to the political process, was delighted to "experience a more alive Democratic party in our conservative county." Alongside the county organization, some supporters organized a "Harvey County Citizens for McGovern" committee.

Old guard conservatives, shut out from leadership in the Harvey County Democratic Party, complained to the Kansas Democratic State Committee in Topeka, headed by Norbert Dreiling, that the McGovern supporters in Harvey County were dividing the party. They were giving all their attention to the national ticket and refusing to support the incumbent Democratic governor, Robert Docking, and the attorney general, Vern Miller. One of the critics charged that "most of this new group will not salute our flag when we have the flag salute, and all they talk about is McGovern."[2] Dreiling sent to Newton some reliable "neutral observers from the outside to check into the matters." These observers reported that the Harvey County Democratic leaders were supporting the entire ticket, including Governor Docking. The controversy in Harvey County reflected a nationwide division in the Democratic Party. The charge that the reformers refused to salute the flag apparently pointed to Mennonite objections to American civil religion. It may also have reflected the broader cultural struggles between generations associated with the Vietnam War. In any case, in the November 1972 presidential election McGovern lost in Harvey County by a wide margin, while Robert Docking won re-election as governor of Kansas, despite the charge that reform Democrat party leaders were not supporting him.

The McGovern reformers controlled the Harvey County Democratic party for just one election cycle. The peace issue faded from local and national politics as the last American troops left Vietnam in March 1973. The Communists took over all of Vietnam two years later and Americans in general turned their attention to other issues. Former peace movement activists experienced "burnout" of various kinds. Student awareness and concern about wider political issues declined to a more "normal" pre-war level. But no one could doubt that the Mennonites, like Americans in general, had been through a transforming experience.

---

[2]Mary Ellen Zimmerman to Norbert Dreiling, 25 September 1972, Merrill Raber personal collection.

Presidential Elections 1968-1972

1968 was a year of stress, upheaval, and violence in American society. Martin Luther King was assassinated April 4 and racial violence broke out in major cities. President Lyndon Johnson, recognizing his failures to unite the country and to achieve his objectives in Vietnam, decided not to run for reelection. Robert Kennedy, campaigning to succeed Johnson, was assassinated on June 6. The Democratic nominating convention in Chicago August 26-29 exploded in violence, as Mayor Richard J. Daley's police battled young people in the streets.

Maynard Shelly, member of the Bethel College Mennonite Church and editor of the *The Mennonite*, official denominational publication of the General Conference Mennonite Church, in the 1960s gave more coverage to the national elections of 1964 and 1968 than did other Mennonite editors. In both of those years Shelly conducted a random political poll of his readers. 32% of the mailings went to Kansas addresses. As of September 1964, 72% of the respondents (nationwide) said they were Republicans, but only 26% had decided to vote for Goldwater.[3] Four years later, in 1968, with Richard Nixon (Republican) running against Hubert Humphrey (Democrat), the number of self-identified Republicans had slipped to 57.3%. But those intending to vote for Humphrey were only 6%. Substantial numbers were undecided. It seemed clear that Nixon, who claimed to have a plan to end the war, was attracting the Mennonite peace vote. Humphrey, who had been vice president under President Johnson, was identified with the war.[4]

The *Mennonite Weekly Review* in 1968 included almost no editorial comment, or letters to the editor, about the presidential candidates or about specific foreign or domestic policy issues. Editor Menno Schrag's reaction to the Democratic convention in Chicago was "one of shock and disbelief. Our violence-ridden nation is clearly in trouble and no real solution is in sight." Schrag dismissed the

---

[3] *The Mennonite*, 13 October 1964, 632-36.
[4] Maynard Shelly, "Nixon Favored by the Mennonites," *The Mennonite*, 8 October 1968, 620-4.

two major candidates (Richard Nixon and Hubert Humphrey) as "skillfully noncommittal on the most urgent foreign and domestic problems." The third candidate (George Wallace) was "an expert in the exploitation of hate and fear." It was more important to pray than to vote.[5]

Orlando Harms, editor of *The Christian Herald* in Hillsboro, like Schrag in Newton, in 1968 spoke more to the cultural crisis than to political candidates or issues. But Harms did print a guest editorial by Larry Kehler from *The Canadian Mennonite*. Kehler said the young protesters should not be dismissed as disgusting "hippies." Kehler said the youth had something to say on important issues: "The sale of arms to underdeveloped nations, the war in Vietnam, the exploitation of the poor, the meager funds made available for the development of the Third World, the growing depersonalization of the educational process, the increasing obsession with the symbols of middle class wealth." Kehler noted a comparison between youth at the Democratic convention, and the anti-communist youth in Prague who denounced the Russian occupation. The American press condemned the former and praised the latter as heroes of freedom.

Kehler's guest editorial got several critical responses. Menno Harms of Cherokee, Oklahoma, wondered whether the editors wanted a "hearing or mob rule." In that same issue, however, Bob Harms, writing from Brussels, was pleased "that there is still someone over thirty who doesn't make a blanket condemnation of young people." God may be using young people "to remind us of some of the sins of our society."[6]

In 1969 Robert Schrag succeeded his father as editor of *Mennonite Weekly Review*. The editorial stance of the paper did not change in the presidential election of 1972. Although "we cannot save the world through the ballot box . . . (W)e still believe that politics–especially in a democracy–should not be the exclusive domain of unbelievers." Christians should be "a leaven." But we

---

[5]Menno Schrag, "Voters–And/Or Intercessors," *Mennonite Weekly Review*, 5 September 1968.
[6]*The Christian Herald*, 8 October 1968, 2, 20.

also "recognize the validity" of the position of Mennonites who abstain from voting. The paper carried little news or editorial comment about the election. The same was true for *The Christian Leader*. These were religious denominational periodicals. They assumed their readers would get news of President Richard Nixon's Watergate crisis from the secular press.

1974 Wheat Centennial

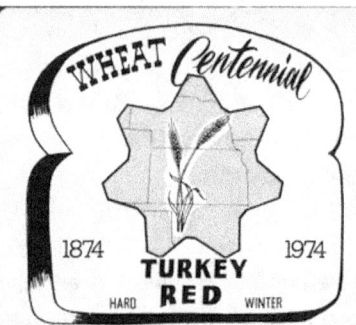

Kansas Wheat Centellial logo featuring threshing stone, and wheat stalks on a loaf of bread.

In 1973 Kansas Mennonites took steps to get support from the state government for upcoming celebrations of the centennial of Mennonite presence in the state. Walter W. Graber, Democratic Mennonite legislator from Pretty Prairie, introduced a "Wheat Centennial" resolution that passed both the House of Representatives and the Senate. The resolution proposed that five agencies, including the Kansas Wheat Commission and the State Board of Agriculture, should cooperate in the celebrations. The legislature directed the Kansas Wheat Commission to give a Mennonite-directed "Wheat Centennial Committee" in Hillsboro $175,000 to promote the centennial of Turkey Red Wheat. The funds were not general tax money, but came from the Kansas Wheat Commission's share of a two mill per bushel tax on wheat. Democratic Governor Robert Docking proclaimed 1974 "The Turkey Hard Red Winter Wheat Centennial." Kansas license plates for 1974 carried the words, "Wheat Centennial." The U.S. Postal Service chose Hillsboro as the place to issue a new ten cent wheat centennial stamp.[7]

---

[7]Information in this section is from documents in the Harley J. Stucky papers, MS.459, MLA, and from the Wheat Centennial archival box at the Center for Mennonite Brethren Studies, Tabor College.

Wesley Prieb, academic dean at Tabor College, and Harley J. Stucky, farmer and teacher from North Newton, were co-directors of the "Wheat Centennial Committee." They used the state endorsement and funding to jump start a range of publications and programs, including educational materials, public meetings, a mobile display unit and float, and an original drama by Thomas H. Broderick, Jr., professional writer and producer. Broderick's drama, "Turkey Red ... Eldorado of the Plains," was performed at the Kansas State Fair in Hutchinson, September 16 and 17. Stucky had dreams for a million-dollar "Wheat Center USA" museum to be located just south of Hutchinson at the crossing of highways 50, 61, and 17/96. A sixteen acre plot for the site was purchased and preliminary architectural plans were distributed. Stucky led in the creation and incorporation of a separate Wheat Centennial Foundation intended to be responsible for the prospective museum beyond 1974.

Walter W. Graber of Pretty Prairie, member of Kansas Wheat Commission, served in the Kansas legislature 1967-77

For Mennonites, who remembered their public disapproval as pacifists in World War II, the Wheat Centennial was in part an exercise to restore their public reputation. The Catholic Germans in western Kansas, who also had migrated from Russia to Kansas in the 1870s but who had not been marginalized as pacifists in World Wars I and II, did not take a lead role in the wheat centennial. An "Inter-Church Centennial Committee" in Marion County created a memorial marker at the town of Peabody. The plaques on the marker thanked the City of Peabody and the Santa Fe Railroad for their help to the immigrants of 1874. They also thanked "our government for respecting conscience, rewarding industry, and granting freedom for Christian outreach." The dedication service in Peabody on July 27 did include a note of prophetic anti-militarism. Peter J. Dyck, the keynote speaker, had been pastor of the Eden Mennonite Church from 1950 to 1957. He reminded descendants of the 1874 migration that they had emigrated in part because of Russian militarism. Now they lived in a country that had a gigantic nuclear arsenal–"the equivalent of 10,000 tons of TNT for every man, woman and child on earth"–and that "uses 55 cents of every tax dollar for military purposes."[8]

1974 memorial of the Swiss Mennonite Cultural and Historical Association at the Hopefield Mennonite Church

In McPherson County, descendants of the Swiss Volhynian immigrants erected a large pillar, twenty feet high and topped with a large globe and a cross, at the Hopefield Mennonite Church. Seven brass plaques told the story of Anabaptist Mennonite history and beliefs from the sixteenth century to the present. The litany at the marker dedication acknowledged "the political and religious liberties and economic opportunities found here in America, along with the warm hospitality and friendship of the American people in the past century."[9]

---

[8]Peter J. Dyck, "Uprooting and Rooting for a Purpose," text of July 26, 1974 keynote address, Kansas Wheat Centennial 1974 box, Kansas Wheat Centennial Santa Fe Railway folder, Center for Mennonite Brethren Studies, Tabor College.

[9]Harley J. Stucky, *The Swiss Mennonite Memorial Monument: Is It Inspirational Art, Symbolic Expression, or History?* (North Newton, KS: Harley J. Stucky, 1999).

references in a three paragraph statement) and the role of the church. Subsequent statements were more focused on public policy and the need to communicate with public officials.

The most strenuous effort came in early 1979. In the election campaign of 1978, John Carlin, the Democratic candidate for governor, had said he would sign a death penalty bill. Polls showed that most Kansans favored the measure so it seemed a sure thing when both the Senate and House of Representatives passed the measure. Mennonites cooperated with a "Coalition to Keep Kansas Free of the Death Penalty" to educate the public, to present testimony at legislative hearings, to write letters to legislators and to the governor, and to write letters to local newspapers. The campaign succeeded on April 4, 1979, when Carlin reversed his campaign position and vetoed the measure on moral grounds.

Mennonites played a greater role in this campaign than their small numbers would suggest. A two-page advertisement in the *Topeka Daily Capital* had the names of 1800 signers and sponsors.[14] Mennonites in twenty congregations had gathered 863 names (48% of the total) and raised $719 in donations. A high proportion of persons who wrote to Governor Carlin on the issue were Mennonites.[15] Clarence Hiebert, chairman of the department of religious/biblical studies at Tabor College at Hillsboro thanked Carlin in behalf of "my colleagues in this community and on this campus."[16] Eight members of the Salina Mennonite Fellowship wrote to congratulate Carlin "for your political and moral courage."[17] Mrs. J. B. Neufeld of Inman wrote, "Thanks to you and praise to God that you vetoed the Death Penalty. And that your reasons for doing so were Christian and moral rather than political."[18] Years later, in retirement, Carlin expressed his

---

[14] *Topeka Daily Capital*, 26 Feb 1979, 6-7.
[15] Constituent Services Subject Files, Capital Punishment, John Carlin administration, Kansas State Historical Society, Box 58-9-2-11.
[16] Clarence Hiebert to Governor John Carlin, 5 Apr 1979, Constituent Services Subject Files.
[17] Salina Mennonite Fellowship to Governor Carlin (undated), Constituent Services Subject Files.
[18] Mrs. J. B. Neufeld to Governor Carlin, 22 April 1979, Constituent Services Subject Files.

appreciation for the Mennonite support: "I always enjoyed going to Newton, McPherson, Hillsboro and Marion. Someone would always come up to me and say 'thank you' for vetoing the death penalty. . . . It was the only place in the state where I felt the majority was with me."[19]

In 1994 Kansas reinstated the death penalty when Governor Kathleen Sebelius allowed it to become law without her signature. Mennonites continued to work with other groups to abolish the death penalty.

Jim Gillmore, Reluctant Politician

Jim Gillmore was one Mennonite in the Kansas legislature who voted against the death penalty in the 1970s. When Jim was a child, his family attended a Newton congregation of the Church of God Anderson.[20] His mother had been a Mennonite, and her mother had been a Mennonite Brethren who opposed Jim's decision to become an attorney. Gillmore joined the Bethel College Mennonite Church in North Newton in 1978, the year that the Republican Harvey County Central Committee selected him to fill out the unfinished term of Richard Walker, who had resigned from the state legislature. In November 1978 Gillmore was handily elected to the legislature in his own right.[21]

Gillmore was a moderate Republican.[22] He voted against liquor by the drink as well as against the death penalty. The latter vote earned him a lot of criticism. He did not enjoy his role in the legislature and he thoroughly "hated" political campaigning. "It was not my personality to enjoy being up front in public," he said.[23] After the legislative term of 1980 Gillmore resigned before completing his two year term and happily went to work full time in his law office in Newton.

---

[19] John Carlin, interview by James Juhnke, 11 Mar 2005.
[20] James Gillmore, interview by James Juhnke, 26 January 2015.
[21] "Gillmore over Modrell for representative," *Newton Kansan*, 8 November 1978, 1.
[22] Richard Walker, interview by James Juhnke, 25 January 2015.
[23] James Gillmore interview.

Approaching the Kansas Republican Norm

The voting results in rural Kansas Mennonite townships in the presidential elections of 1972 and 1976 were notable in terms of comparison with the results in Kansas in general. In the eight presidential elections from 1940 through 1968 voters in townships of substantial Mennonite population voted consistently about fifteen to twenty percent higher for the Republican Party candidate than did voters in Kansas at large. Thus in 1940 Mennonites voted 81% for the Republican candidate Wendell Wilkie, while Kansans in general voted 56.86% for Wilkie. That differential continued until 1968 when Mennonites voted 77.4% for Republican Party candidate Richard Nixon, while Kansans voters in general voted 54.84% for Nixon. With the election of 1972, and again in 1976, the gap between the Mennonites and Kansans in general disappeared. Mennonites and Kansans voted for the Republican candidates in almost exactly the same percentages. A pattern of twenty-eight years came to an end. (See Appendix B.)

What accounts for the loss of Mennonite political distinctiveness? From a sociological viewpoint these results may be taken as a sign of Mennonite acculturation. Ever since their arrival on the Kansas frontier in the 1870s, Mennonites had gradually given up their own social traits and conformed to American ways in language, worship, technology, and a myriad of other folkways. Perhaps that process was now also reflected in political preferences. Kansas Mennonites had been thoroughly Americanized, or more specific to their location, thoroughly Kansanized. They voted a Republican majority, but not more so than their Kansas neighbors.[24]

---

[24]Note that the voting data is from rural townships or precincts. Urban or town Mennonites (Wichita and Newton) are not included. Even in the rural areas, population movements meant that Mennonites became a smaller percentage of the population.

Holdeman Separation from Political World

The Church of God in Christ Mennonites (CGCM), popularly known as "Holdeman Mennonites" after their founding evangelist, were separate-from-the-world people who did not vote in elections or participate in juries. They displayed their separation with distinctive plain dress, women's prayer coverings, male beards, dark-colored cars, and rejection of radio and television. They combined strictly enforced church discipline with a strong emphasis on born-again evangelical revivalism. Unlike the Amish, they did not reject or limit modern agricultural technology. Their mother church was in Lone Tree Township in southern McPherson County, but they founded new congregations in Kansas and other states. They grew more rapidly in numbers than did other Mennonite groups.[25]

In the 1970s the CGCM (Holdeman) Mennonites reinforced their separation from the world in two ways. One was a major disciplinary "cleansing" of the church to remove members who were not conforming to the rules or were judged to be spiritually out of step with the church community. Three hundred church members were excommunicated or "banned" in 1977–including from congregations in Kansas and beyond. Banning involved social exclusion. A banned member was not allowed to eat a meal at the same table with his or her family.[26]

A second and related change was a shift from public to private school primary education. In 1972 the U.S. Supreme Court ruled in the Wisconsin vs. Yoder case that Amish children could not be forced to attend public schools past the eighth grade. CGCM (Holdeman) Mennonites had been sending their children to public primary schools, and in exceptional cases such as nurses for their hospital, to high school or beyond. In the 1970s they took advantage of the Amish initiative. Each congregation, beginning in 1975 with the Alexanderfeld church near Hillsboro, founded its

---

[25]Clarence Hiebert, *The Holdeman People: the Church of God in Christ, Mennonite 1849-1969* (South Pasadena, CA: William Carey Library, 1973).

[26]Chuck Regier, "Discipline and Growth: the Cleansing of the Church of God in Christ, Mennonite 1974-1980" (Mennonite History class paper, Bethel College, 1980).

own private parochial primary school. The state did not require teachers to have education beyond the eighth grade. The schools administered standardized tests that revealed that CGCM (Holdeman) pupils in parochial schools with untrained teachers learned at least as much as pupils in Kansas public schools. Meanwhile they were protected from undesired subjects such as sex education and from athletic activities in which boys and girls wore the same kind of clothing.[27]

Although they did not participate directly in politics, CGCM (Holdeman) Mennonites learned about American political parties and leaders through newspapers, magazines, or word of mouth. Their attitudes were generally conservative. Their preference for Republican Party leaders was strengthened in the latter twentieth century as the issues of abortion and same sex marriage became increasingly prominent.[28] But they consistently stayed away from the ballot box.

---

[27]Tom Kidd "Mennonite Group Starts Public School Exodus," *Wichita Eagle and Beacon*, 8 May 1977, 1A. Conversations of the author with members of the Lone Tree CGCM (Holdeman) congregation, 7 Sept 2014.

[28]Dale Koehn, interview by author James Juhnke, Moundridge, KS, 3 Sept 2014.

Chapter 9

Bicentennial 1976

The national bicentennial celebrations of 1976, held in the wake of America's military defeat in Vietnam and the resignation of President Richard Nixon, attempted to restore national pride in the face of a decade of traumatic upheaval. The master narrative of American history had long linked freedom and warfare. That narrative now needed repair. The bicentennial message claimed that the Declaration and the War of Independence in 1776 were the original source of American freedom.

Mennonites in South Central Kansas, like citizens throughout the nation, were invited to participate in the spirit of the bicentennial. But their involvement was qualified by their pacifist religious commitments. The Anabaptist-Mennonite heritage was at odds with the national master narrative of freedom. During the bicentennial celebrations in 1975 and 1976, Mennonites struggled to navigate the boundaries between appropriate love of country and idolatrous worship of a nation born in warfare.

Official Denominational Statements

Already in 1975 Kansas Mennonites helped to create three official denominational statements about the bicentennial. These statements attempted to balance appreciation for American democracy with criticism of national failures, while strongly affirming that God alone–not any nation–was worthy of worship and veneration.

Most widely distributed was a statement, "Christians and the Bicentennial," adopted by the Peace Section of the Mennonite Central Committee (MCC). Ted Koontz and Delton Franz, both Bethel College graduates, headed the MCC Peace Section offices in Akron, Pennsylvania, and in Washington, D.C. The MCC was an inter-Mennonite agency that accommodated the viewpoints of liberal and conservative constituent groups as they agreed upon "the collective view of the MCC Peace Section (U.S.)."[1] The Peace Section circulated its bicentennial statement with other materials in a "Civil Religion Packet," available to individuals and churches for $1.50. In Kansas it was used by at least one congregation for a Sunday worship litany, and by a symposium at Bethel College as the basis for a public panel discussion.[2]

The MCC "Christians and the Bicentennial" statement was a series of bullet points under six different headings, followed by a set of ten discussion questions. The first point enumerated "reasons to be grateful for our experience here," including freedom of worship, material prosperity, "periods of peace and security," and democratic ideals. The second identified "the nation's failure to be fully what it should be," including the squandering of resources for American consumption, the threats and use of violence, the treatments of Indians and Blacks and giving power to the wealthy few. Additional points of "testimony" and "confession" called for "commitment to put Christ's kingdom above every worldly loyalty, even though conflicts with government will result," and identified the church (not the nation) as "God's primary agent in history." Christians should consider "whether glorification of the nation's birth in war leads us to glorify the sin of war itself." The concluding questions invited readers to list "activities that will occur in your community and the U.S. in which you feel individual Christians and congregations can participate and those that should be avoided," but did not prescribe specific answers. The statement, read in retrospect, seems quite moderate in its references to warfare. It did not refer to imperialism or to the American empire.

In October 1975 the GCMC Western District, meeting in Moundridge, Kansas, in its annual conference, adopted a bicentennial resolution that recommended the MCC Peace Section statement to the congregations. It was shorter than the Peace Section statement, with six "whereas" affirmations and five numbered resolutions. It affirmed that "nationalism tends to blind

---

[1] "Christians and the Bicentennial," Civil Religion Packet distributed by MCC Peace Section, MCC Vertical Files, MLA.V.1.I, MLA.

[2] First Mennonite Church of Christian in Moundridge, worship service bulletin, 4 July 1976.

people to the truth about one's nation, its actions past and present" and that "the supreme lordship of Christ and his kingdom supersedes all national loyalties." It called members to "refrain from participation in those activities that bring glory and honor to the military.... We will refrain from offering speeches, prayers, or use of Christian symbols in such a way as these might be interpreted as support of the evils of nationalism."[3]

The Western District resolution did not have a section of appreciation for American democracy. In the floor discussion some delegates thought the statement was too anti-nationalistic. Also at issue was the question of whether the American flag had a legitimate place in church sanctuaries. Andrew Shelly, former director of the GCMC overseas mission board, said, "While my supreme loyalty is to Christ, it does something to me when I hear 'The star-spangled banner.'" Other comments were: "To me the national flag does not spell war any more than the license tag on my car," and, "I find no conflict as a Mennonite in pledging allegiance to the flag."[4] Even so, the resolution passed by a large margin.

The Southern District of the Mennonite Brethren Conference, meeting in Enid, Oklahoma, authorized its Faith and Life Commission to draft a "Bicentennial Statement for Mennonite Brethren."[5] Wesley Prieb, academic dean and professor of English at Tabor College in Hillsboro, was the chairman of the commission and probably author of the resulting statement. Later it was adopted as the official bicentennial statement for the wider Mennonite Brethren denomination.

The MB statement began with a historical preface that referred to the first century Christian Church and its witness to the priority of

---

[3]"Delegates Pass Bicentennial Resolution," *The Mennonite, Western District Edition,* 11 November 1975, A1-A2.

[4]Ibid.

[5]*Yearbook Southern District Conference of the Mennonite Brethren Churches Convening at Enid, Oklahoma October 31-November 2, 1975.* (Hillsboro: Mennonite Brethren Publishing House, 1975), 54-55. The MB Southern District included churches in Arkansas, Colorado, Kansas, Oklahoma and Texas. "A Bicentennial Statement for the Mennonite Brethren," *The Christian Leader,* 20 January 20 1976, 7.

Christ over against the claims of the Roman Empire. Like the MCC Peace Section statement, the MB statement affirmed "that which is good in the nation," and witnessed "against that which is evil." Among the national evils were "discrimination against minorities, the poor and oppressed," a "general moral decadence which threatens to destroy us like a cancer from within," and "pride in assuming that the citizens of the United States are God's chosen people and His primary agents for saving the world." The statement asked whether Mennonite Brethren had "placed our trust in national survival rather than the return of our Lord? Are we moving in the direction of a civil religion?" Despite the warning against civil religion, the statement endorsed observation of two civil-religious events–"the National Day of Prayer scheduled for March 5 as well as July 4, 1976 . . . focusing attention on the true meaning of freedom as found in Jesus Christ. (Jn. 8:22)."

Engaging Civil Religion

The concept of "civil religion," proposed by Robert Bellah in his landmark essay of 1967, "Civil Religion in America," provided Mennonite intellectuals with a tool to critique nation-worship in the bicentennial.[6] The MCC Peace Section "Civil Religion Packet" included Bellah's essay along with another essay by Herbert Richardson, "Civil Religion in Theological Perspective." Bellah wrote that American civil religion included a transcendent dimension and potential for prophecy, represented by Martin Luther King who effectively called the nation to repentance. Richardson warned that strong powers of national sentiment typically overwhelmed the sense of God's judgment. American political and religious leaders manipulated religious language to invoke God's blessing and to ignore God's wrath. Mennonite leaders generally spoke of the American civil religion in negative terms.

---

[6]Robert Bellah, "Civil Religion in America," *Daedalus: Journal of the American Academy of Arts and Sciences* 96:1 (winter 1967): 1-21.

In January 1976, *The Christian Leader*, the MB denominational periodical published in Hillsboro, printed an article by Paul Toews, graduate of Tabor College and a young professor of history at Fresno Pacific University, a Mennonite Brethren school in California. Toews surveyed the historical rise of civil religion in America and warned Mennonites against the identification of church and nation. "We used to be a pilgrim people; we are now settled and take our cues from American culture. . . . We migrated to America to practice a faith distinctive from national and civic trappings. Have we sold that birthright for civic conformity and national religion?" Toews did briefly acknowledge that civil religion could have salutary effects. It could "improve the moral tone of the nation (and) . . . control the exercise of political power." But his primary thrust was prophetic: "During the Bicentennial year we need to be voices of truthfulness and prophetic dissent."[7]

Donald B. Kraybill, Mennonite sociologist from Pennsylvania, also offered a substantially negative view of civil religion in a popular book for the bicentennial, *Our Star-Spangled Faith*.[8] By 2012 that book had been translated into six other languages and had sold nearly 100,000 copies.[9] In 1976, however, some Kansas Mennonites found Kraybill too negative. Duane Friesen, professor of Bible and Religion at Bethel College, wrote a critical review of Kraybill's book. To support his view of civil religion as "totally evil," wrote Friesen, Kraybill described "the *worst* aspects of civil religion as *practiced*, and the *ideal* aspects of Christianity as it should be believed by true Christians." A more balanced and accurate view would acknowledge that Christianity and civil religion have overlapping values that make it possible for Christians to work for social justice in society.[10] The differences between Friesen, a GCMC Mennonite of Dutch-Russian background, and Kraybill, who was from Pennsylvania and of Swiss-South German background,

---

[7] Paul Toews, "Religion American Style," *The Christian Leader*, 20 January 1976, 2-4.
[8] Donald B. Kraybill, *Our Star-Spangled Faith* (Scottdale, Pa: Herald Press, 1976).
[9] "History book planned for EMU centennial," *Mennonite World Review*, 2 April 2012, 24.
[10] Duane Friesen, review of *Our Star-Spangled Faith* in *Mennonite Life*, September 1976, 29-30.

corresponded to typical social and theological characteristics of those Mennonite branches.[11]

John A. Esau, pastor of the Bethel College Mennonite Church, shared Duane Friesen's unease with the negative use of the civil religion concept.[12] Esau had explored at length the social and theological issues in a Master of Theology thesis at the United Theological Seminary in Minneapolis/St. Paul, MN: "Religion and Culture: A New Model for Understanding Their Changing Relationship."[13] He appreciated Bellah's contribution, but argued that popular discussion of civil religion among Mennonites had so corrupted the term that meaningful conversation around the concept was hardly possible. In January 1976, addressing the "School for Peace" at Lorraine Avenue Mennonite Church in Wichita, Esau proposed an alternative: "The National Ethos: A Better Term for Civil Religion."[14] Perhaps the concept of "national ethos" would help Christians understand how to avoid simple negation of the nation, but to "seek to redeem it toward the Kingdom of God . . . with a full awareness that the chances of success are not by any means overwhelming." Esau did not publish his proposal, so it did not reach a larger audience than his oral presentations.[15]

---

[11] On the differences between the two largest Mennonite ethnic groups in North America, see James C. Juhnke, "Mennonite History and Self Understanding: North American Mennonitism as a Bipolar Mosaic," in *Mennonite Identity: Historical and Contemporary Perspectives*, edited by Calvin Wall Redekop and Samuel J. Steiner (Lanham, MD: University Press of America, 1988), 83-99.

[12] John Esau, "Civil Religion – Or How to Affirm One's Country Without Denying One's Faith," sermon at Bethel College Mennonite Church, 7 July 1974. Esau personal collection. See also Ben Ollenburger, "Mennonites, 'Civil Religion,' and the American Bicentennial: An Interview with James C. Juhnke," *Direction* 5 (July 1976): 15-21.

[13] John A. Esau, "Religion and Culture: A New Model for Understanding Their Changing Relationship," (MTh Thesis, The United Theological Seminary of the Twin Cities, 1972).

[14] Esau's presentation was announced in *The Lorraine Avenue Messenger*, 26 January 1976, 2. Esau's personal file has an undated fourteen-page handwritten manuscript, "National Ethos: A Better Term for Civil Religion."

[15] John Esau, "Civil Religion " sermon. John Esau, interview by James Juhnke, 6 December 2011.

Engaging Conservative Evangelicalism

Conservative evangelical Christians took advantage of the bicentennial to promote their nationalistic views. Some Kansas Mennonite leaders, aware that ordinary Mennonites were often attracted to conservative evangelicalism, spoke out against the excesses of this literature. Robert Kreider, director of the Mennonite Library and Archives and professor of peace studies at Bethel College, wrote a sharply critical review of one popular evangelical book that identified God and country, *America, God Shed His Grace on Thee*, by Robert Flood. Kreider noted that Flood believed that God gave the Americans military victory in the War for Independence, and that Christian evangelical faith accounts for "the country's general prosperity and its position as a great world power." The "beautifully illustrated and exquisitely printed book," wrote Kreider, glorified militarism and "the cult of American riches." "I see this book as like unto a work of pornography which should not be sold in church-related bookstores. I speak with feeling because I love America and I want to be faithful to Jesus Christ who loves America and Canada and Tanzania and the people in every land."[16]

Keith Sprunger, history professor at Bethel College 1963-2001.

Keith Sprunger, Kreider's colleague on the faculty at Bethel College, was decisively dismissive in reviewing two "red-white-and-blue" bicentennial books. The books, by John B. Anderson and James G. Hefly, lamented America's moral decline and called the nation back to its true mission under God. Sprunger found the conservative evangelical books "not very remarkable nor likely to be

---

[16]Robert Flood, *America, God Shed His Grace on Thee* (Chicago: Moody Press, 1975). Robert Kreider, "America Number One in God's Sight?" *Mennonite Weekly Review*, 19 February 1976, 4. After Kreider's negative review, Moody Press stopped advertising books in *Mennonite Weekly Review*. Robert Schrag, interview by James Juhnke, 10 April 2012.

very memorable.... Lincoln's words seem appropriate, 'The world will little note, or longer remember what we say here.'"¹⁷

The influence of conservative evangelicalism was strongest among the Mennonite Brethren. The MB conference had joined the National Association of Evangelicals when it was founded in 1944. Orlando Harms, editor of the MB *Christian Leader,* reported that he had been offended by the excessive patriotic/militaristic displays at one NAE meeting. He had protested to one of the NAE leaders and suggested that perhaps the MBs did not belong there. Harms' editorials in 1976 did not specifically critique conservative evangelical patriotism. In March, however, associate editor Wally Kroeker lamented the ill advised and misinformed evangelical opposition to the Child and Family Services Act introduced by Walter Mondale (MN) and John Brademas (IN). Evangelicals falsely claimed that the bill would restrict the rights of parents to discipline their children, a mistake that, in Kroeker's view, damaged the reputation of evangelicals.¹⁸

Engaging History, Race, and Native Americans

In the face of bicentennial celebrations some Mennonites proposed alternative views of the American War for Independence. Pennsylvania Mennonite historians undertook extensive research to publish a book of documents about the Mennonite experience in the revolutionary era.¹⁹ John Ruth, Mennonite writer from Pennsylvania, completed a popular narrative account of Mennonites during the war, titled *'Twas Seeding Time.* The *Mennonite Weekly Review,* edited in Newton, Kansas, began serial publication of Ruth's book in May 1976. Mennonites in Kansas and

---

¹⁷John B. Anderson, *Vision and Betrayal in America* (Waco, Tx: Word Books, 1975), and James G. Hefley, *America: One Nation Under God* (Wheaton, Il: Victor Books, 1975). Keith L. Sprunger, "On Rekindling the American Dream," *Mennonite Weekly Review,* 11 Mar 1976, 4.

¹⁸Wally Kroeker, "Crying 'Wolf' in Washington," *Christian Leader,* 2 March 1976, 24.

¹⁹Richard K. MacMaster, Samuel L. Horst and Robert F. Ulle, eds., *Conscience in Crisis: Mennonites and other Peace Churches in America 1737-1789* (Scottdale, PA: Herald Press, 1979).

across the country read there about their own people's story two centuries earlier. Ruth's view of the War for Independence was decidedly non-heroic. He showed how the two opposing armies ravaged the countryside and violently exploited ordinary people, including Mennonite farmers, who were in their way. In Ruth's view, the War for Independence was "a tragic adventure in human impatience."[20]

James Juhnke, history teacher at Bethel College, in his classroom and public addresses, re-interpreted United States history from the viewpoint of Anabaptist-Mennonite peace values. He suggested that the conflicts between England and her American colonies could have been managed without resort to warfare. Juhnke's "unsung hero of the Revolution" was Joseph Galloway, leader of the Quaker party in Pennsylvania. At the First Continental Congress in the fall of 1774, Galloway proposed a radical reform of the British Empire–an "American Parliament" to share power with the British Parliament. Galloway's proposal failed to pass by the vote of a single colony. In Juhnke's view, "It would have been far preferable in 1776 to work out an adjustment of competing colonial and imperial claims without destroying the imperial connection and setting loose the dogs of an American nationalistic militarism which two centuries later is one of the world's greatest menaces."[21]

Vincent Harding, director of the Institute of the Black World in Atlanta, was an African-American historian and former Mennonite pastor. In 1976 Harding helped Mennonites see the bicentennial from the viewpoint of African Americans. In a speech at Bethel College, Harding said that the United States was largely "a white success story." The signers of the Declaration of Independence did not include the masses of people in their document. Slaves and poor people struggled for dignity against enormous odds. "If there is anything to celebrate," said Harding, "let it be that long, hard,

---

[20]John L Ruth, *'Twas Seeding Time :A Mennonite View of the American Revolution* (Scottdale, PA.: Herald Press, 1976), 203.

[21]James Juhnke, "Revolution Without Independence" *Mennonite Life*, September 1976, 13. See also James Juhnke, "Freedom and the American Revolution," *The Mennonite*, 22 June 1976, 14-18, and Ben Ollenburger, "Mennonites, 'Civil Religion,' and the American Bicentennial."

costly struggle (of the dispossessed) . . . This will help us see how much is yet undone. It will open our minds to the promise of a nation that sees beauty and joy in diversity." After the assassination of Martin Luther King in 1968, Harding had left the Mennonites in order "to create some new black institutions." But he remained the preeminent Black voice on racial issues heard by Mennonites in Kansas and elsewhere.[22]

Lawrence Hart, a Cheyenne Indian, graduate of Bethel College, and pastor of the Koinonia (Native American) Mennonite Church in Clinton, Oklahoma, represented the Indian viewpoint as Harding did for Blacks. On March 20, 1976, Hart spoke at a study conference on "Mennonites and the Bicentennial," sponsored at Bethel College by the Western District Conference Historical Committee. "What is there to celebrate?" asked Hart. His answer: "We have survived."[23] Hart gave credit to Quakers and Mennonites for contributing to the survival of his people. One of his passions was to bring stories of the Cheyenne tradition of Peace Chiefs together with stories of Anabaptist/Mennonite pacifism to show transcendent common values in both traditions.[24]

Lawrence Hart, Bethel College graduate, Cheyenne peace chief, and Mennonite pastor.

Engaging Imperialism and Militarism

Mennonite academics tended to talk about bicentennial issues in theological, rather than political, terms. None of the three Kansas

---

[22]"Harding calls for American 'second coming,'" *The Mennonite*, 10 February 1976.

[23]Richard Blosser, "Share Views on Bicentennial Year," *Mennonite Weekly* Review, 25 March 1976, 3.

[24]Raylene Hinz-Penner, *Searching for Sacred Ground: The Journey of Chief Lawrence Hart, Mennonite* (Telford, PA: Cascadia Publishing House, 2007).

colleges in Kansas–Tabor, Bethel and Hesston–had academically qualified political scientists on their faculties. Mennonite writing about American government policies in 1976 was not sophisticated. For a pacifist community, there was remarkably little critique of American neo-colonialism and the role of the American armed forces around the world.

But some Mennonites had read the more radical literature. Delton Franz, former pastor serving as director of the MCC Peace Section Office in Washington, D.C., drew upon his reading about American neo-colonialism in an article for Mennonite periodicals. Franz feared that Mennonites were backing away from fundamental critique of the government during the bicentennial year because they were grateful for the privilege of exemption from military service. His essay was a strong indictment of American neocolonialism and the elevation of a corporate elite that oppressed the poor for profit. "The principal reason U.S. corporations get involved in Third World Countries is to utilize cheap labor, expand markets and gain control over raw materials–all for the maximization of profits." Franz drew in part from a book by Richard Barnet and Ronald Muller, *Global Reach: The Power of the Multinational Corporations,* but he did not use the language of social class.[25]

Grass Roots Participation

While Mennonite church leaders and intellectuals drafted resolutions, organized symposia, and wrote books and articles in response to the bicentennial, Mennonites in their local communities took part in bicentennial celebrations in a myriad of ways. In December 1975, Waldo Waltner, owner of Central Kansas Hatchery in Moundridge and president of the Turkey Federation of Kansas, presented a "Bi-Centennial turkey to Kansas Governor Robert

---

[25] Delton Franz, "From 1776 to 1976–the changing style of oppression." *Mennonite Brethren Herald,* 9 July1976. The article also appeared in *Mennonite Weekly Review,* 5August 1976, 12; and in *Mennonite Reporter,* 28 June 1976. Richard Barnet and Ronald Muller, *Global Reach: The Power of the Multinational Corporations* (New York: Simon and Schuster, 1974).

Bennett . . . for the Christmas holidays" in behalf of the Federation.[26] North Newton and Bethel College were on the route of the 82-day and 4,250-mile "Bikecentennial" trail from Yorktown, Virginia, to Reedsport, Oregon. At least two Mennonites, including one Bethel College student, Kent Unrau, made the entire tour.[27] On September 2 the retail committee of the Hesston Chamber of Commerce put a commercial spin on events with a "Buycentennial Sellabration." They blocked off Hesston's Main Street for four hours to feature displays by downtown stores and a flea market or "downtown garage sale" for others.[28] Mennonite civic leaders in the small towns of Buhler, Moundridge, Inman, Goessel, and Hesston joined with non-Mennonites in using the bicentennial theme for their annual community parades and celebrations. There were bicentennial queens, bicentennial tricycle races, bicentennial beard contests, bicentennial golf competitions, bicentennial quilts, and bicentennial middle school essays.

The most highly publicized Mennonite bicentennial artifact was a "Wheat Bell" created in the small town of Goessel. Ben Boese, a retired high school teacher and founding president of the Mennonite Immigrant Foundation at Goessel, made arrangements to create a wheat-straw replica of the Liberty Bell for display at the Smithsonian Museum in Washington, D.C. Hundreds of local folks, including women who put in over a thousand "man-hours," participated in making a six-foot tall wire frame, preparing the wheat straw and weaving it into the final product. Marie and Martha Voth, twin sisters who were nurses at Bethel Deaconess Hospital in Newton, created the bell banner with letters of actual wheat berries mounted on a background of cracked wheat, accented with black thread. Boese and his wife Gertrude attended the opening ceremony at the Smithsonian in June 1976. They took special delight when the Smithsonian director called special attention to the Goessel Bell. In 1978 the bell was returned to Goessel, where it was put on display at the Goessel "Wheat Palace"

---

[26]"Turkey gift to governor," *Moundridge Journal*, 18 December 1975, 1.

[27]Gary Veendorp, "Cross-Country Cyclists Recall Deeds of Kindness," *Mennonite Weekly Review*, 15 July 1976, 12.

[28]*The Hesston Record*, 28 August 1976, 1.

and remained a tourist attraction mentioned in Kansas tour guides.[29]

Washington, D.C., in 1976 attracted Kansas Mennonites in other ways as well. The Smithsonian Folk Life Festival invited Meta Juhnke of the Eden Mennonite Church (Swiss Volhynian) and Esther Schmidt of the Alexanderwohl Church (Dutch-Russian) to display their traditional cheese and cookie-making skills on the National Mall. Also performing on the Mall was a four-member Mennonite "Schweitzer Ensemble" of banjos and mandolins from the Eden Mennonite Church. On July 12 the combined choirs of Tabor College and Bethel College sang in the Bicentennial Parade of Music at the John F. Kennedy Center.[30]

Two grass-roots Mennonite writers wrote historical dramas that drew attention to Mennonite tradition in the bicentennial context. LeAnne Toews of the Tabor Mennonite Church was distressed that the Goessel "Threshing Days" program included a program by the Dalke Family Singers, a group that mixed patriotic and religious music in ways that she found offensive. In response, Toews wrote a historical play, "Mennonite Kaleidoscope," that depicted authentic Mennonite life and faith. Local actors performed the play for two packed audiences in the Alexanderwohl Mennonite Church.[31] Meanwhile William Juhnke of the Eden Mennonite Church wrote and produced a play in Moundridge, sponsored by the Swiss Mennonite Cultural and Historical Association, that brought together Anabaptist/Mennonite symbols and American national icons. A prologue about Anabaptist suffering and steadfastness in Switzerland was followed by an opening act featuring the voices and views of Thomas Jefferson, Ben Franklin, and Abraham Lincoln. One reviewer wrote, "The antiphonal

---

[29]"Kansas Wheat Liberty Bell Still Displayed," *The Hesston Record*, 5 February 1976, 1; "Attend Bicentennial Event in Washington," *Mennonite Weekly Review*, 24 June 1976, 6; "Bell Ready for Long Trip," *Mennonite Weekly Review*, 19 February 1976, 6; Pam Grout, *You Know You're in Kansas When* (Guilford, CT: Insiders' Guide, 2006), 56.

[30]"Choirs join Bicentennial Parade," *Tabor College View*, 9 April 1976, 3.

[31]Leanne Toews, interview by James Juhnke, 8 October 2011.

reading at the end pointed away from narrow nationalism toward a universal loyalty to mankind everywhere."[32]

Affirmations of America

Some Mennonites who could be very critical of their country also took opportunities to describe their love for America. Robert Kreider, in a poetic essay titled "A Hymn of Affection for a Land and a People," listed the specific things he liked about his country: the names of people and places, writers who celebrate the American experience, national parks and monuments, small towns, trees, wild animals, heroic figures (but no military heroes in the list), ethnic diversity, food, technology, clothing, household arts, music, sports, newspapers, comic strips, humor, and artists. Wrote Kreider, "I am intrigued by the ethnic diversity in America. Take, for example, the names in last autumn's World Series of baseball: Evans, Morgan, and Bench, but also Anderson, Driessen, and Johnson, and then Billingham, McEnaney, and Doyle, but also Concepcion, Perez, and Bourbon and–beautiful to the ear–Petrocelli, Yastrzemski, and Geronimo. If only there had also been a Reichenbach, Sawatski, and Tschetter." Kreider's readers recognized the last three as "Mennonite" names.[33]

Robert Schrag, editor of *Mennonite Weekly Review*, approached the bicentennial with an upbeat "Positive View." This would be, Schrag wrote, "an appropriate time for reviewing the whole panorama of the American experience and giving thanks for the many positive and beneficient elements in it." He was not worried that the bicentennial would affect the Mennonite attitude toward the state. He began and ended his editorial with affirmations about the American experience. But along the way he included an admonition for separation from the bicentennial that would not appear in most Protestant denominational newspapers: "Our nonresistant belief certainly excludes us from participation in observances that glorify the martial aspects of the nation. Neither

---

[32]James C. Juhnke, *So Much to be Thankful For*, 173.
[33]Robert Kreider, "A Hymn of Affection for a Land and a People," *The Mennonite*, 13 January 1976, 18-20.

should we give our blessing to religious organizations or gatherings that link God's purposes with those of the country in a kind of civil religion."[34]

In November 1976 the Kansas Mennonite Men's Chorus went on a "bicentennial tour" to eastern Colorado and western Kansas. The tour culminated with a concert on Thanksgiving Day weekend in the Century II Concert Hall in Wichita. The KMMC choir, in its eighth season in 1976, had more than 400 male singers–mostly musically untrained Mennonite farmers, mechanics, teachers, and preachers who had learned to sing four-part harmony in church. Paul Wohlgemuth, the director, composed a special version of the anthem "America, the Beautiful" for the occasion. On November 27, 1976, an overflow crowd of 2,400 packed the Concert Hall and hundreds of late-comers were turned away. The choir sang fourteen numbers, one in German ("Gott ist die Liebe"). "America, The Beautiful," the only nonreligious song in the concert, was in the final section. It was followed by "Stand Up, Stand Up For Jesus" and finally by G. F. Handel's "Hallelujah" Chorus.[35]

On the back page of the printed program, "A Bicentennial Celebration in Song," were notes written by C. Nevin Miller, a teacher from Hesston. Miller gave credit to God, not to the country, for blessings that Mennonites had enjoyed. "In spite of human failures, injustices, and sins, evidenced by dark moments in the nation's two-hundred-year history," wrote Miller, "Mennonites can celebrate, not with the carnival atmosphere of banners and parades, but with the joining of voice to voice to praise Him for His wonderful works to the children of men, in this land of their present sojourn." The KMMC bicentennial concert at the most prominent place of public performance in the region surely highlighted the Mennonite presence in Kansas. But the program notes made clear that America was not the Mennonite final home.

---

[34]Robert Schrag, "The Bicentennial: A Positive View," *Mennonite Weekly Review*, 18 September 1975, 4.

[35]"Concerts by Kansas Men Raise $10,480 for CROP, MCC" *Mennonite Weekly Review*, 2 December 1976, 1. Carol Duerksen, *We Sing That Others May Live, The History of the Kansas Mennonite Men's Chorus 1969-1994* (N.p.: Kansas Mennonite Mens Chorus, 1995).

Even in times of enthusiastic bicentennial celebration, Mennonites found ways to qualify their commitments.[36]

Hillsboro and Tabor College

The town of Hillsboro, population about three thousand, outdid all other towns of south central Kansas in bicentennial celebrations. Governor John Carlin of Kansas designated Hillsboro an official "Bicentennial Town." Hillsboro's civic leaders managed to attract two nationally-sponsored exhibitions–an "Official Bicentennial Wagon Train" in March and the "Armed Forces Bicentennial Caravan" in October. The Bicentennial Wagon Train was one of several in the country that traversed historic national trails and converged at Valley Forge, Pennsylvania, on July 4. The *Hillsboro Star-Journal* estimated that five thousand people attended the Main Street parade, and some four thousand stayed for the evening program in Memorial Park for a program that included a choral group from Pennsylvania University.[37] The Wagon Train had national corporate sponsorship, but the Armed Forces Bicentennial Caravan was a public relations project for the U. S. Department of Defense.[38]

In addition, the local Hillsboro Bicentennial Commission, co-chaired by Carol Wiebe and Ray Baker, organized its own Memorial Day "Bicentennial Birthday Celebration" on May 29. The parade included a 13-man military color guard from Fort Riley, American Legion members, and the Boy Scouts. Garner Shriver, fourth district congressman, spoke at the dedication of a new civic center. Golfers participated in a bicentennial golf tournament, one of many community events. The *Hillsboro Star-Journal* published a special 24-page issue, including a "Special Bicentennial Section." On the first page were illustrations of the signing of the Declaration

---

[36]The J. Harold Moyer papers, MS.323, MLA, has a folder of programs of the Kansas Mennonite Men's Chorus. Vern Zielke also has a copy of the 1976 bicentennial concert program in his personal collection. Vern Zielke, interview by James Juhnke, 6 January 2011.

[37]*Hillsboro Star-Journal*, 28 April 1976, 2-A, 5-A.

[38]"Armed Forces Caravan in Hillsboro Saturday," *Tabor View,*1 October 1976, 2.

of Independence, of Independence Hall, of a fife and drum corps, of a patriot lighting a cannon to shoot ships in the harbor, and of Betsy Ross sewing thirteen stars onto an American flag.[39]

The Mennonites of Hillsboro had mixed reactions to the bicentennial celebrations. One enthusiastic supporter was Elmer W. Flaming, president of the First National Bank and leading member of the Parkview Mennonite Brethren church. Annoyed by articles in the MB denominational periodical, *The Christian Leader*, that were critical of American civil religion, Flaming wrote an essay titled "Why Celebrate the Bicentennial." He said, "The Declaration of Independence is the official and unequivocal recognition by the American people of their belief and faith in God. It is a religious document from the first sentence to the last. It affirms God's existence as self-evident truth which requires no further discussion or debate. The nation it creates is God's country." For Flaming the bicentennial celebrations represented "our opportunity and challenge to revive America with an injection of the same religious faith and dedication that brought about the birth of a great nation."[40]

On the opposite side were some teachers and students at Tabor College, located a few blocks south and east of the center of town. Tabor was wrestling with its identity as a Mennonite Christian liberal arts college. One new faculty member who arrived at Tabor in January 1976 found Tabor to be a "hornet's nest" of controversy.[41] At the center of debate were a number of young idealistic faculty members who urged Tabor to become a distinctively Anabaptist Christian school with a strong peace emphasis. On the other side were teachers and administrators who promoted a conservative evangelical identity that would attract more students of non-Mennonite background. Students in a college forum presentation identified the parties as "the pacifists versus the

---

[39]*Star Journal*, 26 May 1976, A-1.

[40]Elmer W. Flaming, "Why Celebrate the Bicentennial," *The Christian Leader*, 20 July 1976, 16.

[41]Scott Chesebro, interview by James Juhnke, 14 December 2011.

patriots. The alleged Mennonite ethnicists versus Protestantism."[42] One label for the idealists was "radical neo-Anabaptists."[43]

In the fall of 1975 the Tabor College homecoming committee decided on a bicentennial theme, "Highlights of History," for the homecoming parade. The committee invited student groups to create floats portraying events from America's past. Some students and teachers of "neo-Anabaptist" persuasion protested. The student Christian Fellowship Association (CFA), led by Curt Kuhns and Gordon Zerbe, decided to boycott the parade, asking "whether we as a Christian college could celebrate a government that was established by the overthrow of another, has a long history of war, and where so many things are not of God."[44] Don Ratzlaff, editor of the student paper, critiqued the CFA's decision: "At a time when our country needs a moral shot in the arm, CFA proposes we give it a mortal shot in the head. America is in dire need of a Christian influence, not a Christian cop-out."[45]

A year later, in October 1976, the neo-Anabaptist group at Tabor mobilized a public protest when the most militaristic of Hillsboro's bicentennial events, the Armed Forces Bicentennial Caravan, came to town. The caravan consisted of four large semi-truck trailers that contained museum displays for the Army, Navy, Air Force, and Marines "recounting the contributions made to America by her armed forces." An Army spokesman for the display said it was not a recruiting program, but rather "a concerted effort by the Armed Forces to bring the American Revolution Bicentennial closer to the

---

[42]Undated paper by students Daniel Born, Ted Braun, Will Friesen, Charlie Havens, and Gordon Zerbe. From Calvin Redekop personal collection. Key faculty member in the "neo-Anabaptist" group were John E. Toews and Ben Ollenburger of the Bible and Religion department, and Al Dueck, of the psychology department.

[43]Scott Chesebro interview. Chesebro, sociology teacher not in the neo-Anabaptist group, had a reputation as a Marxist. Gordon Zerbe email to James Juhnke, 9 December 2011.

[44]*The Tabor View*, 24 October 1975, 1.

[45]Don Ratzlaff, "How Will We Respond?" *The Tabor View*, 24 October 1975, 2. In other editorials Ratzlaff was critical of militarism and nationalism. He suggested that the national anthem, "The Star Spangled Banner," should be replaced with a less war-like song.

people of Hillsboro and the surrounding communities."[46] In the Air Force Van, said the promotion, "Fifteen projectors and more than 700 slides are used simultaneously in the 17-minute show to highlight the Air Force's role in aviation in its early stages, during the two world wars, in space research and in today's world." The Defense Department was spending a lot of money to refurbish its reputation tarnished by defeat in the Vietnam War.

The Tabor College protesters decided to set up a counter-military display, deliberately crude and low-tech to contrast with the sophisticated and expensive military caravan museums. For a display table for peace literature they rolled in a large wooden utility-wire frame and tipped it on its side. They parked their bicycles in front of the gas-guzzling military semi trailers, and put up a sign, "CHRISTIANS ARE CONCERNED, HAS WAR EVER MADE PEACE?" Visitors to the peace display engaged the protestors in friendly as well as hostile conversation. At his noon break, a young mechanic from the nearby Ford dealership came to argue that the military forces celebrated in the Caravan museums were the reason the protesters had the right to free speech. K. B. Bruce, editor of the *Hillsboro Star-Journal*, made the same point editorially: "The history portrayed in this fine caravan gave those few individuals Saturday their right to distribute material for peace in this country."[47]

Intense reaction to the Caravan confrontation put Roy Just, Tabor College president, in a difficult situation. Elmer Flaming, conservative Main Street banker, called Just and asked him to rein in his protesting students and faculty. On the other side, Ben Ollenburger, professor of religious studies and philosophy, distributed a statement for the "Tabor Forum." The statement scolded the college for failing to support the protesters. They should rather be commended for "an act of courage and faithfulness in giving public testimony to the New Testament message of peace." And, said Ollenburger, the college should renew its commitment "to be faithful to the tradition and theology

---

[46]"Service van visits city," *Hillsboro Star-Journal*, 29 September 1976.
[47]K. B. Bruce, "Missed the Point." *Hillsboro Star-Journal*, 6 October 1976, 2.

which is the reason for this school's existence."[48] President Just attempted to mediate between his radical faculty members and conservative major donors.[49] According to Frank Brenneman, one of the faculty protesters, Just agreed with the ideals of the neo-Anabaptists. But he wanted the radicals to know that Tabor College could not ignore someone like Flaming, a major financial contributor whose bank held the major share of Tabor College's debt.[50]

The "Caravan confrontation" prompted G. George Ens, a medical doctor in Hillsboro, to write out his own version of the underlying issues, and to send them to President Just with copies to three of Tabor's neo-Anabaptists (John E. Toews, Ben Ollenburger, and Al Dueck). In Ens's view, two philosophies were contending for the minds of Tabor students. One was the "Christian capitalist" philosophy that had sustained the Mennonite Brethren Church. It held to an atonement theology with salvation in Christ followed by evangelism and mission work; believed in the validity of capital and benevolence; valued a thrifty and frugal life-style; and respected government as instituted by God. The alternative "socialistic" philosophy, which was threatening to undermine the church, criticized "cheap grace;" thought money was evil; advocated poverty and communalism; was anti-American and avoided involvement in government except for negative prophetic witness.

The Bicentennial-related events and discussions of 1975-76 were one part of an ongoing social and theological process among the Mennonite Brethren and at Tabor College. Roy Just, president of Tabor from 1963 to 1980, was widely perceived as having shifted sharply conservative in the latter years of his presidency. According to Lynn Jost, co-author of the history of Tabor College, President Just after 1973 envisioned Tabor as "a school of evangelistic mission," but the faculty resisted, "insisting on the

---

[48]Untitled statement by Ben C. Ollenburger, 11 November 1976. Calvin Redekop collection.
[49]Ben Ollenburger, email to James Juhnke, 8 December 2011.
[50]Frank Brenneman, interview by James Juhnke, 20 December 2011.

174   People of Two Kingdoms II

historic liberal arts mission."[51] In 1976 Just hired Calvin Redekop to the position of Vice-President, knowing that Redekop would be a strong advocate of Anabaptist identity at Tabor. However, the outspoken neo-Anabaptists, including Redekop, all left Tabor College in the late 1970s, convinced that Tabor had chosen definitively to move in a conservative evangelical, rather than an Anabaptist, direction.[52] The American bicentennial dialogue in Hillsboro illustrated the acculturation process of Mennonite Brethren toward conservative evangelicalism.

The national presidential campaigns of 1976 brought evangelical religion into the political arena in new ways. Jimmy Carter, Democrat candidate from Georgia, identified himself as a "born-again" Christian. Gerald Ford, the incumbent Republican president who was saddled with the burden of the Nixon "Watergate" scandal, said that he too was a man of faith and prayer. Evangelical Christians who were traditionally Republican defensively sought reasons to support Ford. Among Mennonites this was most critical for the Mennonite Brethren.

The editors of both *The Christian Leader* (MB, Hillsboro) and *The Mennonite* (GCMC, Newton) chose to publish an article about Carter's faith by Maynard Shelly, an anti-war and pro-civil rights GCMC writer and editor. Shelly had doubts about Carter's claim to put Jesus Christ "first in my life, even before politics." Shelly noted that Richard Nixon had held highly publicized worship services in the White House. Politicians were unfortunately inclined to use religion for "good feelings" rather than for the Christlike pursuit of justice for the poor.[53] Both periodicals received pushback from readers who thought Shelly's article was too friendly to Carter. *The Christian Leader*, along with *Mennonite Weekly Review*, also published a non-partisan article by John A. Lapp who set forth four principles, including: "The political process lies under the judgment of God; this process is especially susceptible to demonic

---

[51]*Tabor College: A Century of Transformation*, 135. Section three, "A Time of Stability and Growth (1956-1980)," by Lynn Jost, 95-140.

[52]Calvin Redekop, email to James Juhnke, 11 December 2011.

[53]*The Christian Leader*, 14 September 1976, 6-7. *The Mennonite*, 21 September 1976, 545-6.

domination. . . . The place for Christians to discern the will of God on political issues is in the midst of congregational discussion under the guidance of the Holy Spirit."[54]

Robert Schrag, editor of *Mennonite Weekly Review*, qualified the Mennonite preference for "born again" candidates by noting that Ford was preferable to Carter on the issue of abortion. "Certainly our Biblical faith gives us much to say about the growing abortion mania, which is so obviously contrary to humanitarian and Christian values."[55] Meanwhile, Bruce Leichty, an *MWR* staff member, addressed foreign policy issues in an editorial, "National Self-Interest in a Brutal World." Leichty strongly indicted U.S. support of military governments and right-wing dictatorships in developing countries including Brazil, Philippines, Uruguay, and Iran, all of whom engaged in torture. Leichty especially attacked the dictatorial Shah of Iran who was supported by U.S. arms sales and by CIA and AID officials.[56]

Resistance and Welcome

Mennonites in South Central Kansas both resisted and welcomed the national bicentennial celebrations of 1976. Their responses varied among local congregations and communities. Official statements drafted by denominational leaders warned against idolatrous worship of the nation, while expressing appreciation for American freedom. Mennonite folk at the local level embraced opportunities to participate in ways that showed their love of country. All Mennonite responses to the bicentennial demonstrated the extent of their Americanization. Their negative protests and positive affirmations were framed in ways that revealed their character as a distinctive American religious-ethnic group in process of transformation.

---

[54]*The Christian Leader*, 26 October 1976, 5-6. *Mennonite Weekly Review*, 28 October 1976.

[55]Robert Schrag, "Protection of the Unborn a 'Central Issue,'" *Mennonite Weekly Review*, 16 Sept 1976, 4.

[56]Bruce Leichty, "National Self-Interest in a Brutal World," *Mennonite Weekly Review*, 30 Sept 1976, 4.

In December 1976, at the end of the bicentennial year, Robert Schrag, editor of *Mennonite Weekly Review*, captured Mennonite ambivalence by suggesting that Mennonite resistance to American warfare was in its own right a significant contribution to the American democracy. Kansas Mennonites had long been lauded for bringing Turkey Red wheat from Russia to America. In 1976 the Goessel Wheat Liberty Bell celebrated that contribution. But Schrag, with an eye on John L. Ruth's book, *'Twas Seeding Time*, lifted up a different Mennonite gift to America. Ruth's book told the story of colonial Mennonite resistance to participation in the War for Independence–a stark contrast to the nation's bicentennial celebration of that war as the fountain of national freedom. In American wars of the following two centuries, Mennonite refusal of military service had challenged the limits of toleration. Wrote Schrag, "People willing to dissent–to take a stand different from prevailing opinion in order to remain true to their convictions–have an indispensable role in preserving true freedom of conscience." Thus Mennonite resistance to the bicentennial's narrative of American history–freedom obtained through warfare–justified the Mennonite claim to responsible citizenship.[57]

---

[57]Robert Schrag, "Mennonite Contribution," *Mennonite Weekly Review*, 9 Dec 1976, 4.

Chapter 10

Mennonite Politicians I

The most prominent politically active Mennonites were those who ran for state and national office. In chapters ten and eleven we tell the stories of Mennonite politicians whose involvements often extended beyond the time boundaries of other chapters. The differences among these leaders reveal that Mennonites were not all cut from the same mold.

Harold Dyck, Dean of Mennonite Legislators

Harold Dyck of Hesston was a highly respected businessman and philanthropist who served in the Kansas legislature from 1970 to 1988, when he was age 50 to 68. He had come a long way from humble origins. He was born in 1920 into a farm family near Goessel that belonged to the conservative Church of God in Christ (Holdeman) Mennonite Church. Although he did not join the church of his parents, like other Holdeman youth he attended elementary school but did not graduate from high school. During World War II he served as a conscientious objector in Civilian Public Service camps in South Dakota and Pennsylvania. After the war, from 1951 to 1968, he worked as sales manager and vice president of Hesston Corporation, a manufacturer of farm equipment. He was mayor of Hesston from 1969 to 1971.[1]

Harold Dyck

In 1970 the Republican Party appointed Dyck to fill the unexpired legislative term of Raymond King, a building contractor from Hesston (not a Mennonite) who had died in a tragic airline crash that killed most of the players on the Wichita State University

---

[1] Thanks to Robert A. Dueck of Garland, Texas, for sharing a box of materials about his grandfather, Harold Dyck. The box includes an informative scrapbook with many undated clippings. Most of the information in this section is based on this collection.

football team. Dyck was a moderate Republican and an active member of the Hesston Mennonite Church congregation. He had a distinguished gentlemanly bearing and found ways to affirm people of different political points of view. Elected to the legislature in his own right in November 1970, he went on to serve nine full terms–the longest stint of any Mennonite in the Kansas legislature. He became known for his religious identity. It was important to him that the legislature began each day with prayer. For years he led a small group of legislators who met weekly for Bible study and fellowship. That group was expanded into a broader prayer breakfast body. On occasion Dyck travelled to Washington, D.C., to attend national prayer breakfast meetings.

In his second term in Topeka Dyck was appointed chairman of the Education Committee, one of the most important committees in the House of Representatives. The appointment was notable not only for how soon it came to him, but also in view of his not being a high school graduate. Dyck was more interested in competent administration than in the public limelight. "I have not been one to introduce a lot of bills," he said. Three of his bills that failed were one to eliminate the office of lieutenant governor, another to require that contracts be "written in a clear and coherent manner using words with common and every day meaning," and a third to change the Kansas constitution to provide for four-year terms for state legislators. He opposed the death penalty and parimutuel betting. He declined to join the Republican "Conservative Caucus."

In his newspaper column for his constituents Dyck stated his fervent belief in free enterprise. He cosponsored a resolution to direct the State Board of Education to promote courses in the schools about the free enterprise system. But he was not a doctrinaire ideologue. He defended welfare recipients against charges of widespread fraud.[2] He corrected militant opponents of the Equal Rights Amendment who claimed that if the ERA passed women would be drafted into the military. He said his own views on gender relations may be "old fashioned." He agreed with the

---

[2] *Hesston Record*, 13 January 1971.

Bible on the matter, "if properly interpreted and believed."[3] He favored prison reform to encourage community-based correction facilities and programs, and to involve home communities in rehabilitation of offenders. He often met with and assisted representatives from the Prairie View mental health center in Newton.

Dyck took a special interest in national politics. He wrote letters to encourage national leaders, both Republicans and Democrats. In June 1974, after a grand jury had named President Richard Nixon an unindicted co-conspirator in the Watergate affair, Dyck wrote a supportive letter to Nixon saying "We want you to continue to run this country. You have done a most remarkable job even though you have had a very partisan congress to deal with." In January 1977, after Jimmy Carter had been elected, Dyck wrote to the Democratic president-elect, with a copy to Dan Glickman, the newly elected Democratic congressman in Kansas' 4th district, noting, among other things, his support of Carter's energy policies.

Dyck became involved in national organizations for state legislators and enjoyed attending national conferences and meetings. He was a member of the Education Commission of the States, attended meetings for the National Legislative Conference and the Council of State Governments. In August 1981 he was elected vice chairman of the Midwestern Conference of the Council of State Governments meeting in Detroit, Michigan. Occasionally he was frustrated by the tight inner core of Republican leadership. "If you aren't in a certain group," he once wrote, "it is hard to attain anything. . . . (We) wanted to break up some of that within the party so that everyone had a say."[4] In 1976 he hoped to become Republican speaker pro tem, but that plan was undone when the Democrats won a majority in the Kansas House.

Harold Dyck's most lasting legacy was not in the Kansas legislature. In the late 1970s he sold his shares of Hesston Corporation stock in order to make a million dollar gift for an arboretum just south of the town. Because he sold his shares not

---

[3]*Halstead Independent*, 6 March 1975, 9.
[4]Unidentified clipping, Dyck collection.

long before a drastic drop in the value of Hesston Corporation stock, some people accused him of insider trading. He was able to defend himself against the charge with the evidence of correspondence with Hesston College that showed his gift had been planned well in advance. The Dyck Arboretum became a significant natural history gem of the region.[5]

Duane Goossen, Republican Moderate

Duane Goossen, member of Kansas legislature 1983-1996, and budget director for the state of Kansas 1999-2011.

In the spring of 1982, Duane Goossen went from Goessel to Hesston to talk with Harold Dyck about the possibility of running for the 70th district seat in the Kansas legislature. It was a meeting across generations. Goossen at age twenty-two was almost forty years younger than Dyck, who was nearing his sixty-second birthday. The junior was seeking the blessing and endorsement of the senior. They were both Republicans and both Mennonites.

At first Dyck was skeptical. "Are you in this to win?" he asked. "Or is this a lark?"[6] Behind Dyck's suspicion may have been two concerns. Was Goossen a young idealistic prophet who wanted to make a public splash of some kind? In the political upheavals during the Vietnam War, youthful Mennonites were typically more interested in prophetic witness than in viable political candidacy. Moreover, Kansas' 70th legislative district had an incumbent Republican. Bill Novak, a conservative rancher from Lost Springs was running for re-election. Legislators in principle are reluctant to endorse opponents of incumbents from their own party. Would Mennonite identity trump Republican Party identity for Dyck? And what led Goossen to think he had a chance of winning?

---

[5]Harold Dyck, interview by James Juhnke, 2005.
[6]Duane Goossen, interview by James Juhnke, Topeka, KS, 18 January 2013.

Duane Goossen was the son of a Mennonite pastor, steeped in the teachings of peace and service. He also acquired an exceptionally strong passion for public political service. In the year after his graduation from Goessel High school (1973), Goossen spent some time in northern Indiana. There he took a course at Goshen College, "Introduction to Politics," taught by an African-American professor, Leroy Berry. A key concept in that class was "Politics is a way of decision-making."[7] Berry's view was different from traditional Anabaptist-Mennonite notions of politics as a place of compromise with the world.

From 1974 to 1978, Goossen attended Bethel College. He had a double major in religion and peace studies, and became interested in the discipline of conflict resolution. His senior seminar paper, written under his mentor, Duane Friesen, was titled "Faithfulness Versus Effectiveness: A Position on Ethics." The paper outlined and critiqued the ethical positions of theologians Reinhold Niebuhr and John Howard Yoder, finding both of them wanting. Niebuhr, wrote Goossen, rendered the life and teachings of Jesus irrelevant, and Yoder held a view of "being the church" that could lead to "self-righteous minority withdrawal."[8] In a concluding section, Goossen stated his own distinctly humanistic ethical position: "(A) person gains identity by choosing a morality or way of life. . . . We must act shrewdly to implement that vision as <u>effectively</u> as possible." The ethical case mentioned most often in the paper was the refusal to pay income taxes–a position Goossen critiqued as potentially ineffective and a wasted sacrifice involving legal hassles and penalties. During his political career, Goossen became the most ethically articulate and thoughtful of Mennonite politicians. But he was more interested in resolving practical political conflicts than in propagating his theological viewpoints.

By the time of his conversation with Harold Dyck in the spring of 1982, Goossen had started a construction business and served on the city council in the small town of Goessel on the western edge of

---

[7]Goossen interview.

[8]Duane Goossen, "Faithfulness Versus Effectiveness: A Position on Ethics" (seminar paper, Bethel College, 1978).

Marion County. He was a member of the Goessel Mennonite Church congregation. The 70th Kansas legislative district was a rural and small town area with a strong Republican majority. Bill Novak, the incumbent Republican legislator, was a rough-hewn conservative "cowboy," who kept a bust of Ronald Reagan (elected president 1980) on his desk.

Goessen's personality was suited to his rural district. He had a quiet, serious, straightforward demeanor and spoke in measured tones that made him seem older than he was. He kept his ambition under the surface, impressing those he met with genial, but not effusive, good sense. Harold Dyck accepted Goossen's serious intentions, but kept his support muted until after the primary in August. Even more reticent was Carol Wiebe, chairman of the Republican Party in Hillsboro and a member of the Mennonite Brethren Church. Wiebe did help Goossen after he won the August primary.

More important than Dyck and Wiebe for Goossen's campaign was the non-Mennonite Pascal Roniger, Republican political broker in Chase County and former member of the legislature. In their first extended conversation, Roniger quizzed Goossen about the issues. Before the visit ended, Roniger offered to endorse Goossen. He also wrote out a check to help with the campaign. Roniger apparently had been rubbed the wrong way by incumbent Novak. He sent out letters of endorsement to Republican voters, and helped Goossen get the support of Frances Olsen, chairperson of the Chase County Republican party. Olsen gave Goossen important advice: wear cowboy boots while walking in parades, and don't endorse the controversial proposed Tall Grass Prairie Park that was opposed by Flint Hills ranchers.

In his first campaign in 1982 Goossen outlined his positions on policy issues more completely than in any other of his seven campaigns. In part this was a matter of Goossen's self-education; in part it was his generous estimate of how significant policy issues would be for getting elected. Some of his stances were unequivocal and clearly rooted in his Mennonite values. He opposed capital punishment and the liberalization of Kansas liquor and betting laws. He favored restrictions on abortion: "I believe life is sacred, and that a lenient policy toward abortion subtly causes us to value life less. At the same time, I expect that anyone urging me to oppose abortion, would also oppose other things which also devalue the sanctity of life such as child abuse, capital punishment, poverty, etc."[9]

On other issues Goossen took a more equivocal or qualified position. He would support the severance tax only if it were tied to a decrease of property tax. He would favor statewide repeal of the intangibles tax as long as local governments could institute it. He was not for gun control, but would reconsider if the majority in his district wanted it. He was not opposed to the storage of nuclear wastes in Kansas, but they should be strictly regulated. He was for a gas tax increase and for "living within our income."

Kansas politics was not as polarized in 1982 as it became a decade later after the 1991 "Summer of Mercy" controversy on the abortion issue. But there were already important differences between Republican conservatives and progressives. There was a Republican "conservative caucus" to which the incumbent Bill Novak belonged. Goossen said he did not intend to join the conservative caucus. But he benefitted from one of Novak's incautious and controversial comments that "if my daughter insisted on having an abortion, I'd want her to have it under medically approved conditions." The editor of the *Marion County Record* later recalled, with some exaggeration: "That was an honest remark, but it cost Bill the election."[10]

In the three months before the primary in August, Goossen worked more or less full time on his campaign. He knocked on doors of registered Republicans on farm homes and small towns throughout Marion and Chase counties. Nearly all of the money for the primary campaign came out of Goossen's home town of Goessel. He also got help from established Republicans in the moderate wing of the party. Keith Henley, a Bethel College graduate who was on the staff of Wendell Lady, Republican Party

---

[9] Duane Goossen, undated (1982?) document in an unmarked file in Goossen's personal collection.
[10] Bill Meyers, "Common Sense Suggested," *Marion County Record*, 18 March 1992, 2.

leader from Johnson County, helped set up appointments with party leaders. All the work paid off. Goossen won a majority in Chase County, in addition to a decisive majority in his Mennonite base in the western part of Marion County. Mennonites were about one quarter of the voters in the district.

After that first victory in August 1982, for six subsequent election cycles, Goossen was never seriously challenged in the Republican primaries. Nor did he face really strong Democratic challengers in the predominantly Republican 70th district. Never in those campaigns did he say anything negative about his opponent. He joked that he identified with the Texas politician who said, "I am not running on my opponent's demerits. I intend to run on my own demerits!" In the legislature, Goossen preferred to work quietly behind the scenes. At the end of that first term his party colleagues gave him a "Golden Throat Award," a joke prize for speaking less than any other freshman legislator. The *Wichita Eagle-Beacon* newspaper ran a series of articles, "Mr. Goossen Goes to Topeka," which gave him a chance to defend the "compromise" in which the legislature increased the gasoline tax a total of three cents, on top of a five cent tax added by the federal government. "I'm not selling the gas tax to them (his constituents) like an achievement," said Goossen. "I know it's the one that will certainly hit the hardest in my counties, but I'm just reminding them they've complained about the roads for years. This'll be one way to solve that. It was a compromise."[11]

Goossen's election in 1982 gave Mennonites in his district more direct access to a Kansas politician than they had had in the past. Many of them shared their political concerns with him in personal conversations as well as at more formal public forums. Many also wrote letters to him in Topeka about their special concerns. In his first term, January through April of 1983, Goossen received letters from Mennonites on fourteen different issues: pari-mutuel betting, hospital policies, social service funding, medication aides, natural gas prices, farm equipment taxes, liquor laws, solar energy, open

---

[11] Angelia Herrin, "Home Folks Think He Did the Job," *The Wichita Eagle-Beacon*, 30 April 1983, 6A.

meetings, private employment agencies, school finance, local government accounts at savings and loan agencies, and telephone rate increases.[12] Three Mennonite congregations (Goessel, Alexanderwohl, and Tabor), through the Goessel Ministerial Association, gave Goossen $150 to help pay expenses on a trip to Washington, D.C., to attend the National Prayer Breakfast.[13] Goossen's father, Henry, a Mennonite pastor, was especially gratified by the Prayer Breakfast connection. Henry attended the January 10, 1983, inauguration ceremony for Governor John Carlin in Topeka and was most deeply impressed by the Inaugural Prayer Service in the Capitol Rotunda. "We felt this was a very impressive worship experience. We were interacting with God in the setting and atmosphere of state government. . . . My hope for good government and my confidence in those who govern was greatly enhanced."[14]

Compromise for forward movement in progressive public policy was the hallmark of Gosssen's fourteen-year legislative career. He enjoyed the political process, even when the projects he favored took a long time. He devoted major efforts to road and transportation issues, especially improvements on the two major state highways in his district–highway 50 between Newton and Emporia, and highway 56 through Marion and Hillsboro. People in Hillsboro favored, and people in Marion opposed, a plan to re-build highway 56 on a route that bypassed both towns. Goossen voted in favor of the new route, and for an increase in sales tax that in part made it possible. Goossen initially campaigned as a proponent of the severance tax on oil and gas. At times he voted for tax decreases. In the early years of his legislative career, tax issues were not as polarizing as they became in the 1990s. Moderate Republicans were able to cooperate with Democrats.

Most satisfying personally to Goossen was his work in the field of human social services. His leadership in that area was helped by

---

[12]"Correspondence 1983" file in Duane Goossen personal collection.

[13]Duane Goossen to Darrell Ediger (Goessel Mennonite), Jim Schrag (Tabor) and Ken Rupp (Alexanderwohl), February 10 and 11, 1983. Goossen personal collection.

[14]Henry Goossen, "Pastor's Corner" letter, n.d., Duane Goossen political scrapbook.

membership on the House Appropriations Committee. He worked to reduce the domination of large institutional centers in the state mental health system. He tried to move state funding into more community-based mental health settings, including the Mennonite Prairie View Mental Health center based in Newton. Goossen had some success in getting more state money into early childhood and developmental education.

Goossen consistently voted against capital punishment, liquor, and gambling bills. Liquor by the drink and pari-mutuel betting both passed the House, with Goossen voting no. The responses to Goossen's annual questionnaire revealed that most people in the district favored capital punishment, but were conservative on alcohol and gambling. In 1994 the Democratic governor, Joan Finney, allowed a bill reinstituting the death penalty to become law without her signature. Goossen considered himself financially conservative and socially moderate. In 1992 he faced a dilemma for both his social ideals and his Mennonite identity when his Republican colleague in the House of Representatives, Garry Boston, asked for his endorsement. Boston was being challenged in that election by Donna Neufeld, a Mennonite social worker and former social work teacher at Bethel College. Goossen did not know Neufeld personally. He agreed to send a letter to voters in North Newton and Newton endorsing his political colleague as deserving re-election over a Mennonite with whom he shared denominational identity and important value commitments.[15]

The ideological polarization of Kansas politics and the rising power of the conservative wing of the Republican Party were deeply frustrating for Goossen. He had enjoyed the ways that a coalition of Democrats and moderate Republicans were able to pass progressive legislation. But in 1994 the conservative Republicans got a majority and took vindictive action against the moderate Republicans. The new conservative Speaker of the House, Tim Shallenberger, removed Goossen as head of the House Education Committee and replaced him with someone more conservative.

---

[15]Letter from State Representative Duane Goossen to "Dear Friends," 16 October 1992. Author's collection.

Goossen even lost his office in the main part of the capitol building and was banished to an undesirable fifth floor office. Given the new array of political forces that severely reduced the prospects for making progress on matters important to him, Goossen decided to leave the legislature after completing his term in 1996.

He and his wife, Rachel Waltner Goossen, moved to Goshen, Indiana, where she had been hired to teach in the Goshen College department of history. In 1998 he earned a Masters of Public Administration from the Kennedy School of Government at Harvard University. Governor Bill Graves invited him to serve as Kansas' budget director, a post he held for twelve years, including service under Democratic Governors Kathleen Sebelius and Mark Parkinson. In that role he was able to make an even greater contribution to public policies than he had done in his fourteen years as a legislator.[16]

Duane Goossen had a clear understanding of the relationship between his political work and his Mennonite ideals. Government, he said "can be a useful tool in helping Mennonites carry out a mission of service to others and a mission of peacemaking." He saw lawmaking as "conflict resolution constantly in motion. Individuals and groups bring their conflicts and competing desires to government, using the legislative process to reach nonviolent solutions." Yes, government's role was limited and the decisions were often partisan and narrow-minded. That only made Mennonite intentional involvement on issues of deep moral concern even more urgent. To pay state income taxes, Goossen argued with exaggeration beyond his accustomed style, was as worthy as contributing to Mennonite Central Committee, the primary church agency for Mennonite benevolence. Goossen believed in government and committed his career to public service.[17]

---

[16] Goossen interview.
[17] Duane Goossen, "The Politics of Peace and Service: Calling All Mennonites," *Mennonite Life* (September 1996), 5. See also Goossen's reflections on public service in a sermon, "It Takes All Kinds of People to Make a World," presented at Southern Hills Mennonite Church, October 2011.

Jesse Harder, Democrat Moderate

Along with Duane Goossen in the 1982 class of freshmen in the Kansas House was Jesse Harder of Buhler.[18] Harder was a Democrat, thirty-nine years older than Goossen. But the two Mennonite legislators were remarkably similar in personal style, church identity, and social values. They were both non-demonstrative moderates and social progressives, Mennonites in predominantly non-Mennonite districts. They both opposed the death penalty, contrary to the majority will of their districts.

Jesse Harder

Harder had grown up in Oklahoma and during World War II had served in Civilian Public Service as a conscientious objector to war.[19] After the war he taught social studies in Buhler High School, and then for thirteen years (1969-1982) at Hutchinson Community College. Milo Stucky, the principal at Buhler High School, convinced Harder to become a Democrat. Stucky was a Mennonite of Swiss-Volhynian ethnic background, a group more inclined to Democratic Party identification than were Harder's Dutch-Russian Mennonite forebears. In coffee-room discussions, Stucky convinced Harder that the Democrats were the party of the people and that Roosevelt's New Deal had been good for the country. Harder served as mayor of Buhler from 1957 to 1961, and as moderator of his Mennonite Brethren Church congregation for twenty-five years or more. Nearly everyone in that congregation was Republican. Indeed, the 103rd district was strongly Republican, with only 27% of voters registered as Democrats.[20]

---

[18] Also in that freshman class was Steven Ediger from Hutchinson, a Democrat of Mennonite background and friend of Jesse Harder. Ediger was not at the time a member of a Mennonite church. He served just one two-year term in the Kansas House.

[19] Jesse Harder, interview by James Juhnke, Buhler, KS, 13 November 2009.

[20] Jesse Harder, *Beyond Isabella: A Harder Family Story* (N.p.: author, 1999), 77.

In 1982 when Harder announced his candidacy, another Mennonite Democrat, Reno County Commissioner Ralph Krehbiel, said he "didn't have a Chinaman's chance" of being elected. Bert Chaney, Democrat state senator who had encouraged Harder to run, and who was Harder's teaching colleague at Hutchinson Community College, was more optimistic. The overconfidence of the three-term Republican incumbent, Dean Hinshaw, proved to be Harder's advantage. The political newcomer ran an under-the-radar campaign. Rather than seeking publicity and speaking at large public gatherings, he covered the 103rd district door to door, concentrating on three precincts west of Main Street in Hutchinson. He spent only $3,200 for the campaign. In his campaign brochure he did not mention his party affiliation, church membership, or his wartime Civilian Public Service history. He won with 54% of the vote.

In his first term in Topeka Harder faced one of the most difficult voting decisions of his ten-year political career. The issue was a severance tax on gas and oil, proposed by the Democrat Governor, John Carlin, to improve general fund revenues. Harder voted for the bill the first time it passed in the House of Representatives. But after the Senate appended a severance tax on salt to the bill–a measure strongly opposed by Hutchinson salt-mine interests in his district–Harder decided to vote against the bill. He remained embarrassed that he had compromised his own (and his party's) preference in order to conform to the wishes of his constituents. In his memoir, he confessed he may have been "concerned about their response in the next election."[21]

On the issue of the death penalty, a matter of passionate concern for this Mennonite pacifist, Harder took a consistent position he knew was against the opinion of the majority in his district. Although he considered himself a "support person, not a leader, not a point person, in the legislature," he did rise to speak from the House podium on capital punishment.[22] After one such speech, Duane Goossen came across the aisle from the Republican side and

---

[21]Harder, *Beyond Isabella*, 80.
[22]Harder interview.

thanked him. Harder's position was both pragmatic and moral. The death penalty was not a deterrent to crime, and was often unfair. "Only God has the right to take a life," he said.[23] Harder wrote to Dan Glickman, fourth district congressman, about death penalty provisions in the federal crime bill.[24]

Surveying his ten-year career in the Kansas legislature, Harder later identified his two most important votes. One was for a 1989 highway bill that included funding for an improved four-lane highway between Wichita and Hutchinson. The second was a school funding bill in 1992. Opponents of the 1989 highway bill (including the Democrat Party caucus) were concerned about increased user fees and an $890 million bond. Also opposing the bill were Amish folk southeast of Hutchinson whose communities would be divided by closed roads and by fast-moving traffic that endangered horses and buggies. Some Amish men came to public meetings to protest the highway plan. Sam E. Bontrager of Rt. 2, Haven, wrote a handwritten letter to Harder in Topeka, in a distinctively Amish voice:

> We plead for mercy for our community which is in jeapordy. (*sic*) Our transportation is Horse & buggy. We use them daily, traveling on & crossing K-96 Hiway. To wait for traffic while setting in the median with traffic Buzzing by in front of & Behind, I feel, is much too dangerous & will test a well broke horse. Please hear our plea. If you will not drop this project. Please. We ask you to be so considerate as to put overpasses at every intersection, not closing any roads. We request this in Jesus Holy Name.[25]

Harder did not respond to the Amish protest. As it turned out, his vote was essential for the 1989 highway bill. The bill passed by only one vote.

---

[23]Harder, *Beyond Isabella*, 86.

[24]Dan Glickman to Jesse Harder, 1 November 1991, Jesse Harder papers, Center for Mennonite Brethren Studies, Tabor College, Hillsboro, KS.

[25]Sam E.Bontrager to Jesse Harder, undated, Jesse Harder papers.

A second "most important" vote was the school finance reform bill of 1992. That bill passed after the Democrats in the 1990 election had won a one-vote majority in the Kansas House, and had elected a Democratic governor, Joan Finney. The bill, in Harder's judgment, "helped equalize per pupil spending state wide, and shifted some of the school tax burden from property tax to sales tax and income tax." It also resolved a conflict between the legislature and the state Supreme Court that had long threatened school finance law.[26]

Harder retired from the legislature in 1992, proud that legislative achievements of his final term had ranked, in the judgment of one Associated Press reporter, as the "most productive in the last 25 years."[27] Two years later, however, at age 78, Harder decided to run again, after district boundaries had been redrawn in the reapportionment process. He was the oldest candidate in Kansas in that election. For the first time he lost an election, with 43% of the vote.[28]

Harder paid special attention to his Mennonite constituents. He was a regular speaker at the "Legislative Awareness Seminars" sponsored by the Western District Mennonite (GC) and the Southern District Mennonite Brethren groups. Harder had little sympathy for the traditional Mennonite resistance to political involvement with politics. When Wesley Prieb, English professor at Tabor College and also an active churchman, asked him, "How do you reconcile your political work with your Anabaptist heritage?" he said, "Somebody is going to make the decisions. If I help in the process, I don't think it is a violation of my Christian principles."[29]

---

[26]Harder, *Beyond Isabella*, 93.
[27]Harder, *Beyond Isabella*, 94.
[28]Harder, *Beyond Isabella*, 95.
[29]Harder interview.

Tom Bishop, Mennonite Housing Entrepreneur

Tom Bishop 1990

Tom Bishop was a first-generation Mennonite originally from Ohio. After marrying a young woman from the Smithville Mennonite Church, Bishop worked for a term in a Mennonite Voluntary Service Unit in Pendleton, Oregon. In 1980 he was appointed to the staff of the Mennonite Board of Missions in Elkhart, Indiana, and became director of recruitment and training for Mennonite Voluntary Service. Influenced by radical Christian leaders such as Tony Campolo and Gene Stoltzfus, Bishop developed a strong interest in social concerns and political issues. Ronald Reagan's election in 1980, he believed, portended "the bottom falling out of things." Some people in his Voluntary Service orientation group thought he was too political.[30]

In 1986 Bishop moved to Wichita, Kansas, to become director of Mennonite Housing. His successful administration and expansion of the program got favorable attention from local government and from the press. He became known as "a problem-solver, with an amazing capacity for keeping track of details of different projects in his head."[31] In 1990 Bishop, at age 35, turned his energy to Kansas politics. Encouraged by Harold Dyck, Republican from Hesston, he ran as a Democrat for the state legislature in the 91st district in urban Wichita, a district with an open seat and a large Republican majority. His Republican opponent, Steve Cisneros, was, according to the Wichita *Eagle,* an ambitious 24-year old with "a pretty face and empty head." The *Eagle* endorsed Bishop: "His priorities include education, property taxes, and health care. His proven record at Mennonite Housing and other community activities would make him an effective voice for the 91st district."[32]

---

[30]Tom Bishop, interview by James Juhnke, Holton, KS, 28 November 2013.
[31]Howard Keim, "Rhetorical Strategies and Self-Definitions of Local Leaders: Four Case Studies" (PhD dissertation, University of Kansas, 1996), 77.
[32]*Wichita Eagle*, 31 October 1990, 8A.

Bishop won the 1990 general election with 59% of the vote. His success was part of a general Democrat tide that gave the Democrat party a one-vote majority in the Kansas House. Not since 1978 had the Democrats had a majority in the House. In 1992 Bishop won a second term. His Republican opponent in that election, Darrel Thorpe, supported capital punishment and opposed abortion rights. Bishop opposed capital punishment, casino gambling, and assault weapons. He favored open admissions policy for state universities, and a state revenue stream in equal thirds for sales taxes, property taxes, and income taxes. In his second election, he increased his majority to 61%.

Bishop was exceptionally active as a new legislator in drafting bills and gaining support for his measures. He said that his goal in life was to "wreak havoc, protect the constitution, change the world, and revolutionize state government as we know it."[33] Among his achievements was a bill to make drive-by shooting a felony instead of a misdemeanor. He also introduced a bill, and secured votes for its passage, to protect Super Fund designation for a large area of contaminated groundwater in the city of Wichita, and to enable tax increment financing for environmental remediation. That bill was later replicated in other states. A third bill reformed the process for sale of properties that were deficient in payment of local property tax–a process that often benefitted "slumlords" or business interests whose plans did not benefit the local city or county. Bishop's major disappointment was his failure to get the legislature to authorize creation of a state housing finance agency. The Kansas Bankers Association and bond firms kept the bill from passing, leaving Kansas the only state in the nation lacking a state housing finance agency.[34] One leadership study characterized Bishop as a "pragmatic visionary." He articulated high ideals and advocated far-reaching reform while "settling for what was possible at the moment."[35]

---

[33] Keim, "Rhetorical Strategies," 54.

[34] Thomas A. Bishop, "Legislative Reflections," undated memorandum (December 2013), author's collection.

[35] Keim, "Rhetorical Strategies," 100.

Were the values of the Mennonite-Anabaptist-Christian faith relevant to Bishop's political activity? "Yes," he responded to that question. "To all of it!" It was important to him to work hard in behalf of the people he represented, rather than to serve his personal business interests or those of special businesses or constituencies. He was discouraged that local voters were not knowledgeable about the issues, and that "money rules the day" in the legislature through well paid professional lobbyists.[36] Bishop served just one year of his second term, resigning in January 1994. His resignation was related to divorce and remarriage. He returned to full time work as leader of Mennonite Housing.

---

[36] Thomas A. Bishop, "Learnings and Lessons," undated memorandum (December 2013), author's collection.

Chapter 11

Mennonite Politicians II

Charles Benjamin, Academic Activist

In the fall of 1979 Bethel College hired Charles Benjamin, a Ph.D. candidate from the University of Southern California, to teach government and political science classes. Benjamin was the first professionally trained political scientist to teach government classes at a Kansas Mennonite college. He was a conscientious objector to war, attracted to Bethel College for its peace heritage. He was a Jew and a political activist. He planned to teach at Bethel for two years and then move on to a more prestigious school. But two events intervened to keep him at Bethel. He married a Mennonite woman (Jean Hershey) and he became successfully involved in local and state politics.[1]

Charles Benjamin, "outsider" county commissioner

Less than a year after arriving in Kansas, Benjamin decided to challenge an incumbent Democrat for a seat on the three-man Harvey County Commission. Five things made this quest apparently hopeless: Benjamin was a recent youthful arriver to a district that presumably shared a typical Kansas mistrust of outsiders. He taught at a college in a community long afflicted with town-gown tensions. He was a Jew among Protestants. He was a Democrat in a majority Republican district. And he had a dark black beard. Nevertheless, to everyone's surprise, Benjamin won both the August Democratic primary and the November general election by comfortable margins. It was one of the most amazing political outcomes in the history of Harvey County.[2]

---

[1] The following account is based on unprocessed materials in the Charles Benjamin papers, MS.447, MLA, and in part on memories of the author as Benjamin's colleague at Bethel College and as a helper in Benjamin's political campaigns.

[2] Buzz Ball, "Benjamin, Griffiths post wins," *Newton Kansan*, 6 August 1980, 1.

How was Benjamin able to win in 1980? He campaigned under the radar. He went door to door in all eight precincts of the second district, greeting people and asking if they didn't agree that it was "time for a change." Voters had sensed that the Harvey County commission was an old boys' network and that this earnest, soft-spoken, well-dressed, smiling young man could be a breath of fresh air. Perhaps Benjamin benefitted from something of the same desire for change that in 1980 elected Ronald Reagan as national president. Perhaps Harvey County was not as narrow-minded and intolerant of outsiders as people often assumed. His opponent, the second district Democratic incumbent Clayton Dey, was indeed elderly and did not bother to campaign at all for re-election. The Republican Party, comfortable with its two-to-one majority on the commission, conceded the seat to the Democrats and did not nominate their own candidate in the Republican primary. When Benjamin won the primary over Dey (472 to 333), the surprised Republicans named a write-in candidate, Jack Kline, and mounted a belated campaign. But Benjamin won the general election with a majority in each of the eight precincts. In North Newton he won 102 to 14.

Benjamin did not take long to shake up the old boys' network. In February 1981 he proposed two policy changes to make decision-making more open and public, and to abide by the Kansas Open Meetings Act of 1977. He said he did not accuse the county commission of violating the law, but "We must avoid the appearance of a closed meeting." His proposed changes died for lack of a second.[3] But the editor of the local newspaper, the *Newton Kansan*, apparently annoyed by secretive procedures in the past, strongly endorsed Benjamin proposals.[4] The commission's procedures changed and there were no more decisions behind closed doors. Benjamin got consistent support from the local press as he went on to establish a solid reputation for his mastery of issues and the law. He was re-elected to the Harvey County

---

[3]"Benjamin proposes board policy changes," *Newton Kansan*, 18 February 1981, 1.

[4]"The public's business," *Newton Kansan*, 19 February 1981, 4A.

Commission in 1984, 1988, and 1992. In 1990 he summarized eleven "significant accomplishments" of his time on the county commission. Among these were lower taxes, budget reforms, a long-range plan for roads and bridges, a Community Development Block Grant, a 911 Emergency Response System, and "strict adherence to Kansas open meetings laws."

While on the Harvey County Commission, Benjamin soon had his eye on the U. S. Congress. Harvey County was on the western edge of Kansas' 5th Congressional District at that time, a 25-county rural district in southeastern Kansas. In 1985 the incumbent Republican congressman, Robert Whittaker from Augusta, announced that he was considering leaving his position to run for the governor of the state. Enticed by the prospect of an open congressional seat, Benjamin geared up for a campaign in 1986–raising money, outlining policy positions and speeches, and drafting a biographical introduction and announcement of his candidacy. His three major issues would be "jobs, farm policy, and senior citizen concerns." He presented himself as a family man, married to Jean Hershey, a nurse clinician, and father of an adopted daughter and a one-year old son. Indicating how much he had been integrated into the Mennonite community, and perhaps to deflect concern about his Jewishness, the proposed brochure noted that "The family attends the Bethel College Mennonite Church."[5] On January 3, 1986, however, Congressman Whittaker announced that he was going to run for re-election after all. Benjamin promptly withdrew. He knew he could not come close to rivaling the incumbent's huge advantages of name recognition and campaign funding.

Four years later, in 1989, Whittaker definitively announced his retirement from Congress, and Benjamin once again geared up a professionally organized campaign. The open seat attracted four Democratic and six Republican candidates to the August primary. In 1990 Benjamin's issues included jobs, low taxes, national health

---

[5]"Announcement of Candidacy for Charles Benjamin, candidate for Congress in Kansas Fifth District, Jan 8, 1986," Charles Benjamin papers, MLA. Benjamin was a non-observant Jew who attended a Mennonite church, but was not a baptized member or active in congregational or denominational concerns.

care, campaign reform, and reduction of the federal deficit. He proposed to reduce the deficit by cutting money wasted in the defense budget. In addition to such scandals as $600 toilets, it was long past time, he said, for both Europe and Japan to pay for their own military defense rather than depending upon billions of dollars from the United States. Benjamin was an officer in the Wichita branch of the Freeze the Arms Race. To deflect potential criticism of his peace activism, he noted that both his parents were veterans of World War II and that he supported funding for veterans hospitals. The problem of his Jewish identity did not keep him from going to Kansas City to raise funds from the local Jewish community there. An article in *The Kansas City Jewish Chronicle* noted that some towns in the 5th district had been "hotbeds for such anti-Semitic groups as the Posse Comitatus and the Ku Klux Klan." Benjamin acknowledged to the writer that Jewishness could be a problem, but "I don't go around beating the drum, so to speak, about being Jewish but I also don't hide it. . . . I don't think it should make any difference."[6]

As it turned out, neither Benjamin's Jewishness nor his pacifism became open issues in the campaign. He was endorsed by the Kansas National Education Association and by the United Mine Workers. Geographic location was more relevant. As he campaigned in the southeastern counties of the district, he became aware that some voters saw him as too much associated with the city of Wichita, which was outside the district. Also, it was not helpful to be an academic from Bethel College. In the August primary Benjamin won in Marion, Butler, McPherson, and Harvey counties, but it was not enough to overcome his opponent George Wingert's advantage in the eastern counties. Wingert was an Ottawa rancher who had name recognition advantage from having served in the Kansas House of Representatives and on the Kansas Board of Regents. Wingert got 11,343 votes (32.7%), while Benjamin got 9,750 votes (28%) and two other candidates shared the rest.

---

[6] Ruth Baum Bigus, "Jewish man view for 5th District House seat," *The Kansas City Jewish Chronicle*, 8 June 1990.

Dick Nichols, a Republican banker from McPherson, won the general election over Wingert in November.

Even though he lost in his campaign for Congress, Benjamin's political career demonstrated that south-central Kansas was not necessarily as parochial and suspicious of outsiders as was commonly assumed. He made himself at home in his adopted community and promoted progressive peace values that were widely shared. Although he did not convert and become a member of the Mennonite church, his integration into the Mennonite world and its surrounding community gave him a special role in the history of Mennonite political acculturation. In 1992 Benjamin left Harvey County to take a position in Topeka as lobbyist with the Sierra Club and the Natural Resources Council. The family lived in Lawrence, where his wife, Jean Hershey, worked in Student Health Services at the University of Kansas.[7]

Donna Neufeld, Liberal Social Worker

Donna Neufeld's father, Menno Simons (M. S.) Kaufman, was named after the founder of the denomination. Her uncle Jacob "Jake" Kaufman, businessman in Moundridge and an active Democrat, in the 1970s used his political influence, at least according to family lore, to get two interstate highway exits for Moundridge on I-35. Donna graduated from Bethel College in 1955 with a major in music. By 1992 she had become a liberal feminist social worker and lived in North Newton with her husband Harry. They both had master's degrees in social work from Washington University in St. Louis. Donna was a member of NOW, the National Organization for

Donna Neufeld, Democratic candidate for the state legislature in 1992 and 1994

---

[7]Bill Wilson, "Longtime commissioner says goodbye," *Newton Kansan*, 18 December 1996, 1.

Women. She had worked at Menninger Foundation in Topeka and had taught in the social work department at Bethel College. During the 1991 "Summer of Mercy" in Wichita she had stood with others on a "Clinic Watch" to protect George Tiller's clinic from attack by anti-abortion protesters. There she met Colleen Kelly Johnston, a leader in the Wichita chapter of NOW. Johnston was a Democrat Party activist who recruited liberal Democratic candidates like Neufeld to run for office. Charles Benjamin also encouraged Neufeld to run.[8]

Neufeld won the August 1992 Democratic primary over Roberta "Bobby" Seger, Harvey County Democrat party chairman and longtime party activist in Harvey County and in state politics. In the November general election Neufeld faced Garry Boston, a one-term incumbent Republican legislator who headed an insurance business on Main Street in Newton. She came within 357 votes (47%) of winning, out of 9,517 total votes cast. Neufeld's remarkable success encouraged her to try again two years later, in 1994. Again she lost in a close race, but by a somewhat larger margin. The abortion issue hurt her more in 1994 than in 1992.

Even though she lost both times, Neufeld's relative success against apparently great odds demands explanation. Her disadvantages were formidable: The 72nd district had a strong majority of registered Republicans. Garry Boston, the Republican incumbent, was a mild- mannered affable businessman, popular on Main Street and with the Chamber of Commerce. He was what later would be called a "moderate" Republican, who listened to his constituents and voted against the death penalty. Neufeld lived in North Newton and was identified with Bethel College and its long history of town-gown tensions with the much larger town of Newton. She was a social worker, feminist, and pro-choice activist—all of which were potential disadvantages in conservative small-town Kansas. And she was Mennonite—identified with a people who were only 15% to 20% of the district and too divided among themselves on social issues to serve as a substantial political

---

[8]Donna and Harry Neufeld, interview by James Juhnke, North Newton, KS, 9 January 2013.

base. Duane Goossen, the Mennonite legislator that most Mennonites knew and trusted, publicly endorsed Garry Boston. How was Neufeld able to come close to upsetting the incumbent?

Neufeld was an attractive, articulate and entertaining person. She was 59 years old, but could have passed for 39. She ran an energetic campaign, together with her close friend and campaign director, Ruth Ann Hiebert. Neufeld and Hiebert not only went door to door throughout the district; they created a musical comedy routine consisting of old time mountain music and homely jokes that they performed at public events. She was a newcomer to politics, perhaps helped by her unintimidated political innocence. "I was naïve," she later said. "I barely knew who Garry Boston was, or the status of partisan registrations in the 72nd district."[9] Neufeld ran a more aggressive campaign than did Boston, who may have underestimated his opponent.

Neufeld in 1992 successfully branded herself as a mainstream candidate, rather than a feminist social worker. The vital issues, she said, were taxes, property assessment, education, health care and family life. Her brochure noted her role in "farm and rental management" and her membership in the Newton Chamber of Commerce and the Newton-North Newton Area Planning Commission. If anyone asked about abortion she said she was "pro-life, pro-family, and pro-choice."[10] She supported the U. S. Constitution (Roe v. Wade) and Kansas law. In her view, no new laws were needed. Neufeld's earlier involvement in the defense of the George Tiller clinic during the "Summer of Mercy" protests did not become an issue. Garry Boston, if he knew about Neufeld's radical activities and associations, did not raise them in his campaign.

Neufeld in 1992 also benefitted from a wider Democratic momentum. That year the Democrat Bill Clinton won the national presidency over the Republican incumbent George H. W. Bush, and the Democrat Joan Finney won the Kansas governorship over the Republican incumbent Mike Hayden. In 1992 the Democrats were

---

[9]Neufeld interview.
[10]Donna Neufeld handwritten campaign notes, n.d., Neufeld campaign file.

looking to expand their thin majority in Kansas House of Representatives. The state party helped Neufeld with money, on-site campaign strategy counsel, and a list of Boston's legislative votes that people in Newton would not like. After the election, Boston complained in a letter to the *Newton Kansan* that Neufeld's last-minute campaigning had unfairly taken his voting record out of context and highlighted "only one feature of a comprehensive bill."[11] Even in victory, Boston was on the defensive.

Two years later, in 1994, the political climate had shifted away from the Democrats to Neufeld's disadvantage. President Clinton's missteps (gays in the military, national health insurance, etc.) resulted in major Republican gains in the national Congress. Republicans increased their majorities in the Kansas House and Senate. Neufeld again ran an aggressive campaign. Her campaign literature called her "A Strong Active Voice"—in contrast with the more low-key incumbent. She wrote letters to fellow members of her Bethel College Mennonite Church, asking for campaign help and noting her Mennonite family credentials.[12] But in 1994 Neufeld had to struggle to maintain a mainstream image. She found herself increasingly on the defensive. In the face of anti-abortion criticism, she said, "I will represent people of District #72, not the Tiller Clinic."[13] The *Newton Kansan*, declining to endorse either candidate, summarized Neufeld's positions in somewhat critical terms: "She is pro-choice, against the death penalty, and believes more preventive programs would help society deal with a variety of ills, including crime, homelessness, hunger and broken families. . . . While Neufeld is compassionate and intelligent, we still are unsure whether she can temper her compassion with a good dose of economic reality."[14]

Despite her two defeats, Neufeld's remarkable showing demonstrated that Newton and Harvey County were not simple

---

[11]Garry Boston, "The Rest of the Story," letter to the editor of the *Newton Kansan*, 19 November 1992, 4.

[12]Donna Neufeld letter to "Dear Fellow Church Member," undated.

[13]Neufeld note to "Dear Discerning Voter," n.d., Neufeld campaign file.

[14]"The Newton Kansan 72nd District a tossup," *Newton Kansan*, 1 November 1994, 4.

conservative Republican strongholds. Virginia Iserhardt, a leading conservative Republican activist in Harvey County, later complained, "Harvey County is harder to work in than many other places in Kansas. This is not a conservative county. I don't know why."[15] Mennonites voters, most of whom (but by no means all) voted for Neufeld, were part of the progressive liberal fabric in the 72nd district and also part of the reason for Iserhardt's frustration.

Cedric Boehr, Insurgent from the Right

In 1994 Cedric Boehr, a conservative evangelical Christian and a member of the Emmaus Mennonite Church congregation in Butler County, registered to run for the Kansas 74th district House seat. The primary and general election campaigns made history. In the August Republican primary Boehr upset Ellen Samuelson, incumbent in the 74th House district. Then in the November general election Samuelson upset Boehr with a write-in campaign. The result was unprecedented not only among Mennonites but in Kansas political history. Never before had an incumbent Kansas legislator been re-elected to office despite having been defeated in the primary. The result apparently demonstrated, among other things, that conservative evangelicals were not in the majority among Kansas Mennonites in the 74th district.[16]

Boehr campaign ad

Cedric Boehr and his wife, Sandi, like Donna Neufeld, had participated in the 1991 "Summer of Mercy" demonstrations in Wichita—but on the opposite side from Donna Neufeld. The Boehrs were passionate opponents of abortion. Boehr's family had deep roots in the conservative evangelical wing of the Mennonite

---

[15]Virginia "Jinny" Iserhardt, interview with the author, 23 September 2003.
[16]James C. Juhnke, "Moderates, Mennonites, and the Religious Right, A Hot Contest in the Seventy-fourth House District, 1994," *Kansas History* (Autumn 2004): 180-93.

denomination. Cedric's grandfather had been a missionary in China. His father taught music at Grace Bible Institute in Omaha, Nebraska, a school founded in 1942 as a conservative evangelical alternative to Bethel College. After their marriage in 1977, Cedric and Sandi's movements included a four-year term for Cedric in the U.S. Navy. They moved to Kansas in 1991 and quickly became involved in conservative Christian social causes. In behalf of religious foundations for their three children, Cedric and Sandi chose home schooling over public schooling.

The 74th House district consisted of twenty-four small-town rural townships in McPherson, Harvey and Butler counties. The district surrounded the city of Newton. There were twenty-six active Mennonite congregations in the district, and some people from the district attended Mennonite congregations in Newton. This number of Mennonites in the district—estimated at twenty-five to thirty percent—was greater than in any other Kansas legislative district.

Ellen Samuelson, the 74th district Republican incumbent, had served three terms in the Kansas House. She was so popular that the dispirited Democrats in 1994 did not even bother to field a candidate to oppose her. She had Mennonite credentials and associations. Although she was a member of a Methodist church, her grandparents (named Banman) had belonged to the First Mennonite Church of Hillsboro. She was a home economics teacher and had taught at both Hesston College and Bethel College. Her husband, Armin, was well known among Mennonites through work as a 4-H extension agent and as a development officer at Prairie View Mental Health Center. In the legislature Ellen served on the Education Committee, the Public Health and Welfare Committee, and as chairman of the Joint Committee on Children and Families.

In the August primary of 1994, Cedric Boehr and his wife, who served as campaign director and was more articulate and dynamic than her husband, chose to run what they called a "sleeper campaign." They avoided publicity and quietly visited the homes of every registered Republican in the district. They found supporters in the towns of Moundridge, Hesston and Sedgwick. The Grace Community Church south of Newton and the Garden

Church south of Moundridge were conservative evangelical congregations inclined to support Boehr's platform. In the final days of the campaign Boehr invested in an advertising push on the abortion issue. Samuelson complained that the portrayal of her position was unfair, and that it was too late for her to respond. Boehr's strategy worked to perfection. Some of Samuelson's friends, confident of her victory, did not bother to vote. The voter turnout was low, an advantage to Boehr's highly motivated supporters. He won by a margin of 107 votes. In the conservative wave of that Republican primary, religious conservatives in Harvey County elected enough precinct committeemen and women, some of whom were conservative Mennonites never before involved in politics, to wrest control from the moderates, who had long been in power. Virginia Iserhardt, who said she "worked my tail off" for Boehr, in the post-primary party meeting was elected chairperson of Republican Party in Harvey County. Sandi Boehr was elected chairperson of the Republican Party in Butler County.[17]

Shocked by Samuelson's loss in the primary, her supporters urged her to run a write-in campaign for the general election. It was an advantage for her that the Democrats did not have a candidate on the ballot. Oswald Goering, a Democrat from Moundridge who contributed money to Samuelson's campaign, joked in a letter to the editor that he had asked Ellen "to cash the check after dark as I did not want my Democrat friends to know that I was supporting a Republican."[18] Other letter writers identified themselves as "Democrat for Samuelson." John Waltner, the Democratic mayor of Hesston, served as Samuelson's campaign co-chairman, along with Vernon Nikkel, a Republican businessman. Waltner was a member of the Bethel College Mennonite Church in North Newton and Nikkel was a former Mennonite who had joined the United Methodist Church in Hesston.

---

[17]Juhnke, "Moderates," 187.

[18]Oswald and Elaine Goering, letter to the editor, *Harvey County Independent* (Halstead), 24 August 1994; Samuelson campaign clipping notebook, private collection of Ellen Samuelson, Newton, KS.

Cedric Boehr was a true believer, a man of conviction who said what he believed and refused to moderate his stand on any issue in order to get elected. Early in the campaign he spoke about integrity. Before the primary election, Samuelson had signed the standard Republican Party pledge to support the winner of the primary. Then she reneged on that promise. For his part, Boehr had refused to sign the pledge, knowing he would never support someone who disagreed with his core values. He put the issue of abortion front and center, but he also advocated a radical reform of school finance. He proposed that the state provide tax credits for people who schooled their children at home. He also called for an end to state aid for public schools. Let each local board of education decide on its own, he said, how to offset the loss of state aid. The Samuelson campaign warned that Boehr's proposal would result in a catastrophic depletion of local school budgets—from sixty-nine percent in Moundridge to eighty-four percent in Sedgwick.[19]

A key turning point early in the campaign had little to do with policy issues. Before the primary election the Grace Hill Mennonite Church, seven miles east of Newton, had invited Samuelson to speak to a combined Sunday School class. After Samuelson's decision to run a write-in campaign, Sandi Boehr contacted a Grace Hill church leader and asked that Cedric also be invited to speak lest the congregation lose its tax-exempt status. Sandi denied that she had made a threat about the congregation's tax exemption, but Doug Anstaett, a moderate Republican and editor of the *Newton Kansan*, got wind of the issue and used it to take sides and discredit the Boehr campaign.[20]

The Boehr-Samuelson battle generated an unprecedented blizzard of letters to editors of newspapers inside and outside the district. About half the letters were written by Mennonites, and they were on both sides. The editor of the *Ledger*, a weekly paper serving Buhler, Inman and Moundridge, reported receiving seventy letters, far more than could be printed. The city of Wichita

---

[19]Juhnke, "Moderates," 190.
[20]Doug Anstaett, "Church had a right to hear who it had invited," *Newton Kansan*, 17 August 1994.

was outside the 74th district, but the *Wichita Eagle* published more letters for and against Boehr and Samuelson than it did for any of the legislative districts in the city. Abortion was the most frequent topic. Kirsten Kliewer identified Samuelson with George Tiller's clinic: "Ellen Samuelson is endorsed by our state's most liberal pro-abortion group, Pro-Choice Action League. This group is the personal lobbying arm of George Tiller's late term abortion business."[21] At issue was Samuelson's vote to support House Bill #2778, a measure that did not satisfy the pro-life lobby. Adolf Neufeld of Inman, supporting Samuelson, wrote that the intent of that vote was to limit abortions. "Many of us would have liked a bill restricting abortion even more but this was a lot better than no control at all which was what we had before."[22] Both candidates complained that their opponents were distorting their record and positions.

In joining the navy, Cedric Boehr had deviated from the official Mennonite denominational position of opposition to military service. But the anti-Boehr Mennonites could not use military service as a negative issue in an American political campaign, so they neglected to raise that topic in public. When Boehr's campaign literature claimed that he was a "veteran of the Gulf War," he left an opening for criticism. He had been in the navy during the Persian Gulf War of 1991 but not in a combat zone. One Boehr opponent, himself a World War II veteran, found Boehr's claim "reprehensible" and "extremely disgusting."[23]

The voter turnout in the hotly contested general election was high–71% of registered voters. Samuelson won with 4,118 votes (54%) to Boehr's 3,435 (46%). Cedric and Sandi Boehr, as surprised and disappointed as Samuelson had been in the primary, charged election fraud. They said that some election officials had helped voters write Samuelson's name on the ballot, that some people campaigned at the polling places, and that some people voted more than once. They thought they could have had the result overturned

---

[21]*Harvey County Independent,* 29 September 1994.
[22]*Newton Kansan,* 3 November 1994.
[23]Undated clipping from the *McPherson Sentinel,* Samuelson campaign clippings notebook.

if they had taken the issue to court. In 1998 they left the Republican Party and joined the U.S.Taxpayers Party, which in 1999 changed its name to the Constitution Party. Cedric Boehr became the state chairman of that party. In 1998 both Cedric and Sandi ran for statewide office with the Constitution Party, with no hope of winning.

A tally of votes in the 74th district shows that neither candidate dominated a particular region of the district. Boehr and Samuelson both got majorities in some townships of all three counties—McPherson, Harvey and Butler. The final result demonstrated that Mennonite conservative evangelicals were a minority concentrated in a few congregations—Emmaus and the Swiss Church of Whitewater, the Garden Township and the Hopefield churches south and west of Moundridge, and the Grace Community Church south of Newton. These congregations were on the margins of the Mennonite denominational mainstream. Most Mennonite congregations in the region, however, were led by folk who had gotten Christian liberal arts education at their denominational colleges, Bethel College and Hesston College. Samuelson had lived and worked in the district for several decades. Although she was not a member of a Mennonite congregation, she was probably known by more Mennonites than was Boehr, a relative newcomer to the district. In any case, Boehr's victory in the primary demonstrated that citizens who held views normally considered "moderate" or "progressive" in Kansas may have been part of a majority establishment, but that they were vulnerable to challenges from a rising and dissenting conservative evangelical religious right.

Eric Yost, Marginal Mennonite

Eric R. Yost, member of the Lorraine Avenue Mennonite Church in Wichita, in 1990 and 1992 challenged the long term fourth district U.S. Congressman,

Eric Yost of Wichita, Republican candidate for the US House of Representatives in 1990 and 1992

Democrat Dan Glickman, who had first been elected in 1976. Yost lost both times, but he got more votes than most Republicans who had run against Glickman. Yost had grown up in a nominally Methodist family, "mainly an Easter-and-Christmas churchgoer."[24] In 1981 he married Teresa Penner, a Mennonite who had grown up in Burrton and who had graduated from Bethel College. They joined the Lorraine Avenue Church and attended worship there regularly.

Already before marriage Yost had become an active politician. He graduated from Wichita State University in 1977 and, the following year, at age twenty-three, was elected to the Kansas House of Representatives. He served two terms in the House, then went to law school and in 1984 was elected for the first of two terms in the Kansas Senate. He worked for the law firm of Triplett, Woolf and Garretson. At the time of his races with Glickman he was the Senate vice-president.

Yost was a conservative Republican. His platform in 1990 included reduction of the federal debt, with cuts to Social Security and to welfare programs. He supported tax breaks for private school parents, and prayer in public schools. Yost admitted that he was "more hawkish" than most Mennonites on military defense issues. Jesus' teachings of love for the enemy, he said, applied to personal life—not to national policy. Yost supported the Strategic Defense Initiative ("Star Wars") and opposed the Peace Tax Fund bill, a measure strongly advocated by Mennonites and endorsed by Glickman, the Democratic incumbent.[25]

On national health care, however, Yost took a moderate position that in later years would be considered anathema on the Republican right. He favored the "Basicareplan," a proposal by Nancy Kassebaum, a moderate Republican Senator. That plan would have required insurance companies to offer basic coverage to everyone, regardless of age, health, or ability to pay.

---

[24]Donald Williams, "Challenger Yost strives for magical balance," *Wichita Eagle*, 1 November 1990, 5B.
[25]Rich Preheim, "Mennonite Politicians May Face Challenges When They Take Beliefs into Politics," *Mennonite Weekly Review*, 29 October 1992, 1-2.

In his 1992 campaign, after the "Summer of Mercy" had put abortion at the top of political agenda, Yost became a strong pro-life candidate. He attempted to mobilize religious support by speaking to conservative churches and to pastors' groups about his opposition to abortion. Glickman, the incumbent, acknowledged that he was pro-choice, but said that government should "stay out of his relationship with God and moral decisions."[26] Yost also attacked Glickman for having written 105 bad checks in the U.S. House bank scandal, and for supporting the regulation of cable company rates. Yost's challenge to Glickman was a strong one, perhaps weakening the incumbent who lost two years later to Todd Tiahrt. (Tiahrt was not a Mennonite, but he had remote Mennonite ancestors and he consistently reminded Mennonite audiences of that connection.)

While Yost was aggressively courting the votes of conservative churches in Wichita, he was not invited to speak at his own congregation, the Lorraine Avenue Mennonite Church. Church members there were divided on the abortion issue, but most of them probably leaned toward a pro-choice position. Don Steelberg, the pastor, did not address the abortion issue from the pulpit but members knew that he and his wife, Elsie, were pro-choice. Eric and Teresa Yost increasingly felt marginal to the congregation. They eventually stopped attending the Mennonite church and changed their membership to the Eastminster Presbyterian Church, where the more conservative theological and social atmosphere was more congenial to their interests. Eric Yost's sojourn with the Mennonites had been temporary. His departure was another indication that Mennonites, especially in urban congregations, did not fit easily in the camp of the emerging Republican right.

Don Klassen, Reform Party

In 1996 Donald R. Klassen, a member of the Lorraine Avenue Mennonite Church in Wichita, ran on the Reform Party ticket for an

---

[26]Robert Wuthnow, *Red State Religion, Faith and Politics in America's Heartland* (Princeton: Princeton University Press, 2012), 299.

open seat in the U. S. Senate. The Reform Party was identified with Ross Perot, presidential candidate who had gotten 19% of the national vote in 1992, running against Bill Clinton and George H. W. Bush. Klassen was a businessman with Pizza Hut, Inc., and became a founding member and organizer of the Reform Party in Kansas. The open Senate seat had been vacated by Bob Dole in order to challenge President Bill Clinton, who was running for a second term. Klassen expected Perot in 1996 to sweep the election for the U.S. presidency. It was, he and other party members believed, an opportune time to ride into political office on Perot's coat tails.

Donald Klassen of Wichita, Reform Party candidate for the US Senate in 1996

Klassen and the Reform Party were primarily concerned about business and economics issues. They avoided social issues such as abortion, believing that government should not attempt to legislate morality. Trade policy was a top priority. The Reform Party platform called for major increases in tariff rates ("America for Americans") and reduction of the income tax. They advocated closing military bases in Japan and Germany as a business cost-saving measure. They proposed major fees ($50,000 to $100,000) for immigrants to America to become citizens.

The 1996 campaign proved a great disappointment for Klassen and the Reform Party. In his view, the Republicans and Democrats teamed up to freeze out the Reform Party's access to media outlets. Perot got just 8% of the presidential vote. Klassen got only 2.8% of the vote in his race for the Senate. Sam Brownback, the Republican candidate, won the vacant seat with 53.9% of the vote. Klassen was disillusioned. He had invested nine months of his life and $15,000 of his personal wealth to establish the Reform Party of Kansas and to run for the U. S. Senate. And there was nothing to show for it. He was never tempted to run for office again.

Klassen had a more cordial relationship with the Lorraine Avenue Mennonite Church than did his fellow church member,

Eric Yost. One church member, Ed Peters, helped with great success to get signatures for the Reform Party petition drive for legal recognition in Kansas. Dan Bergen, earlier Lorraine member, did Don's official photo for the campaign. Peter Bartel offered to organize a meeting at the church for Don, but the candidate declined because he "did not want to make this a religious candidacy." Klassen strongly believed in separation of church and state. He saw his political platform as exclusively secular, not an expression of spiritual values. In this regard he was different from other Kansas Mennonites in politics.

Robert E. Krehbiel, Attorney Rancher

In 1988 Robert E. Krehbiel, a 42 year old Democratic attorney and rancher from Pretty Prairie, was elected to the state legislature from the 101st district in Reno County, the same position held from 1968 to 1976 by his mentor Walter W. "Sprig" Graber. Like Graber, Krehbiel was a member of the First Mennonite Church of Pretty Prairie. Graber served as treasurer for Krehbiel's campaign. The two men shared a populist-oriented interest and expertise in budget and financial matters. In his first campaign, Krehbiel accused his opponent, incumbent Republican Robert Wunsch of Kingman, with being controlled by the insurance industry.

One theme of Krehbiel's five terms in the legislature was his defense of the interests of small-town and rural Kansans against the domination of urban eastern Kansas, especially Johnson County. "I was sent to Topeka," he wrote in 1992, "by the people of Reno County to lower property taxes and reduce government intervention in our lives and business." As a member of the Assessment and Taxation Committee, he helped craft a new funding method for public education that "shifted some of the property tax burden to sales and income tax on very high incomes, giving a much fairer and balanced tax policy for Kansas."[27]

---

[27]Robert E. "Bob" Krehbiel, "Krehbiel wants to set his voting record straight," *The Hutchinson News*, 6 October 1994.

Krehbiel opposed capital punishment, but took strong positions against crime. To critics who accused him of being soft on crime he wrote, "I believe very strongly that murderers should never leave prison except in a pine box and that other violent criminals must not be paroled before serving their time."[28] The issue of abortion complicated Krehbiel's later campaigns. His basic position, consistent with his general opposition to government intervention, was that abortion was an issue to be dealt with by churches and families, not by state government. In the 1994 campaign he said his pro-life opponent, Steve Graber, who believed "that women with problem pregnancies should die trying to give birth and that state law should require them to do so." In his last term in the legislature, the spring of 1998, Krehbiel voted against a controversial bill, eventually signed into law by Governor Bill Graves, that placed further restrictions on women's abortion rights.[29]

The Hutchinson News editors supported Krehbiel with campaign endorsements. In the 1996 *News* editors described him as a "conservative Democrat," who helped "lead the charge during the last legislative session against conservative House Republicans, whom he accused of trying to dismantle the state's school system." In the editors' view, "Krehbiel has been a consistent defender of education during his eight years in the House."[30] Krehbiel retired from the Legislature in 1998.

Jerry Moran, Temporary Mennonite

In 1996 Jerry Moran of Hays, Kansas, was elected as a Republican to the U.S. House of Representatives. Moran had been raised in a Quaker family, then moved to town where he became a Methodist. In 1992 or 1993, when he was serving in the Kansas State Senate, he

---

[28] Robert E. "Bob" Krehbiel, "Krehbiel sets the record straight," *The Hutchinson News*, 5 November 1994, 4.

[29] "Graves signs controversial abortion law," *The Hutchinson News*, 28 April 1998, A1. Dwight Jurgens, "Reactions—like the abortion issue—divided," *The Hutchinson News*, 28 April 28 1998), A2.

[30] *The Hutchinson News*, 25 October 1996, 4.

and his wife, Robba, had joined the North Oak Community Church in Hays. That congregation did not have "Mennonite" in its name, but it officially belonged to the Mennonite Brethren Southern District conference. The denominational identity at North Oak was far in the background.

Some Mennonites were eager to claim Moran as one of their own. A front page article in *The Mennonite Weekly Review* acclaimed Moran as the first Mennonite to be elected to Congress since Edward Clayton Eicher, a Democrat from Iowa who served three terms in the 1930s.[31] But was Moran really a Mennonite? When he moved to Washington, D.C. he kept his Mennonite identity hidden. Congressional information sources, presumably informed by Moran's office, listed him as a Methodist.[32] "I've tried to describe myself more as a Christian instead of as a Mennonite," he said. The Mennonite label could be a problem when people identified it with horse-and-buggy separatism.[33]

However, when Moran visited the predominantly Mennonite small towns in his district, he made use of his Mennonite connection. At the Crusader Café in Buhler in 1997, someone asked him about military budget cuts. "Ah, the Mennonite perspective," he said as the audience laughed. "I'm a Mennonite, so I know our perspective." He told the folks that he opposed cutting the defense budget. With the Cold War over, Russia was no longer a threat, but "China is around the corner." That, of course, was not a preferred "Mennonite" answer. But Moran did reach out to this audience by favoring the Peace Tax Fund bill to allow conscientious objectors to pay all their taxes for non-military purposes.[34] Later, for a retirement-home fundraiser in Buhler, Moran donated to the highest bidder an invitation to have a meal with his family in Hays. Jesse Harder, leader in the Buhler Mennonite Brethren Church and

---

[31]Rich Prehcim, "Kansas MB Wins Election to Congress," *Mennonite Weekly Review*, 7 November 1996, 1.

[32]J. Daryl Byler, email message, 30 Aug 1999.

[33]Robert Rhodes, "Kansas MB re-elected to 5th term in Congress," *Mennonite Weekly Review*, 8 November 2004, 1, 3.

[34]Paul Schrag, "Listening to the People, MB Congressman Supports Peace Tax Fund, Strong Defense," *Mennonite Weekly Review*, 28 August 1997, 1.

former Democrat member of the Kansas House of Representatives, bought the meal and had a wonderful cross-party time with Moran in Hays.[35]

After Moran was elected to the U.S. Senate in 2012, he and his wife, Robba, moved from Hays to Manhattan. They left the North Oak Community Church in Hays, and did not join the Mennonite Church in Manhattan. His status as a Mennonite politician slipped away.

---

[35]Jesse Harder, interview by author, 13 November 2009, Buhler, KS.

Chapter 12

Activity Church

In the half-century after World War II the Kansas Mennonites increasingly became what may be called an "activity church." They were not alone in this trend. Robert Wuthnow, in his book on faith and politics in Kansas, suggested that the public school consolidation movement, together with "better cars, fewer people doing farm chores, an improved economy, and children in the home" prompted small town churches in the post-war era to begin new activities. Churches went beyond their traditional worship services, Sunday school classes, and prayer meetings or revival services. In Kansas' small towns, including those with substantial Mennonite population (Buhler, Inman, Hesston, Moundridge, Goessel, Hillsboro), Protestant congregations competed with the schools by organizing youth groups and sports teams, by hosting guest lectures and community-wide meetings, and by cooperating with local ministerial alliances that sponsored special events. Wuthnow says the "activity church" fit well with the "quiet conservatism" that Dwight D. Eisenhower, a Kansan in the White House, represented in those years.[1]

The Anabaptist-Mennonite tradition had long linked Christian doctrine and worship to daily life in community. Cornelius H. Wedel, president of Bethel College, pointed to the Mennonite heritage of communal discipleship as "a model experiment in so-called social Christianity."[2] This heritage had been extended during and after World War I in a remarkable surge of benevolent activity. Mennonites who had been scorned for their lack of patriotism undertook programs of generous giving that met their need for a pacifist moral equivalent for military service. A new Mennonite Central Committee, created in 1920, became the primary inter-Mennonite agency for this overseas and domestic benevolent work. This surge of denominational institutional activity extended

---

[1] Robert Wuthnow, *Red State Religion*, 189.
[2] C. H. Wedel, *Geleitworte an junge Christen* (Newton, KS: Schulverlag von Bethel College, 1912), 33-4.

beyond Wuthnow's definition of "activity church," but was related to the same dynamic.[3]

After World War II Mennonites in Kansas and elsewhere created a host of new inter-Mennonite voluntary associations that brought together members of the separate groups in cooperative activities. Many of these were outgrowths of World War II Civilian Public Service–a well-organized activity that spawned dozens of additional well-organized activities. By one account, sixty-nine inter-Mennonite agencies, associations, and voluntary societies were created between 1941 and 1974.[4] This organizational flowering marked an important stage in Mennonite Americanization. Over time the new organizations established relationships with the public arena, often taking advantage of government funding for social services. Government funding had implications for organizational mission and for the agency's relationship with the founding churches or denomination.

Notable in Kansas was Mennonite Disaster Service (MDS) which began in 1950-1 when a group of laymen from Hesston organized to provide disaster relief to victims of tornados, floods, and other problems.[5] Other churches in Kansas and beyond picked up the idea so quickly that by 1954 a national Disaster Service Coordinating Committee was put in place. In the public mind Mennonites became known for cleaning up after tornados as much as for refusing military service. The nationwide work of MDS led it into a partnership agreement with the Federal Emergency Management Agency (FEMA). The Disaster Relief Act of 1974 listed MDS along with the Red Cross and Salvation Army as agencies that agreed "to operate under the advice or direction" of the FEMA federal coordinating officer.[6] MDS and other Mennonite church

---

[3] James C. Juhnke, *Vision, Doctrine, War*. James C. Juhnke, "Mennonite Benevolence and Civic Identity: The Post-War Compromise," *Mennonite Life* (January 1970): 34-7.

[4] Paul Toews, *Mennonites in American Society*, 268.

[5] Lowell Detweiler, *The Hammer Rings Hope: Photos and Stories from Fifty Years of Mennonite Disaster Service* (Scottdale, Pa: Herald Press, 2000), 19-23.

[6] Disaster Relief Act of 1974, http://www.hsdl.org/?view&did=458661 Thanks to John Pannabecker for this reference.

activity agencies brought both renewal within denominational circles and unprecedented relationships with the outside world.

Kansas Mennonite colleges in North Newton, Hesston, and Hillsboro, and hospitals in Newton, Hillsboro, and Goessel had been founded before World War II. After the war new retirement homes for the elderly sprouted up in all the central Kansas "Mennonite" small towns. New inter-Mennonite voluntary agencies were founded in the fields of mass media (Mennonite Publishers Fellowship, 1960), wealth management (Mennonite Foundation, 1953), recreation (Mennonite Camping Association, 1960), professional associations (Mennonite Medical Association, 1948), and benevolence (Mennonite Relief sales, in Hutchinson, 1968), Offender-Victim Ministries (1986), and more. Common work in private associations and agencies tended to hold different kinds of Mennonites together despite their differences in church theology and polity.

Mennonite agencies and associations brought Mennonites into public life in new ways. In some cases, such as Mennonite Disaster Service, the agencies remained strictly private. In other cases they took advantage of available public funding to grow in ways that met their mission goals. But the acceptance of government funds raised questions about independence and self-control. At what point did a Mennonite institution become so separate from the churches and so dominated by outside funding and by non-Mennonite administration and staff that it was no longer a Mennonite agency? The experiences of Kansas Mennonite agencies in the fields of higher education, mental health, and public housing illustrate alternative courses of Mennonite institutional development in the context of the American welfare state democracy.

Government Aid for Education

The three Mennonite colleges in Kansas all chose not to become private sectarian Bible colleges. They rather became liberal arts colleges with programs accredited first by state, and later by national, education agencies. Bethel, Hesston (two-year junior college), and Tabor were accredited by the regional North Central Association respectively in 1938, 1964, and 1965. The G.I. Bill of 1944 provided educational benefits for returning World War II veterans, a few of whom attended Mennonite colleges. In 1963 the federal government passed a Higher Education Facilities Act, followed in 1965 by another Higher Education Act. The new laws provided funding for dormitory and library facilities as well as scholarships and low-interest loans for students. The three colleges all applied for and received federal funds. Bethel expanded the men's and women's dormitories; Hesston built a new library; and Tabor built a new "cafeteria" building–all with substantial federal funds.

The federal funds came on favorable terms. Bethel was able to cover its new debt by student rents at the rate of 3½% per year over forty years. The Bethel board and faculty did not protest the new relationship with government.[7] The Hesston board, more inclined toward traditional doctrines of separation from the world, was more suspicious. President Tilman Smith, who had had an earlier career as a public school administrator, made the case for government funding: "The federal government is not a monster. We are citizens and it is our government." Moreover, refusal of federal funding would put Hesston at a competitive disadvantage: "We have no right to stand by and watch Christian education . . . being priced out of the market."[8] In the 1980s Hesston received a Title IV grant with funding from the USAID of the State Department to participate in a program to educate poor foreign students and promote international understanding.[9]

Some members of the Tabor College board also expressed fears that federal aid would mean federal control.[10] But pressures to take advantage of federal funding were irresistible. As members of the

---

[7] Keith Sprunger, *Bethel College of Kansas 1887-2012* (North Newton: Bethel College, 2012), 149-50.
[8] John E. Sharp, *School on the Prairie*, 281.
[9] Sharp, *School on the Prairie*, 362.
[10] Lynn Jost, "A Time of Stability and Growth (1956-1980)," 95-140 in *Tabor College: A Century of Transformation*, 95-140. Wilmer Harms, interview by James Juhnke, North Newton, KS, 19 June 2014.

Associated Colleges of Central Kansas, Tabor and Bethel received benefits from funding under Title III of the Higher Education Act to fund joint academic programs, library services, faculty development, and other programs.

The Mennonite colleges did not necessarily lose independence in significant ways because of strings attached to the federal aid. They were required to carefully account for the use of funds–an addition to administrative bureaucracy. But the colleges did not face federal government pressure regarding curriculum or free expression of ideas. At the state level, however, a different story unfolded. In 1972 Kansas adopted a program of tuition grants to private college students who were residents of the state. Church-related colleges were eligible to participate as long as they were not "sectarian"–a distinction that needed definition. The grants went directly to the students–not to the colleges–which protected the program against charges of state aid to religious institutions. The amount of the grants was based on need–up to $1,000, raised to $1,200 in 1978. The Mennonite colleges, as other private schools in the state, benefitted from the tuition grant program in the recruitment of students.[11]

A court challenge to the Kansas tuition grant program forced some changes in actual programs at the Mennonite colleges. Americans United for Separation of Church and State brought suit to challenge the program on the grounds that it violated the U.S. constitution's first amendment requirement of separation of church and state. In February 1974 a panel of federal judges in Wichita ruled against Americans United and held the tuition grant program constitutional. However, the ruling said that five Kansas colleges, including all three Mennonite schools, were not eligible because they required specific sectarian religious practices for graduation. (The other two were Sterling and St. John's.) At Tabor and Hesston the issue was religious chapel attendance. At Bethel it was a required senior oral comprehensive examination. The judges' decision was based solely on a reading of the colleges' catalogs, not

---

[11]For the tuition grant story see Sprunger, *Bethel College*, 175-6; Sharp, *School on the Prairie*, 322-3; and Juhnke, *Small Steps*, 118-9.

upon evidence of actual practice. Bethel administrators and faculty believed the judges had misread the catalog requirement. But the prospect of a legal appeal by Bethel was not attractive. The Kansas private colleges in general had won their case, and were not inclined to join Bethel in a challenge to part of a court ruling that had upheld the tuition grant program.

Why had the federal court judges chosen to discipline the Mennonite colleges? Some Mennonites noted that one of the three judges, Wesley Brown, three years earlier (April 1971) had been the judge in the trial of Dennis Koehn for refusing to register for the draft. Brown's rigorous examination of Mennonite leaders on that occasion had led the attorney for the defense to wonder if "the Mennonite Church itself might be on trial here this morning."[12] Now in the tuition grant case Judge Brown singled out Bethel College for its rigid "adherence to sectarian dogmas." Brown claimed to have knowledge of, and respect for, the Mennonites. It was not a great leap to conclude that his negative view of Mennonite pacifism was in the background of his tuition grant decision.

The Mennonite colleges all changed their programs to meet the court's requirements and to remain eligible for state tuition grants. The debate over the changes was most intense at Bethel, where some faculty considered the changes to be an unwarranted compromise with a domineering state. Hesston and Tabor continued to require attendance at all-school convocations, but changed the chapel attendance policy so that students intent upon avoiding religious indoctrination could skip all the religious "chapel" gatherings and still meet the graduation requirement. In 1995 Bethel reintroduced the senior oral comprehensive examination by folding it into the requirements of a new course for seniors–Basic Issues of Faith and Life.[13] The tuition grant court case of 1974 had been a dramatic test of separation of church and state.

---

[12]Transcript of Trial Proceedings 15 April 1971 in United States District Court for the District of Kansas, folder 3, 34, Dennis Koehn papers, MS.137, MLA.

[13]Sprunger, *Bethel College*, 199.

But it had not fundamentally changed the mission or the practices of the Mennonite colleges.

Government Aid for Mental Health

Mennonites traditionally cared for mentally ill people in their home families and communities. Over the decades in Kansas, Mennonites began to take advantage of state-provided mental health institutions that would accept mentally ill people who were too great a burden for private home care. Some Mennonites believed they should not be so dependent upon the state and proposed to create an institution of their own for care of the mentally ill. In 1937 a church committee led by C. E. Krehbiel and H. J. Dyck investigated possibilities. They reported that "a large number of our Mennonite people" were among the mental patients at the state hospitals at Larned, Topeka, and Ossawatomie. Dyck reported that Mennonites were reluctant to place their people in state institutions, in part because it discredited or embarrassed the family and in part because of potential negative influences from different persons there. Mennonites in the Ukraine in 1910 had established a mental health institution in the Chortitza district, but it had closed in 1927 because of the disruptions of World War I and the Communist Revolution. Immigrants from the Ukraine to Canada in the early 1920s had created a mental health institution in Ontario. The committee in Kansas visited mental hospitals and conducted a survey of General Conference Mennonite churches throughout North America. But they were unable to establish a new mental hospital before being diverted by World War II.[14]

The wartime experience of Mennonite conscientious objectors in state mental hospitals generated a new movement for Mennonite activity in mental health care. Robert Kreider, who in January 1944 at age twenty-five had become the director of the MCC-CPS hospital section, became convinced that "the most lasting contribution of CPS" would be in the field of mental health. That

---

[14]Miscellaneous papers, folder 90, C. E. Krehbiel papers, MS.11, MLA. A. J. Dyck, "Eine Anstalt für Nerven-und Geisteskranke," *Christlicher Bundesbote*, 8 June 1937.

expectation came true in two ways. First was the impact of CPS worker reports that exposed the shocking inhumane treatment of mentally ill people in many state hospitals.[15] Popular articles such as "BEDLAM 1946" in *Life* magazine, based on information from CPS workers, raised the public's consciousness about mental health care and contributed to reform efforts.[16]

A second contribution of CPS was the movement to build mental hospitals and treatment centers in states with a substantial Mennonite population. By 1966 the Mennonites had established six mental health facilities in five states from Maryland to California–a remarkable display of institutional activity by a small rural denomination. At the outset Mennonites had no professionally trained and accredited psychiatrists of their own available for leadership.[17] But the CPS-generated movement to establish mental health institutions had inexorable momentum. In Kansas the new mental hospital opened in 1954. It was located just east of Newton and named Prairie View. In 1957 Elmer Ediger, who had gone to Mennonite Biblical Seminary in Chicago after CPS, and then (1951) moved to Newton to take a position as executive secretary of the General Conference Mennonite Board of Christian Service, became administrator of Prairie View.[18]

Under Ediger's leadership, the ministries of Prairie View extended far beyond the pre-war dreams of C. E. Krehbiel and of the supporting Mennonite groups represented on the local Prairie View board. Government legislation and funding prompted the new directions. In 1961 the Kansas legislature passed a Community Health Law, and in 1963 the federal government passed a Community Mental Health Center Act. Mennonites, traditionally more involved with practical work on the ground than with

---

[15] Alex Sareyan, *The Turning Point: How Men of Conscience Brought About Major Change in the Care of America's Mentally Ill* (Washington, D.C.: American Psychiatric Press, 1994), 189-206.

[16] Albert Q. Maisel, "BEDLAM 1946," *Life*, May 6, 1946, 102-18.

[17] Robert S. Kreider, *My Early Years*, 390-2.

[18] On the general history of Prairie View see "Eyewitness to Prairie View History, 1954-1984," a videodisk documentary of interviews with former employees compiled by Merrill Raber.

political lobbying in the state and federal capitals, were not involved with the proposing and passing of this legislation. But they moved decisively to take advantage of government program recommendations and government funding–county, state, and federal. Prairie View shifted from being primarily a voluntary service oriented mental hospital for Mennonites to becoming a provider of professional diversified mental health care for the wider community. Ediger later confessed that the flowering of the community mental health emphasis "was clearly dependent upon public funds becoming available from the counties beginning in 1963, the federal government in 1966, and the state in 1975."[19]

The shift to wider visions and programs of community mental health (while continuing the original private hospital) was consistent with Prairie View's mission. Early in his administration Ediger anticipated the community mental health emphasis that soon became a popular nationwide movement. He and his medical director met with caretakers in the community–physicians, ministers, county welfare directors–to assess possibilities for Prairie View to meet community needs. When the Kansas legislature in 1961 passed a law allowing counties to contract with local nonprofit agencies for local health care services, Prairie View was well positioned to get government officials in the three counties with substantial Mennonite population–Harvey, McPherson, and Marion–to choose Prairie View as their provider of mental health services. Prairie View was on the way to becoming a "Comprehensive" Center with a high goal of "making the whole community therapeutic." The community served was not limited to Mennonite church members but extended to the wider public. And the burgeoning staff was made up increasingly of non-Mennonites.[20]

The movement beyond the Mennonite base was met with skepticism and resistance by some leaders in the original sponsoring churches. One issue was the church's ideal of voluntary

---

[19]Elmer M. Ediger, "Prairie View Newton, Kansas," in *If We Can Love: The Mennonite Mental Health Story*, ed. by Vernon H. Neufeld (Newton, KS: Faith and Life Press, 1983), 133.

[20]Ediger, "Prairie View," 134-5.

service that expected workers to subsist on minimal wages. That ideal was not compatible with the requirements of competitive wages for qualified staff. Another issue was the increasing role of non-Mennonites on the Prairie View staff. Bill Juhnke, by then a farmer and teacher in McPherson County and a generous contributor to the fund drive for the original Prairie View hospital, was offended when non-Mennonite solicitors came around in subsequent drives. Juhnke wanted to know if Prairie View was still "our" institution.[21] Would the churches lose control of Prairie View if it became heavily dependent on outside funding? In 1964 or 1965 when the board discussed for the first time Elmer Ediger's proposal to accept a major federal grant to build a new center for administration, some board members protested. The board finally agreed to accept federal funds, "so long as we don't become dependent upon federal funds." In the view of Larry Nikkel, who in 1983 succeeded Ediger as director, "Of course, Prairie View very soon crossed the dependency line."[22]

The contribution of local, state, and federal funds to Prairie View's revenue streams varied over the years of its development and expansion. In the 1970s federal funds could pay staff salaries, but not treatment costs, on a ten-year schedule, reduced each year by ten per cent. The first check from the Kansas state government came in 1975. Mennonite legislators, especially Harold Dyck from Hesston (1970-88) and Duane Goossen from Goessel (1982-94) helped Prairie View to pursue their interests in Topeka, the state capital. "When the legislature was in session," reported Larry Nikkel, "I would go to Topeka every week. We had special dinners to wine and dine the key legislators." Prairie View had competitive advantages over other mental health care providers in Kansas, both because of its head start in the field of community mental health care and also because it had a hospital in addition to other services.[23]

---

[21]On Bill Juhnke's strong ethnic/religious Mennonite commitments, see James C. Juhnke, *So Much to be Thankful For*, 149-50, 171-76.
[22]Larry Nikkel interview by James Juhnke, Wichita, KS, 17 June 2013.
[23]Nikkel interview.

Even as the churches lost control of Prairie View, Mennonites could take pride in the worldly success of something they had initiated. The American Psychiatric Association granted Prairie View one of seven Gold Awards for model programs in community mental health. One acclaimed program, quite beyond therapy for the mentally ill, was a "Growth Associates" division, led by Merrill Raber. That division provided consultation to business, industry, education, and community leaders, in the area of organization development, management, supervisory training, and conflict resolution. Additionally, retreats addressed issues of racism, poverty, town/gown tensions, and needs for public school and recreational facilities.[24] Prairie View was instrumental in establishing the Kansas/Paraguay Partnership, a program under John F. Kennedy's "Alliance for Progress" that matched states with foreign countries. That partnership was of special interest to Mennonites because of their connections with their people who had migrated to the Paraguayan Chaco and other parts of that country. The Kansas/Paraguay Partnership involved cultural and professional exchanges, including the exchange of mental health professionals.[25]

In the mind of the general public, Prairie View remained at least vaguely associated with Mennonites, perhaps in the way a large hospital bearing the name "Wesley" would be identified with Methodists. Prairie View endeavored to cultivate its connections with the Mennonite constituency through special publications and celebratory events that recalled the origins and history of the institution. The number of Mennonites on the staff, while a decreasing minority, still was higher than the proportion of Mennonites in the region. But the momentum away from the religious-ethnic base and towards a broader American public presence was undeniable.

---

[24]Merrill Raber, email to James Juhnke, 26 June 2014.
[25]Merrill Raber and Boots Raber, *A 40-Year History of Kansas-Paraguay Partners: Making a Difference Through Volunteerism, 1968-2008* (West Conshohocken, PA: Infinity Publishing, 2013).

Government Aid for Housing

Mennonites in Kansas were publicly known for Turkey Red wheat, for pacifism, and for disaster service. From the late 1980s, especially in the city of Wichita, they were also identified with low-cost housing programs. Ironically, as the name "Mennonite Housing" became prominent, the Mennonite character of the agency was gradually eclipsed by non-Mennonite administration, by a mostly non-Mennonite board, and by dependence on funding from city and federal sources.

Mennonite Housing grew out of an intentional community, Fairview Mennonite House, formed in 1971-72 by members of the Lorraine Avenue Mennonite Church. Four families and one single member shared their resources and lived together in a large house in Wichita's midtown area. In mid-1974 the Fairview group worked with a Midtown Citizens Association to remodel residences for low-income people in the area. The Fairview intentional community enabled Willard Ebersole, a skilled carpenter and builder, to leave his job as a teacher to lead the remodeling project. Ebersole supervised members of a Voluntary Service unit. In 1977 the voluntary service program was granted non-profit status as a community-based non-profit organization. It was guided by a board of directors and took on the new name of Mennonite Housing. In 1978 the non-profit program completed 148 home repair projects.[26] By 1986 there were ten employees and $300,000 in revenue.[27] But the ethos of the agency remained oriented to voluntary service and low-cost administration. The headquarters was housed in a garage.

By 1986, Mennonite Housing Rehabilitation Services needed more professional administration. They invited Tom Bishop from Indiana to become executive director. Bishop had been an administrator of voluntary service programs for the MC (Old) Mennonite Board of Missions. In Wichita he joined the Church of

---

[26]David A. Haury, *A People of the City: A History of the Lorraine Avenue Mennonite Church, 1932-82* (Wichita: Lorraine Avenue Mennonite Church, 1982), 190.

[27]"Tom Bishop of Homestead Affordable Housing," http://www.kshousingcorp.org/tom-bishop-named-2011-trailblazer.aspx (accessed 26 Jan 2013).

the Servant Mennonite congregation on Fairview Avenue. Under Bishop's leadership, Mennonite Housing's home repair work expanded. They painted fifty to sixty houses per year and organized a "Paint the Town" project that mobilized the temporary work of many volunteers. Bishop was highly successful in public relations and in innovative combinations of fundraising from private as well as public sources. One observer found that Bishop "cut an imposing figure–large in stature, intense in gesture and manner, with a strong voice."[28] His mastery of administrative details, of budgetary issues, and of creative ways of financing projects enabled the successful growth of Mennonite Housing.

In November 1990 Mennonite Housing broke ground for a 52-unit new housing development, Riverfront Residences for Senior Living. That development marked a shift from home repair to comprehensive housing. The project raised $1.7 million with "a grant from the City of Wichita Housing Task Force, proceeds from the sale of federal low income housing tax credits (approved by the Kansas Department of Commerce for this project), a 30-year mortgage written by Railroad Savings Bank and a direct subsidy by the Federal Home Loan Bank in Topeka."[29] That project was followed in subsequent years by other housing developments, each of which involved some federal financing, and some of which required the city to adapt zoning requirements. Mennonite Housing's annual report for 1997, the last year of Bishop's administration, said that the agency had developed "over 500 units of affordable rental housing for senior citizens and families at 60% or less of the area's median income."[30] The development agency expanded to more than fifty employees and, from 1994 to 1998, had annual revenues of more than four million dollars. Funding came from the federal Housing and Urban Development, as well as from the city of Wichita and from other sources including Koch Industries. Under Bishop's leadership, Mennonite Housing built

---

[28] Howard Keim, "Rhetorical Strategies," 67.
[29] Mennonite Housing Rehabilitation Services Inc. Annual Report, 1990. Report by J. Michael Lehman, President of the Board of Directors, 2.
[30] Mennonite Housing Annual Report 1997, 10.

and sold over 165 homes for low-income households, and developed 565 units of affordable rental housing.

Bishop used his prominence as a popular public figure to seek election to the Kansas legislature. In 1990 and 1992 he was elected on the Democratic ticket in a Wichita district with a large Republican majority. His contributions in the legislature included bills to reform procedures for the sale of properties deficient in payment of property tax, as well other bills related to his role as director of Mennonite Housing.

Mennonite Housing underwent a time of reorientation after Bishop resigned. His eventual successor, Andy Bias, had been a chairman of the board of directors but was not a Mennonite. Bias was a gifted administrator and under his leadership Mennonite Housing continued to build low-cost housing developments, primarily with federal funding–though the expansion was not at the breakneck speed that characterized Bishop's tenure. Time and funding applied to home repair, as well as the use of volunteer and short term work camp labor, gradually declined. The contributions of Mennonite congregations and church members became nominal rather than substantive. Three Mennonite churches in Wichita had two members each on a board of fourteen. They did not contribute to policy decisions in distinctive ways. The congregations' gifts to Mennonite Housing, which had become a multi-million dollar agency dependent on outside funding, were relatively insignificant.

Given the fact that Mennonite Housing had moved so far beyond the denominational character of its origins, did it make sense to keep the name "Mennonite"? CEO Bias was adamant on the point: "The name 'Mennonite' is golden in this community." The name would not be changed.[31] It was ironical that an agency that had moved so far from its Mennonite roots kept a name that secured its Mennonite identity in the mind of the public.

---

[31] Andy Bias, presentation to Mennonite Men's breakfast, Lorraine Avenue Mennonite Church, 23 March 2013.

Government Aid, Expansion of Mission, and Loss of Mennonite Identity

The relationships of Mennonite agencies to their founding churches reflected typical patterns in broader American faith-based organizations. Dozens of American Protestant colleges, founded by deeply religious people intent upon propagating their faith, gradually gave up their religious and denominational identities.[32] Some scholars have proposed to measure the depth of a faith-based institution's commitment to the original religious or denominational identity by examining a range of factors. These included financial support, mission statement, board member and staff selection, religious program content, and expectation of religious outcomes.[33] Detailed research into each of the many Mennonite agencies founded after World War II would need to be done to identify their places on such a religious-secular continuum. As for the institutions discussed in this chapter, such a standard would place Kansas Mennonite colleges toward the faith-based end of the continuum, Mennonite Housing toward the secular or "faith-secular partnership" end of the continuum, and Prairie View somewhere between. The general tendency over time of all of these agencies has been to move in the direction of Americanization. Acceptance of federal and state funding has been an important, though variable, impetus in that process.

Mennonite agencies that expanded beyond their denominational origins were able to achieve missions that far exceeded what they would have been able to do with just Mennonite resources. If Mennonite Housing in Wichita had chosen to hold the line on its voluntary service ethos and primary service of home repair, many people of low income who received their help would have remained in sub-standard housing. If Prairie View in Newton had

---

[32]George Marsden, *The Soul of the American University: From Protestant Establishment to Established Nonbelief* (New York: Oxford University Press, 1994), 415-16.

[33]"Categories of Faith-Based Organizations," Berkeley Center for Religion, Peace and World Affairs, Georgetown University. http://berkeley-georgetown.edu/essays/categories-of-faith-based-organizations (accessed June 25, 2014).

not chosen to use tax money and to hire qualified personnel regardless of Mennonite heritage, its expansive mission for mental health in the wider community would have been severely curtailed. Prairie View became the only surviving private psychiatric hospital in the state of Kansas. Without tax money it might not have survived at all.

Erosion of Mennonite identity was one of the hazards of the choice to become an "Activity Church." The social achievements of Mennonite agencies, often made possible by funding from the government, were paradoxical. The national legislation that provided generous funding for education, mental health, and housing was passed by Democratic administrations. These initiatives of John F. Kennedy's and Lyndon Johnson's administrations were extensions of Roosevelt's New Deal that most Mennonites had opposed. It is ironical that Democratic welfare state liberalism helped Mennonites achieve their agency objectives as an activity church while they remained predominantly Republican on other grounds. Beyond the irony, however, was the fact that Mennonite agencies founded after World War II enabled the denomination to make contributions to the public order far beyond what might be expected from a religious group of so few members.

Chapter 13

1980s: Farm Crisis, Legislative Awareness

Farm Crisis

In the 1980s a national farm crisis forced thousands of American family farmers into bankruptcy and off their farms. One Mennonite response was a book of twenty-one essays edited by La Vonne Godwin Platt from North Newton, a teacher and writer on world hunger concerns. The book was titled *Hope for the Family Farm, Trust God and Care for the Land.*[1] It might have been titled *Lament for the Disappearing Family Farm*. Platt's own historical essay, "As Family Farms Flower and Fade," reviewed the history of agriculture from colonial times to the present. In recent times the family farm had been "slowly declining for more than half a century." Like the other essayists, Platt called for a new vision "in line with our Judeo-Christian faith and a land stewardship ethic that borrows from the native peoples who once cherished this land."[2] Readers were bound to be impressed with the earnest Mennonite spiritual and prophetic concerns for land and conservation. One essay linked the farm crisis to militarism.[3] But the book offered no convincing prospects for reversing the underlying dynamics of mechanization, marketing, and government policy that were destroying the American family farm.

LaVonne Godwin Platt of North Newton, writer on environmental and hunger issues.

---

[1] LaVonne Godwin Platt, ed., *Hope for the Family Farm, Trust God and Care for the Land* (Newton, Ks: Faith and Life Press, 1987). Two of the twenty-one essays were written by non-Mennonites, but members of historic peace church congregations.

[2] Margaret Epp Hiebner and LaVonne Godwin Platt, "As Family Farms Flower and Fade," in *Hope for the Family Farm*, 73.

[3] Robert O. Epp, "Farmers Everywhere Burdened by Militarism," *Hope for the Family Farm*, 162-8.

The social and cultural implications for Mennonite farm-based communities were profound. Kansas Mennonite rural congregations once had been made up primarily of diversified self-sufficient farm families. Now farming had become modern business enterprise.[4] Big machines replaced the labor of children and parents. Specialized production of crops and animals replaced diversified production for local consumption and the sale of small surpluses of eggs, milk, and vegetables. Use of fertilizer and pesticides doubled and tripled crop production levels. Farm sizes increased as the large efficient farmers bought out the smaller inefficient operations. Between 1940 and 2000 the average size of farms in Kansas grew from 303 acres to 736 acres.[5] The surplus population of large Mennonite families moved to the towns and cities and found wage-earning, professional, and business employment. In McPherson County William Juhnke counted himself among those who could remain farmers by working as teachers nine months of the year.[6] The Hesston Corporation, manufacturer of agricultural machinery, provided jobs to hundreds of part-time farmers and administered a generous vacation policy during harvest and other times of farm activity. Even so, all farmers remained vulnerable to unpredictable business cycles and increasingly dependent upon federal government subsidies.

The two great crises in the American farm economy were the great depression of the 1930s and the overexpansion debt crisis of the 1980s. President Franklin D. Roosevelt's New Deal program included the Agricultural Adjustment Act (AAA) of 1933, the first federal government program of massive direct payments to struggling farmers. Menno Schrag, editor of *Mennonite Weekly Review*, lamented the rise of big government. But neither he nor any Mennonite farmers suggested that they should refuse government

---

[4]For a general survey of the transition see John Sjo, "The Family Farm Becomes a Business Enterprise: 1860 to 1980," in *The Rise of the Wheat State: A History of Kansas Agriculture*, ed. George E. Ham and Robin Higham (Manhattan, Ks: Sunflower University Press, 1987), 115-122.

[5]Kansas Statistical Abstract 2001, Institute for Policy and Social Research. http://www.ipsr.ku.edu/ksdata/ksah/KSA46.pdf (accessed 7 Nov 2014).

[6]James C. Juhnke, *So Much to be Thankful For*, 105-23.

payments. Mennonite farmers became increasingly dependent upon the government. Each new government program to subsidize farmers was promoted as a way to save the family farm, but the payments benefitted primarily the wealthy farms and high-income non-farm investors.[7]

Farmstead of Sam Regier, northwestern Harvey County, ca. 1950

A measure of the impact of federal subsidies is found in the careful records of farm income and expenses kept by the Mennonite farmer Sam Regier and his son Raymond Regier from 1933 to the 1990s.[8] (Raymond took over the farm in 1957.) For most of those years the Regier farm consisted of 240 owned acres in Alta Township of Harvey County, plus additional rented land. In the 1930s it was a diversified farm, with beef cattle, milk cows, sheep, pigs, chickens, and grain crops–primarily wheat. Sam Regier's first federal subsidy check arrived in January 1934. The amount of the

---

[7]Roger Claassen, "Make Public Policy Work for Justice," in *Hope for the Family Farm*, ed. by La Vonne Godwin Platt (Newton, Ks: Faith and Life Press, 1987), 144-58.

[8]Records in Raymond Regier personal collection, North Newton, KS.

federal subsidies varied over succeeding years and decades, but the subsidies were helpful to the Regier farm budget–at times about ten percent of total cash receipts.

Sam Regier worked closely with the Kansas State College Extension Service and with its Farm Management Association that sent a field man to visit the farm four times a year. Regier often visited the Extension Service offices in Newton, and occasionally was paid for work for the Agricultural Administration Act office in the same building. Mennonite farmers in the 1940s and 1950s who were employed by the United States Department of Agriculture included Jacob Wedel in McPherson County and Jonas Voran in Harvey County. Regier and Wedel also worked closely with farmers' cooperative organizations.

Walter W. "Sprig" Graber, wheat and cattle farmer of Pretty Prairie in Reno County, was the most prominent and influential Mennonite engaged in public agricultural policy formation.[9] Graber joined the Reno County Farm Bureau and became chairman of its legislative committee. In 1949 he testified in the state capitol in Topeka for the Farm Bureau in favor of a severance tax on the oil industry. He accused the oil industry of using its "virtually unlimited" financial resources to exercise "dictatorial" power to promote taxes on everything except gas and oil.[10] That same year Graber met with a group of farmers in Greensburg, Kansas, to form a new organization, the Kansas Wheat Growers Association. Kansas Governor George Docking in 1957 appointed Graber one of the seven commissioners of the Kansas Wheat Commission. Among his proudest achievements was getting wheat purchasers for the international market to pay premium prices for high quality wheat. In 1968 Graber was elected to the first of two terms in the Kansas legislature.

---

[9]Tim Stucky and Nancy Stucky, "Walter W. "Sprig" Graber: A Man for All Seasons," *Ninnescah Valley News*, July 11, 2003, reprinted in the Swiss Mennonite Cultural and Historical Association online newsletter http://www.swissmennonite.org/featlure_archive/2003/200308.html.

[10]"Oil Interests Said Holding Up Severance Tax," undated, unidentified newspaper clipping, March 1949, in scrapbook of Helen Graber Unruh, Hutchinson, KS.

Some Mennonite farmers, like Graber, joined the Farm Bureau. Others joined the Farmers' Union and the National Farmer's Organization (NFO) to influence public agricultural policies in more progressive directions. Sam Regier and William Juhnke for many years were members of the Farm Bureau, in part attracted by their good insurance programs. Both of them left the Farm Bureau when they decided its public policy positions became too conservative. In 1967, when the price of wheat had dropped to an unprofitable level, William Juhnke and Clarence Schrag joined the NFO in McPherson County.[11] The NFO gained notoriety for its producer strikes or "holding actions" and for its large tractor protest drive to Washington, D.C.

Not until the 1980s did Kansas Mennonites take collective denominational action in behalf of beleaguered farmers. An "export bubble," triggered by large Soviet grain purchases in the early 1970s, led to inflated grain prices and land values. When the boom collapsed in the early 1980s farmers who had made major purchases of land and equipment were caught by insupportable debt and high interest rates. Many Kansas farmers, including Mennonites, faced bankruptcy–a matter of embarrassment and shame in the community. Raymond Regier, whose farm was debt free, took an active role in efforts of the Western District Conference to mobilize assistance for hurting farmers and to influence public policies to help the family farms. Regier was a leading member of the bi-national Mennonite Central Committee Farm Crisis Committee and of a Kansas branch of that committee.

In 1985 the MCC Farm Crisis Committee sponsored public meetings and distributed a "Statement of Concern" to be sent to "district conference ministers, congressmen, senators, state legislators, and the governor of Kansas."[12] The statement called the state governments to do five things: undertake studies to examine the effects of tax policies on family farm ownership; create a family farm development fund for low interest loans to beginning farmers; require agricultural research and educational programs to focus on

---

[11] James C. Juhnke, *So Much to be Thankful For*, 161-2.
[12] The statement was included in *Hope for the Family Farm*, 183-6.

small and moderate sized operations, especially minority farmers; open market opportunities and provide market information and training for farmers; and support the family farm by advocating that the federal government "provide a fair price for farm products." The statement provided an equal list of five policy objectives for the federal government. The MCC Farm Crisis Committee policy recommendations may have been too broad and diffuse to be translated into an effective lobbying agenda. In any case, the Mennonites were a very small part of the economic and political agricultural upheaval of the 1980s.[13]

From 1985 to 1994 Raymond Regier, who had attended Bethel College for two years and graduated with an agricultural major from Kansas State University in 1950, represented the Western District Peace and Social Concerns Committee on the Interfaith Rural Life Committee (IRLC) of Kansas Ecumenical Ministries. For several years Regier served as chairman of this ecumenical committee. The IRLC provided training seminars to help farmers plan their operations and cope with banks and other agencies. It also distributed to farmers some Farm Aid funds raised by popular country music singer Willie Nelson and routed through the National Council of Churches. A report of May 1989 for *Western District Conference News* said that "Farm Aid funds totaling $7,525 have been distributed to seventy-seven Western District Conference member families from 16 congregations between October, 1985 and December, 1988." As Regier wrote in one report, "$100 for a farm family seems like a small amount when their debts may have been in the hundreds of thousands. However, these tokens were meaningful showings of care to hurting families."

Mennonite farmers who considered or declared bankruptcy faced extraordinary social pressures from their rural and small town communities as well as from their church congregations and families. Bankruptcy represented a kind of moral failure. To default on debts owed to people with whom one worshiped on Sunday morning was a problem. Mark Janzen, farmer near Elbing, said he

---

[13]Information in this section based upon conversation with Raymond Regier and research in Regier's personal files.

could have saved $125,000 by declaring bankruptcy but chose not to do so. Bankrupt farmers often left the church and community.[14] Duane Friesen, religion and ethics teacher at Bethel College, in 1987 presented an essay, "The Ethics of Bankruptcy," at a regional meeting of Mennonite Economic Development Associates in Newton. The presumption against bankruptcy, Friesen suggested, was based upon the understanding that refusal of debt payment is a "break of one's word" that harms other people. On the other hand, bankruptcy could be a legal and orderly way out of hopeless situations and a means of protection from total poverty. Lester Ewy, a farmer from Partridge, Kansas, who barely escaped bankruptcy himself, took a job with Mennonite Central Committee to offer emotional support and financial counsel to farmers in trouble in Kansas and other states.

Legislative Awareness

Kansas Mennonites in the 1980s, prompted in part by the agricultural crisis, showed an exceptionally strong interest in Kansas state politics. More Mennonites were elected to the Kansas House of Representatives in the 1980s than in any other decade. The Mennonite and Mennonite affiliated representatives elected in the 1980s included Harold J. Dyck (R) of Hesston, Jesse Harder (D) of Buhler, Duane Goossen (R) of Goessel, Steve Ediger (D) of Hutchinson, Bill Goering (D) of McPherson, and Eric Yost (R) of Wichita. Dyck, Harder, Goering, and Goossen were members of Mennonite congregations. Ediger and Yost were of Mennonite background, carried traditional "Mennonite" names, and had the advantage of Mennonite ethnic and family connections. But their relationships with local Mennonite congregations were more marginal. Mennonites were a minority in each of the six legislative districts that these Mennonite politicians represented.

Another sign in the 1980s of growing Kansas Mennonite interest in politics was a series of "legislative awareness" seminars held each spring in the state capital. From 1981 to 1988 the pastors of the

---

[14]Mark Janzen, interview by James Juhnke, Wichita, KS, 20 July 2014.

Southern Hills Mennonite Church (GC) and the Fairview Mennonite Brethren Church of Topeka (MB) cooperated in organizing and hosting an annual "Legislative Awareness Seminar" in Topeka. The seminars were primarily a form of adult education in the political process and current issues, and secondarily an opportunity for Mennonites to make their views known to Kansas public officials.[15]

The Peace and Social Concerns of the Western District Conference (GC), with headquarters in North Newton, was the primary sponsor of the Topeka legislative awareness seminars. Pastors Ron Flaming (1981-83) and Ray Reimer (1984-88) of the Southern Hills Church in Topeka, along with Phil Esau of the Fairview Mennonite Brethren Church, were the volunteer organizers and coordinators. The seminars ran on a minimal budget of a few hundred dollars per year. Out of town participants were invited to bring their own bedding and to sleep on the floors of the churches, or to be hosted by Mennonites who lived in Topeka. There was a modest registration fee or, in the first years, no registration fee at all. Public officials who addressed the seminars offered their services without charge. Fifteen pastors from Western District Conference churches attended the seminar in the first four years.

The first Legislative Awareness Seminar, held March 15-17, 1981, began on Sunday evening and continued for full days on Monday and Tuesday. The focus for the first day was on criminal justice and corrections (treatment of offenders, the death penalty, etc.) For the second day the focus was on family issues (care for dependent children, child abuse, etc.) No fewer than eleven elected public officials addressed the gathering, headlined by John Carlin, governor; Ross Doyen, president of the Senate; and Wendell Lady, speaker of the House. In addition there were eight representatives from state and private agencies who spoke on panels or in plenary sessions. The meeting was held in the First Presbyterian Church, adjacent to the Capitol building. Each day time was allotted for seminar attendees to walk over to the capitol building to observe

---

[15]Western District Peace and Social Concerns Committee minutes, II.3.e.9, MLA.

the legislative process–the House of Representatives on Monday and the Senate on Tuesday.

The legislative seminars offered the opportunity for Kansas Mennonites to meet, to learn from, and to express their opinions to Mennonite legislators. At the 1986 seminar, participants had breakfast in the State Office Building Cafeteria with four "Mennonite-related legislators": Senator Eric Yost, and Representatives Harold Dyck, Duane Goossen, and Jesse Harder. Later that day (Feb. 10) Harold Dyck, who was chairman of the Commercial and Financial Institutions Committee, addressed the group on the topic, "How can the state respond to bank failures?" Another session consisted of speeches by, or in behalf of, announced and prospective candidates for the 1986 gubernatorial campaign. Duane Goosen spoke in behalf of candidate Mike Hayden, Republican Speaker of the House. Participants at the 1986 meeting included thirty-seven adults plus fifteen students from Bethel College.[16] When Ray Reimer left Topeka in 1988 the Legislative Awareness Seminar series came to an end. Kansas Ecumenical Ministries did not pick up the project, and the Mennonite interest and ability to carry on had declined. Much had depended upon Reimer's volunteer labors. His congregation, the Southern Hills Church, in the 1990s and into the twenty-first century, continued to take leadership in monitoring the status of legislation in Kansas.

What accounts for the flowering of Mennonite interest in Kansas politics in the 1980s? The agricultural crisis had a role. The eight years of the seminars coincided with the eight years of the presidency of Ronald Reagan. Many Mennonites were part of the peace movement which came to life in response to the Reagan administration's belligerent foreign policy and military arms buildup. President Reagan's shift of government responsibility from the national to the state and local level had consequences for issues of finance and budget in Kansas. During the years of the Topeka legislative awareness seminars, Kansas Mennonites were involved in other events of political education and witness,

---

[16]Ray Reimer personal collection.

including seminars in Washington, D.C., and protests related to the Titan II missiles in the Wichita area. By the end of the 1980s the organizing leaders and supporters had moved on, both from the Topeka Mennonite churches and from the Western District Peace and Social Concerns committee. The continuation of the seminars would have depended upon a more substantial and institutionalized base of support. The budget of the Peace and Social Concerns committee decreased rather than increased in the late 1980s and the 1990s. In any case, the Topeka legislative awareness seminars had been a remarkably effective project to have been carried out by such a small denomination.

Income Tax Refusal

Cornelia Lehn

In 1975 Cornelia Lehn, employee in the education department of the General Conference Mennonite Church (GCMC) headquarters in Newton, Kansas, asked that federal taxes not be withheld from her salary. The church should be able to say to the government, "We will not give you our sons and daughters and we will not give you our money to kill others."[17] Lehn's request triggered an intense eight-year denominational policy debate. In 1980 the GCMC convened an extraordinary "mid-triennium" meeting to address only this issue. By 1983 the denomination had gained a strong majority, if not a complete consensus, to take a radical step of civil disobedience. The church informed the United States Internal Revenue Service that it would no longer withhold money for federal income tax from monthly salaries of seven employees who were conscientiously opposed to paying the tax. The legal consequences were potentially

---

[17]Cornelia Lehn, "My Pilgrimage With War Tax Resistance," appended to a letter by Elmer Neufeld, President of the General Conference Mennonite Church, to GCMC pastors, 14 Oct 1976.

momentous. Would the IRS enforce its authority with a law suit against the Mennonites?

The GCMC action of 1983 was the culmination of decades of discussion, debate, article-writing, and resolution-passing at Mennonite conferences about the payment of income tax for military purposes. The Cold War arms race after World War II, and the dedication of a major portion of the national budget to military expenditures, substantially increased the portion of the federal budget that went for military purposes. Donald D. Kaufman, a Bethel College graduate and Mennonite pastor, in 1969 reviewed the history of tax resistance and analyzed the Biblical issues in a path breaking book, *What Belongs to Caesar?*[18] Stories of tax resistance multiplied. David Janzen of Newton, for example, in 1972 owed the IRS $31.32 but conscientiously refused to pay. The IRS took possession of Janzen's 1963 Ford Falcon station-wagon and sold it at auction to recover the money. A group of Janzen's friends bought the vehicle and returned it to him. In most cases the IRS got the money from resisters' bank accounts.[19] In 1975 the Peace and Social Concerns Committee of the General Conference Mennonite Church began publishing *God and Caesar*, a new "forum newsletter" for the church and the wider tax-resistance community. For two decades *God and Caesar* carried articles about tax resistance, told the stories of individual resister's encounters with the Internal Revenue Service, and charted the high and low points of the movement.[20]

One national legislative proposal to resolve the problem of pacifists paying for war was the "Peace Tax Fund." That proposal would have allowed conscientious objectors to pay their income tax into an alternative fund that would be spent for civilian purposes. In the 1970s Kansas Mennonites influenced their Kansas Fourth District congressmen, Republican Garner Shriver and (after 1976)

---

[18]Donald D. Kaufman, *What Belongs to Caesar?* (Scottdale, Pa: Herald Press, 1969).

[19]Internal Revenue Service, "Notice of Seizure," and "Notice of Public Auction Sale," Newton, Ks, 22 May 1972. Published with an undated letter by David Janzen. In the author's files.

[20]Harold Regier and Peter Ediger were the first editors of *God and Caesar*. Robert Hull was editor from 1989 to 1994. See copies in Mennonite Library and Archives.

or moved on to other jobs, the number of GCMC employees requesting the church's civil disobedience declined to zero. It was a remarkably un-dramatic outcome to a tension-fraught problem or crisis.

Realist Pacifism

Although Kansas Mennonites throughout the twentieth century sustained a strong heritage of peace teaching and witness, they produced very little systematic theological reflection on the relationship of church and state. They were better at discipleship than at theology. For more than half a century there were well qualified Bible and Religion teachers at the three Mennonite colleges in central Kansas. But not until 1986 did one of them produce a book that engaged contemporary theological peace issues in comprehensive detail. The book was *Christian Peacemaking & International Conflict, A Realist Pacifist Perspective*, and the author was Duane Friesen, Bible and Religion professor at Bethel College.[25] Friesen had earned a Th.D. degree in social ethnics from Harvard Divinity School with a dissertation on the social ethics of the German theologian Ernst Troeltsch (1865-1923). At Bethel College Friesen was the founder in 1973 of a new Peace Studies Program and organizer of a Peace Lecture Series that brought leading scholars of the emerging Peace Studies discipline to the campus. He was also active in the national Consortium of Peace Research, Education and Development, an organization that for several years had its headquarters at Bethel College.

Friesen's book was interdisciplinary. He took into account the best recent scholarship of the social sciences together with the literature of theology and ethics. He rejected the common claim, most influentially stated by Reinhold Niebuhr in *Moral Man and Immoral Society* (1932), that pacifism based on the New Testament was not realistic. Pacifists, said Friesen, were more realistic than the so-called "realists" who failed to see the dimensions of cooperation

---

[25]Duane K. Friesen, *Christian Peacemaking & International Conflict: A Realist Pacifist Perspective* (Scottdale, Pa: Herald Press, 1986).

in international politics, and whose endorsement of the military power interests of modern nations had helped to bring the world to the brink of nuclear catastrophe. The goal of peacemaking is justice. That goal should be pursued nonviolently, but "coercion" and "pressure" were appropriate. Christian pacifist ethics could make sense on non-Christian grounds.

Friesen also argued with theologians of his own Mennonite tradition, most notably John Howard Yoder who rejected "effectiveness" as a valid goal for Christian ethics. When Christians work for justice, Friesen argued, "the question of effectiveness and the careful social scientific inquiry which tries to predict the consequences of a course of action are absolutely essential in enabling a Christian to fulfill the Christian ethic of discipleship."[26] A distinctive Mennonite note in *Christian Peacemaking and International Conflict* was Friesen's emphasis upon the role of the church. The final chapter, co-written by Elizabeth Schmidt, one of Friesen's students, explored the "spiritual resources for empowerment" that could sustain a long-term peace witness both for individuals and for the church.

In terms of inter-Mennonite peace dialogue, Friesen's book was a breakthrough statement that thoroughly revised a traditional church-state dualism. From World War II until the 1980s the definitive Mennonite statement on war/peace and church/state issues had been the book by Guy F. Hershberger, *War, Peace and Nonresistance* (1944).[27] That book was written from a Mennonite Church (MC) perspective most familiar at Goshen College in Indiana and Hesston College in Kansas. Over the years numbers of Mennonite scholars attempted to challenge or modify Hershberger's church-state dualism. One important moment was in 1957 when Elmer Neufeld, a native of Inman, Kansas, presented a paper that, in the assessment of scholar Perry Bush, represented a "theological breakthrough" for inter-Mennonite conversation and behavior. Neufeld affirmed the two kingdom doctrine while calling the church to ministries of reconciliation, service, and mission to

---

[26]Friesen, *Christian Peacemaking*, 156.
[27]See Theron F. Schlabach, *War, Peace and Social Conscience*, 117-62.

the world, including "proclaiming the righteousness of God" to those in power.[28] J. Lawrence Burkholder, a young faculty member at Goshen College, wrote a Th.D. dissertation in 1958 at Princeton Theological Seminary that thoroughly challenged Hershberger's views as too oriented toward sectarian withdrawal. The dissertation was titled "The Problem of Social Responsibility from the Perspective of the Mennonite Church." Hershberger turned defensive and combative. With his supporters he made sure that Burkholder's dissertation would not be published in Goshen's scholarly series, "Studies in Anabaptist and Mennonite History."[29]

One reviewer observed that Duane Friesen's work was "to some degree at least . . . parallel to Hershberger's *War, Peace and Nonresistance*."[30] In fact Friesen did an end run around the old Hershberger debate. He did not engage Hershberger's ideas or even mention *War, Peace and Nonresistance* in his text. A new Mennonite generation, more oriented to prophetic activism for justice than to quietistic nonviolence, had come on the scene by the time of Friesen's 1986 book.[31] That book was a break-through not only in terms of Mennonite peace theology and ethics, but also in an ecumenical inter-Mennonite sense. It was a book by a GCMC Mennonite of Dutch-Russian heritage, published (albeit with some reluctance) by Herald Press of Scottdale, Pennsylvania–a Mennonite Church (MC) press of the Swiss-South-German Mennonite tradition. The Kansas Mennonite GCMC heritage of engagement with the political world had taken a long time to find its theological voice.

---

[28]Perry Bush, *Two Kingdoms, Two Loyalties*, 198-201.

[29]Schlabach, *War, Peace and Social Conscience*, 367-85. Schlabach's account, friendly to Hershberger, says the Hershberger/Burkholder confrontation was "tragic," and that a synthesis of the two men's thoughts might have been possible.

[30]Ted Koontz, review of *Christian Peacemaking and International Conflict*, in *Mennonite Life* (September 1987), 36. See also the review by Edward Learman in *Mennonite Quarterly Review* (July 1987): 341-2.

[31]This transition was explored in detail in Driedger and Kraybill, *Mennonite Peacemaking*.

1980s Resistance and Witness

In the latter 1970s, after the end of military conscription and the Vietnam War, the peace movement on Kansas Mennonite college campuses was relatively quiet. Two events brought the movement back to life. One was President Jimmy Carter's renewal in 1980 of Selective Service registration for the military draft. The other was President Ronald Reagan's military buildup in 1981-82, the first years of his presidency.

Carter's renewal of draft registration was intended to threaten the Soviet Union. Russia had invaded Afghanistan in 1979. The United States withdrew from the Russian Olympics in 1980, placed trade embargo on certain commodities, and funded the mujahedeen rebels who fought against Russia. A significant number of Mennonite young men, not wanting to participate in a clear military threat, refused to register. The Selective Service registration form did not allow them to indicate that they were conscientious objectors to war.

On September 21, 1980, the government indicted two Bethel College students, Kendal Warkentine and Charles "Chuck" Epp, for refusing to register. Both were tried in district court in Wichita. The trials got local and national publicity. Sam Crow, the judge in Warkentine's case, sentenced the young offender to two years of unsupervised labor. The judge directed Selective Service to provide a special form that allowed him to "declare that I am conscientiously opposed to serving in the armed services." Warkentine was willing to sign the form. The judge said that this decision should not be a precedent for any other cases. Meanwhile Chuck Epp refused to sign *any* registration form. Frank Theis, the judge in Epp's case, arranged for the charges to be dismissed. Theis noted that Epp was different from the thousands of men who had secretly refused to register. Epp had clearly informed Selective Service about his birth date and the reasons for his refusal. That action, said the judge, essentially constituted "constructively registering." The decisions of judges Crow and Theis to avoid confrontation with the resisters had something in common with the decision of the Internal Revenue Service to avoid a legal battle with the General Conference Mennonite Church over the issue of tax withholding. The government's punishment of civil disobedience in both cases could have been much more severe. In 1983 the federal government passed a law cutting off college financial aid to non-registrants. The GCMC and the Mennonite Church (MC) both

Kendal Warkentine (middle) and Charles Epp (right) at a press conference regarding their nonregistration for the draft.

set up student aid funds to assist conscientious objectors to registration.[32]

President Reagan's military buildup in 1981 brought the national peace movement to life in the form of a popular movement to "Freeze the Arms Race." In Kansas the Freeze campaign was linked to the fate of eighteen Titan II missile sites that surrounded the city of Wichita. The Titans, with warheads carrying explosive power some 250 to 300 times the bombs that destroyed Hiroshima and Nagasaki, were aimed at highly populated "soft targets" overseas. In August 1978 an accident at a Titan II missile site near Rock, Kansas, killed two men, injured twenty-five others, and sent toxic fumes into the air. In the ensuing controversy, Kansas Mennonites played a role in getting Congressman Dan Glickman to come out in favor of dismantling the over-aged Titan II sites.[33] Then the military proposed that a new generation of MX missiles be located in the old Titan II sites or along a massive "racetrack" for protection against a first strike from Russia. Robert Bennett, Republican governor of Kansas, spoke out sharply against basing the MX in Kansas. Miriam Wiebe, Bethel College student, and Fred Loganbill of Newton served with peace activists from Wichita on the executive committee of a group called "Kansans Against the MX."[34]

Emerging political issues during the Reagan years pulled Mennonites in different directions. On the "conservative" side Mennonites were inclined to oppose abortion and homosexual marriage–Republican issues. On the "liberal" side Mennonites were inclined to oppose militarism and imperialism–positions more identified with Democrats. Editors of Mennonite newspapers, desiring to appear non-partisan, took both sides. Before the 1980 election, editor Wally Kroeker of *The Christian Leader* printed a "tract for justice" published by Evangelicals for Social Action to guide the election choice between President Jimmy Carter and challenger Ronald Reagan. The article's "basic Christian principles"

---

[32]James C. Juhnke, *Small Steps Toward the Missing Peace*, 117-8; Keith L. Sprunger, *Bethel College of Kansas*, 183.

[33]Juhnke, *Small Steps*, 130-2.

[34]Newsletter titled "Kansans Against the MX, a Project of Kansans for Peace and Justice/Freeze the Arms Race," 27 Nov 1981, in the author's collection.

opposed abortion and homosexual marriage while endorsing peacemaking and God's concern for the poor.[35] Mennonite editors were generally more liberal than their conservative constituencies. Before the 1984 election, *The Christian Leader* ran two articles by Mennonite volunteers who had worked in Nicaragua and were sharply critical of the Reagan administration's support of the *Sandinista* rebels who were trying to overthrow the Nicaraguan government.[36]

The rising role of the religious right in the Republican Party also came up for discussion among the Mennonite Brethren. John H. Redekop, a Canadian political scientist who had studied and taught in the United States, in 1984 was the moderator of the Canadian Mennonite Brethren Conference. He was offended by the religious rhetoric at the Republican national convention in Dallas that fall. Redekop wrote a sharply worded editorial for *The Christian Leader* warning his American Mennonite Brethren friends not to turn God into an American, a Republican, a capitalist, a militarist, or "your mascot." No one party has "any particular claim on God."[37] When the editorial resulted in a storm of protest from Mennonite Republicans, editors Wally Kroeker and Don Ratzlaff said they stood by the editorial. It had not mentioned any candidate nor was it intended as a partisan endorsement. All political rhetoric needs "critique from a biblical perspective."[38] The timing of Redekop's editorial, just before an election, may have been controversial. (Reagan was re-elected over Mondale in a landslide.) But in the Mennonite editors' message biblical values trumped nationalistic rhetoric.

---

[35]"Making Christ Lord of our Politics" *The Christian Leader*, 21 Oct 1980, 2-5.

[36]J. R. Burkholder, "Whom can we believe about Central America?" *The Christian Leader*, 16 October 1984, 12-13. Lauren Martens, "Nicaragua–the rebuilding continues." *The Christian Leader*, 30 October 1984, 15-17.

[37]John H. Redekop, "Editorial," *The Christian Herald* , 30 October 1984, 24.

[38]Editors' Response, *The Christian Herald*, 27 November 1984, 9.

Chapter 14

1990s: Desert Storm, Summer of Mercy

Desert Storm

"It seems like every generation has its war," said Aaron Rittenhouse in January 1991 when America bombed and invaded Iraq. "This one is ours." Rittenhouse was a senior at Bethel College. He joined in the anti-war protests. Then, when the war ended in American victory, he and a classmate, Jalane Schmidt, conducted an oral history project of tape-recorded interviews with eighty-four Mennonites–leaders, lay folks, senior citizens, and youth–to document what they had experienced during the Persian Gulf War. The interviews, along with documents donated by the informants, showed that the war, despite its brevity, was an intense experience for Kansas Mennonites. It was difficult (and sometimes energizing) to be against war when patriotic enthusiasm dominated the community, and when everyone rejoiced in an American military triumph.[1]

The twentieth century had been defined by "total wars" that demanded the entire nation's full participation through military service, income tax payment, and moral affirmation. The Persian Gulf War, in contrast, was notable for what it did *not* ask of the American people. President George H. W. Bush did not ask for money or for conscripted military service. He asked the people for *permission* to fight the war. Mennonites, accustomed to responding to the country's direct wartime demands, faced a new situation. In August 1990 Saddam Hussein had invaded and conquered Iraq's oil-rich neighbor, Kuwait. The world's supply of cheap oil was threatened. With the support of the United Nations, and a vote in the United States Senate, Bush assembled an international coalition to join the fight and to pay for most of the costs. Once the war was

---

[1] "Bethel Students Document Gulf War Reaction," *Mennonite Weekly Review*, 3 October 1991, 7. The documents from the Persian Gulf War Oral History Collection are at Mennonite Library and Archives (OH.3). Interviews were conducted in Indiana and Missouri as well as Kansas.

under way, the people of the United States gave him enthusiastic support, at least in the short term.

Before, during, and after the Persian Gulf War, Mennonites in their own way denied President Bush their permission to make war. Denominational newspapers, especially *Mennonite Weekly Review*, covered the war with news, editorials, and anti-war columns.[2] The colleges held "Teach-Ins" that critically examined the causes and context of the war. Students from Hesston College and Bethel College organized a "Walk and Mail" protest in Newton. The Newton Area Peace Center published an "Open Letter to the People of Iraq from Citizens of Kansas" in the *Newton Kansan*, along with the names of 460 signers, mostly Mennonite.[3] The Mennonite Central Committee raised funds to buy mattresses, blankets, and food for war refugees.[4] A delegation of representatives from Christian Peacemaker Teams visited Baghdad where they engaged in conversations with Iraqi leaders.[5] Dennis Koehn, who had served time in prison for refusing to register during the Vietnam War, went to Frankfurt, Germany, with a team to counsel soldiers who had conscientious objections to this war.[6] The numbers of Mennonite tax resisters increased.[7] Church leaders held well-attended seminars for young men and women in the colleges and churches about how to prepare for a possible military draft. Robert Hull, secretary for peace and justice of the GCMC, a first-generation Mennonite who had grown up in a military family, was in demand as a draft counselor.

---

[2] See for example Paul Schrag, "Will Americans Pay for Oil with Blood?" *Mennonite Weekly Review*, 15 November 1990, 1.

[3] "Open Letter to the People of Iraq from the Citizens of Kansas," *The Newton Kansan*, 22 September 1990, 7.

[4] "Iraq, Kuwait Refugees Get Assistance From MCC," *Mennonite Weekly Review*, 30 August 1990, 1.

[5] Gene Stoltzfus, "Team Promotes Peace Dialogue," *Mennonite Weekly Review*, 20 December 1990, 1. Ron Rempel, "CPT Urges Release of Hostages, Prays for Peace, Talks to Iraqis," *Mennonite Weekly Review*, 20 December 1990, 1.

[6] "Soldiers Questioning Mideast War, MCCers in Germany Counseling COs in US. Army," *Mennonite Weekly Review*, 10 January 1991, 1.

[7] Paul Schrag, "Gulf War Swells Ranks of War-Tax Resisters" *Mennonite Weekly Review*, 14 March 1991, 4.

Not everyone in Mennonite churches and institutions was clearly opposed to the war. Everyone agreed that Saddam Hussein's invasion of Kuwait was iniquitous, but some doubted that anything short of military force would induce him to withdraw. Students at Tabor College and Bethel College put strongly opposing views on their student opinion bulletin boards. In December 1990, a month after Bethel's and Hesston's students had organized an anti-war "Walk and Mail," a group of forty "Students Believing in America" held their own march protesting against the protesters. The spectacle of students at a Mennonite college supporting war garnered exceptional TV and newspaper media coverage in Wichita, Hutchinson, and Newton. Byron Rupp, a Bethel sophomore and son of two Mennonite pastors, joined the "Students Believing in America" to support the troops because they were willing to die for something they believed in. Rupp said he was a conscientious objector, but he also believed there was no way to stop Saddam Hussein other than the use of force.[8] Keith Hand, a student from Arkansas not of Mennonite background complained that "The whole school system [at Bethel] propagates the peace philosophy. They [the anti-war groups] have no sense of reality."[9]

One reality of the war hit the Bethel community when news arrived that the husband of Christina Waller, a student in the nursing department, had been killed in Iraq.[10] Depressing at another level was anticipation that the war would promote the power and popularity of American militarism in the future. President Bush proudly claimed that the successful war had "kicked the Vietnam Syndrome." Darrell Fast, pastor of the Bethel College Mennonite Church, said "I think we were fighting Vietnam the whole time we were in the Persian Gulf." A swift military

---

[8]Byron Rupp, "Desert Storm is a Just War," *In Search*, March 1991, 1-3. See notes by Patty Shelly on Byron Rupp's statement at a Bethel College student convocation, folder 27, box 2, Persian Gulf War Oral History Collection.

[9]Jim Holm, "Politics of the Kingdom," *Christian Leader*, 20 October 1992, 12.

[10]Note in Patty Shelly folder, folder 26, box 2, Persian Gulf War Oral History Collection.

victory would make it more likely that America would turn to military invasion in future crises.[11]

Before the war was over, the GCMC Commission on Education published a book of Mennonite essays titled *Weathering the Storm Christian Pacifist Responses to War*. Church leaders and academics in the fields of theology, economics, history, and psychology offered their reflections. James M. Harder, professor of economics at Bethel, challenged the prevailing image, a legacy of World War II prosperity, that war was good for the American economy. George Dyck, a psychiatrist at Prairie View Mental Health Center, examined the human psychological mechanisms that perpetuate violence. Doug Penner, a social psychologist who had taught at Bethel College, noted the special stresses that pacifist workers faced in wartime as they related to war-supporting co-workers. Other pastors, church administrators, journalists, and public school teachers wrote about the fears and dilemmas faced by pacifists in wartime. Absent from the collection was the perspective of political science–an academic discipline in which Mennonites were notably weak.[12]

Town-gown relationships between Newton and Bethel College were not as tense during the Persian Gulf War as they had been in World Wars I and II and the Vietnam War. Pastors of different denominations in the Newton Ministerial Alliance found ways to cooperate in response to the war. Administrators in Newton High School responded positively to suggestions from Mennonite teachers who were concerned that school assemblies and public address messages not be used to beat the war drums. The community ignored Pastor Vern Bender of the People's Bible Baptist church when he put up an inflammatory sign offering a thousand dollars reward "for information leading to arrest and conviction of college 'peace' (?) protesters who shoot us and steal our flag." But the *Newton Kansan* gave full coverage to an encounter of peace protesters and war supporters led by Bender on the Harvey County Courthouse lawn.

---

[11]Darrell Fast, interview by Jalane Schmidt, Persian Gulf War Oral History Collection.

[12]*Weathering the Storm: Christian Pacifist Responses to War* (Newton, KS: Faith and Life Press), 1991.

256 People of Two Kingdoms II

The war ended quickly. It was barely six weeks from the beginning of U.S. bombing in mid-January to the withdrawal of U.S. troops at the end of February. The prospect of a military draft disappeared and Mennonite youth suddenly stopped coming for draft counseling. President Bush, whose popular wartime approval rating had gone over 80%, came under criticism for failing to invade Baghdad, to capture Saddam Hussein, and to help Iraqi dissidents who rebelled against Hussein. Bush lost the 1992 presidential election to Bill Clinton. The Mennonites remained predominantly Republican, but the old charge that the Democrats, not the Republicans, got the country into war was no longer convincing. As for the peace movement, one of Aaron Rittenhouse's senior citizen oral interview informants, Rachel Kreider, who had been a teacher's wife at Bethel College during World War II, offered her Anabaptist-Mennonite pacifist wisdom: "Let the other organizations have the mighty flames. Somebody has to keep the steady glow between the upsurge of flames. You can't keep the flames leaping for 450 years."[13]

Summer of Mercy

In the summer of 1989 Michelle Ruebke, a member of Hesston Inter-Mennonite Fellowship, took action against the abortion clinic of Dr. George Tiller in Wichita.[14] Ruebke infiltrated Tiller's operation by pretending to be a woman coming for an abortion. Gaining access to the hotel where 98 women were awaiting late-term abortions, she successfully counseled nine women to save their babies. Together with another anti-abortion activist, Ruebke locked herself to a cement block on the driveway to the Tiller clinic. She was arrested then, and at many other times. Her home congregation, and Mennonites generally, did not openly support her radical action. But a few Mennonites did take part in the 1991 "Summer of Mercy," a dramatic event sponsored by "Operation Rescue" that brought thousands of members from across the

---

[13]"Bethel Students Document Gulf War Reaction." See also the summary report by Aaron Rittenhouse of the Persian Gulf War Oral History Collection.

[14]Michelle Ruebke, interview by James Juhnke, Newton, KS, 9 September 2014. Michelle Ruebke email to James Juhnke, 12 September 2014.

that "those hospitals with which we are affiliated to disallow elective (on demand) abortion."[22]

During the six-week volatile confrontations of the "Summer of Mercy" in Wichita, July-August 1991, the leaders and members of Mennonite churches, for the most part, kept a distance from the action. There were five Mennonite congregations in the city. Their leaders had reservations about Randall Terry, the abrasive charismatic-fundamentalist director of Operation Rescue, and his confrontational tactics of civil disobedience. Don Steelberg, pastor of the Lorraine Avenue Mennonite Church, said he was pro-life but respected people who made other choices. He opposed abortion as a means of birth control, but did not believe that life with a soul happens at the moment of conception. Marvin Zehr, pastor of Hope Mennonite Church, said most of his congregation leaned pro-life but didn't see abortion as a simple black-and-white issue. Zehr observed that the anti-abortion protesters quoted the same Bible verses that Mennonites did about killing in war. Why were the anti-abortionists willing to accept killing of innocent lives in wartime? John Warkentin, pastor First Mennonite Brethren Church, was concerned that the single issue focus on abortion defined pro-life too narrowly.[23] Gordon Bergman, pastor of a small East Wichita Mennonite Brethren Church, was more positively engaged. He saw Operation Rescue as a positive "wake-up call" for his small congregation–to prevent "the murder of life" and "this holocaust." The congregation agreed to hold a two-hour prayer vigil at an abortion clinic on September 23, the month after the Operation Rescue protestors had gone home.[24]

Cedric and Sandi Boehr of the Emmaus Mennonite Church (GCMC) near Whitewater joined the anti-abortion picketers. That event inspired them to run a political campaign in 1994 for the Kansas legislature 74th district, primarily on the abortion issue. Carol Harrison, Mennonite Brethren member in Wichita who had

---

[22]Willard S. Krabill, M.D. "Directive on Abortion from Health and Welfare Committee," *Mennonite Medical Messenger*, July-September 1976, 17-18.

[23]Don Ratzlaff, "Ministry amid a 'Summer of Mercy," *Christian Leader*, 10 September 1991, 17-19.

[24]Paul Schrag, "Abortion Battle Prompts Kansans to Confront Issue, Pro-Life Advocate Says Movement Gets Little Support from Mennonites," *Mennonite Weekly Review*, 26 September 1991, 1-2.

been assistant editor with *The Christian Leader*, was deeply moved by Operation Rescue. She adopted Randall Terry's rhetoric about "the legalized murder of 4,300 unborn babies each day across this nation." Harrison could not fathom "why so many Mennonites, long known for the radical stands in their early history, remain largely passive on this issue."[25]

On the other side of the picket lines in Wichita was Donna Neufeld, a social worker and social work teacher, who was a member of the Bethel College Mennonite Church in North Newton. Neufeld was a pro-choice feminist. She joined the people who lined up outside of George Tiller's clinic to protect abortion-seeking women who were threatened by the Operation Rescue activists. Neufeld's pro-choice activism was in the background in her later campaigns for the Kansas legislature. In 1994 and 1996 Neufeld ran against the pro-life Republican incumbent Gary Boston in the 72nd district which included the city of Newton.[26]

In the weeks after the Summer of Mercy, Mennonites who were put off by the movement's militant rhetoric and civil disobedience had opportunities to protest abortion in less confrontational ways. On October 6, 1991, people in cities around the country lined up in "Life Chains" along streets holding signs, "Abortion Kills Children." Jim Dunn, pastor of the First Mennonite Church in Newton, helped organize the Life Chain in Newton. The line extended eastward from First Mennonite Church about one mile toward the interstate highway 35. More than 1,500 people stood in line. Included were 855 from the Emmaus Mennonite Church of Whitewater; 80 from Grace Community Church in Newton; 53 from Koerner Heights Mennonite Brethren Church; and 52 from First Mennonite.[27] In 1994, three years later, some of these folks helped Cedric Boehr in his campaign for the state legislature.

In the judgment of Paul Schrag, editor of *Mennonite Weekly Review* and member of the First Mennonite Church in Newton, the Operation Rescue protests in Wichita were so undisciplined that they hurt the pro-life cause. While disagreeing with Randall Terry's

---

[25]Carol Harrison, "Mennonite for life, 'Mennonite for Life'," *The Christian Leader*, 10 September 1992, 10-11.

[26]Donna and Harry Neufeld interview.

[27]"Life Chain Gives Anti-Abortion Witness in Newton, Kan." *Mennonite Weekly Review*, 10 October 1991, 1.

tactics, Schrag agreed with the goal to reduce the number of abortions in the country. He called Mennonites to support adoption programs and centers where pregnant women could get help.[28]

One measure of the growing power of the religious right in central Kansas, and the polarization of the Republican Party into moderate and right wings, was manifest in the primary election of August 1994. For the first time the conservative evangelicals, led by Jinny Iserhardt and energized by Cedric Boehr's primary victory over the incumbent Ellen Samuelson, gained control of the Harvey County Republican Party. Iserhardt was a former Baptist who had joined the Grace Community Church south of Newton. That congregation was affiliated with the Evangelical Mennonite Church, a branch of the denomination with headquarters in Fort Wayne, Indiana. Iserhardt succeeded by recruiting conservative evangelicals, many previously politically uninvolved, to serve as Republican precinct committeemen and committeewomen. These folks were concerned about social issues, including abortion, homosexuality, and prayer in public schools.

Among Iserhardt's recruits were Elmer Klassen and Leonore Friesen Klassen, fellow members at the Grace Community Church. The Klassens were elected three times–1992, 1994, and 1996. They had both served as overseas missionaries and were married in 1988 after retirement. They were pro-family, anti-abortion conservative evangelicals. Before the 1990s they had not been involved in politics. But what they saw as the social and cultural deterioration of American life forced them to react. Things had changed drastically, Elmer Klassen said, since the years of his youth in a Krimmer Mennonite Brethren congregation near Hillsboro. "Back then we were in charge of our own education. Nobody complained when we had prayer in the public schools of Marion County. But take away the freedom of people to teach their children, and you really cause trouble." The Klassens were disappointed when Cedric Boehr, conservative, lost to Ellen Samuelson, moderate, in the general election of 1994. That outcome, Elmer believed, was due to Boehr's personal characteristics rather than to popular

---

[28]Paul Schrag, "Wichita Protests Aren't Best Pro-Life Witness." *Mennonite Weekly Review*, 22 August 1991, 4.

disagreement with his position on the issues. "He had no charisma, was not a leader, just didn't have the zip."[29]

The conservative evangelical control of the Harvey County Republican Party lasted only one election cycle. The Republican shift back to the moderate center was parallel to the course of the Harvey County Democrat Party two decades earlier, in 1972, when the left wing supporters of George McGovern gained control temporarily of the local party. The struggle between the polarized wings of the local Republican Party continued for at least the next two decades. The fact that Mennonites were engaged on the left and right wings of the movements–Democrats in 1972 and Republicans in 1994–suggested something of Mennonite political polarization.

Anabaptist Martyrs in Washington, D.C.

In the fall of 1990 a new exhibit on the Anabaptist martyr tradition, titled "Mirror of the Martyrs," opened at Kauffman Museum at Bethel College.[30] Robert Kreider was the exhibit curator. Featured in the exhibit were recently acquired copper plates with etchings done by the Dutch artist Jan Luyken for the 1685 edition of the *Martyrs Mirror*. In 1993 Kreider received an invitation from the Experimental Gallery of the Smithsonian Institution to showcase the museum exhibit in Washington, D.C., that spring and summer. It was a unique opportunity. Never before had the central symbols of the Anabaptist/Mennonite story been brought together so closely with the central symbols of America on the national mall. Kreider ambitiously planned for Mennonite artists, story tellers, and dramatists to perform at the exhibit.[31]

On March 4, less than a month before the planned exhibit opening, Smithsonian officials announced that it would be cancelled. Kreider had not been consulted in advance. Robert McC.

---

[29]Elmer Klassen and Lenore Friesen Klassen, interview by James Juhnke, North Newton, KS, 19 December 2000.

[30]James C. Juhnke, "Shaping Religious Community through Martyr Memories" (Unpublished presentation at "Walls and Windows" symposium, Bethel College, 20 November 1998).

[31]Robert S. Kreider, *Coming Home: An Autobiography of my 1952-2011 Years* (North Newton, KS: CreateSpace/Mudcreek Press, 2012), 217-9.

Adams, the Smithsonian's Secretary, sent a letter that vaguely spoke of bad timing in view of recent terrorist events–presumably the recent attacks on the World Trade Center in New York City and the Branch Davidian crisis in Waco, Texas. The letter also mentioned bureaucratic procedures in the Smithsonian, and the exhibit's narrow focus and inappropriateness for children. Kreider was nonplussed that the Mennonite tradition would be identified with terrorism and religious fanaticism. He asked Kansas politicians–Senators Bob Dole and Nancy Kassebaum and Representative Dan Glickman–to intercede in behalf of the exhibit. The politicians were polite, but did not offer effective pressure on the Smithsonian. The incident illustrated the relative political powerlessness of Kansas Mennonites.

Word eventually leaked out that the decision to cancel the exhibit was the result of petty bureaucratic infighting at the Smithsonian. Kreider was deeply disappointed. He took the opportunity to remind Mennonites of their separate identity: "Group worth is not predicated on achieving this stamp of national cultural approval. Actually it may be in one's marginality, living on the edges, that in the long run one can influence most profoundly the whole."[32]

Liquor by the Drink

Kansas historically had some of the strictest alcohol laws in the country. From 1881 to 1948 Kansas had statewide prohibition. The rules were gradually relaxed in a series of votes at the state and local levels. When given the opportunity, Mennonites voted to maintain strict controls in their counties and towns. By 1986 Kansans could purchase alcohol in liquor stores and in private clubs, and counties could make local decisions to allow purchase of "liquor by the drink" in restaurants that derived at least thirty percent of revenue from the sale of food.

Votes on liquor by the drink in 1986 and 1996 showed apparent changes in attitude. Voters in Harvey and McPherson counties voted against liquor by the drink in 1986, with Mennonites leading the opposition. But those same counties in 1996 voted to adopt

---

[32]Robert S. Kreider, "Reflections on the Smithsonian Experience" (unpublished manuscript, 17 February 1994).

liquor by the drink, with Mennonites still in opposition, but by a smaller margin. Marion County voted against liquor by the drink both times. Some observers speculated that the results revealed Mennonite acculturation over the decade–gradual liberalization of attitudes toward alcohol.[33] There were other factors at play, however, that made the vote results difficult to interpret. The 1986 vote was held in a non-presidential election year. In 1996 there was a presidential election (Bob Dole vs. Bill Clinton). And in 1996 the Chamber of Commerce and restaurant owners were far better organized to argue for the economic benefits of liquor by the drink.

In any case, in 1996 the anti-alcohol Mennonite forces in Harvey County did not go down without a vigorous fight. Clarence Rempel, pastor of First Mennonite Church in Newton, served as secretary and spokesman for the "Citizens for a Better Harvey County."[34] That committee put up signs, wrote letters to the editor, and bought newspaper advertisements. Steve Schmidt, pastor at New Creation Fellowship, asked "How Would Jesus Vote?" and answered that, although Jesus drank wine, he would vote "no" in a society of drunk drivers and rampant drug abuse. James D. Rutschman, a Mennonite restaurant owner, wrote that "Most restaurant operators believe liquor by the drink is a burden, not a boon," especially in a small town noted for good family restaurants with mid-scale casual dining.[35] Some Mennonites from opposite ends of the political spectrum found themselves agreeing on this issue. Donna Neufeld, liberal Democratic social worker, and Leonore Klassen, conservative Republican retired missionary and pastor, both opposed any measure that would increase consumption of alcohol in the community.[36] The tide of history was not on their side, despite events of local resistance. In 2003 the

---

[33]Foulke,"Shaping of Place," 241-6.
[34]Bill Wilson, "Anti-liquor by the drink signs vandalized," *The Newton Kansan*, 23 October 1996, 1.
[35]James D. Rutschman, letter to the editor, *The Newton Kansan*, 2 November 1996, 15.
[36]Lenore Klassen, letter to the editor, *The Newton* Kansan, 29 October 1996, 5. Lisa Elliott, "Liquor by the Drink," *The Newton Kansan*, 12 October 1996.

voters in Hesston, in an advisory referendum, soundly defeated (63% to 37%) a proposal to sell beer at the Hesston Golf Park.[37]

Evolution

From 1999 into the twenty-first century some Mennonites became involved in a statewide controversy about the teaching of the subject of evolution in Kansas public schools. On Aug. 11, 1999, the Kansas State Board of Education voted to allow science teachers to criticize the theory of evolution and to offer alternative explanations for human origins. That decision reflected the rise of the religious right in Kansas culture and politics. It made Kansas "a laughingstock among scientists, educators, and journalists across the nation."[38] Harold Voth, member of Burrton Mennonite Church and former superintendent at Haven High School (1966-1994), was a member of the Kansas State Board of Education. He had been actively involved in the field of education, including service on the boards of Bethel College, the Kansas State High School Activities Association, and the Hutchinson Community College Board of Trustees. He voted with the conservatives against the teaching of evolution. Despite his vote with the conservatives, Voth did not want to be identified with doctrinaire religious right anti-evolutionists. He said he had no disagreement with the theory of evolution. He thought the Board of Education's decision was a compromise and that his vote helped avoid an impasse. The decision had left to local boards of education the power to decide how the theory of evolution should be taught.[39]

On the other side of the issue was Wayne Wiens, professor of biology at Bethel College and member of the Bethel College Mennonite Church. He had been teaching evolution from the beginning of his career in the 1960s. Wiens found Voth's explanation of his quest for "compromise" to be weak and unconvincing. "I can't believe the state of Kansas is doing this,"

---

[37] Amanda Balzer, "Hesston says no to beer," *The Newton Kansan*, 11 November 2003, 1. Palmer Becker, "Why the 'no' vote on beer," *The Newton Kansan*, 13 November 2003, 4.

[38] Robert Wuthnow, *Red State Religion*, 269.

[39] Harold Voth, interview by James Juhnke, Burrton, KS, n.d. Wuthnow, *Red State Religion*, 308-9.

said Wiens. Why was science "the only area of the curriculum to be given over to the locals to control?"[40] Wiens critiqued the evangelical fundamentalist right for distorting the meaning of the words "fact" and "theory." He was alarmed when one publisher of a Kansas history textbook responded to the State Board's decision by removing a chapter on Kansas geology and paleontology from their book. The book omitted references to the inland sea that covered Kansas sixty million years ago and to the fossils that were on display in Kansas museums.[41]

In February 2001, after two conservative members of the board of education had been ousted, the new board reinstated evolution in the science teaching standards. By 2005 the conservatives were back in control and the board returned to standards similar to those of 1999. This time the argument shifted to the case for "intelligent design." Harold Voth was no longer on the board, but Wayne Wiens vigorously spoke out in public and wrote in newspapers about evolution. He argued against the notion that the theories of intelligent design and of evolution were both faith positions backed by relatively equivalent evidence. "There is very, very little real scientific evidence in favor of intelligent design," he wrote, "certainly in comparison to the massive weight of evidence for evolution accumulated over the past 150 years."[42] In 2007 the Kansas board of education pendulum shifted once again and criticisms of evolution were eliminated from the science standards.

Death Penalty

In 1994 Kansas reinstated the death penalty when Governor Kathleen Sebelius allowed it to become law without her signature. Mennonites continued in the following years to work with other groups for abolition. In 2012 Steven Becker, a former district court

---

[40]Jennifer Newton, "Educators troubled by board's vote on evolution," *The Newton Kansan*, 16 August 1999, 1, 5. Wayne Wiens, "Consequences of the Evolution Furor: What Must be Changed" (paper at "Friday at Four Forum," Bethel College, 27 October 2000), 1. Wiens collection shared by Gail Lutsch.

[41]John Ellis, "Book on state history altered after evolution vote," *The Wichita Eagle*, 21 August 1999, 1A, 4A.

[42]Wayne Wiens, "Intelligent design should be tested," *The Newton Kansan*, 28 June 2005, 6A.

judge and a member of the Buhler First Mennonite Church, was elected on the Republican ticket to the Kansas House of Representatives. Becker became a sponsor of death penalty repeal and an advisor to the End the Death Penalty Task force of the Western District Conference. The Kansas Coalition Against the Death Penalty, in its "Volunteer Spotlight," in the spring of 2014 officially commended the Western District Mennonite Task force for generating more letters to legislators in the campaign for death penalty repeal than any other group in the Coalition.[43]

Political Identification Dilemma

The politics of the 1990s put Mennonites on the horns of a dilemma. Their opposition to militarism and warfare led them toward the Democrats. The Republicans, initiators of the Persian Gulf War and supporters of big defense budgets, seemed on the side of militarism. At the same time, Mennonite opposition to abortion and homosexual rights led them toward the Republicans.

Marvin Hein, former pastor of the Mennonite Brethren Church of Hillsboro, wrote that "we Anabaptists stand in a unique but difficult position. We are morally and theologically conservative like Republicans tend to be, but we are also sensitive to social justice and peace issues which seem to be the hallmarks of Democrats. I accept that dichotomy as a strength, not a weakness." Hein was responding to a question during the 1996 presidential campaign about whether Mennonites should prefer a candidate who lacked a record of military service (Bill Clinton) or a candidate who was a military veteran (Bob Dole). Dole had made that an issue in the campaign. Hein said Mennonites should not be single issue voters. In the context of the 1990s, Hein's advice could be seen as an admonition to church members who had been newly politicized over the abortion issue.[44]

There were indeed many other issues. Richard Kyle, teacher of history at Tabor College, in 1992 listed twelve important issues in the presidential contest between George Bush and Bill Clinton. The

---

[43]"Volunteer Spotlight: The Mennonite Western District Conference," *Kansas Coalition Against the Death Penalty Newsletter*, Spring 2014.

[44]Marvin Hein, "Inquiring Minds," *The Christian Leader*, October 1996, 15.

most important issue, Kyle said, was limited government versus expansive government. Abortion and abortion rights belonged to emotion-laden "single-issue politics" that attracted "single-minded people and extremists."[45] The National Association of Evangelicals that same year listed the positions of Bush and Clinton on seventeen issues, without indicating their relative importance. The *Christian Leader*, Mennonite Brethren denominational publication in Hillsboro, published the NAE listing before the election of 1992.[46]

Sociological studies of Mennonites all across America showed that Mennonites in general were becoming more politically involved. Comprehensive church member surveys in 1972 and 1989 revealed that increasing numbers of Mennonites were ready to identify with both Republicans and Democrats. Leland Harder, Mennonite sociologist who collected and surveyed the data, wrote that the results reflected increased urbanization and education. More highly educated Mennonites tended to be more identified with the Democrat Party. Harder predicted greater political pluralism in the future. The church member surveys did not compare Kansas with other states. Kansas Mennonites had long been more politically involved than more culturally conservative Mennonites in Indiana, Ohio, Pennsylvania, and Virginia. But the increasing polarization in Kansas wrought in the 1990s in the wake of the Persian Gulf War and the Summer of Mercy in Wichita was consistent with the results of the church member surveys in 1972 and 1989.[47]

---

[45]Richard Kyle, "The Issues Beyond the Rhetoric," *Christian Leader*, 20 October 1992, 7-9.

[46]"Bush, Clinton: Where They Stand," *Christian Leader*, 20 October 1992, 10-11.

[47]Leland Harder, "Taking a more political approach," *The Christian Leader*, 9 October 1990, 10-11. J. Howard Kauffman and Leland Harder, *Anabaptists Four Centuries Later: A Profile of Five Mennonite and Brethren in Christ Denominations* (Scottdale, PA: Herald Press, 1975); J. Howard Kauffman and Leo Driedger, *The Mennonite Mosaic: Identity and Modernization* (Scottdale, PA: Herald Press, 1991); Leland Harder, *The Discerning People of God: Doors to Lock and Doors to Open* (Scottdale, PA: Herald Press, 1993).

Chapter 15

Turn of Century: Flags, Same-Sex Marriage

9-11 and the Flag at Hesston

The terrorist attack on the World Trade Center in New York on September 11, 2001, galvanized American patriotic militarism and once again put the pacifist Mennonites on the defensive. Three thousand people died and the shocked American people demanded vengeance. Less than a month later, on October 7, President George Bush bombed and invaded Afghanistan in an attempt to capture Osama bin Laden, the leader of Al Qaeda, who took credit for the 9-11 atrocity. Bin Laden escaped. A year and a half later, on March 20, 2003, President Bush militarily attacked Iraq, claiming that President Saddam Hussein was associated with Al Qaeda and was developing weapons of mass destruction. Both claims proved false. In both Afghanistan and Iraq, the U.S. became mired in expensive and destructive long-term civil wars that had the unintended effect of energizing terrorist groups.

The immediate response to 9-11 by Kansas Mennonites was to lament the tragedy, to call for justice for the perpetrators, and to warn against a spirit and policy of vengeance. Clarence Rempel, pastor of the First Mennonite Church in Newton, in his sermon the Sunday after 9-11 suggested that "the United States refuse in Jesus' name to retaliate for these horrific terrorist acts." The Muslim world would be more impressed with restraint than with violence.[1] Paul Schrag, editor of *Mennonite Weekly Review,* wrote that "We must seek justice. . . . But do not retaliate. Do not destroy more lives. Do not return evil for evil." Retaliation was not in the national interest. "We do not expect the government to adopt the peaceful ways of Jesus. But we can expect the government to do what serves its people best."[2] In letters to the editor and other public protests during the debate leading up to the invasion of Iraq, Mennonites repeatedly returned to the theme of violence begetting violence. Gordon Allaby, pastor of the First Mennonite Church of

---

[1] Melanie Zuercher, "Across the country, a Sunday for peace," *Mennonite Weekly Review*, 20 September 2001, 1.
[2] Paul Schrag, "'In God we trust' means no revenge," *Mennonite Weekly Review*, 20 September 2001, 4.

Christian in Moundridge wrote, "Our violent aggressiveness will not stop terrorism; it will cause more terrorism."[3] Leonard Wiebe, interim pastor of Whitestone Mennonite Church in Hesston said, "If we destroy Iraq in a war, my concern is that we will create a whole new group of enemies and terrorists."[4]

The Mennonite witness against approaching war in 2002-3 had much in common with their contribution to public debate before the Persian Gulf War in 1990-1. Thousands of church members signed a letter from Jim Schrag, executive director of the Mennonite Church USA, to President Bush calling for alternatives to war. A Christian Peacemaker Team delegation visited Baghdad to seek possibilities of dialogue. There were public peace demonstrations and advertisements in newspapers. The Mennonite Central Committee raised funds to help war victims.

Some of the peace protest techniques were new and different. In the face of rampant American flag veneration, the Mennonite Church USA produced alternative white flags printed in green, "Pray for Peace, Act for Peace." Those flags appeared in church yards and sanctuaries, in peace marches and demonstrations, and in the front of some Mennonite homes. Hesston College students joined other protestors in sending envelopes with half cups of rice to President Bush asking him to send food, not bombs, to Iraq. Some groups, such as the Kansas Institute for Peace and Conflict Resolution at Bethel College, opened conversations with local Muslims and hosted events that brought Muslims and Christians together.[5]

Local American patriots pushed back against the Kansas Mennonite peace witness. One anti-pacifist from Sedgwick had a sense of history repeating itself. "During World War II," wrote Mary Coslett, "buildings at Bethel College were painted yellow by people who were proud to be Americans. Those were the days."[6]

---

[3]Gordon Allaby, "Christians, have you forgotten who you are?" *Newton Kansan*, 27 September 2002, 7.

[4]Phil Richard, "Stories highlight Hesston Peace Week" *Mennonite Weekly Review*, 17 February 2003, 7.

[5]For a summary of the Mennonite peace witness in 2002 see Paul Schrag, "2002 year in review," *Mennonite Weekly Review*, 30 December 2002, 6.

[6]Mary Grace Coslett, "She supports Curtis on signs," *The Newton Kansan*, 10 January 2003, 4.

Coslett's implied threat of violence did not deter Mennonites from outspoken challenges to Americans' claims of God's support for Bush's wars. David Janzen, writing to the *Newton Kansan*, critiqued the U.S. conviction "that power may defile other nations, but our superpower status proves that we are favored by God with a calling to conquer evil by means of a war that cannot be evil, because opposing evil makes us good. This is the illusion of American innocence and messianic destiny that is so dangerous to the world."[7]

Hesston College became the prime target for anti-pacifists who venerated the American flag.[8] In 1970, amid controversy over the Vietnam War, the college had removed the flagpole from in front of the administration building. Now, thirty-two years later, in the wake of the 9-11 terrorist attacks, some Kansas legislators took offense at the absence of a flagpole. They undertook a campaign to declare Hesston College ineligible for state tuition grant funding if the college did not display an American flag on an outdoor flagpole. At that point Hesston received about $143,000 yearly in the tuition grant program. The anti-Hesston legislators claimed as legal basis a state law passed in 1939 (K.S.A. 73-707) which required private and parochial schools to "provide a suitable flag . . . for every schoolhouse." In fact, the American flag was on display each year in the Hesston's student center cafeteria during the international festival along with the national flags of international students.

Garry Boston, a Newton businessmen who represented the 72nd district in the legislature, was one leader in the Hesston flag controversy. The 72nd district included Newton, but not Hesston. Boston was joined by Melvin Neufeld of Ingalls, a farmer of Mennonite background who had attended Tabor College in the 1960s, and by Bob Bethell of Alden. Bethell introduced a measure to the House Appropriations Committee to deny Hesston tuition grant funding until it put up a flagpole. In Bethell's view, "If you accept state money, you accept it with strings attached. . . . I don't think we ought to be thumbing our nose at people who have

---

[7]David Janzen, "Jesus overcame fear of death; we can too," *The Newton Kansan*, 24 April 2003, 4.
[8]John Sharp, *School on the Prairie*, 403-7.

fought and died to provide the freedoms that we enjoy."[9] Loren Swartzendruber, president of Hesston College, with the support of the college board and faculty, decided to keep up the flag display in the cafeteria year round, but to refuse the demanded outdoor flagpole. One former student, who had become a constitutional lawyer, volunteered pro bono legal services if the college chose to challenge the state's action as a violation of freedom of religion.[10]

For three months, March to May, versions of Bethell's proposal wended through the Kansas House and Senate. Meanwhile the media, including a local TV station and a nationally syndicated radio program, the *Neal Boortz Show*, picked up the story, well aware of its potential to outrage patriots in the overheated post 9-11 climate. Hesston College received a blizzard of protests. Asked one e-mail message to President Swartzendruber, "Why couldn't you people have been in the Twin Towers on Sept. 11th?"[11] Swartzendruber said that for too long the tuition grant flag issue absorbed ninety percent of his administrative time. The Kansas legislature finally sent to Governor Bill Graves a strange compromise as part of the budget bill that would have offered Hesston College $500 from one legislator's unused postal funds to put up a flagpole. On the final day of the session, May 31, 2002, Governor Bill Graves used his line-item veto to remove the provision. Hesston College was still eligible for Kansas tuition-grant funds.

Garry Boston's outspoken role in the flag-flying case, offensive as it was to his Mennonite constituency, endangered his political support from Mennonites in the upcoming 2002 election. Most damaging was an encounter on March 13 in Boston's Topeka office with Matt Schloneger. Schloneger, grant writer for Hesston College and a resident of Newton, had come to thank Boston for the Kansas Arts Commission's past support of the Hesston-Bethel Performing Arts Series and to lobby for future support. When Schloneger introduced himself as from Hesston College, Boston condemned Hesston for not flying the flag. He refused to accept Schloneger's

---

[9]Susan Balzer, "Bill would cut Hesston aid for not flying flag," *Mennonite Weekly Review*, 15 April 2002, 1-2.

[10]Sharp, *School on the Prairie*, 405.

[11]Rich Preheim, "Unflagging pursuit of faithfulness," *The Mennonite*, 2 July 2002, 11.

folder of materials and ordered him out of the office. Schloneger, at that point completely unaware of the flag issue, was surprised and shocked. He asked for an explanation. Boston said, "Will you leave my office, or do I have to call security?" The confrontation was covered in the Mennonite press and circulated in the Mennonite community.[12]

On October 4, 2002, during his campaign for re-election, Garry Boston spoke at a Bethel College convocation. He invited Matt Schloneger from the audience to join him on stage in order to correct what he called distortions in the published accounts of the March 13 encounter in Topeka. In the process Boston confused and alienated his audience. He did not deny that he had threatened to call security if Schloneger did not leave his office.[13] One Bethel student wrote to the *Newton Kansan* complaining that Boston's speech was "bizarre" and "distressing."[14] Another student sent an angry message to Bethel's "student announce" web site telling fellow students that "It is not necessary for us to be represented in Topeka by a total a—hole." A group of politically active students organized to help Boston's opponent, Tom Thull, with door-to-door campaigning in Newton.[15]

Thull was a banker in Newton and mayor of North Newton. He campaigned as a Democratic fiscal conservative who favored a balanced budget, reduced tax burden on middle class families, and restored "state funding for education, health care and senior services."[16] He was Catholic, but not as strong against abortion as was Boston. The *Newton Kansan* endorsed Thull, criticizing Boston for weak leadership in behalf of social service agencies such as Prairie View Mental Health Center. The endorsement did not mention Boston's effort to deny tuition grant funds to Hesston College. That issue remained an unacknowledged anti-Republican elephant in the room. In the election on November 5 Thull defeated Boston 53.1% to 46.8%. The *Kansan* noted that Boston "was unable to overcome North Newton's overwhelming support of Democrat

---

[12]Preheim, "Unflagging pursuit," 11.

[13]James Juhnke, personal notes from the 4 October 2002 convocation.

[14]Sam Schrag, "Boston visit to Bethel 'bizarre,'" *The Newton Kansan*, 7 October 2002, 4.

[15]Alex Gingerich, Bethel College Student Announce email list, 4 October 2001.

[16]Tom Thull campaign flyer, October 2002.

Tom Thull."[17] The outcome demonstrated, in part at least, Mennonite political power to punish a politician who had offended them.

Gerrymander Fight

In October 2001 a Kansas House Redistricting Committee, charged with adjusting the boundaries of congressional districts to achieve equal population per district, proposed a plan that put North Newton into the big rural first district of western Kansas. The plan was an obvious political "gerrymander." It was a Republican strategy to take North Newton's Democratic votes out of the fourth district (including Wichita) where elections were often closely contested, and put them into the strongly Republican first district of rural western Kansas where they would make no difference. In separating North Newton (1st district) from Newton (4th district) the plan violated the redistricting guidelines, which said that "communities of interest" should not be divided. Moreover, on the map the city of North Newton was barely contiguous in its northwestern tip with the proposed new 1st district boundary.[18] Mennonites in North Newton assumed that the plan was payback for their peace activism as well as for voting Democratic.

Community leaders of both political parties at Bethel College, North Newton, and Newton united in a nonpartisan campaign of opposition to the proposed gerrymander. Doug Anstaett, editor of the *Newton Kansan*, denounced the plan as a "blatant political move," and called for a veto by Governor Bill Graves.[19] North Newton held several public meetings and invited legislators Garry Boston (from Newton) and Carl Krehbiel (from Moundridge) to hear their protests. Students at Bethel College sent some ninety letters to members of the redistricting committee. City administrators from Newton and North Newton travelled to

---

[17]Chris Strunk and Amanda Balzer, "North Newton Democrat defeats 12-year incumbent," *The Newton Kansan*, 6 November 2002, 2.

[18]June Krehbiel, "'Gerrymander' not welcome at Bethel," *Mennonite Weekly Review*, 20 December 2001, 12.

[19]Doug Anstaett, "Redistricting plan is blatant political move," *The Newton Kansan*, 19 March 2002, 4.

Topeka to make their case for their mutual common interests and for the importance of staying in the same district with Wichita to the south. James Juhnke, North Newton Democratic precinct committeeman, designed an alternative plan to keep all of Harvey County in the 4th district by putting a number of rural townships in western Kingman County into the 1st district.[20]

In May 2002 the Redistricting Conference Committee agreed to a plan that kept Harvey County intact and in the 4th district. Portions of rural Greenwood County were put into the 1st district. Mike O'Neal, Republican chairman of the House Redistricting committee, publically congratulated Krehbiel and Boston for their leadership in overturning the original proposal, without acknowledging the partisan scheming that created it in the first place.[21]

Same-Sex Marriage

A Kansas political referendum in 2005 on gay marriage exposed a sharp polarization of attitudes among Mennonites on homosexual rights. The issue had been vigorously debated in Mennonite church circles, especially the Western District Conference (GC). Mennonite denominations had adopted official statements that God approved only marriages between one man and one woman. State law already prohibited same-sex marriage, but religious conservatives wanted to join in a national movement for an amendment to the United States constitution. In an April 2005 election, Kansas voters overwhelmingly approved the amendment banning same-sex marriage by a 70 to 30 percent margin.[22] The South Central counties of substantial Mennonite population also voted overwhelmingly for the amendment.

There was one notable exception. In North Newton, home to Bethel College and the Bethel College Mennonite Church, opponents of the amendment opposed the strong majority tide. They voted 59% to 41% in favor of legal same-sex marriage.

---

[20]Matt Moline, "Professor takes redistricting personally," *The Topeka Capital-Journal*, 17 December 2002. http://cjonline.com/stories/121701/kan_juhnke.shtml.

[21]Mike O'Neal, "Chair cites Boston, Krehbiel for work," *The Newton Kansan*, 28 May 2002, 4.

[22]Wuthnow, *Red State Religion*, 330 6.

Douglas County, which included the University of Kansas, was the only county in Kansas to vote against the amendment.[23] North Newton was the only precinct in Harvey County to do so. In the days before the election, Mennonite supporters of same-sex marriage had written many letters to the editor of the *Newton Kansan*. They argued their case in eloquent detail. Ruth Linscheid, member of the Bethel College Mennonite Church, told her story as the mother of a gay son who had been in a healthy monogamous same-sex marriage for twenty years. Walter S. Friesen, who had been pastor of a number of Mennonite churches, reviewed the Bible texts from Leviticus and the letters of Paul. Friesen said that the sexual relationships condemned in the Bible had nothing in common with same-sex relationships in modern America. Anne Showalter of Hesston argued that homosexuals should not be blamed for the breakdown of marriage in American society. A number of writers made the point that homosexuality was a birth characteristic, not a matter of choice.[24]

The distinctiveness of North Newton opinion and voting showed a dramatic difference both from Kansas and local public opinion in general, and from the positions of more rural and conservative evangelical Mennonites. Voters in Marion County voted against same-sex marriage by a margin of 82% to 18%. Those results included many votes of conservative evangelical Mennonite Brethren in Hillsboro, and the votes of Mennonites of various branches in rural parts of the county. In McPherson County voters opposed same-sex marriage by a margin of 74% to 26%. The polarization of Mennonite opinion was substantially along rural/urban lines. There is no voting record available for the Lorraine Avenue Mennonite Church, where at least two lesbian couples were regular worshippers in the congregation. It is likely that a strong majority there voted against the amendment. The same would be true for the Peace Mennonite Church in Lawrence,

---

[23]Scott Rothschild, "Douglas County Alone Rejects Ban," *Lawrence Journal World*, 6 April 2005, 1A, 8A.

[24]See the letters on the editorial pages of *The Newton Kansan* for March 3, 22, 24 29, 30 and April 1, 2005.

a congregation that "Opens Doors to Gays" according to the local newspaper.[25]

Judging by letters to the editor of the *Newton Kansan*, Mennonites were far more agitated by the same-sex marriage issue than about the casino/gambling issue that came up for a vote later that same year, December 2005. The vote in December was a non-binding referendum designed by casino supporters to promote their cause. The referendum failed in Marion County and won in Harvey County, both by small margins of 52% to 48%. In neither case did local Mennonites organize letter-writing campaigns or other protests. As it turned out, a casino was built at Mulvane south of Wichita, well outside of the territory of Mennonite settlement.[26]

Don Dahl, Conservative Republican

In 1996 Don Dahl, a conservative Republican and member of the Mennonite Brethren Church in Hillsboro, was elected state representative in the 70th district. Dahl replaced Duane Goossen, who had retired in frustration with the growing power of the Republican right wing and the marginalization of moderates in the party. Dahl had graduated from Tabor College in 1968 majoring in history and social sciences. He then had spent twenty-two years in the U.S. Navy. Dahl was part of the religious right wing. His political advertisements called for "defeat of the Homosexual Agenda." He cited a text from the Old Testament book of Leviticus that said that men who lie down with each other should be put to death. But, he said, "I don't go that far." Dahl favored legislative action to limit abortion, but also claimed to favor a "hands off" approach by government. Though he was never married, he said that "the family unit is the backbone of American society." He wanted to lower taxes, but also favored using state funds to support private, parochial, and home-based schools.[27]

---

[25]"Church Opens Doors to Gays," *Lawrence Journal-World*, 20 April 2004. Cited in Wuthnow, *Red State Religion*, 438.

[26]"Harvey, Sumner counties want casino development," *Hillsboro Star-Journal*, 21 December 2005, 1.

[27]Notes and clippings in a Don Dahl file at the Center for Mennonite Brethren Studies at Tabor College.

The 70th district Republican Party primary in 1996 illustrated the rising importance of issues of sexuality in Kansas politics. Dahl's opponent in that election was David Mueller, 35, a Lutheran who lived with another man near Tampa. When Dahl's supporters accused Mueller of being gay, they responded that it was strange that Dahl, a 51-year-old never-been-married man, lived with his widowed mother in Hillsboro. Dahl said he was straight. Mueller refused to deny that he was gay. Mueller's position on other issues aligned with moderate Republicans. Dahl won the election by only twenty-six votes, less than one percent of the total. Mueller won outside of Hillsboro, but overwhelming support in his home town gave Dahl the primary victory. There was no Democratic candidate in the 1996 general election. Dahl won the following five elections without serious opposition. He retired from the legislature in 2008.[28]

John Waltner, Town Mayor and History Teacher

In 1998 Ellen Samuelson retired from her position in the Kansas House of Representatives, district 74. Four years earlier, in 1994, John Waltner, mayor of the town of Hesston and history teacher at Hesston High School, had helped Samuelson win a write-in campaign after she had lost the Republican primary, though he was a Democrat and she was a Republican. When he announced his candidacy for the open seat in 1998, Waltner hoped that Samuelson and other Republicans would reciprocate his support. That hope was not realized.[29]

Waltner had been elected mayor of Hesston in 1985, a non-partisan position he held for twenty-five years. One challenge had been to oversee the recovery of the town from a devastating tornado in 1990. A longer-term challenge was managing the growth of the town in the 1980s and 1990s. In his 1998 campaign, Waltner hoped that his years of leadership in the community would help overcome the 60% to 40% advantage that Republicans had over

---

[28]Dave Ranney, "Sex, politics mingle in race," *The Wichita Eagle*, 13 October 1996, 21A.

[29]John Waltner, interview by James Juhnke, North Newton, KS, 28 January 2015.

Democrats as registered voters. He was disappointed when Samuelson took a position on his opponent's campaign staff.

Waltner's Republican opponent in 1998 was Carl Krehbiel, president of an independent telephone company in Moundridge. Waltner and Krehbiel had traditional "Mennonite" names, but Krehbiel's family had left the Mennonite church in an earlier generation. Waltner was a member of the Bethel College Mennonite Church. Both candidates were middle aged (52 and 49) political moderates who agreed on the major issues. Both were pro-choice on abortion, supporters of a new state highway plan, and advocates of funding for public education. Krehbiel had the advantages of a majority of registered Republicans in the district, and of superior funding resources. The Democrats, in a last-minute campaign blitz of radio advertisements and printed flyers, questioned how out-of-district contributions by supporters in the telephone industry would affect Krehbiel's judgment in office. But Krehbiel won the election handily by 3,509 (55%) to 2817 (45%) of the votes.[30]

Waltner went on to a number of different positions of public service. For nine years he served as Harvey County special projects coordinator, and as chairman of the Regional Economic Area Partnership. In December 2009 he was appointed Harvey County Administrator.

Christine Downey, Catholic Mennonite

At the turn of century Kansas Mennonites were for the first time represented in the state legislature by two women, one in the Senate and one in the House of Representatives. Christine Downey, a sixth grade teacher from Newton, served as Kansas Senator for District #31 from 1993 to 2004. Downey had been raised in a Catholic farm family near Abilene, and had been an observant and active member of the St. Mary Catholic Church in Newton while her three children were growing up. Her youngest child was a freshman in high school when Downey was elected to the senate in

---

[30]Chris Strunk, "Campaign finance at issue in House," *The Newton Kansan*, 24 October 1998, 15. Chris Strunk, "Krehbiel Overcomes Waltner for 74th District House Seat," *The Newton Kansan*, 4 November 1998, 5. Doug Anstaett, "Race didn't have to go negative," *The Newton Kansan*, 4 November 1998, 4.

280   People of Two Kingdoms II

Downey campaign ad

November 1992. A month after the election her husband told her he was leaving the marriage. Two and a half years later, in July 1995, Downey married Gordon Schmidt, a Mennonite farmer and member of the Hoffnungsau Mennonite Church in southwestern McPherson County. Downey had her first marriage annulled. She and Schmidt regularly attended the Hoffnunsau church. Although she became alienated from the St. Mary Church–in part because the priest wanted to annul Schmidt's first marriage and in part because St. Mary supported her opponents in subsequent elections–she did not officially leave the Catholic Church. For practical and political purposes, however, her identity was Mennonite. She told one persistent casino supporter who wanted her vote, "Look. I'm married to a Mennonite. I worship with the Mennonites. I live in a Mennonite community. I'll never vote for gambling!"[31]

The 31st Senate district included all of Harvey County and part of southeast Sedgwick County (Bel Aire, Kechi, Park City). Only about a quarter of the registered voters were Democrats. Downey won all three of her elections (1992, 1996, and 2000) by narrow margins. Martin Hawver, political commentator in Topeka, attributed Downey's success in a dominantly Republican district to her "unique personality."[32] She was an engagingly self-confident, articulate, and well-informed person. She listened well to opponents, stated her own positions clearly, and sought bi-partisan compromise. The Democrats were a declining minority in the Senate–falling from eighteen to eight members of the forty-member body. But Downey was pleased that the Democrats were often able

---

[31]Christine Downey-Schmidt, interview by James Juhnke, North Newton, KS, 6 October 2014.
[32]*Hawver's Capitol Report* (27 October 2004), 3.

to cooperate with moderate Republicans to get progressive legislation passed. One important bill that got her bipartisan support was a tax increase supported by the moderate Republican governor Bill Graves in 2002.[33]

Downey was a member of the Chamber of Commerce and Industry. In 2000 she received a Chamber "Friend of Business" award for her pro-business voting record. A three-term member of the Senate Education Committee, and ranking minority member in her third term, Downey strongly supported funding for education. She introduced a bill for monitoring pollution in the Equus Beds water supply. Governor Graves enacted her proposal by executive order. Downey opposed voucher programs to give public tax dollars to private schools. She criticized the National Rifle Association's positions on guns: "After 20 years in elementary classrooms teaching kids how to solve problems in nonviolent ways, I'm having difficulty understanding how we will make Kansas safer by encouraging citizens to carry and conceal weapons." Downey consistently opposed the death penalty.[34]

The issue of abortion dominated Downey's third election campaign in 2000. Downey had opposed abortion. She had voted for a 24-hour waiting period, for parental notification bills, and to ban the procedure known as "partial birth abortion." However, she had voted against one anti-partial-birth abortion bill that was "clearly unconstitutional" and would have involved the state in expensive litigation. Her opponent, Steve Brunk of Park City, supported by the Kansans for Life organization, attacked her on the abortion issue. Virginia Iserhardt, a pro-life crusader in Newton, wrote to the Newton *Kansan* that partial birth abortions were still being done in Kansas, and that Downey's vote was in part responsible. The Wichita *Eagle* and the Newton *Kansan* endorsed Downey for re-election. She won with 52% of the vote.[35]

Downey declined to run for a fourth term in 2004. Ten years after her retirement, in the wake of a right wing Republican purge of

---

[33]Downey-Schmidt interview. "Leadership worked hard to find solution," *The Wichita Eagle*, 19 May 2002, n.p. from Downey files.

[34]Christine Downey, "Death penalty not the answer to crime," *The Newton Kansan*, 1 February 1994, 4.

[35]Information about the 2000 campaign from two folders in possession of Christine Downey-Schmidt.

progressive legislators from their party under the administration of Governor Sam Brownback, Downey lamented that the bipartisan political cooperation that characterized her terms in the Kansas Senate had become impossible.

Judy Loganbill, Urban Educator

Loganbill campaign ad

In November 2000 Judy Loganbill, a 47-year old elementary school teacher in Wichita, became the first Mennonite woman to be elected to the Kansas House of Representatives. She was an active member at Lorraine Avenue Mennonite Church. She served as a Democrat in district 86 for six terms–through 2012. In that year she lost in the primary to a popular fellow Democrat after changes in the district boundaries.[36]

Loganbill was proud to be the only elementary school teacher in the Kansas House. She was an activist teacher who had become known through her work for the local teachers union and for the Wichita affiliate of the National Education Association. Her most important legislative concern was adequate funding for education. She also gave special attention to "the social issues"–social welfare, immigration, voter registration, and unemployment. The National Rifle Association usually rated her at the bottom of their list–an "F minus minus"–as she put it. Loganbill did favor allowing a casino vote in Sedgwick County, a position that most of her fellow church members probably disagreed with.

One time that Loganbill voted against her own convictions was on the issue of gay marriage. Her district was more conservative than she was on that issue. A bill came before the House to force a popular vote for an amendment to the state constitution outlawing gay marriage. Thinking of her constituents, she "wimped out and

---

[36]Judy Loganbill presentation at Lorraine Avenue Mennonite Church, 29 January 2012.

voted to put the issue on the ballot. I was literally in tears when I did it." Later that same issue came back to the House from the Senate, and she voted against the amendment. She did get a few letters of protest from her constituents. She also was honored by Wichita Pride with one of their Gay and Lesbian Awards for "most supportive public official."[37]

Loganbill's Mennonite identity made her vulnerable to charges of not being sufficiently patriotic. In the 2004 campaign her opponent distributed a flyer accusing her of not saying the pledge of allegiance and of not supporting American troops in Iraq. In fact she often had not gotten to her seat in the House chamber in time to participate in the morning opening pledge of allegiance. She was not opposed to reciting the pledge, but she always concluded under her breath: "with peace and justice for all (some day)." Loganbill did not like to see the American flag in church sanctuaries. "God is not an American," she said.

During the six terms she served in the legislature (through 2012), Loganbill spoke up at congregational sharing times to keep her fellow church members informed about state politics. Asked in 2012 about how her Christian and Mennonite values affected her politics, she pointed to the banners in front of the church: "Love, Hospitality, Service." The hospitality theme was immediately relevant in view of a crusade by the Kansas secretary of state, Kris Kobach, to restrict voting by immigrants.

Immigrant Farm Workers

Beginning in 2001 Kansas Mennonites and the Kansas Department of Health and Welfare (KDHW) cooperated in a unique social welfare project. In the late 1990s substantial numbers of non-Latino, Low German-speaking farm workers began arriving in Kansas. These workers were from "Old Colony" Mennonite settlements in Mexico whose ancestors had migrated from Ukraine to Canada and to Mexico. They left Mexico in part because of an economic downturn there in the 1990s, and because of burgeoning Mennonite population with large families. Some of these migrant

---

[37]"Wichita Pride Hosts Gay and Lesbian Awards," *The Wichita Eagle*, 16 June 2007, 1B.

workers stayed in Kansas. Others moved to Canada or back to Mexico. Many were impoverished, uneducated, and in need of health care. The KDHW had long been providing services for needy Hispanic immigrant farm workers. But they had no staff members with Low German speaking skills. The Mennonite Western District Conference, lacking their own program to meet the needs of the Mennonite farm worker families from Mexico, did have some people with requisite language skills who were willing to volunteer. A Western District Conference task force responded to an appeal by KDHW for funding and for volunteers.[38]

Surveys of Old Order people to learn their needs had to be conducted in the Low German language. Tina Block Ediger and Rosemary Wyse of North Newton conducted the first extensive social survey of the Mennonite farm workers for the Kansas Department of Health and Welfare. They discovered that wives of the Old Colony farm workers were especially isolated and needy, sometimes victims of domestic violence and lacking any professional health care when pregnant. Funding grants for Mennonite volunteer workers came from the Schowalter Foundation and from the Kansas Health Foundation, channeled through the Peace and Social Concerns Committee of the Western District Conference. Some of the money was used to employ young Old Colony Women as "health promoters." These women, trained and supervised by KDHW, helped poor people to access health programs, fill out the necessary forms, and go to the right places. All the money paid to the health promoters went through the Mennonites rather than through a state agency. In 2004 the Kansas Statewide Farmer Health program served 1,426 Low German people–44% of the total of 3,275 persons assisted in the program.

The cooperation between Mennonites and the state agency to assist poor Old Order farm workers in western Kansas was a remarkable collaboration in a country that claimed an ideology of separation of church and state. Cindi Treaster, the social worker who directed the state program and met regularly with her

---

[38]This account is based on interviews with Cindi Treaster and Tina Block Ediger on 7 February 2005, and a public presentation by Treaster at a Western District Conference meeting at Bethel College, July 2011. Details checked with Harold Thieszen in a telephone conversation 15 May 2015.

Mennonite partners, reported that there was no public criticism of this church-state arrangement. By the twenty-first century Mennonite institutions for higher education, hospitals, and retirement communities also received public funding that enabled them to fulfill their missions. The Farm Worker Program revealed again that the Mennonite ideal of "separation from the world" was increasingly difficult to sustain in the American welfare-state democracy.

Chapter 16

A People of Dual Citizenship

Population Stability and Change

At the dawn of the twenty-first century, there were 15,650 Mennonites in south central Kansas, according to data reported in *Religious Congregations & Membership in the United States 2000*.[1] That number, when corrected for over-reporting by congregations that counted absentee and out of state church members on their official lists, was not far from the total of 12,676 in 1940, sixty years earlier. The stability of overall numbers masked significant social and economic changes in the wider Mennonite community. The small family farm that had been the mainstay of Mennonite life in 1940 virtually disappeared. Thousands of Mennonites sought economic opportunities elsewhere. For those who stayed in south-central Kansas, the number in wage-earning occupations increased markedly.

Group	1940 membership		2000 membership	
GCMC	8,355	66%		
MC	890	7%		
MCUSA			10,135	64.8%
MB	1,666	13%	2,789	17.8%
KMB	549	4.3%		
CGCM	1,216	9.6%	1,983	12.7%
Independent			743	4.7%
total	12,676		15,650	

There had been two church mergers. In 1960 the Krimmer Mennonite Brethren (KMB) joined with the Mennonite Brethren (MB). At the end of the century the General Conference Mennonite

---

[1] Dale E. Jones, et. al., *Religious Congregations & Membership in the United States 2000* (Nashville, Tn: Glenmary Research Center, 2002). The numbers are of congregation members, not of the entire population.

Church and the Mennonite Church MC (formerly known as "Old" Mennonite) merged to form the MCUSA. The combined MCUSA groups in 2000 constituted a decreasing percentage of all Mennonites in this region. Members of the General Conference Mennonite churches were the most politically active, and supplied most of the Mennonites elected to the state legislature, in the time covered in this study.

The Church of God in Christ Mennonite group maintained the greatest separation from the American public order. They did not vote in elections, serve on juries, or attend public schools–and hence do not often appear in the narrative of this book. They did succeed in growing their membership by planting new churches in south central Kansas, elsewhere in Kansas, and in the United States and Canada.

A new category of "independent" Mennonite churches accounted for 4.7% of Mennonite members in 2000. These were more conservative evangelical congregations who had withdrawn from "mainstream" Mennonites that they considered too liberal on issues such as abortion, same-sex marriage, and evolution. The "independent" Mennonite churches reflected the polarization of religious and political attitudes that turned Kansas into one of the reddest (i.e. Republican) of red states in the country.

Red State Mennonites

Robert Wuthnow concluded his study of the role of religion in the history of Kansas politics, *Red State Religion* (2012), by identifying two dominant motifs that characterized the region. The first was "a pervasive skepticism toward big government."[2] That motif also characterized the Mennonites. Both in their European Anabaptist-Mennonite sectarian heritage and in their acculturation to typical political attitudes in Kansas, Mennonites doubted the efficacy of big government. At best big governments agreed to protect special privileges of Mennonites, but the fate of German-speaking people in Russia showed that those privileges could be withdrawn.

---

[2] Robert Wuthnow, *Red State Religion*, 364-5.

The editorials of *Mennonite Weekly Review*, the largest inter-Mennonite periodical in the country, were a good barometer of Kansas Mennonite political attitudes. Menno Schrag, editor from 1923 to 1969, wrote against what he considered the totalitarian tendencies of President Franklin Roosevelt's New Deal. That view was typical in Kansas. But Mennonites, unlike typical Kansans, also stood against big government militarism. Mennonites were pacifists. In the 1964 presidential election, Schrag, without great enthusiasm, voted for the incumbent Democratic President, Lyndon Johnson, over the Republican challenger Barry Goldwater, largely because Goldwater spoke out for escalated warfare in Vietnam. President Johnson' subsequent decision to wage a major land war in Asia confirmed Schrag's aversion to big government as means to promote the ideals of God's kingdom.

Paul and Robert Schrag, editors of *Mennonite Weekly Review*, 2011

Menno Schrag's son and grandson, Robert Schrag and Paul Schrag, succeeded him as editors of *Mennonite Weekly Review*–a three-generation journalistic succession of more than eighty years. Over the decades their editorial position on the proper biblical way to witness for peace and justice was consistently cautious. They persistently warned against putting unwarranted faith in government and in political involvement. But their language and emphases did change over the years from traditional nonresistance toward endorsement of proactive peacemaking. The Civil Rights movement in the 1960s prompted the change from nonresistant avoidance of conflict to an endorsement of public demonstrations for justice. An editorial by Robert Schrag, then assistant editor, in the June 13, 1963, issue, "Peacemaking in Birmingham," marked the change. Schrag was influenced by Martin Luther King's philosophy of loving nonviolence, and by the role of Vincent Harding as a peace negotiator for groups in conflict in Birmingham. "Bro. Harding, and the MCC Peace Section to whom he is accountable," wrote

Schrag, "are to be commended for a courageous effort to help make the Gospel relevant in an area the church has long neglected."[3]

The Schrags long refused to endorse peace demonstrations against the Vietnam War, a position that put them in some tension with public protesters at the Mennonite colleges. But by the spring of 1968, six weeks after the Tet Offensive in Vietnam, Menno and Robert Schrag moved to denounce the United States' war policy. To be sure, they wrote, "The church never was established to order the affairs of mankind, much less does it hold jurisdiction over its wars and conflicts." But the time had come for Mennonites to appeal to the government to withdraw troops from Vietnam. The American public had turned against the war. Mennonites, who had often petitioned the government when their own interests were at stake, should now take a position on general war policy.[4] By the time of the Persian Gulf War (1990-1) and the Iraq War (2001-3), the Schrags more decisively called the government to policies of peace rather than war.[5] The *Mennonite Weekly Review*'s shifting viewpoint was part of a larger Mennonite denominational peace witness movement from quietism to activism.[6]

Robert Wuthnow's second "enduring motif" that shaped Kansas' "Red State Religion" was "the heartland's faith in associational grassroots democracy." At the local level of church, school, and community organization, Mennonites joined other Kansans in enhancing civic life. In the small towns with substantial Mennonite population–Hillsboro, Goessel, Hesston, Moundridge, Halstead, Buhler and Inman–Mennonites served on non-partisan city councils, school boards, and innumerable committees for community uplift and celebration. In McPherson and Marion

---

[3] Robert Schrag, "Peacemaking in Birmingham," *Mennonite Weekly Review*, 13 June 1963, 4.

[4] Menno Schrag, "An Unparalleled Tragedy," *Mennonite Weekly Review*, 14 March 1968, 4.

[5] Robert Schrag, "Peace Efforts May Vary; Uniformity Not Required," *Mennonite Weekly Review*, 29 November 1990, 4. Paul Schrag, "The forgotten moral crisis," *Mennonite Weekly Review*, 22 March 2001, 4. Paul Schrag, "'Just war' and civilian casualties," *Mennonite Weekly Review*, 8 November 2001, 4. Robert Rhodes, "The immorality of manufacturing a war," *Mennonite Weekly Review*, 23 September 2002, 4. Paul Schrag, "Opposing war: means and ends," *Mennonite Weekly Review*, 7 April 2003, 4.

[6] Driedger and Kraybill, *Mennonite Peacemaking*.

counties Mennonites more or less continuously represented their districts on the county commissions.

In the late nineteenth and early twentieth century central Kansas Mennonites founded three religious liberal arts colleges that benefitted from the financial gifts, organizational energies, and teaching skills of succeeding generations. There were Mennonite hospitals in Newton, Goessel, Hillsboro, and Moundridge. In the years after World War II, Kansas Mennonites organized and supported a remarkable array of new associations that promoted the public good in the fields of mental health, housing for the poor, emergency disaster relief, overseas mission and development aid, insurance and investment programs, retirement homes, victim-offender reconciliation, and professional associations. The local congregations of worshiping believers provided the undergirding spiritual basis for all this associational activity. Ever since their Anabaptist origins in Europe, Mennonites had believed that the Christian faith must be rooted in the life of the congregation and expressed in daily living. In Kansas, and elsewhere in North America, this resulted in voluntary benevolent organizations that contributed to what Wuthnow called "the core of civic life."[7]

A third major motif in the Mennonite story, not typical for Kansans in general, was the role of Mennonite pacifism in determining attitudes and behavior. The teaching and practice of nonresistance in a century of warfare was critical to Mennonite identity. In a world of ongoing warfare from World Wars I and II to the Korean War to the Vietnam War to the Persian Gulf and Iraq Wars, Mennonites always knew that the call of the country could contradict the call of Christ. When American wars were very popular among the general public, Mennonite anti-war attitudes placed them on the margins, not likely to run for, or to hold, political office. But when America's wars became unpopular, as happened in the war in Vietnam, Mennonites could become part of a wider anti-war movement in the country. Mennonite anti war activism in the Vietnam War, and in the subsequent Persian Gulf and Iraq Wars, grew out of the Mennonite peace tradition. It also took its shape from the wider American civil rights and anti-war movements.

---

[7]Wuthnow, *Red State Religion*, 365.

The Activist 1980s

A timeline of Kansas Mennonite political activity reveals an ebb and flow rather than a straight line of increasing engagement. During and immediately after World War II, as was the case for World War I, pacifist Mennonites were largely excluded from electoral politics. In peacetime there were new opportunities. Mennonite engagement in the political world reached a peak in the 1980s. During that decade three strong Mennonite candidates served in the state legislature–Harold P. Dyck (R) from Hesston, Duane Goossen (R) from Goessel, and Jesse Harder (D) from Buhler. These men were invited to speak at the annual "Legislative Awareness Seminars" in the state capital sponsored from 1981 to 1988 by General Conference and Mennonite Brethren. In these seminars Mennonite pastors, lay leaders and students learned about the legislative process and expressed their concerns in the offices of their representatives. More than before and after these years, Mennonites seemed to be aware of state politics.

The same dynamic expressed itself at the national level. The Washington office of the Mennonite Central Committee Peace section, directed by a Kansan, Delton Franz, organized meetings for concerned Mennonites to come to Washington, D.C., to learn from important government officials, and to meet with their senators and representatives. One factor driving Mennonite political activism in the 1980s was the farm crisis of those years. Some Mennonites turned to government for solutions to the precipitous decline in the farm economy. At the same time, Mennonite peace activists joined the national "Freeze the Arms Race" movement in response to President Ronald Reagan's military buildup. In south central Kansas the movement focused on the aging Titan 2 missile system located in a large ring around Wichita.

From the early 1980s onward Kansas Mennonites typically had two or three elected representatives in Kansas legislature. In 1990 four Mennonites (Duane Goossen from Goessel, Robert Krehbiel from Pretty Prairie, Jesse Harder from Buhler, and Tom Bishop from Wichita) were elected to the legislature. That year the average population for each of the 125 House districts was 19,820 persons, a number slightly above the total Mennonite population in south central Kansas. Given their population numbers, the Mennonites would have been entitled to just one legislator. The "overrepresentation" of Mennonites in the Kansas legislature, while not dramatic in effect, was remarkable for a religious ethnic group that over much of its history had been reluctant to become involved in politics.[8]

Red State Democrats

Kansas Mennonites were not as "Red" or Republican as commonly assumed. To be sure, most Kansas Mennonites in most elections voted for Republican candidates. This was especially true in rural communities represented by such congregations as Alexanderwohl, Hoffnungsau, and Ebenfeld. Nevertheless, the partisan identification of the Kansas Mennonite politicians whose stories are told in this book is surprisingly more Democratic than Republican. From World War II to 2014 a total of thirty Kansas Mennonites ran for state or national political office. Of these, seventeen (57.7%) were Democrats, twelve (40.0%) were Republicans, and one (3.3%) was Independent (Reform Party). Nine of the twelve Republicans, and six of the seventeen Democrats, were elected to office.[9]

The Republican total is actually inflated because it includes two politicians, Eric Yost and Jerry Moran, who were not raised Mennonite, whose careers in elective office began before they joined Mennonite churches, and who eventually left the Mennonites to join other churches. The total also includes two Republican politicians who later left their party. Cedric Boehr joined the Taxpayers Party after his defeat in 1994, and Duane Goossen changed his registration to the Democratic Party in 2008.

Twenty-five (83.3%) of the thirty Mennonite candidates for state and national office were members of, or related to, congregations of the General Conference Mennonite Church. Four (13.3%) were members of the Mennonite Brethren Church. One (3.3%) was a member of the (Old) Mennonite Church.

---

[8]Thelma Helyar, ed., *Kansas Statistical Abstract 2000* (Lawrence, Ks: Policy Research Institute, 2001), 2-3.
[9]See the list of candidates in Appendix A.

What accounts for the high Democratic numbers of politicians among a people who were predominantly Republican? The answer is elusive and depends upon the stories of the individual candidates and office holders. Issues of social welfare and what Mennonites called the "peace witness" were relevant to partisan identity. All of the Mennonite Democratic candidates and office holders had social concerns for poor and disadvantaged people. All of them opposed the death penalty. As surely as the Mennonite peace witness influenced national policies of military conscription, Kansas Mennonites exercised influence beyond their numbers in the ongoing debate regarding capital punishment.

There was an ethnic component to Mennonite partisan choices. The "Swiss Volhynians," a minority of Mennonites in Kansas, were mostly Democrats from their early years in the state. They produced more than their share of political candidates. Walter W. "Sprig" Graber and Robert E. Krehbiel were from the Swiss Volhynian Pretty Prairie community. Donna Kaufman Neufeld and James Juhnke were reared in Swiss Volhynian families from the Moundridge area. Jesse Harder, himself of Dutch-Russian ethnic background, was convinced to register Democrat by a Swiss Volhynian high school administrator who said that the Democrats were the "party of the people" and that Roosevelt's New Deal was good for the country.

In the years around turn of the twenty-first century the Mennonite contribution to Kansas politics was shaped by a "three-party" system. An increasing number of Kansans were registered Republicans who elected an increasingly Republican legislature. Kansas was called "the reddest of the red states." But Kansas Republicans were divided into two groups–moderate and right wing. It was possible for moderate Republicans to join with Democrats to oppose right wing legislation and to elect Democratic governors. Coalitions of Democrats and moderate Republicans elected the Democratic governors John Carlin in 1980 and 1984, and Kathleeen Sebelius in 2004 and 2008. It was possible for Mennonite Democrats such as Walter W. Graber, Jim Bishop, Robert Krehbiel, Christine Downey, and Judy Loganbill to influence the legislative process more than the numbers of their minority party would imply.[10]

A People of Dual Citizenship

Mennonites were deeply influenced by the context of American denominationalism. In the 1870s most of them had arrived on the Kansas frontier as German-speaking subjects in a Russian empire that was threatening to take away their special privileges as a people separated unto God. They were a people of two kingdoms, subject first of all to the Kingdom of Christ and secondarily to the kingdoms of this world. When the claims of the two kingdoms conflicted, as it did on the state's requirement of military service, they chose to serve Christ, whatever the cost. But tolerant American democracy proved to be a powerful solvent. In America the Mennonites gradually came to see themselves not as a tolerated sect with special privileges, but as a denomination alongside other denominations in a democracy that protected religious freedom for all. Each denomination had its distinctive characteristics–Baptists, Methodists, Congregationalists, and the rest. The Mennonites could see themselves as Protestants whose distinctiveness was an emphasis upon peace, discipleship, and simple living.

The "Goshen School" of Anabaptist-Mennonite historiography, most notably the writings of Harold Bender and Guy F. Hershberger, articulated the doctrine of nonresistance for the post-World War II generation. Bender portrayed Anabaptists as church-minded Christian disciples who carried the message of the sixteenth century Protestant reformers to its logical conclusion. The Anabaptists had suffered martyrdom, but they had been the quintessential Protestants. Bender's "Anabaptist Vision" synthesis was well suited for a generation of Mennonites who wanted to be legitimately at home in America at the same time that they were in some real sense separate from the world. Hershberger made the case for Mennonite "nonresistance" over against "pacifism" in a volume that defined the "state" as essentially violent while

---

[10]Michael Smith, "Kansas, the Three-Party State," *Campaigns and Elections* (Oct/Nov 2003): 36.

affirming a place for Mennonite local rural communities as contributors to American democracy.[11]

At the beginning of the twenty-first century, Duane Friesen, the preeminent Kansas Mennonite theologian, set forth a new "Anabaptist Theology of Culture" for another generation in language quite different from that of Bender and Hershberger.[12] Friesen made a case for the church as a people of "dual citizenship," attentive to the call by the prophet Jeremiah to the Children of Israel exiled in Babylon to "Seek the peace (shalom) of the city where you dwell" (Jer. 29:7). Friesen set aside Bender and Hershberger, not even mentioning them in his book. He built upon, and at points critiqued, the ideas of the two pre-eminent Mennonite theologians of the second half of the twentieth century, Gordon Kaufman and John Howard Yoder. Glen Stassen, promoter of the concept of "Just Peacemaking," credited Friesen with "a consistent, Trinitarian and Christologically embodied theology of culture." For a Mennonite people whose peace witness was historically tied to the refusal to engage in military service, Friesen offered a more expansive set of "Guidelines for Christian Citizenship" that included "Compassion and Wholeness Toward the Weak and Powerless," "Religious Liberty," "Restorative Justice," and "Nonviolent Resolution of Conflict." Mennonites, in Friesen's view, were aliens living in a modern Babylon, but they were called to contribute to the functioning of American democracy.

Mennonites stood in need of a new theological foundation for thinking about church and state in part because the American government ended the military draft in 1972. The end of conscription was significant for Mennonite identity. Refusal of military service had long been a key marker of Mennonite identity as a people separate and not conformed to the world. Without that marker it became less obvious to Mennonites and to the people among whom they lived that Mennonites were a distinctive people. Church congregations and denominational agencies struggled to maintain a sense of two kingdoms and dual citizenship. In the twenty-first century issues of war and peace were pushed aside as

---

[11] Albert Keim, *Harold S. Bender*; Theron Schlabach, *War Peace and Social Conscience*.
[12] Duane K. Friesen, *Artists, Citizens, Philosophers: Seeking the Peace of the City* (Scottdale, Pa. Herald Press, 2000), 7, 242-250.

Mennonites, much like their Kansas neighbors, became increasingly absorbed by polarizing issues of sexuality–gay marriage and abortion. And yet a distinctive Mennonite identity persisted well into the twenty-first century. Their view of the role of the state and of their obligations to the civic order would be important to maintaining their identity and their public mission in the future.

Appendix A

Below is a list of Mennonites who campaigned in Kansas and U.S. national political elections and who served in Kansas state political office between 1940 and 2014. Candidates and office holders were included if they were Mennonite church members or if they regularly attended a Mennonite congregation and received significant Mennonite support. They were not included if they were not Mennonite church members and did not attend a Mennonite congregation during the time of their political involvement.

The list includes thirty names. Of these seventeen (57.7%) were Democrats, eleven (40.0%) were Republicans, and one (3.3%) was a member of the Reform Party. Nine of the twelve Republicans, and six of the seventeen Democrats, were elected to office.

Twenty-five (83.3%) of the politicians were members of, or related to, congregations of the General Conference Mennonite Church. Four (13.3%) were members of the Mennonite Brethren Church. One (3.3%) was a member of the (Old) Mennonite Church.

Mennonite Politicians

Becker, Steven. Served in Kansas House from 2013 to present. Reno County. Republican.

Benjamin, Charles. Candidate for U. S. House 1986. Harvey County. Democrat.

Bishop, Tom. Served in Kansas House from 1991 to 1994. Sedgwick County. Democrat.

Boehr, Cedric. Candidate for Kansas House 1994. Butler County. Republican.

Dahl, Don. Served in Kansas House from 1997 to 2009. Marion County. Republican.

Downey, Christine Schmidt. Served in Kansas Senate from 1993 to 2005. Harvey and McPherson Counties. Democrat.

Dyck, Harold. Served in Kansas House from 1970 to 1989. McPherson County. Republican.

Friesen, Jacob V. Served in Kansas House from 1941 to 1943. Harvey County, Republican.

Gillmore, Jim. Served in Kansas House 1978-1980. Harvey County. Republican.

Goering, J. D. C. Candidate for Kansas House, 1940. McPherson County. Democrat.

Goering, William J. "Bill." Served in the Kansas House, 1981-1983. McPherson County. Democrat.

Goossen, Duane. Served in the Kansas House, 1983 to 1997. Marion County. Republican.

Graber, Walter. Served in the Kansas House from 1967 to 1977. Reno County. Democrat.

Harder, Jesse. Served in the Kansas House, 1983 to 1993. McPherson County. Democrat.

Hiebert, Paul W. Candidate for Secretary of State, 1966. Marion County, 1966.

Juhnke, James. Candidate for U. S. Congress, 1970. Harvey County. Democrat.

Klassen, Don. Candidate for U. S. Senate. 1996. Sedgwick County. Reform Party.

Krehbiel, Robert E. Served in Kansas House from 1989 to 1989. Reno County. Democrat.

Loganbill, Judy. Served in Kansas House from 2001 to 2013. Sedgwick County. Democrat.

Mace, Jack. Candidate for Kansas House, 2010. Reno County. Democrat.

Moore, Carol. Candidate for Kansas House, 2012. Reno County. Democrat.

Moran, Jerry. Served in U. S. Congress, 1997 to 2011. Ellis County. Republican. (Left Mennonite Brethren Church after 2012.)

Neufeld, Donna. Candidate for Kansas House, 1992 and 1994. Harvey County. Democrat.

Peters, James "Jim." Candidate for the Kansas House, 1968. Marion County. Democrat.

Peters, Marjorie Klassen. Candidate for Kansas House, 1966. Marion County. Democrat.

Schowalter, Jacob A. Served in Kansas House from 1935 to 1941. Harvey County. Democrat.

Schroeder, Don. Served in Kansas House from 2008 to present. McPherson County. Republican.

Tieszen, Walter E. Candidate for Kansas House, 1968. Sedgwick and Sumner Counties. Republican.

Unruh, Ernest Arthur. Served in Kansas House from 1953 to 1963. Harvey County. Republican.

Yost, Eric. Candidate for U. S. Congress, 1990 and 1992. Sedgwick County. Republican.

Appendix B

Kansas Mennonite Voting Statistics
1940-1976

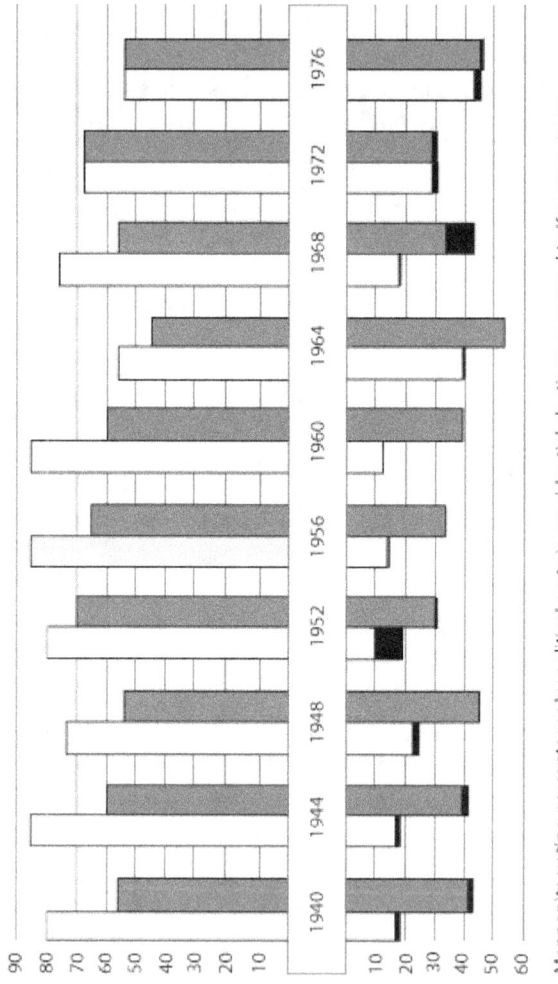

Mennonite voting percentages by political party in presidential elections compared to Kansas average, 1940-1976. Mennonite vote on the left (white) and Kansas vote on the right (gray) for each year. Republican percentage above the center. Democratic percentage below the center. Third party percentage black below the Democratic percentage

Bibliography

Published items

"72nd District a tossup." *Newton Kansan,* 1 November 1994, 4.
Allaby, Gordon. "Christians, have you forgotten who you are?" *Newton Kansan,* 27 September 2002, 7.
"America Gathers under a Sign of Peace." *Life,* 24 October 1969, 32-41.
Anderson, John B. *Vision and Betrayal in America.* Waco, TX: Word Books, 1975.
Anstaett, Doug. "Church had a right to hear who it had invited." *Newton Kansan,* 17 August 1994.
— — —. "Race didn't have to go negative." *Newton Kansan,* 4 November 1998, 4.
— — —. "Redistricting plan is blatant political move." *Newton Kansan,* 19 March 2002, 4.
Appleby, Joyce, Lynn Hunt, and Margaret Jacob. *Telling the Truth About History.* New York: Norton, 1994.
"Armed Forces Caravan in Hillsboro Saturday." *Tabor View,* 1 October 1976, 2.
"Attend Bicentennial Event in Washington." *Mennonite Weekly Review,* 24 June 1976, 6.
Awbrey, Stuart. Editorial. *Hutchinson News,* 31 January 1976, 4.
Ball, Buzz. "Benjamin, Griffiths post wins." *Newton Kansan,* 6 August 1980, 1.
Balzer, Amanda. "Hesston says no to beer." *Newton Kansan,* 11 November 2003, 1.
Balzer, Susan. "Bill would cut Hesston aid for not flying flag." *Mennonite Weekly Review,* 15 April 2002, 1-2.
Barnet, Richard, and Ronald Muller. *Global Reach: The Power of the Multinational Corporations.* New York: Simon and Schuster, 1974.
Baskir, Lawrence M., and William A. Strauss. *Chance and Circumstance: The Draft, the War and the Vietnam Generation.* New York: Knopf, 1978.
Bassett, David R., Steve Ratzlaff, and Tim Godshall, eds. *Persistent Voice: Marian Franz and Conscientious Objection to Military Taxation.* Telford, PA: Cascadia Publishing House, 2009.
Beatty, Bob, ed. "Be Willing to Take Some Risks to Make Things Happen: A Conversation with Former Governor John Carlin." *Kansas History* 31 (summer 2008): 114-140.
Bechler, Le Roy. *The Black Mennonite Church in North America, 1886-1986.* Scottdale, Pa: Herald Press, 1986.
Becker, Palmer. "Why the 'no' vote on beer." *Newton Kansan,* 13 November 2003, 4.
"Bell Ready for Long Trip." *Mennonite Weekly Review,* 19 February 1976, 6.
Bellah, Robert. "Civil Religion in America." *Daedalus: Journal of the American Academy of Arts and Sciences* 96:1 (winter 1967): 1-21.
Bender, Harold S. "The Anabaptist Vision." *Mennonite Quarterly Review* 18 (April 1944), 67-88.
"Benjamin proposes board policy changes." *Newton Kansan,* 18 February 1981, 1.
"Bethel Students Document Gulf War Reaction." *Mennonite Weekly Review,* 3 October 1991, 7.
"Bethel's Concern." four-page flyer, *We Protest,* n.d.
"A Bicentennial Statement for the Mennonite Brethren." *The Christian Leader,* 20 January 20 1976, 7.
Bigus, Ruth Baum. "Jewish man view for 5th District House seat." *The Kansas City Jewish Chronicle,* 8 June 1990.

Blosser, Richard. "Share Views on Bicentennial Year." *Mennonite Weekly* Review, 25 March 1976, 3.
Boston, Garry. "The Rest of the Story." letter to the editor of the *Newton Kansan*, 19 November 1992, 4.
Brokaw, Tom. *The Greatest Generation*. New York: Random House, 1998.
Bruce, K. B. "Missed the Point." *Hillsboro Star-Journal*, 6 October 1976, 2.
Burkhart, Allen. letter to the editor, *Mennonite Weekly Review*, 3 November 1960, 6.
Burkholder, J. R. "Whom can we believe about Central America?" *The Christian Leader*, 16 October 1984, 12-13.
"Bush, Clinton: Where They Stand." *Christian Leader*, 20 October 1992, 10-11.
Bush, Perry. *Two Kingdoms, Two Loyalties: Mennonite Pacifism in Modern America*. Baltimore: Johns Hopkins University Press, 1998.
— — —. "We have Learned to Question Government." *Mennonite Life* 45 (June 1990), 13-17.
"Campuses Set for Moratorium." *Wichita Eagle*, 13 November 1969.
Carroll, James. *House of War: The Pentagon and the Disastrous Rise of American Power*. Boston: Houghton Mifflin, 2006.
"Choirs join Bicentennial Parade." *Tabor College View*, 9 April 1976, 3.
"The Christian and Nuclear Power." General Conference Mennonite Church Minutes, 1959, 24-5.
"Christians and the Bicentennial," Civil Religion Packet distributed by MCC Peace Section, MCC Vertical Files, MLA.V.1.I, Mennonite Library and Archives.
"Church Opens Doors to Gays." *Lawrence Journal-World*, 20 April 2004.
"Concerts by Kansas Men Raise $10,480 for CROP, MCC," *Mennonite Weekly Review*, 2 December 1976, 1.
Conference on Life and Human Values. Harrisonburg, VA: Mennonite Medical Association, 1973.
Conscience and Conscription: Papers from an MCC Peace Section Assembly, November 20-22, 1969. Akron, PA: MCC, 1970.
Coslett, Mary Grace. "She supports Curtis on signs." *Newton Kansan*, 10 January 2003, 4.
"Declaration of Christian Faith and Commitment," a flyer with the delegates and resolutions of the Study Conference on Nonresistance, Winona Lake, Indiana, November 9-12, 1950. Akron, PA: MCC Peace Section, 1950.
"Delegates Pass Bicentennial Resolution." *The Mennonite, Western District Edition*, 11 November 1975, A1-A2.
Detweiler, Lowell. *The Hammer Rings Hope: Photos and Stories from Fifty Years of Mennonite Disaster Service*. Scottdale, PA: Herald Press, 2000.
Dick, Sue. "Court Decision Questioned." *Bethel Collegian*, 30 April 1971, 2.
"Docking Sweeps Aside Tradition to Defeat Avery." *Newton Kansan*, 8 November 1966, 1.
Downey, Christine. "Death penalty not the answer to crime." *Newton Kansan*, 1 February 1994, 4.
Driedger, Leo. *Fallout Shelters: A Discussion*. Newton, KS: Board of Christian Service, General Confererce Mennonite Church, 1962.
Driedger, Leo, and Donald B. Kraybill. *Mennonite Peacemaking: From Quietism to Activism*. Scottdale, PA: Herald Press, 1994.
Duerksen, Carol. *We Sing That Others May Live: The History of the Kansas Mennonite Men's Chorus 1969-1994*. N.p.: Kansas Mennonite Mens Chorus, 1995.

Dyck, A. J. "Eine Anstalt für Nerven- und Geisteskranke." *Christlicher Bundesbote*, 8 June 1937.
Dyck, John M. *Faith Under Test: Alternative Service During World War II in the U.S. and Canada*. Moundridge, KS: Gospel Publishers, 1997.
Ediger, Elmer. "A Christian's Political Responsibility." *Mennonite Life* 11 July 1956, 143-4.
― ― ―. "Is It Right to Accept CPS?" *The Snowline* 3:4 (Apr. 1945), 2.
Editors' Response. *The Christian Herald*, 27 November 1984, 9.
Eitzen, Dirk W., and Timothy D. Falb. "An Overview of the Mennonite I-W Program." *Mennonite Quarterly Review* 56 (October 1982), 365-81.
"Election Results." *Hillsboro Journal*, 7 November 1940, 1.
Elliott, Lisa. "Liquor by the Drink." *Newton Kansan*, 12 October 1996.
Ellis, John. "Book on state history altered after evolution vote." *Wichita Eagle*, 21 August 1999, 1A, 4A.
Enz, Jacob J. "Editorials." *The Mennonite*, 7 December 1948, 3.
Ewert, Lydia Siemens. *Lydia's Letters & Messages*. Hillsboro, KS: author, 1984.
First Mennonite Church of Christian in Moundridge, worship service bulletin, 4 July 1976.
Flaming, Elmer W. "Why Celebrate the Bicentennial." *The Christian Leader*, 20 July 1976, 16.
Flood, Robert. *America, God Shed His Grace on Thee*. Chicago: Moody Press, 1975.
Flowers, Charles. "Services Well Attended." *Bethel Collegian*, 16 October 1959, 3.
Foulke, Steven Vail. "Shaping of Place: Mennonitism in South-Central Kansas." Ph.D. dissertation, University of Kansas, 1998.
Franz, Delton. "From 1776 to 1976—the changing style of oppression." *Mennonite Brethren Herald*, 9 July1976. The article also appeared in *Mennonite Weekly Review*, 5 August 1976, 12; and in *Mennonite Reporter*, 28 June 1976.
Fretz, J. Winfield. "Should Mennonites Participate in Politics?" *Mennonite Life* 11 (July 1956): 139-140.
Friesen, Duane K. *Artists, Citizens, Philosophers: Seeking the Peace of the City*. Scottdale, PA: Herald Press, 2000.
― ― ―. *Christian Peacemaking & International Conflict: A Realist Pacifist Perspective*. Scottdale, PA: Herald Press, 1986.
― ― ―. review of *Our Star-Spangled Faith*. *Mennonite Life* 31 (September 1976): 29-30.
Friesen, Gerhard. "The Flag in the Church." *The Mennonite*, 26 June 1945, 8.
Funk, Ray N., comp. *Bruderthal 1873-1964 90th Anniversary*. Hillsboro, KS: Bruderthal Mennonite Church, 1964.
Gaeddert, Albert. "Why Civilian Public Service Work?" *Pike View News* 1:3 (4 October 1941), 5.
Gaustad, Edwin Scott. *Historical Atlas of Religion in America*. New York: Harper & Row, 1962.
General Conference Mennonite Church. *Minutes and Reports of the Twenty-Eighth Session of the General Conference of the Mennonite Church of North America, 1938*.
"Gillmore over Modrell for representative." *Newton Kansan*, 8 November 1978, 1.
Gingerich, Melvin. *Service for Peace: A History of Mennonite Civilian Public Service*. Akron, PA: Mennonite Central Committee, 1949.
Goering, Oswald and Elaine. letter to the editor, *Harvey County Independent* (Halstead), 24 August 1994.
Goering, Paul. "Not Peace But a Sword." *The Mennonite*, 20 December 1966, 780.

Gold, Matea. "'Sons of Wichita' explores Koch brother's lives." *Wichita Eagle,* May 23, 2014, 3B.
Goossen, Duane. "The Politics of Peace and Service: Calling All Mennonites." *Mennonite Life* 51 (September 1996): 4-9.
Goossen, Rachel Waltner. *Women Against the Good War: Conscientious Objection and Gender on the American Homefront, 1941-1947.* Chapel Hill, NC: University of North Carolina Press, 1997.
"Graves signs controversial abortion law." *The Hutchinson News,* 28 April 1998, A1.
Grimsrud, Theodore Glenn. "An Ethical Analysis of Conscientious Objection to World War II." PhD dissertation, Graduate Theological Union, 1988.
Grout, Pam. *You Know You're in Kansas When.* Guilford, CT: Insiders' Guide, 2006.
Ham, George E., and Robin Higham, eds. *The Rise of the Wheat State: A History of Kansas Agriculture.* Manhattan, KS: Sunflower University Press, 1987.
Harder, Jesse. *Beyond Isabella: A Harder Family Story.* N.p.: author, 1999.
Harder, Leland. *The Discerning People of God: Doors to Lock and Doors to Open.* Scottdale,PA: Herald Press, 1993.
―――. *The Houses I Lived In: Memoirs of my Life.* North Newton, KS: Harder Graphics, 2008.
―――. "Taking a more political approach." *The Christian Leader,* 9 October 1990, 10-11.
"Harding calls for American 'second coming.'" *The Mennonite,* 10 February 1976.
Harms, Orlando. "The Editor's 'Uneasy Chair.'" *The Christian Leader,* 24 November 1964, 1.
Harrison, Carol. "Mennonite for life, 'Mennonite for Life.'" *The Christian Leader,* 10 September 1992, 10-11.
Harshbarger, Emmett L. "Can America Be Neutral?" *The Southwestern Social Science Quarterly* (March 1938), 1-10.
Hart, Lawrence. "Student Protests." *Bethel College Collegian,* 30 March 1961, 2.
"Harvey Political Campaign in Last Lap." *Newton Kansan,* 2 November 1966, 3.
"Harvey, Sumner counties want casino development." *Hillsboro Star-Journal,* 21 December 2005, 1.
Haury, David A. *A People of the City: A History of the Lorraine Avenue Mennonite Church, 1932-82.* Wichita, KS: Lorraine Avenue Mennonite Church, 1982.
―――. *The Quiet Demonstration: The Mennonite Mission in Gulfport, Mississippi.* Newton KS: Faith and Life Press, 1979.
Hefley, James G. *America: One Nation Under God.* Wheaton, IL: Victor Books, 1975.
Hein, Marvin. "Inquiring Minds." *The Christian Leader,* October 1996, 15.
Helyar, Thelma, ed., *Kansas Statistical Abstract 2000.* Lawrence, KS: Policy Research Institute, 2001.
"Here is What Others Say About Peacetime Conscription." *Fellowship* (August 1944), 142.
Herrin, Angelia. "Home Folks Think He Did the Job." *Wichita Eagle-Beacon,* 30 April 1983, 6A.
Hershberger, Guy F. *Christian Relationships to State and Community.* Akron: PA: Mennonite Central Committee, 1942.
―――. *War, Peace and Nonresistance.* Scottdale, PA: Herald Press, 1944, rev. ed. 1953 and 1969.
Hiebert, Clarence. *The Holdeman People: The Church of God in Christ, Mennonite 1849-1969.* South Pasadena, CA: William Carey Library, 1973.

Hinz-Penner, Raylene. *Searching for Sacred Ground: The Journey of Chief Lawrence Hart, Mennonite*. Telford, PA: Cascadia Publishing House, 2007.

"History book planned for EMU centennial." *Mennonite World Review*, 2 April 2012, 24.

Holm, Jim. "Politics of the Kingdom." *Christian Leader*, 20 October 1992, 12.

Huber, Tim. "Pastor Nudged Church to Act on Civil Rights." *Mennonite World Review*, 9 June 2014, 1, 13.

"Iraq, Kuwait Refugees Get Assistance From MCC." *Mennonite Weekly Review*, 30 August 1990, 1.

Jackson, Jeanette. "Jeers Greet Protest Marchers." *The Hutchinson News*, 19 October 1969.

Janzen, David. "Jesus overcame fear of death; we can too." *Newton Kansan*, 24 April 2003, 4.

Janzen, Reinhild. "The Mennonite Settler Receives National Register Nomination." *Kansas Preservation* (March-April 1998), 1, 4-5.

Jones, Dale E., et. al. *Religious Congregations & Membership in the United States 2000*. Nashville, TN: Glenmary Research Center, 2002.

Juhnke, James C. "Clashing Symbols in a Quiet Town: Hesston in the Vietnam War Era." *Kansas History* 23 (Autumn 2000): 142-153.

———. *Dialogue With a Heritage, Cornelius H. Wedel and the Beginnings of Bethel College*. North Newton, KS: Bethel College, 1987.

———. "Edmund G. Kaufman, Minister of Peace in a World of War." *Kansas History* 18 (Spring 1995): 48-58.

———. "Freedom and the American Revolution." *The Mennonite*, 22 June 1976, 14-18.

———. letter to the *Hutchinson News*, with copy to the *Peabody Gazette-Herald*, 19 December 1961.

———. "Mennonite Benevolence and Civic Identity: The Post-War Compromise," *Mennonite Life* 25 (January 1970): 34-7.

———. "Mennonite Benevolence and Revitalization in the Wake of World War I." *Mennonite Quarterly Review* 60 (January 1986): 15-30.

———. "Mennonite History and Self Understanding: North American Mennonitism as a Bipolar Mosaic." In *Mennonite Identity: Historical and Contemporary Perspectives*, edited by Calvin Wall Redekop and Samuel J. Steiner, 83-99. Lanham, MD: University Press of America, 1988.

———. "A Mennonite Runs for Congress." *Mennonite Life* 26 (January 1971): 8-11.

———. "Moderates, Mennonites, and the Religious Right, A Hot Contest in the Seventy-fourth House District, 1994." *Kansas History* 27 (Autumn 2004): 180-93.

———. *A People of Two Kingdoms: The Political Acculturation of the Kansas Mennonites*. Newton, KS: Faith and Life Press, 1975.

———. "Revolution Without Independence." *Mennonite Life* 31 (September 1976): 10-13.

———. *Small Steps Toward the Missing Peace: A Memoir*. Wichita, KS: Flying Camel Publications, 2011.

———. *So Much to be Thankful For: The Bill and Meta Juhnke Story*. Wichita, KS: Juhnke, 2009. Available online at http://www.juhnke.com/family/thankful.htm

———. "The Victories of Nonresistance: Mennonite Oral Tradition and World War I." *Fides et Historia* 7 (Fall 1974): 19-25.

———. "Vietnam and the Politics of Repentance." *The Mennonite*, 13 October 13 1970, 616-18; *Lutheran Forum*, February 1971, 16, 25-27; *The Presbyterian Outlook*, 5 October 1970, 5-6; and *The Guardian: A Christian Weekly Journal of Public Affairs*, 28 January 28 1971, 7-8.

———. *Vision, Doctrine, War: Mennonite Identity and Organization in America 1890-1930*. Scottdale, PA: Herald Press, 1989.

Juhnke, Roger. "The Perils of Conscientious Objection, An Oral History Study of a 1944 Event." *Mennonite Life* 34 (September 1979): 4-9.

Jurgens, Dwight. "Reactions–like the abortion issue–divided." *The Hutchinson News*, 28 April 28 1998, A2.

"Kansan 'Never Captive" Missionary Leaving Vietnam." *Kansas City Star*, 23 Jan 1976, 4.

"Kansas Campuses Will Participate In Vietnam Plans on October 15." *Bethel Collegian*, 10 Oct 1969.

"Kansas Wheat Liberty Bell Still Displayed." *Hesston Record*, 5 February 1976, 1.

Kauffman, J. Howard, and Leland Harder. *Anabaptists Four Centuries Later: A Profile of Five Mennonite and Brethren in Christ Denominations*. Scottdale, PA: Herald Press, 1975.

Kauffman, J. Howard, and Leo Driedger. *The Mennonite Mosaic: Identity and Modernization*. Scottdale, PA: Herald Press, 1991.

Kauffman, Milo. "The Challenge of the Second Mile," in booklet "Peace Conference Lectures," Tabor College, 1953.

Kaufman, Donald D. *What Belongs to Caesar?* Scottdale, PA: Herald Press, 1969.

Kaufman, Ed. G. "Editorial." *Bethel College Bulletin*, 15 March 1945, 1.

Kaufman, Edward E. "The Bible in Public Schools." *Mennonite Weekly Review*, 30 October 1940, 3.

Kaufman, Gordon. "Should Mennonites Register for the Draft?" *The Mennonite*, 8 June 1948, 4-5.

Keim, Albert. *The CPS Story: An Illustrated History of Civilian Public Service*. Intercourse, PA: Good Books, 1990.

———. *Harold S. Bender, 1897-1962*. Scottdale, PA: Herald Press, 1998.

Keim, Albert N., and Grant M. Stoltzfus, *The Politics of Conscience: The Historic Peace Churches And America at War, 1917-1995*. Scottdale, PA: Herald Press, 1988.

Kidd, Tom. "Mennonite Group Starts Public School Exodus." *Wichita Eagle and Beacon*, 8 May 1977, 1A.

"King Well Received." *Bethel Collegian* , 19 January 1960, 3.

Klassen, James R. *Jimshoes in Viet Nam: The Eyewitness Account of an American Christian Who Stayed Behind after the "Fall" of Saigon*. Scottdale, PA: Herald Press, 1986.

Klassen, Lenore. letter to the editor, *Newton Kansan*, 29 October 1996, 5.

Klassen, Marjorie, ed. "Hillsboro High School Oracle." *Vorwaerts*, Nov 18, 1938, 4.

Koller, Jeffery W., ed. *The Eden Peace Witness, A Collection of Personal Accounts*. Moundridge, KS: Jebeko Publishing, 2004.

Koontz, Ted. review of *Christian Peacemaking and International Conflict*, in *Mennonite Life* 42 (September 1987), 36.

Koppes, Clayton. "Students March in South." *Bethel Collegian*, 2 April 2 1965, 2.

Krabill, Willard S. "Directive on Abortion from Health and Welfare Committee." *Mennonite Medical Messenger*, July-September 1976, 17-18.

Krahn, Cornelius. "Centennial Calendar of Events, U.S. and Canada." *Mennonite Weekly Review*, 20 June 1974, 10-11.
Kraybill, Donald B. *Our Star-Spangled Faith*. Scottdale, PA: Herald Press, 1976.
Krehbiel, C. E. "Peacetime Conscription." *The Mennonite*, 2 January 1945, 4.
Krehbiel, June. "'Gerrymander' not welcome at Bethel." *Mennonite Weekly Review*, 20 December 2001, 12.
Krehbiel, Leona. "Peacetime Military Conscription." *The Mennonite*, 17 April 1945, 1-2.
Krehbiel, Nicholas A. *General Lewis B. Hershey and Conscientious Objection during World War II*. Columbia, MO: University of Missouri Press, 2011.
Krehbiel, Robert E. "Krehbiel sets the record straight." *Hutchinson News*, 5 November 1994, 4.
― ― ―. "Krehbiel wants to set his voting record straight." *Hutchinson News*, 6 October 1994.
Kreider, Robert S. "America Number One in God's Sight?" *Mennonite Weekly Review*, 19 February 1976, 4.
― ― ―. *Coming Home: An Autobiography of My 1952-2011 Years*. North Newton, KS: CreateSpace/Mudcreek Press, 2012.
― ― ―. "CPS: 'A Year of Service with Like-Minded Christian Young Men': CPS Camp No. 5, Colorado Springs, Colorado, 1941-42." *Mennonite Quarterly Review* 66 (October 1992): 567-68.
― ― ―. "The 'Good Boys of CPS.'" *Mennonite Life* 46 (September 1991), 4-11.
― ― ―. "A Hymn of Affection for a Land and a People." *The Mennonite*, 13 January 1976, 18-20.
― ― ―. *My Early Years: An Autobiography*. Kitchener, ON: Pandora Press, 2002.
Kroeker, Wally. "Crying 'Wolf' in Washington." *Christian Leader*, 2 March 1976, 24.
Kyle, Richard. "The Issues Beyond the Rhetoric." *Christian Leader*, 20 October 1992, 7-9.
Landauer, Jerry. "Church Pressure Aids Chances for a Strong Civil Rights Measure." *Wall Street Journal*, 17 September 1963, 1.
"Leadership worked hard to find solution." *Wichita Eagle*, 19 May 2002.
Learman, Edward. Review of *Christian Peacemaking and International Conflict*, in *Mennonite Quarterly Review* 61 (July 1987): 341-2.
Lehn, Cornelia. "My Pilgrimage With War Tax Resistance," appended to a letter by Elmer Neufeld, President of the General Conference Mennonite Church, to GCMC pastors, 14 Oct 1976.
Leichty, Bruce. "National Self-Interest in a Brutal World." *Mennonite Weekly Review*, 30 Sept 1976, 4.
"Letter to Members of Congress." *The Mennonite*, 3 Oct 1939, 3.
"Local News." *Mennonite Weekly Review*, 17 September 1942, 5.
Loewen, Esko. "Church and State." *Mennonite Life* 11 (July 1956): 141-142.
Loewen, Royden. *Diaspora in the Countryside: Two Mennonite Communities and Mid-Twentieth Century Rural Disjuncture*. Urbana: University of Illinois Press, 2006.
― ― ―. *Family, Church and Market: A Mennonite Community in the Old and New Worlds*. Urbana: University of Illinois Press, 1993.
Loewen, Royden, and Steven M. Nolt. *Seeking Places of Peace*. Global Mennonite History Series: North America. Intercourse, PA: Good Books, 2012.
Lyttle, Bradford. *You Come With Naked Hands: The Story of the San Francisco to Moscow March for Peace*. Raymond, NH: Greenleaf Books, 1966.

MacMaster, Richard K. *Land, Piety, Peoplehood: The Establishment of Mennonite Communities in America*. Scottdale, PA: Herald Press, 1985.

MacMaster, Richard K., Samuel L. Horst and Robert F. Ulle, eds., *Conscience in Crisis: Mennonites and other Peace Churches in America 1737-1789*. Scottdale, PA: Herald Press, 1979.

Maisel, Albert Q. "BEDLAM 1946." *Life*, May 6, 1946, 102-18.

"Making Christ Lord of our Politics." *The Christian Leader*, 21 Oct 1980, 2-5.

Marsden, George. *The Soul of the American University: From Protestant Establishment to Established Nonbelief*. New York: Oxford University Press, 1994.

Martens, Lauren. "Nicaragua–the rebuilding continues." *The Christian Leader*, 30 October 1984, 15-17.

Martin, Earl. *Reaching the Other Side: The Journal of an American Who Stayed to Witness Vietnam's Postwar Transition*. New York: Crown Publishers, 1978.

Memo from the Peace Section Washington Office, January and June 1969.

Mennonite Brethren Statement Regarding Political Involvement Accepted at the 26-29 November 1966 General Conference, Corn, Oklahoma.

"Mennonite Worker says No Blood Bath." *Hutchinson News*, 19 May 1976, 1.

"Mennonites Testify at Hearings on Post-War Military Policy." *The Mennonite*, 10 July 1945, 5-6.

Meyers, Bill. "Common Sense Suggested." *Marion County Record*, 18 March 1992, 2.

Miller, Douglas B., ed. *Tabor College: A Century of Transformation 1908-2008*. Hillsboro, KS: Center for Mennonite Brethren Studies, 2008.

Miller, Melissa, and Phil M. Shenk, *The Path of Most Resistance*. Scottdale, PA: Herald Press, 1982.

"Missile Sites Under Study." *Mennonite Weekly Review*, 3 September 1959, 7.

"Missionary Saw No Reprisals in Saigon." *Kansas City Times*, 11 May 1976, 47.

Moline, Matt. "Professor takes redistricting personally." *Topeka Capital-Journal*, 17 December 2002. http://cjonline.com/stories/121701/kan_juhnke.shtml

Morrow, Darrell. "Two Demos Completely at Odds." *Wichita Eagle*, 10 July 10 1970, 5c.

Neufeld, Vernon H., ed. *If We Can Love: The Mennonite Mental Health Story*. Newton, KS: Faith and Life Press, 1983.

– – –. letter to the editor, *The Mennonite*, 27 December 1966, 799.

Newton, Jennifer. "Educators troubled by board's vote on evolution." *Newton Kansan*, 16 August 1999, 1, 5.

"No Bloodbath, Executions in Saigon, Four Mennonite Missionaries Report." *The Ephrata Review* (19 June 1975), B-5.

Ollenburger, Ben. "Mennonites, 'Civil Religion,' and the American Bicentennial: An Interview with James C. Juhnke." *Direction* 5 (July 1976): 15-21.

O'Neal, Mike. "Chair cites Boston, Krehbiel for work." *Newton Kansan*, 28 May 2002, 4.

"Open Letter to the People of Iraq from the Citizens of Kansas." *Newton Kansan*, 22 September 1990, 7.

"Operation 600." *The Mennonite*, 23 June 1959, 400.

Opiyo, John Serapi. "Wheat and Chaff." *Bethel Collegian*, 14 April 1961.

Partin, John W. "The Dilemma of 'A Good, Very Good Man': Capper and Noninterventionism, 1936-1941." *Kansas History* 2 (Summer 1979): 86-95.

"Peacetime Conscription." *The Christian Century*, 18 October 1944, 1190-1.

Peachey, Paul. "The Church Cannot Align Herself, The 1964 Elections." *The Christian Leader,* 27 October 1964, 3, 21.
— — —. "Church Cannot Align with Any Political Program." *Mennonite Weekly Review,* 1 October 1964, 9.
Peters, Frank C. "Principles of Peace" and "The Maladjusted Christian," in a booklet, "Peace Conference Lectures," printed by Tabor College. Copy in the Wesley Prieb collection at the Center for Mennonite Brethren Studies, Tabor College.
Platt, LaVonne Godwin, ed. *Hope for the Family Farm, Trust God and Care for the Land.* Newton, KS: Faith and Life Press, 1987.
Preheim, Rich. "Kansas MB Wins Election to Congress." *Mennonite Weekly Review,* 7 November 1996, 1.
— — —. "Mennonite Politicians May Face Challenges When They Take Beliefs into Politics." *Mennonite Weekly Review,* 29 October 1992, 1-2.
— — —. "Unflagging pursuit of faithfulness." *The Mennonite,* 2 July 2002, 11.
"Presidential Poll Conducted on Campus." *Bethel Collegian,* 11 November 1960, 1.
"Program for the Bible Week at Bethel College." *Bethel College Bulletin,* Feb. 1934.
"The public's business." *Newton Kansan,* 19 February 1981, 4A.
Raber, Merrill, and Boots Raber. *A 40-Year History of Kansas-Paraguay Partners: Making a Difference Through Volunteerism, 1968-2008.* West Conshohocken, PA: Infinity Publishing, 2013.
Ranney, Dave. "Sex, politics mingle in race." *The Wichita Eagle,* 13 October 1996, 21A.
Ratzlaff, Don. "How Will We Respond?" *The Tabor View,* 24 October 1975, 2.
— — —. "Ministry amid a 'Summer of Mercy.'" *Christian Leader,* 10 September 1991, 17-19.
Redekop, John H. "Editorial." *The Christian Herald*, 30 October 1984, 24.
Regier, Austin. "Christianity and Conscription as Viewed by a Nonregistrant." *The Mennonite,* 30 November 1948, 13-15.
— — —. *The Courage of Conviction: The Correspondence of a Conscientious Objector.* North Newton, KS; Raymond Regier, 2000.
Rempel, Ron. "CPT Urges Release of Hostages, Prays for Peace, Talks to Iraqis." *Mennonite Weekly Review,* 20 December 1990, 1.
"Resolution on Abortions." *Mennonite Medical Messenger,* January-March 1973, 18.
Rhodes, Robert. "The immorality of manufacturing a war." *Mennonite Weekly Review,* 23 September 2002, 4.
— — —. "Kansas MB re-elected to 5th term in Congress.," *Mennonite Weekly Review,* 8 November 2004, 1, 3.
Richard, Phil. "Stories highlight Hesston Peace Week." *Mennonite Weekly Review,* 17 February 2003, 7.
Richmond, Robert. *Kansas: A Land of Contrasts,* 4th ed. Wheeling, IL: Harlan Davidson, 1999.
Rothschild, Scott. "Douglas County Alone Rejects Ban." *Lawrence Journal World,* 6 April 2005, 1A, 8A.
Rupp, Byron. "Desert Storm is a Just War." *In Search,* March 1991, 1-3.
Ruth, John L. *'Twas Seeding Time: A Mennonite View of the American Revolution.* Scottdale, PA.: Herald Press, 1976.
Rutschman, James D. letter to the editor, *Newton Kansan,* 2 November 1996, 15.

Sareyan, Alex. *The Turning Point: How Men of Conscience Brought About Major Change in the Care of America's Mentally Ill.* Washington, D.C.: American Psychiatric Press, 1994.
Saul, Norman E. "The Migration of the Russian-Germans to Kansas." *The Kansas Historical Quarterly 40* (Spring 1974): 38-62.
― ― ―. "Myth and History: Turkey Red Wheat and the 'Kansas Miracle.'" *Heritage of the Great Plains* 22 (Summer 1989): 1-13.
Sawatsky, Rodney James. *History and Ideology: American Mennonite Identity Definition through History.* Kitchener, ON: Pandora Press, 2005.
Schellenberg, Ernest, ed. "Tabor College Bulletin." *Vorwaerts*, May 3, 1940, 7.
Schlabach, Theron F. *Peace, Faith, Nation: Mennonites and Amish in Nineteenth-Century America.* Scottdale, PA: Herald Press, 1988.
― ― ―. *War Peace and Social Conscience: Guy F. Hershberger and Mennonite Ethics.* Scottdale, PA: Herald Press, 2009.
Schrag, Menno. "Reader Response About the Problem of the Right and Left." *Mennonite Weekly Review*, 24 September 1964, 5.
― ― ―. "The Religious Issue." *Mennonite Weekly Review*, 13 October 1960, 6.
― ― ―. "An Unparalleled Tragedy." *Mennonite Weekly Review*, 14 March 1968, 4.
― ― ―. "Voters–And/Or Intercessors." *Mennonite Weekly Review*, 5 September 1968.
― ― ―. "Wheat Fields and Missiles." *Mennonite Weekly Review*, 9 July 1959, 6.
― ― ―. "Which Is It?" *Mennonite Weekly Review*, 6 July 1950, 4.
Schrag, Paul. "2002 year in review." *Mennonite Weekly Review*, 30 December 2002, 6.
― ― ―. "Abortion Battle Prompts Kansans to Confront Issue, Pro-Life Advocate Says Movement Gets Little Support from Mennonites." *Mennonite Weekly Review*, 26 September 1991, 1-2.
― ― ―. "The forgotten moral crisis." *Mennonite Weekly Review*, 22 March 2001, 4.
― ― ―. "Gulf War Swells Ranks of War-Tax Resisters." *Mennonite Weekly Review*, 14 March 1991, 4.
― ― ―. "'In God we trust' means no revenge." *Mennonite Weekly Review*, 20 September 2001, 4.
― ― ―. "'Just war' and civilian casualties." *Mennonite Weekly Review*, 8 November 2001, 4.
― ― ―. "Listening to the People, MB Congressman Supports Peace Tax Fund, Strong Defense." *Mennonite Weekly Review*, 28 August 1997, 1.
― ― ―. "Opposing war: means and ends." *Mennonite Weekly Review*, 7 April 2003, 4.
― ― ―. "Wichita Protests Aren't Best Pro-Life Witness." *Mennonite Weekly Review*, 22 August 1991, 4.
― ― ―. "Will Americans Pay for Oil with Blood?" *Mennonite Weekly Review*, 15 November 1990, 1.
Schrag, Robert. "The Bicentennial: A Positive View." *Mennonite Weekly Review*, 18 September 1975, 4.
― ― ―. "Mennonite Contribution." *Mennonite Weekly Review*, 9 Dec 1976, 4.
― ― ―. "Peace Efforts May Vary; Uniformity Not Required." *Mennonite Weekly Review*, 29 November 1990), 4.
― ― ―. "Peacemaking in Birmingham." *Mennonite Weekly Review*, 13 June 1963, 4.
― ― ―. "Protection of the Unborn a 'Central Issue.'" *Mennonite Weekly Review*, 16 Sept 1976, 4.
Schrag, Sam. "Boston visit to Bethel 'bizarre.'" *Newton Kansan*, 7 October 2002, 4.

"Service van visits city.," *Hillsboro Star-Journal*, 29 September 1976.
Sharp, John. *A School on the Prairie, A Centennial History of Hesston College*. Telford, PA: Cascadia Publishing House, 2009.
Shearer, Tobin Miller. *Daily Demonstrators: The Civil Rights Movement in Mennonite Homes and Sanctuaries*. Baltimore: Johns Hopkins University Press, 2010.
Shelly, Javan. "Peace Marchers Converge in Washington for Protest." *Bethel Collegian*, 21 November 1969, 1, 5.
Shelly, Maynard. "Editorial." *The Mennonite*, 13 December 1966, 765.
— — —. "For us the bell tolled." *The Mennonite* 4 November 1969, 663.
— — —. "Nixon Favored by the Mennonites." *The Mennonite*, 8 October 1968, 620-4.
— — —. "Peace Walk Baffles Peace Church." *The Mennonite*, 13 December 1966, 758.
Sibley, Mulford Q., and Philip Jacob. *Conscription of Conscience: The American State and the Conscientious Objector, 1940-1947*. Ithaca, NY: Cornell University Press, 1952.
Siemens, Curt. "Outside power structure," letter to the editor, *The Mennonite*, February 17, 1970, 118.
Smith, Michael. "Kansas, the Three-Party State." *Campaigns and Elections* (Oct/Nov 2003): 36.
"Soldiers Questioning Mideast War, MCCers in Germany Counseling COs in US. Army." *Mennonite Weekly Review*, 10 January 1991, 1.
Southern District Conference of the Mennonite Brethren Churches. *Yearbook Southern District Conference of the Mennonite Brethren Churches Convening at Enid, Oklahoma October 31-November 2, 1975*. Hillsboro, KS: Mennonite Brethren Publishing House, 1975.
Sprunger, Keith L. *Bethel College of Kansas 1887-2012*. North Newton: Bethel College, 2012.
— — —. *Campus, Congregation, and Community: The Bethel College Mennonite Church 1897-1997*. North Newton: Bethel College Mennonite Church, 1997.
— — —. "The Most Monumental Mennonite," *Mennonite Life* 34 (September 1979), 10-15.
— — —. "On Rekindling the American Dream." *Mennonite Weekly Review*, 11 Mar 1976, 4.
Sprunger, Keith L., James C. Juhnke and John D. Waltner. *Voices Against War: A Guide to the Schowalter Oral History Collection on World War I Conscientious Objection*. North Newton: Bethel College, 1973, 1981.
Stoltzfus, Gene. "Team Promotes Peace Dialogue." *Mennonite Weekly Review*, 20 December 1990, 1.
Strunk, Chris. "Campaign finance at issue in House." *Newton Kansan*, 24 October 1998, 15.
— — —. "Krehbiel Overcomes Waltner for 74th District House Seat." *Newton Kansan*, 4 November 1998, 5.
Strunk, Chris, and Amanda Balzer, "North Newton Democrat defeats 12-year incumbent." *Newton Kansan*, 6 November 2002, 2.
Stucky, Harley J. "Should Mennonites Participate in Government?" *Mennonite Life* 14 (January 1959), 34-8, 12.
— — —. *The Swiss Mennonite Memorial Monument: Is It Inspirational Art, Symbolic Expression, or History?* North Newton, KS: Harley J. Stucky, 1999.
Stucky, Tim, and Nancy Stucky, "Walter W. "Sprig" Graber: A Man for All Seasons." *Ninnescah Valley News*, July 11, 2003, reprinted in the Swiss

Mennonite Cultural and Historical Association online newsletter http://www.swissmennonite.org/featlure_archive/2003/200308.html.
"Students March in Topeka." *Bethel Collegian,* 14 April 14 1965, 1.
Stumpf, David K. *Titan II: A History of a Cold War Missile Program.* Fayetteville, AR: University of Arkansas Press, 2000.
Suderman, Dale. "One week in Saigon." *The Mennonite,* 12 May 1970, 332.
Taylor, Steven J. *Acts of Conscience: World War II, Mental Institutions, and Religious Objectors.* Syracuse, NY: Syracuse University Press, 2009.
Templin, Lawrence. "On the serious side, on registration." *Bethel Collegian,* 27 March 1942, 4.
Toews, Paul. *Mennonites in American Society 1930-1970: Modernity and the Persistence of Religious Community.* Scottdale, PA: Herald Press, 1996.
— — —. "Religion American Style." *The Christian Leader,* 20 January 1976, 2-4.
Trillin, Calvin. "A Reporter at Large, The War in Kansas." *The New Yorker,* 2 April 1967, 82.
"Turkey gift to governor." *Moundridge Journal,* 18 December 1975, 1.
Veendorp, Gary. "Cross-Country Cyclists Recall Deeds of Kindness." *Mennonite Weekly Review,* 15 July 1976, 12.
Vogt, J. W. "Peacetime Military Conscription." *The Christian Leader,* November 1944, 2.
"Volunteer Spotlight: The Mennonite Western District Conference." *Kansas Coalition Against the Death Penalty Newsletter,* Spring 2014.
Walters, LeRoy. "The Life Man Controls: A Perspective on Abortion and Euthanasia." *Mennonite Medical Messenger,* October-December 1972.
Waltner, Erland. "Numbered with the Transgressors." *The Mennonite,* 1 February 1949, 4.
Weathering the Storm: Christian Pacifist Responses to War. Newton, KS: Faith and Life Press), 1991.
Weaver, J. Denny. *Keeping Salvation Ethical, Mennonite and Amish Atonement Theology in the Late Nineteenth Century.* Scottdale, PA: Herald Press, 1997.
Wedel, C. H. *Geleitworte an junge Christen.* Newton, KS: Schulverlag von Bethel College, 1912.
Weinbrenner, Reynold. "Peacetime Conscription." *The Mennonite,* 5 December 1944, 3.
Wernicke, Günther, and Lawrence S. Wittner. "Lifting the Iron Curtain: The Peace March to Moscow of 1960-1961." *The International History Review* (December 1999): 900-917.
Western District Conference. *Report of 45th annual meeting, Beatrice, Nebraska, 21-23 October 1936.*
— — —. *Minutes and Reports of the Seventy-Eighth Annual Session of the Western District Conference, October 10-12, 1969.*
Wiens, Wayne. "Intelligent design should be tested." *Newton Kansan,* 28 June 2005, 6A.
Williams, Donald. "Challenger Yost strives for magical balance." *Wichita Eagle,* 1 November 1990, 5B.
Wilson, Bill. "Anti-liquor by the drink signs vandalized." *Newton Kansan,* 23 October 1996, 1.
— — —. "Longtime commissioner says goodbye." *Newton Kansan,* 18 December 1996, 1.

Wuthnow, Robert. *Red State Religion: Faith and Politics in America's Heartland.* Princeton: Princeton University Press, 2012.
"Youth Accepts Challenge," Tabor College Bulletin. *Hillsboro Journal,* 17 October 1940, 7.
Zuercher, Melanie. "Across the country, a Sunday for peace." *Mennonite Weekly Review,* 20 September 2001, 1.

Web sites

Ballotpedia: The Encyclopedia of American Politics, Kansas State Legislature. http://www.ballotpedia.org/Kansas_State_Legislature (accessed 23 April 2015)
"Categories of Faith-Based Organizations," Berkeley Center for Religion, Peace and World Affairs, Georgetown University. http://berkeley-georgetown.edu/essays/categories-of-faith-based-organizations (accessed June 25, 2014).
The Civilian Public Service Story: Living Peace in a Time of War. http://www.civilianpublicservice.org/ (accessed 25 March 25 2013).
"Guidelines on Abortion (General Conference Mennonite Church, 1980)." http://anabaptistwiki.org/mediawiki/index.php?title=Guidelines_on_Abortion_(General_Conference_Mennonite_Church,_1980) (accessed 15 August 2014).
Homeland Security Digital Library, Disaster Relief Act of 1974. http://www.hsdl.org/?view&did=458661 (accessed 31 Dec 2015).
Kansas Statistical Abstract 2001, Institute for Policy and Social Research. http://www.ipsr.ku.edu/ksdata/ksah/KSA46.pdf (accessed 7 Nov 2014).
"List of Nike missile sites," Wikipedia, http://en.wikipedia.org/wiki/List_of_Nike_missile_sites#Kansas (accessed 15 Oct 2015).
"Mennonite Church Abortion Statement 1975" http://anabaptistwiki.org/mediawiki/index.php?title=Abortion_(Mennonite_Church,_1975) (accessed 15 August 2014).
"Project Nike," Wikipedia, http://en.wikipedia.org/wiki/Project_Nike (accessed 15 Oct 2015).
"Resolution on Abortion (Mennonite Brethren Church)" http://anabaptistwiki.org/mediawiki/index.php?title=Resolution_on_Abortion_(Mennonite_Brethren-Church-1975) (accessed 15 Aug 2014).
"Tom Bishop of Homestead Affordable Housing." http://www.kshousingcorp.org/tom-bishop-named-2011-trailblazer.aspx (accessed 26 Jan 2013).

Unpublished items

Bargen, Helen. Personal collection.
Bargen, Helen. Conversation with James Juhnke, North Newton, KS, 17 February 2014.

Bargen, Helen, and David Habegger. "The Life of Eldon Bargen." Unpublished paper, 28 August 2010 (MLA).
Benjamin, Charles, papers, MS.447, MLA.
Bethel College Peace Club Records, III.1.A.29.e, MLA
Bias, Andy. Bias, presentation to Mennonite Men's breakfast, Lorraine Avenue Mennonite Church, 23 March 2013.
Bishop, Tom. Interview by James Juhnke, Holton, KS, 28 November 2013.
Bogard, Michael. "The Flag: A Symbol of Patriotism Among American Mennonites." Paper for Great Plains Seminary, December 1990.
Brenneman, Frank. Interview by James Juhnke, 20 December 2011.
Carlin, John. Interview by James Juhnke, 11 Mar 2005.
Chesebro, Scott. Interview by James Juhnke, 14 December 2011.
Dirks, Debra L. "The United States vs. Carl J. Stucky." Unpublished paper, n.d.
Downey-Schmidt, Christine. Interview by James Juhnke, North Newton, KS, 6 October 2014.
Dueck, Robert. Collection of Harold Dyck papers, Garland, TX.
Dyck, Cornelius J. "Unity Amidst Diversity." Unpublished presentation at the Mennonite Central Committee 75th anniversary symposium, Fresno, CA, March 10, 1995.
Dyck, Harold. Interview by James Juhnke, 2005.
Eden Mennonite Church Record Book, Congregational Meeting Minutes 1926-1980.
Ediger, Elmer papers, MS.334, MLA.
Ediger, Elmer, papers held by Carol Ediger Peters.
Esau, John A. "Civil Religion – Or How to Affirm One's Country Without Denying One's Faith." Sermon at Bethel College Mennonite Church, 7 July 1974.
— — —. Interview by James Juhnke, 6 December 2011.
— — —. "Religion and Culture: A New Model for Understanding Their Changing Relationship." MTh thesis, The United Theological Seminary of the Twin Cities, 1972.
Fast, Henry A. Interview by Keith Sprunger, March 21, 1973, 940.5316 #3, MLA.
"Financial Audit Report, Kansas Wheat Commission for the Fiscal Year Ended June 30, 1975." Kansas State Archives, Topeka, KS.
J. Winfield Fretz papers, MS. 69, MLA.
Friesen, Duane K. "A Moral Justification for War Tax Resistance." Unpublished paper, American Society of Christian Ethics, 19 Jan 1980. Copy at MLA.
Friesen, Jacob V., file, Center for Mennonite Brethren Studies at Tabor College, Hillsboro, KS.
General Conference Mennonite Church Board of Christian Service records, MLA.
Gillmore, James. Interview by James Juhnke, 26 January 2015.
Goering, Erwin. Interview by Trent Shipley, November 13, 1987, 940.5316 #146-147, MLA.
Goering, Joseph D. C. Interview by James Juhnke, 31 July 1966.
Goering, Terence. "A History of the Bethel College Peace Club." Social Science Seminar paper, Bethel College, 1975.
Goossen, Duane. "Faithfulness Versus Effectiveness: A Position on Ethics." Seminar paper, Bethel College, 1978.
— — —. Interview by James Juhnke, Topeka, KS, 18 January 2013.
— — —. "It Takes All Kinds of People to Make a World." Sermon presented at Southern Hills Mennonite Church, October 2011.

———. Personal collection.
Harder, Jesse. Interview by James Juhnke, Buhler, KS, 13 November 2009.
———, papers, Center for Mennonite Brethren Studies, Tabor College, Hillsboro, KS.
Harder, Leland. Interview by Fred Fransen, 10 March 1988, 940.5316 #155, MLA.
———. "A Joint Study of Four Hillsboro-Lehigh Area Churches in Kansas." Unpublished paper, 1964.
Harms, Wilmer. Interview by James Juhnke, North Newton, KS, 19 June 2014.
Henley, Keith R. "The Jim Juhnke Congressional Campaign of 1970." Seminar paper, Bethel College, 1975.
Hiebert, Paul. Interview by James Juhnke, 1 April 2015.
Houser, Gordon. Interview by James Juhnke, 15 August 2014.
International Relations Institute records, V.14, MLA.
Iserhardt, Virginia "Jinny." Interview by James Juhnke, 23 September 2003.
Janzen, Mark. Interview by James Juhnke, Wichita, KS, 20 July 2014.
Juhnke, James C., papers, MS.136, MLA.
———. Personal collection.
———. "Shaping Religious Community through Martyr Memories." Unpublished presentation at "Walls and Windows" symposium, Bethel College, 20 November 1998.
Kansans Concerned about Vietnam records, VI.2, MLA.
Kaufman, E. G., presidential records, III.1.A.1.g, MLA.
———. Papers, MS.108, MLA.
Keim, Howard. "Rhetorical Strategies and Self-Definitions of Local Leaders: Four Case Studies." PhD dissertation, University of Kansas, 1996.
Kingsley, Judy Hilty. Interview by James Juhnke, September 8, 1996.
Klassen, Elmer, and Lenore Friesen Klassen. Interview by James Juhnke, North Newton, KS, 19 December 2000.
Klassen, James. Interview by James Juhnke, 21 May 2014.
Koehn, Dale. Interview by author James Juhnke, Moundridge, KS, 3 Sept 2014.
Koehn, Dennis, papers, MS.137, MLA.
Krehbiel, C. E., papers, MS.11, MLA.
Krehbiel, Doug. Interview by James Juhnke, North Newton, Ks, 11 Nov 2012.
Kreider, Robert S. Email message to James Juhnke, 3 June 2003.
———. Interview by Keith Sprunger, 19 October 1988, 940.5316 #178, MLA .
———. Interview by James Juhnke, 22 July 2008.
———. Interview by James Juhnke, 11 November 2008.
———. "Reflections on the Smithsonian Experience." Unpublished paper, 17 February 1994.
Loewen, Esko. Interview by Keith Sprunger, Oct. 9, 1973, 940-5316 #1-2, MLA.
Loganbill, Judy. Presentation at Lorraine Avenue Mennonite Church, 29 January 2012.
Lorraine Avenue Mennonite Church bulletin/newsletter, 30 September 1945. LAMC archives.
Mennonite Housing Rehabilitation Services Inc. Annual Report, 1990, 1997.
Miller, Joseph S. "German POWS at Peabody and Concordia, Kansas During World War II." Social Science Seminar paper, Bethel College, 1978.
Moyer, J. Harold, papers, MS.323, MLA.
Neufeld, Donna, personal collection.

Neufeld, Donna and Harry. Iinterview by James Juhnke, North Newton, KS, 9 January 2013.
Nikkel, Larry. Interview by James Juhnke, Wichita, KS, 17 June 2013.
Ollenburger, Ben. Email to James Juhnke, 8 December 2011.
Persian Gulf War Oral History Collection, OH.3, MLA
Raber, Merrill, comp. "Eyewitness to Prairie View History, 1954-1984." Videodisk documentary of interviews with former employees.
— — —. Email to James Juhnke, 26 June 2014.
— — —. Interview by James Juhnke, 15 May 2013.
— — —. Personal collection.
Redekop, Calvin. Email to James Juhnke, 11 December 2011.
— — —. Personal collection.
Regier, Austin. "The General Conference and World War II." Student paper for Mennonite history class taught by Cornelius Krahn, Bethel College, May 1948.
Regier, Chuck. "Discipline and Growth: the Cleansing of the Church of God in Christ, Mennonite 1974-1980." Mennonite History class paper, Bethel College, 1980.
Regier, Harold. Interview by James Juhnke, 10 April 2014.
Regier, Raymond. Personal collection, North Newton, KS.
Reimer, Ray. Personal collection.
Ruebke, Michelle. Email to James Juhnke, 12 September 2014.
— — —. Interview by James Juhnke, Newton, KS, 9 September 2014.
Samuelson, Ellen. Personal collection.
Schrag, Edwin. Interview by Tim Schrag, Sept 13, 1974, 940.5316 #17, MLA.
Schrag, Robert. Interview by James Juhnke, 10 April 2012.
— — —. Interview by James Juhnke, 15 October 2014.
Schroeder, Sue, and Michelle Friesen, "A Case of Non-Registration." Student research paper, Bethel College, 21 March 1972.
Shriver, Garner E., Papers, MS 77-01, Wichita State University Libraries Special Collections.
Stucky, Dale. Interview by James Juhnke and Keith Sprunger, 3 August 1993, 940.5316 #258-259, MLA.
Stucky, Harley J. "Carl J. Stucky's Witness for the Christian Gospel of Love and Non-resistance." Unpublished paper, n.d.
— — —. Letter to United States District Court Office of the Clerk, 14 September 1944.
— — —. Papers, MS.459, MLA.
Stucky, Mark E. "James C. Juhnke and Political Involvement." Seminar paper, Bethel College, 1971.
Suderman, Dale. Interview by James Juhnke, 13 May 2014
— — —. Interview by James Juhnke, 24 May 2014.
— — —. Papers, MS.560, MLA.
Thieszen, Barbara. "Voting Trends in Selected Mennonite Townships." Student research paper, Bethel College, 6 December 1979.
Toews, Leanne. Interview by James Juhnke, 8 October 2011.
Unruh, Ernest. Interview by James Juhnke, Newton, KS, 24 February 2005.
Unruh, Helen Graber. Scrapbook of Graber political clippings, Hutchinson, KS.
Voth, Harold. Interview by James Juhnke, Burrton, KS, n.d.
Walker, Richard. Interview by James Juhnke, 25 January 2015.
Waltner, John. Interview by James Juhnke, North Newton, KS, 28 January 2015.

Wedel, David C. Interview by Fred Fransen, March 24, 1988, 940.5316 #160, MLA.
Western District Peace and Social Concerns Committee minutes, II.3.e.9, MLA.
Wheat Centennial records, Center for Mennonite Brethren Studies, Tabor College.
"Wichita Pride Hosts Gay and Lesbian Awards," *The Wichita Eagle*, 16 June 2007, 1B.
Wiebe, Ray. Interview by James C. Juhnke, Hillsboro, 4 April 2014.
Wiens, Wayne. "Consequences of the Evolution Furor: What Must be Changed." Paper at "Friday at Four Forum," Bethel College, 27 October 2000.
Yoder, Gene. Interview by Tim Schrag, 19 January 1975, 940.5316 #23b, MLA.
Zerbe, Gordon. Email to James Juhnke, 9 December 2011.
Zielke, Vern. Interview by James Juhnke, 6 January 2011.

Index

Abortion, 182, 200, 201, 202, 207, 210, 213, 256-61, 281
Allaby, Gordon, 270
Al Qaeda, 269
Agnew, Spiro, 135
Americanization, 217, 230, 294
American Legion, 43, 107, 170
Anabaptist Martyr Exhibit, 262-3
Andreas, Paul, 128
Anstaett, Doug, 206, 274-5
A People of Two Kingdoms, vol. 1, 1-9
Armed Forces Bicentennial Caravan, 172
Army Corps of Engineers, 95-6
Avery, William, 88
Awbrey, Stuart, 7
Babson, Roger W., 52
Bachman, Ernest, 135
Baird, Carson, 133
Baker, Ray, 170
Ball, William Bentley, 244
Bargen, Eldon, 62, 63
Bargen, Ralph, 62, 63
Bartel, Peter, 212
Bartel, Roland, 41
Baukhage, H. R., 14
Beachy, Alvin, 112, 113
Becker, Steven, 266-7, 297
Bellah, Robert, 157
Bender, Harold S., 37, 54, 58-59, 294
Bender, Urie, 147
Bender, Vern, 113, 114, 255
Benjamin, Charles, 195-9, 297
Bennett, Robert, 165
Berg, Peter H., 23, 25-26, 28
Bergen, Dan, 212
Bergman, Gordon, 259
Berry, Leroy, 181
Bethel College, 6, 17-18, 60, 68-9, 87, 88, 92, 104, 219, 221, 254
Bethel College Mennonite Church, 35
Bethell, Bob, 271
Bicentennial 1976, 125-6, 153-76
Bishop, Tom, 192-4, 228-9, 291, 293, 297
Boehr, Cedric, 203-8, 259, 261, 292, 297
Boehr, Sandi, 203-6, 259
Boese, Anita, xii

Boese, Ben, 165-6
Boese, Gertrude, 166
Bontrager, Sam, 190-1
Boston, Garry, 186, 200, 201, 260, 271-4, 275
Brenneman, Frank, 173
Brown, Wesley, 121-22, 221
Brownback, Sam, 212, 282
Bruce, K. B., 172
Brunk, Steve, 281
Burkholder, J. Lawrence, 247
Bush, George, 267, 269
Bush, George H.W., 252-3, 256
Bush, Perry, 246
Campolo, Tony, 192
Carlin, John, 149, 169, 185, 189, 293
Carter, Jimmy, 174, 179, 248
Casino gambling, 277
Catholic, 279-80
Chaney, Bert, 189
Chesebro, Scott, 171
Church of God in Christ Mennonite, 28, 35, 152-3, 287
Civilian Public Service, 16, 29-45, 50-56, 59-65, 83, 119, 177, 188-9, 217, 222-3
Clinton, Bill, 201, 256, 267
Constitution Party, 208
Coslett, Mary, 270-1
Crow, Sam, 248-9
Dahl, Don, 277-8, 297
Death Penalty, 148-150, 182, 186, 188, 190, 266
Desert Storm, 252-6
Dey, Clayton, 196
Dole, Robert, 263, 267
Downey, Christine, 279-82, 293, 297
Dueck, Al, 173
Dunn, Jim 260
Dutch-Russians, 188, 247
Dyck Arboretum, 179-80
Dyck, George, 255
Dyck, Harold, 177-80, 192, 225, 238, 291, 297
Dyck, H. J., 222
Dyck, Peter J., 142
Ebersole, Willard, 227
Ediger, Tina Block, 284

Eicher, Edward Clayton, 214
Eisenhower, Dwight, 215
Elections, 1908, 2;
1924, 3, 4;
1930, 3;
1932, 4;
1936, 25;
1940, 17, 23-27, 79, 151;
1944, 53;
1948, 126;
1952, 70, 80;
1956, 81;
1960, 97-99, 126-7;
1964, 99-101, 142, 288;
1968, 102, 128, 142-3, 151;
1970, 126-138, 139-40;
1972, 102, 140, 143, 151;
1976, 102, 138, 151, 174;
1978, 149;
1980, 196, 250;
1982, 182-4; 188-9;
1984, 250-1;
1988, 212;
1990, 138, 193, 209, 229, 291;
1992, 138, 200, 201, 209; 256, 267;
1994, 203-8;
1996, 211-2, 214, 267;
1998, 279;
2000, 282;
2002, 272-4
Epp, Charles, 248-249
Equal Rights Amendment, 178-9
Esau, Phil, 239
Evolution, 265-6
Ewert, Jacob Gerhard, 2
Ewert, Lydia, 75
Farm crisis, 231-8, 291
Fast, Darrell, 254
Fast, Henry A., 40-41, 44
Fellowship of Reconciliation, 15
Feminism, 199
Finney, Joan, 186, 191, 201
First Mennonite Church of Christian Moundridge, 94
flag American, 76, 141, 156, 269-73, 283
Flaming, Elmer, 170, 172-3

Flaming, Ron, 239
Flowers, Charles, 84
Flowers, Dorothy, 84
Ford, Gerald, 174
Foulke, Seven Vail, 7
Franz, Delton, 85, 103, 153, 164, 243, 291
Franz, Jay, 107
Franz, John P., 80
Franz, Marian, 243-4
Freeze the Arms Race, 249-50, 291
Fretz, Winfield, 36, 68
Friesen, Duane, 158, 181, 244, 295
Friesen, Jacob V., 298
Friesen, Walter, S., 276
Funk, Arnold, 95, 107
Funk, John F., 2
Gaeddert, Albert, 33-34, 36, 39, 44
Gaeddert, John, 55
Galloway, Joseph, 162
Gandhi, Mahatma, 15
Gay marriage (see same-sex marriage)
General Conference Mennonite Church, 8, 9, 37, 44, 57, 86, 92, 286
Gerrymander, 274
German language, 23
Gillmore, Jim, 150-1, 298
Glickman, Dan, 138, 179, 209, 243, 263
Goering, Bill, 238, 298
Goering, Erwin, 44
Goering, J. D. C., 27, 101, 298
Goering, Oswald, 205
Goering, Paul, 108
Goering, Peter W., 77
Goertzen, Peggy, xii
Goldwater, Barry, 99-100
Goossen, Duane, 180-8, 190, 201, 225, 238, 291, 292, 298
Goossen, Henry, 185
Goossen, Rachel Waltner, 187
Government aid for education, 218-22
Government aid for immigrants, 283-5
Government aid for mental health, 222-6
Graber, Delia, 107
Graber, Steve, 213
Graber, Walter W., 72-4, 144-5, 212, 235, 293, 298

Grace Bible Institute, Omaha, 204
Grant, Ulysses S., 1
Graves, Bill, 187, 213, 272, 275, 281
Gulfport Mission, 83-5
Gun control, 183, 281
Hall, Fred, 72, 73
Harder, James, 255
Harder, Jesse, 188-192, 215, 238, 291, 293, 298
Harder, Leland, 54, 268
Harding, Rosemary Freeney, 86
Harding, Vincent, 84, 85-7, 163, 288
Harms, Bob, 143
Harms, Leon H., 4
Harms, Menno, 143
Harms, Orlando, 52, 98-9, 100, 143
Harrison, Carol, 259-60
Harshbarger, Emmet, 10, 11, 18-20, 54
Hart, Lawrence, 87, 163
Hawver, Martin, 280
Hayden, Mike, 201
Hein, Marvin, 267
Henley, Keith, 183-4
Hershberger, Guy F., 37-8, 54, 58, 246, 294
Hershey, Jean, 197
Hershey, Lewis B., 40-41, 64
Hesston College, 6, 89, 113-6, 220, 221, 254, 270, 271-3
Hesston Corporation, 233
Hiebert, Clarence, 133, 149
Hiebert, John, xiii
Hiebert, Paul, 97, 298
Hiebert, Ruth Ann, 201
Hillsboro Journal, 23
Hilty, Judy, 91
Hinshaw, Dean, 189
Historic peace churches, 22
Historiography, x
Holdeman, see (Church of God in Christ Mennonite)
Holt, Arthur E., 36
Homosexuality, 275-6, 277, 278
Hope, Clifford, 16
Hopefield Mennonite Church, 50
Hostetter, Doug, 112
Houston, John M, 12, 14, 47
Hull, Robert, 253
Humphrey, Hubert, 109, 140

Hutchins, Robert, 17
Ichikawa, Yoshihiro, 124
Immigrant farm workers, 283-5
Income tax refusal, 241-5
Intermennonite cooperation, 217-8
Iraq War, 269-71
Iserhardt, Virginia, 203, 205, 261, 281-2
I-W Program, 64-5
Jackson, Gregory, 111
Janzen, David, 242, 271
Janzen, Louis, 51
Janzen, Mark, 238
Johnson, Lyndon, 80, 89, 102, 109, 231
Johnston, Colleen Kelly, 200
Jost, Lynn, 174
Juhnke, Bill (William), 12-14, 38, 45-6, 53, 55, 60, 80-1, 82, 126, 129, 167, 225, 233, 236
Juhnke, James, x, 13, 126-38, 162, 275, 293, 298
Juhnke, Marvin, 54
Juhnke, Meta Goering, 13-14, 129, 166
Juhnke, Walter, 38-9, 53
Juhnke, William Jr., 88
Just, Roy, 172, 174
Kauffman, Milo, 67-8
Kansas Institute of International Relations, 11
Kansas Mennonite Men's Chorus, 168-9
Kansas Wheat Growers Association, 73
Kassebaum, Nancy, 210, 263
Kaufman, Donald, 242
Kaufman, Edmund G., 12, 16, 46-7, 49, 54, 58, 63, 111
Kaufman, Edward E., 14-15
Kaufman, Gordon, 60-1, 67, 244, 295
Kaufman, Jacob, 199
Kaufman, M. S., 199
Kaufman, Orlo, 83, 87
Keeney, William, 121
Kehler, Larry, 143
Kelly, Patrick, 129
Kennedy, John F., 90, 92, 128, 231
Kennedy, Robert, 142
King, Martin Luther, Jr., 84, 85, 86, 90, 142, 157, 288

King, Raymond, 177
Klassen, Elmer, 261-2
Klassen, Don, 211, 298
Klassen, George, 20
Klassen, James, 123-6
Klasssen, Lenore Friesen, 261, 264
Kliewer, Jerry, 118
Kliewer, Kirsten, 207
Kliewer, Paul, 30, 31
Kobach, Kris, 283
Koch, Charles, G., 105
Koehn, Dennis, 119-22, 221, 253
Koontz, Ted, 153
Korean War, 64, 80
Kosch, Lewis F., 41
Kraybill, Donald, I, 158
Krehbiel, Carl, 275, 279
Krehbiel, Christian E., 49, 222
Krehbiel, Henry Peter, 2, 21, 22, 23
Krehbiel, Leona, 58
Krehbiel, Ralph, 189
Krehbiel, Robert E., 212-4, 291, 293, 298
Kreider, Amos E, 17
Kreider, Anna, 128
Kreider, Rachel, 256
Kreider, Robert, 7, 12, 16-18, 26, 36, 37, 38, 39-40, 44, 55, 66, 160, 167, 222, 262-3
Kroeker, Wally, 161, 250, 251
Kunkel, Howard, 107
Krimmer Mennonite Brethren, 1, 8, 3
Kuhns, Curt, 171
Kyle, Richard, 267-8
Lady, Wendell, 184
Langenwalter, R. G., 135
Lapp, John, 112, 175
Legislative awareness seminars, 191, 239-40, 291
Lehman, Ralph, 42
Lehn, Cornelia, 241, 245
Leichty, Bruce, 175
Linscheid, Ruth, 276
Liquor by the Drink, 263-4
Loganbill, Judy, 282, 293, 298
Loewen, Esko, 16, 18, 89, 121
Loewen, Royden, ix
Lorraine Avenue Mennonite Church, 35, 59-60, 277

Lynch, James, xii
MacArthur, Douglass, 49
Mace, Jack, 298
MacMaster, Richard,
Martin, Pat Hostetter, 114
Mayer, Robert, 110
McCarthy, Eugene, 128, 139
McCuish, John, 72
McGovern, George, 139, 140, 262
Mennonite Brethren, 1, 8, 103, 155-6, 286
Mennonite Church, see (Old) Mennonite Church
Mennonite Disaster Service, 55, 217
Mennonite Central Committee, 3, 39, 44, 66, 291
Mennonite Housing, 192-4, 227-9
Mennonite Settler Monument, 30-31
Mennonite Weekly Review, 3, 23
Mennonite World Conference, 76
Mental health reform, 42-4
Miller, C. Nevin, 168-9
Miller, Jenilee, 140
Miller, Leo L., 77
Miller, Vern, 141
Missile base Nike Hercules, 77-8
Missile base Titan II sites, 79, 291
Moore, Carol, 299
Moran, Jerry, 214-5, 292, 299
Moratorium 1969, 109-13
Mueller, David, 278
Muste, A. J., 61, 91
National Association of Evangelicals, 161
National Organization of Women, 200
National Prayer Breakfast, 178, 185
National Service Board for Religious Objectors, 33
Neufeld, Adolf, 207
Neufeld, Donna, 186, 199-203, 260, 264, 293, 299
Neufeld, Elmer, 246-7
Neufeld, Harry, 199
Neufeld, Melvin, 271
Neufeld, Mrs. J. B. , 150
Neufeld, Vernon, 107, 108
Neufeld, Walter, 69, 76-7, 94
Newton Chamber of Commerce 31, 46
Nguyen, Cao Ky, 130

Nichols, Dick, 199
Niebuhr, Reinhold, 116, 181, 245
Nikkel, Larry, 225
Nikkel, Vernon, 205-6
Nixon, Max, 30
Nixon, Richard, 99, 109, 124, 128, 174, 179
Nolt, Steven, ix
Nonregistration, 60-3, 119-22, 248-9
North Atlantic Treaty Organization, 126
Nossaman, Mike, 129
Novak, Bill, 180, 182
Nuclear weapons, 77-9, 92-3
Old Colony Mennonites, 284-5
(Old) Mennonite Church, 8, 37, 54, 83, 120, 286
Ollenberger, Ben, 173
Olsen, Frances, 182
Olsen, Victor, 40
O'Neal, Mike, 275
Opiyo, John, 87
Ottoson, Robin, xiii
Pamba, Hannington, 88
Parkinson, Mark, 187
Pax Service, 64
Peace Pilgrim, 90-1
Peace Section MCC, 66-7, 103
Peace Tax Fund, 209-10, 215, 242-5
Peace Walk to Moscow, 91-2
Peachey, Paul, 100-1
Pearson, Betty, 137
Pearson, Charles, 137
Pearson, James, 89
Peine, Arthur, 106
Penner, Doug, 255
Peters, Ed, 212
Peters, Frank C., 67
Peters, Jim, 97, 299
Peters, Marjorie Klassen, 96-7, 299
Penner, H. D., 2
Penner, Mil, 147
Penner, Teresa, 209
Persian Gulf War, 252-6
Platt, Dwight, 62, 63
Platt, LaVonne Godwin, 231
Platt, Selma Rich, 45
Pledge of allegiance, 283

Prairie View Mental Health Center, 186, 223-226
Prisoners of war, 51
Prohibition, 4
Politics, xi
Preheim, Vern, 89
Pretty Prairie, 72
Prieb, Wesley, 145, 156, 191
Quakers, 22
Raber, Merrill, 139-40
Racism, 82-3
Rahn, Ben, 89
Ratner, Payne, 14, 23
Ratzlaff, Don, 147, 171, 251
Reagan, Ronald, 240-1, 248, 291
Redekop, John H., 251
Reed, Clyde, 59
Rees, Edward H., 59
Reform Party, 211-212
Regier, Austin, 61-2, 67
Regier, Harold, 82, 85, 87
Regier, Raymond, 234, 236-7
Regier, Robert, 92, 108, 109, 133
Regier, Sam, 234-5
Reid, Tom, 139
Reimer, Ray, 239, 240
Rempel, Clarence, 264, 269
Repentance Walk 1966, 105-9
Retirement homes, 218
Rich, Mardy, 91
Richardson, Herbert, 157
Richert, Peter H., 10, 21
Robinson, Thomas, 128
Roniger, Pascal, 182
Roosevelt, Eleanor, 23, 43-4
Roosevelt, Franklin Delano, 3, 10, 14, 22, 25, 32, 51, 52, 57, 72, 80, 231, 233
Ross, John, 43
Ruebke, Michelle, 256-7
Rupp, Byron, 254
Ruth, John, 162, 176
Rutschman, James D., 264
Same-sex marriage, 275-7, 283
Samuelson, Armin, 204
Samuelson, Ellen, 203, 204, 205, 261, 278
Saul, Norman, 148
Sawatsky, Rodney James, 22
Schellenberg, Ernest, 20

Index 323

Schlabach, Theron, ix
Schloneger, Matt, 272-3
Schmidt, Carol, 147
Schmidt, Elizabeth, 246
Schmidt, Esther, 166
Schmidt, Gordon, 280
Schmidt, Melvin, 107, 129
Schmidt, Steve, 264
Schoeppel, Andrew, 96
School of Living, 16, 46
Schowalter, J. A., 4, 299
Schrag, Clarence, 236
Schrag, Don, 136
Schrag, Edwin, 42
Schrag, Jim, 270
Schrag, Menno, 23, 24, 28, 52, 77, 80, 97-8, 142-3, 233-4, 288-9
Schrag, Paul, 260-1, 269, 288
Schrag, Robert, 143, 167-8, 175, 176, 288-9
Schroeder, Don, 299
Schultz, Renetta, 24
Sebelius, Kathleen, 150, 187, 293
Seger, Roberta, 200
Selective Service, 39-40, 42, 60, 63, 119-23, 248-9
Shallenberger, Tim, 186-7
Sheldon, Charles M., 15
Shelly, Maynard, 108, 142, 174
Showalter, Anne, 276
Shriver, Garner 114, 126-7, 129, 131, 134-5, 170, 243
Sibanda, Enos, 87
Siemens, Curt, 14, 133
Slocombe, Lawrence, 96
Smucker, Bert, 32
Smucker, Jesse N., 10
Socialist, 17, 18, 26, 38, 53, 61
Soil Conservation Service, 39, 40
Sommerfeld, Harold, 115
Southern Hills Mennonite Church, 239
Sprunger, Keith, 160-1
Starnes, Joe, 44
Stassen, Glen, 295
Steelberg, Don, 210
Steelberg, Elsie, 210
Stoltzfus, Gene, 192
Stone, Barton, 91

Stucky, Carl J, 39, 48-50
Stucky, Dale, 50-1, 96
Stucky, David T., 27
Stucky, Harley, 49, 69-70, 145, 148
Stucky, Milo, 188
Students for a Democratic Society, 128
Suderman, Dale, 116-8
Suderman, John C., 30
Suderman, Karl K., 135
Summer of Mercy, 200, 203, 256-260
Swartzendruber, Loren, 272
Swiss-Volhynian Mennonites, 2, 26, 50, 72, 79, 146, 188, 293
Swomley, John, 106
Tabor College, 6, 20-21, 67, 88, 112, 149, 169-74, 219-220, 221
Templin, Lawrence, 16, 46-7, 60
Templin, Ralph, 16
Terry, Randall, 259
Thant, U, 106
Theis, Sam, 248-9
Thierstein, John, 17, 25
Thieu, Nguyen Van, 130
Thiesen, John, xii
Thomas, Norman, 17, 38, 53, 61
Thull, Tom, 273
Tiahrt, Todd, 210
Tieszen, Walter E., 299
Tiller, George, 207, 256
Toews, Irvin E., 30
Toews, John E. 173
Toews, LeAnne, 166
Toews, Paul, i, 122, 158
Tran, Thi Ly, 126
Treaster, Cindi, 285
Truman, Harry, 63-4, 80
Tuition grant program, 220-1
Unrau, Kent, 165
Unruh, Ernest Arthur, 70-2, 81, 90, 139, 299
Unruh, Henry F., 72
Vietnam War, 86, 103-126, 289
Vogt, J. W., 58
Vogt, Vernard, 12, 13
Vogt, Vernon, 20-21
Voran, Jonas, 235
Voth, A. J., 23
Voth, Harold, 265

Voth, Marie, 166
Voth, Martha, 166
Voth, Orville, 107, 112
Walker, Richard, 140, 150
Waller, Christina, 254
Waltner, Erland, 62, 67
Waltner, James, 77, 107
Waltner, John, 205-6, 278-9
Waltner, Waldo, 165
Warkentin, Bernhard, 147
Warkentin, John, 259
Warkentin, Kendal, 248-9
Weber, Ralph, 94
Wedel, David C., 41, 50, 68
Wedel, Cornelius H., 21-22
Wedel, Jacob A., 27, 235
Weinbrenner, Reynold, 57
Western District Conference, 120, 155
Western District Peace Committee, 21, 77, 89, 94, 148
Wheat centennial 1974, 144-8
Wheat bell, 165
Whittaker, Robert, 197
Wiebe, Carol, 170, 182
Wiebe, Elizabeth Pauls, 83
Wiebe, Henry Pauls, 83
Wiebe, Peter, 115
Wiens, Wayne, 265-6
Willkie, Wendell, 23, 25
Willms, Gerhard, 23, 24
Wilson, Woodrow, 3, 80
Wingert, George, 198-9
Winrod, Gerald B., 4
Wohgemuth, Paul, 168
World War I, 2-3, 12, 45
World War II, 29-55, 56
Wormhoudt, Gerrit, 121
Wunsch, Robert, 212
Wuthnow, Robert, 215, 287
Wyse, Rosemary, 284
Yoder, John Howard, 246, 295
Yost, Eric, 209-11, 292, 299
Zehr, Marvin, 25
Zerbe, Gordon, 171
Zerger, Gerhard, 27, 49, 80
Zerger, Kirsten, 111, 112